ABORTION

ISSN 2332-3728

ABORTION

Stephen Meyer

INFORMATION PLUS® REFERENCE SERIES
Formerly Published by Information Plus, Wylie, Texas

GALE
CENGAGE Learning®

Farmington Hills, Mich • San Francisco • New York • Waterville, Maine
Meriden, Conn • Mason, Ohio • Chicago

GALE
CENGAGE Learning®

Abortion

Stephen Meyer
Kepos Media, Inc.: Steven Long and Janice Jorgensen, Series Editors

Project Editors: Tracie Moy, Laura Avery

Rights Acquisition and Management: Ashley Maynard, Carissa Poweleit

Composition: Evi Abou-El-Seoud, Mary Beth Trimper

Manufacturing: Rita Wimberley

WCN: 01-100-101

Cover photograph: © Education Images/UIG/Getty Images.

Gale
27500 Drake Rd.
Farmington Hills, MI 48331-3535

ISBN-13: 978-0-7876-5103-9 (set)
ISBN-13: 978-1-5730-2664-2

ISSN 2332-3728

This title is also available as an e-book.
ISBN-13: 978-1-5730-2709-0 (set)
Contact your Gale sales representative for ordering information.

Printed in the United States of America
1 2 3 4 5 20 19 18 17 16

TABLE OF CONTENTS

also presents opposing perspectives from other public figures and the Obama administration on the Pain-Capable Unborn Child Protection Act, a law that would prohibit abortion after 20 weeks of pregnancy.

PREFACE

Abortion is part of the *Information Plus Reference Series*. The purpose of each volume of the series is to present the latest facts on a topic of pressing concern in modern American life. These topics include the most controversial and studied social issues of the 21st century: capital punishment, care for senior citizens, education, the environment, health care, immigration, national security, social welfare, sports, women, youth, and many more. Although this series is written especially for high school and undergraduate students, it is an excellent resource for anyone in need of factual information on current affairs.

By presenting the facts, it is the intention of Gale, Cengage Learning, to provide its readers with everything they need to reach an informed opinion on current issues. To that end, there is a particular emphasis in this series on the presentation of scientific studies, surveys, and statistics. These data are generally presented in the form of tables, charts, and other graphics placed within the text of each book. Every graphic is directly referred to and carefully explained in the text. The source of each graphic is presented within the graphic itself. The data used in these graphics are drawn from the most reputable and reliable sources, such as from the various branches of the U.S. government and from private organizations and associations. Every effort has been made to secure the most recent information available. Readers should bear in mind that many major studies take years to conduct and that additional years often pass before the data from these studies are made available to the public. Therefore, in many cases the most recent information available in 2016 is dated from 2013 or 2014. In the case of abortion statistics, and in particular worldwide abortion statistics, the data are sometimes older. Older statistics are sometimes presented in this series if they are landmark studies or of particular interest and no more-recent information exists.

Although statistics are a major focus of the *Information Plus Reference Series*, they are by no means its only content. Each book also presents the widely held positions and important ideas that shape how the book's subject is discussed in the United States. These positions are explained in detail and, where possible, in the words of their proponents. Some of the other material to be found in these books includes historical background, descriptions of major events related to the subject, relevant laws and court cases, and examples of how these issues play out in American life. Some books also feature primary documents or have pro and con debate sections that provide the words and opinions of prominent Americans on both sides of a controversial topic. All material is presented in an evenhanded and unbiased manner; readers will never be encouraged to accept one view of an issue over another.

HOW TO USE THIS BOOK

Few topics rouse as much dissension and disagreement as the topic of abortion. Some people assert that it is a woman's right to choose to have an abortion, whereas others assert that abortion is tantamount to murder. This book attempts to provide both sides of the divisive argument. Also included is information on the number and types of abortions performed in the United States, the number of abortion clinics, teen pregnancy and abortion, views of abortion from around the world, religious thoughts on abortion, and legal rulings pertaining to abortion.

Abortion consists of 10 chapters and three appendixes. Each chapter is devoted to a particular aspect of abortion. For a summary of the information that is covered in each chapter, please see the synopses that are provided in the Table of Contents. Chapters generally begin with an overview of the basic facts and background information on the chapter's topic, then proceed to examine subtopics of particular interest. For example, Chapter 5: Teen Pregnancy and Abortion begins with an overview of teen pregnancy in the United States, analyzing demographic factors that account for variations in teen pregnancy outcomes among different racial and ethnic groups. The chapter proceeds to discuss pregnancy prevention initiatives aimed at teenagers, paying particular attention to the politics behind abstinence-only education programs. The chapter goes on to examine sex education policies on the state level, outlining approaches to teaching teens the importance of using contraception properly and consistently, as well as how to communicate about sexuality openly and effectively with their peers. The chapter concludes with a detailed analysis of data relating to teen birth and abortion rates both in the United States and abroad, while considering the issue of parental involvement in the abortion decisions of minors, and also relinquishment for adoption. Readers can find their way through a chapter by looking for the section and subsection headings, which are clearly set off from the text. They can also refer to the book's extensive Index if they already know what they are looking for.

Statistical Information

The tables and figures featured throughout *Abortion* will be of particular use to readers in learning about this issue. These tables and figures represent an extensive collection of the most recent and important statistics on abortion and related issues—for example, graphics cover the chronology of major U.S. Supreme Court abortion cases, Americans' positions on abortion by political party affiliation, teenage birth rates, states with near-total abortion bans, the number of legal abortions worldwide, and public opinion on whether abortion should be legal. Gale, Cengage Learning, believes that making this information available to readers is the most important way to fulfill the goal of this book: to help readers understand the issues and controversies surrounding abortion in the United States and to reach their own conclusions.

Each table or figure has a unique identifier appearing above it for ease of identification and reference. Titles for the tables and figures explain their purpose. At the end of each table or figure, the original source of the data is provided.

To help readers understand these often complicated statistics, all tables and figures are explained in the text. References in the text direct readers to the relevant statistics. Furthermore, the contents of all tables and figures are fully indexed. Please see the opening section of the Index at the back of this volume for a description of how to find tables and figures within it.

Appendixes

Besides the main body text and images, *Abortion* has three appendixes. The first is the Important Names and Addresses directory. Here, readers will find contact information for a number of government and private organizations that can provide further information on abortion. The second appendix is the Resources section, which can also assist readers in conducting their own research. In this section, the author and editors of *Abortion* describe some of the sources that were most useful during the compilation of this book. The final appendix is the detailed Index. It has been greatly expanded from previous editions and should make it even easier to find specific topics in this book.

COMMENTS AND SUGGESTIONS

The editors of the *Information Plus Reference Series* welcome your feedback on *Abortion*. Please direct all correspondence to:

Editors
Information Plus Reference Series
27500 Drake Rd.
Farmington Hills, MI 48331-3535

CHAPTER 1
ABORTION: AN ETERNAL SOCIAL AND MORAL ISSUE

WHAT IS ABORTION?

An abortion—which is also called induced abortion—is a procedure performed to end a pregnancy before birth occurs. It is not the same as a spontaneous abortion, which occurs when a fetus or embryo dies in the mother's uterus and is expelled by the body. Spontaneous abortion is also called miscarriage.

The length of a pregnancy is measured in weeks from the first day of a woman's last menstrual period. A normal pregnancy lasts about 40 weeks. Pregnancy is also described in trimesters. There are three trimesters in a pregnancy, and each trimester is about three months long.

According to Karen Pazol et al. of the Centers for Disease Control and Prevention, in "Abortion Surveillance—United States, 2011" (*Morbidity and Mortality Weekly Report*, vol. 63, no. 11, November 28, 2014), 91.6% of induced abortions in 2011 were performed during the first trimester of pregnancy—the time of least risk to the health of the mother. Few abortions (7.1%) were performed between 14 and 20 weeks, and fewer (1.4%) at 21 weeks or later.

Abortion may be induced using surgery or a combination of medications. The most commonly performed medical abortions involve the use of two oral drugs: mifepristone (also known as RU-486) and misoprostol. In some cases misoprostol may be administered vaginally rather than taken by mouth. Early medication abortions can be done safely at home under the care of a physician, whereas early surgical abortions can be performed safely in a physician's office or clinic.

Surgical abortions up to the 12th week of pregnancy are generally performed using vacuum aspiration (suction to remove the contents of the uterus). For pregnancies of 15 to 24 weeks' duration the dilation and evacuation method is common, which in addition to suction often entails passing a forceps into the uterus to remove its contents. Later abortions are often performed in hospitals or in special clinics where labor may be induced using drugs so that the fetus is expelled or surgical evacuation may be performed.

Abortions have been performed since the beginning of recorded history. There have always been women who, for a variety of reasons, wanted to terminate their pregnancies. In the 21st century the abortion issue has developed into a conflict about whether an embryo or fetus is entitled to legal rights, and whether a woman's right to control her life and body includes the right to end an unwanted pregnancy. Although abortion has been debated for centuries, motivations to condemn or support it have varied with changing political and social conditions.

ANCIENT TIMES

Abortion is mentioned in the ancient Code of Assyria (in Mesopotamia) of the 12th century BC. Provision 53 explicitly ordered that any woman who had an abortion should be impaled on stakes without the dignity of burial. If the woman did not survive the abortion, her body was to be similarly impaled, again without burial. Likewise, ancient Jewish law strictly forbade abortion, although it allowed the sacrifice of the fetus to save the life of the mother.

Conversely, in ancient Greece and Rome abortion was often used to limit family size. It was socially acceptable, as was the practice of disposing of deformed and weak infants through exposure (leaving babies outdoors to die). Males were favored; parents who did not want the expense of raising a female infant often resorted to exposure.

The Greek philosophers Plato (428–348 BC) and Aristotle (384–322 BC) both approved of abortion and exposure as a means of population control. Plato wrote in *The Republic* that any woman older than 40 years (an age when the rate of birth defects increases sharply) should be compelled to abort a pregnancy.

The Hippocratic Oath is generally thought to have been first developed by the Greek physician Hippocrates (c. 460–c. 377 BC) or his students. It has been influential throughout history as a set of medical ethics, and in modified forms is still held in esteem today. Scholars disagree on whether it forbids abortions. It mentions them in the context of not giving a woman a pessary (a device that is inserted into the vagina to support the pelvic region or to serve as a contraceptive) to induce an abortion. However, at the time a pessary could often cause infections in a woman leading to her death, so the proscription against their use may have more to do with the health of the woman than opinions on abortion. The original Hippocratic Oath did not mention other methods used to induce abortion, which was legal at the time.

The consequences of adultery or prostitution were compelling reasons for a woman or her family to end a pregnancy. In the ancient Roman household the father determined the ethical life of the family. He alone had the authority to order or forbid an abortion. When abortions were performed, Romans were not concerned with the life of the child but with the health of the mother, because improper mixtures of abortion-inducing drugs poisoned some women. Thus, fathers usually opted for infanticide (killing an infant after birth) rather than for abortion.

TABLE 1.1

Religious affiliations in the United States, 2007 and 2014

	2007	2014	Change[a]
	%	%	%
Christian	**78.4**	**70.6**	**−7.8**
Protestant	51.3	46.5	−4.8
Evangelical	26.3	25.4	−0.9
Mainline	18.1	14.7	−3.4
Historically black	6.9	6.5	—
Catholic	23.9	20.8	−3.1
Orthodox Christian	0.6	0.5	—
Mormon	1.7	1.6	—
Jehovah's Witness	0.7	0.8	—
Other Christian	0.3	0.4	—
Non-Christian faiths	**4.7**	**5.9**	**+1.2**
Jewish	1.7	1.9	—
Muslim	0.4	0.9	+0.5
Buddhist	0.7	0.7	—
Hindu	0.4	0.7	+0.3
Other world religions[b]	<0.3	0.3	—
Other faiths[b]	1.2	1.5	+0.3
Unaffiliated	**16.1**	**22.8**	**+6.7**
Atheist	1.6	3.1	+1.5
Agnostic	2.4	4.0	+1.6
Nothing in particular	12.1	15.8	+3.7
Don't know/refused	**0.8**	**0.6**	**−0.2**
	100.0	**100.0**	

[a]The "change" column displays only statistically significant changes; blank cells indicate that the difference between 2007 and 2014 is within the margin of error.
[b]The "other world religions" category includes Sikhs, Baha'is, Taoists, Jains and a variety of other world religions. The "other faiths" category includes Unitarians, New Age religions, Native American religions and a number of other non-Christian faiths.

SOURCE: "Christians Decline as Share of U.S. Population; Other Faiths and the Unaffiliated Are Growing," in *America's Changing Religious Landscape*, Pew Research Center, May 12, 2015, http://www.pewforum.org/files/2015/05/RLS-08-26-full-report.pdf (accessed September 21, 2015)

THE CHRISTIAN POSITION ON ABORTION

Christianity is a system of beliefs and practices founded in Palestine by the followers of Jesus (4? BC–AD 29?) approximately 2,000 years ago and is based on the Old and New Testament of the Bible. There are a variety of Christian religions, including Catholicism, and a variety of Protestant denominations. Likewise, there are a variety of Christian positions on abortion.

Catholicism has existed since the earliest days of Christianity. Protestantism, however, dates back only to the Reformation, a 16th-century movement in western Europe that aimed at reforming some doctrines and practices of the Catholic Church and resulted in the establishment of the Protestant churches. There is disagreement about which religions the term *Protestant* encompasses. One organizational structure of religious affiliations is shown in Table 1.1. This table is from *America's Changing Religious Landscape* by the Pew Research Center (May 12, 2015, http://www.pewforum.org/files/2015/05/RLS-08-26-full-report.pdf).

As Table 1.1 shows, the U.S. population is predominantly Christian. In 2014, 46.5% of U.S. adults considered themselves Protestant and 20.8% considered themselves Catholic. Another 3.3% considered themselves Mormon (1.6%), Jehovah's Witness (0.8%), Orthodox Christian (0.5%), or some other Christian affiliation (0.4%). As Table 1.2 shows, older Americans were far more likely to identify as Christian in 2014. Conversely, more than one-third of Americans born during the 1980s or later professed no religious affiliation that year.

Early Christian Position on Abortion

The first written works of Christianity hardly mention abortion. The earliest known Christian document that declared abortion a sin was the *Didache*, which was written in approximately AD 100. *Didache* 2:2 states, "You shall not kill the embryo by abortion and shall not cause the newborn to perish." Early church leaders agreed that if an abortion was performed to hide the consequences of fornication and adultery, then it was a sin that required penance. This sparked the debate about whether abortion was murder.

The Roman Catholic Position

During the first six centuries of the Roman Catholic Church, theologians debated about the starting point of human life. St. Augustine of Hippo (354–430), whose teachings helped establish the church's theological foundation, taught that abortion is not the murder of an infant (infanticide). He wrote, "The law does not provide that the act [abortion] pertains to homicide, for there cannot

TABLE 1.2

Religious affiliations, by generation, 2014

	Silent generation (born 1928–1945)	Baby Boomers (born 1946–1964)	Generation X (born 1965–1980)	Millennials (born 1981–1989)	Millennials (born 1990–1996)
	%	%	%	%	%
Christian	**85**	**78**	**70**	**57**	**56**
Protestant	57	52	45	38	36
Evangelical	30	28	25	22	19
Mainline	22	17	13	10	11
Historically black	5	7	7	6	6
Catholic	24	23	21	16	16
Other Christian groups	3	3	4	3	3
Other faiths	**4**	**5**	**6**	**8**	**8**
Unaffiliated	**11**	**17**	**23**	**34**	**36**
Don't know/refused	*	**1**	**1**	**1**	**1**
	100	**100**	**100**	**100**	**100**

Notes: 2014 Religious Landscape Study, conducted June 4–Sept. 30, 2014. Figures may not add to 100%, and nested figures may not add to subtotals indicated, due to rounding. The "other Christian groups" category includes Mormons, Orthodox Christians, Jehovah's Witnesses and a number of smaller Christian groups.

SOURCE: "Generational Replacement Helping Drive Growth of Unaffiliated, Decline of Mainline Protestantism and Catholicism," in *America's Changing Religious Landscape*, Pew Research Center, May 12, 2015, http://www.pewforum.org/files/2015/05/RLS-08-26-full-report.pdf (accessed September 21, 2015)

yet be said to be a live soul in a body that lacks sensation when it is not formed in flesh and so is not endowed with sense." Reflecting a similar viewpoint, the *Irish Canons* (c. 675) noted that the penalty for illicit intercourse (a minimum of seven years on bread and water) was far more severe than the penance for abortion (three and a half years on the same diet).

The Catholic theologian St. Thomas Aquinas (c. 1225–1274) developed the concept of hylomorphism, which defines a human being as the unity of body and soul. This resulted in the belief that there could be no human being without the presence of both elements. In other words, the soul can exist only in a fully formed body, which he noted did not occur until the fifth or sixth month of fetal development. In *Summa Theologica* (Part 1, Question 90, Article 4), Thomas Aquinas wrote, "The soul, as a part of human nature, has its natural perfection only as united to the body."

However, not all Catholic theologians agreed with Thomas's position. Some theologians taught that hominization (the point at which a fetus acquires a soul and becomes a human being) occurred at 40 days (slightly more than one month) after conception for males and 80 days (not quite three months) for females.

In 1312, at the Council of Vienne, the Catholic Church officially adopted Thomas's hylomorphic theory of human life and upheld this traditional doctrine through the 16th century. Although the church endorsed Thomas Aquinas's theory, theological discussions about abortion continued. From the 12th through the 16th centuries various popes issued differing pronouncements on abortion and the fetal status. In some cases they imposed excommunication (exclusion from church membership) as a penalty for purposefully aborting a fetus.

In *Apostolicae Sedis Moderationi* (1869), Pope Pius IX (1792–1878) declared abortion a homicide and, therefore, grounds for excommunication. This decision was reaffirmed in 1917 with the issuance of *Code of Canon Law*. Canon 2350, Paragraph 1, stated, "Persons who procure abortion, mothers not excepted, automatically incur excommunication reserved to the Ordinary at the moment the crime takes effect: if they are clerics, they shall also be deposed." Recent popes have firmly upheld this canon. Pope Pius XII (1876–1958), who was deeply concerned about abortion, wrote in *Allocution to Midwives* (October 29, 1951, http://www.ewtn.com/library/PAPALDOC/P511029.HTM) that "every human being, even the child in the womb, has the right to life directly from God and not from his parents, not from any society or human authority. Therefore, there is no man, no human authority, no science, no 'indication' at all—whether it be medical, eugenic, social, economic, or moral—that may offer or give a valid judicial title for a direct deliberate disposal of an innocent human life, that is, a disposal which aims at its destruction, whether as an end in itself or as a means to achieve the end, perhaps in no way at all illicit."

The Second Vatican Council (1962–1965), the largest Roman Catholic Church gathering in Christian history, declared in *Gaudium et Spes* (December 7, 1965, http://www.vatican.va/archive/hist_councils/ii_vatican_council/documents/vat-ii_cons_19651207_gaudium-et-spes_en.html) that abortion is a "supreme dishonor to the Creator." The council further observed that "from the moment of its conception life must be guarded with the greatest care while abortion and infanticide are unspeakable crimes."

In *Humanae Vitae* (July 25, 1968, http://www.vatican.va/holy_father/paul_vi/encyclicals/documents/hf_p-vi_enc_25071968_humanae-vitae_en.html), Pope Paul VI (1897–1978) stated, "We are obliged once more to declare that the direct interruption of the generative process already begun and, above all, all direct abortion, even for therapeutic reasons, are to be absolutely excluded as lawful means of regulating the number of children."

Pope John Paul II (Karol Jozef Wojtyla; 1920–2005) proclaimed his firm stance against contraception, abortion, and euthanasia (mercy killing) in *Evangelium Vitae* (March 25, 1995, http://www.vatican.va/holy_father/john_paul_ii/encyclicals/documents/hf_jp-ii_enc_25031995_evangelium-vitae_en.html). He claimed that modern society promoted a "culture of death." In 1998 the National Conference of Catholic Bishops of the United States issued "Living the Gospel of Life: A Challenge to American Catholics" (http://www.usccb.org/issues-and-action/human-life-and-dignity/abortion/living-the-gospel-of-life.cfm). The conference stated that "direct abortion is *never* a morally tolerable option. It is *always* a grave act of violence against a woman and her unborn child. This is so even when a woman does not see the truth because of the pressures she may be subjected to, often by the child's father, her parents or friends."

Pope Benedict XVI (Joseph Cardinal Ratzinger; 1927–), the successor of Pope John Paul II, stated shortly after assuming the papacy that he and the Catholic Church would continue to stand firmly against abortion. This statement was in keeping with Ratzinger's earlier stance as evidenced in *Donum Vitae* (February 22, 1987, http://www.cin.org/vatcong/donumvit.html), which was issued by the Congregation for the Doctrine of the Faith (CDF) and which Ratzinger signed. *Donum Vitae* focused on biomedical techniques such as in vitro fertilization; the embryo and fetus were once again affirmed to be "a person from the moment of his conception." Ratzinger, as Pope Benedict XVI, and the CDF issued an update of *Donum Vitae* in 2008. *Instruction Dignitas Personae: On Certain Bioethical Questions* (June 20, 2008, http://www.vatican.va/roman_curia/congregations/cfaith/documents/rc_con_cfaith_doc_20081208_dignitas-personae_en.html) stated that "the human being is to be respected and treated as a person from the moment of conception."

Pope Francis (Jorge Mario Bergoglio; 1936–), who became pope in March 2013, upholds the church's long-standing opposition to abortion. In his biography, *Pope Francis: Conversations with Jorge Mario Bergoglio* (Sergio Rubin and Francesca Ambrogetti, 2013), he explains his belief that life begins at conception, "The pregnant woman doesn't carry a toothbrush in her womb, nor a tumor. Science teaches that from the moment of conception, the new being has all the genetic code. It's impressive. It's not, therefore, a religious question but clearly a moral one, based on science." At the same time, however, Francis also showed signs of establishing a more compassionate attitude within the church toward women who had had abortions. In "Letter of His Holiness Pope Francis According to Which an Indulgence Is Granted to the Faithful on the Occasion of the Extraordinary Jubilee of Mercy" (September 1, 2015, https://w2.vatican.va/content/francesco/en/letters/2015/documents/papa-francesco_20150901_lettera-indulgenza-giubileo-misericordia.html), Francis grants all priests "the discretion to absolve of the sin of abortion those who have procured it and who, with contrite heart, seek forgiveness for it." The decree was intended to coincide with the Catholic Church's Holy Year of Mercy, a period from December 8, 2015, to November 20, 2016, during which the church would offer "great amnesty" toward individuals who had sinned against the faith. Francis explains, "The forgiveness of God cannot be denied to one who has repented, especially when that person approaches the Sacrament of Confession with a sincere heart in order to obtain reconciliation with the Father."

The Protestant Position

Until the late 1960s almost all Protestant churches opposed abortion. However, the changing social climate, as well as the U.S. Supreme Court decision in *Roe v. Wade* (410 U.S. 113 [1973]), which legalized abortion in the United States, spurred a change in Protestant positions on abortion.

Since 1970 the Presbyterian Church has supported free and open access to abortion without legal restriction. At about the same time, the United Methodists, the Lutheran Church in America, the United Church of Christ, the Disciples of Christ, and the Southern Baptist Convention adopted policies allowing abortion as a decision of the woman or the couple. In 1980 the Southern Baptist Convention began to reverse its stance, first by opposing the use of tax money to fund abortions. By the late 1980s the Southern Baptist Convention made its opposition to abortion, except to prevent the death of the mother, a firm policy. It reaffirmed this policy in 2003 on the 30th anniversary of the *Roe v. Wade* decision. Many evangelical, fundamentalist, and independent Bible churches also oppose abortion. However, several Protestant denominations still support open access to abortion.

THE ISLAMIC POSITION

Islam has more than 1 billion followers worldwide, but as Table 1.1 shows, in 2014 it accounted for only 0.9% of the U.S. population. The Koran, which Muslims believe to contain God's revelations to Muhammad (c. 570–632), the founder of the religion of Islam, describes the development of the fetus, "O Mankind! If ye are in doubt concerning the Resurrection, then lo! We have created you from dust, then from a drop of seed, then from a clot, then from a little lump of flesh shapely and shapeless, that We may make [it] clear for you. And We cause what We will to remain in the wombs for an appointed time, and afterward We bring you forth as infants" (Koran 22:5, as translated by

Mohammed Marmaduke Pickthall, in *The Meaning of the Glorious Qur'an*, 1938).

The Koran teaches that fetal development is divided into three 40-day stages. At the end of the third stage, the soul enters the fetus. Muslims, who are divided into different sects, differ in their beliefs as to when—or if—abortion is permissible. Most sects believe it is permissible to abort a pregnancy up to four months, at which point a fetus is thought to become a living soul. Others argue that God forbids the killing of both the born and unborn, even those who have not received a soul. They claim the Koran (6:140) specifically teaches, "They are losers who besottedly have slain their children without knowledge, and have forbidden that which Allah bestowed upon them." Despite these differences, many Muslims feel that abortion is acceptable to save the mother's life.

THE JEWISH POSITION ON ABORTION

Table 1.1 shows that Jewish Americans made up 1.9% of the U.S. population in 2014. Like Christianity and Islam, Judaism has no one position on abortion. In the United States most Jews belong to one of three groups: Orthodox, Conservative, or Reform Judaism. Conservative and Reform Jews generally believe that abortion is the choice of the woman. Jewish law does not recognize a fetus, or even an infant younger than 30 days old, as having legal rights. The laws of mourning do not apply to an expelled fetus or a fetus that does not survive to its 30th day. The biblical text that is the basis for this states, "If a man strikes and wounds a pregnant woman so that her fruit be expelled, but no harm befall her, then he shall be fined as her husband shall assess, and the matter placed before the judges. But if harm befall her, then thou shalt give life for life" (Exodus 21:22).

The Mishnah is the code of Jewish law that forms the basis of the Talmud, the most definitive statement of Jewish law. The Mishnah, which dates back to the second century BC, states, "If a woman is having difficulty in giving birth, it is permitted to cut up the child in her womb and take it out limb by limb because her life takes precedence. However, if the greater part of the child has come out, it must not be touched, because one life must not be taken to save another."

Orthodox Judaism takes a restrictive position on abortion, teaching that a fetus is an organic part of the mother and, as such, does not have legal status. Nonetheless, termination of a pregnancy is strongly condemned on moral grounds. Although a mother's life takes precedence over the unborn, Orthodox Jews believe that the fetus, particularly after the 40th day from conception, has a right to life that cannot be denied. Cases of rape or fetal deformity do not give a mother permission to terminate a pregnancy unless they threaten her mental health (e.g., if the mother becomes suicidal as a result of the pregnancy).

THE MORMON POSITION ON ABORTION

The Church of Jesus Christ of Latter-Day Saints (LDS; also known as the Mormon Church) had its beginnings in 1820 with the founder Joseph Smith (1805–1844). Section 59:6 of *The Doctrine and Covenants of the Church of Jesus Christ of Latter-Day Saints* (2015, http://www.lds.org/scriptures/dc-testament?lang=eng) states, "Thou shalt not steal; neither commit adultery, nor kill, nor do anything like unto it." This statement translates into an LDS position that abortion is wrong and people who support or facilitate elective abortions risk excommunication from the church. Exceptions may be made when the life or health of the mother is in jeopardy or if the pregnancy is the result of incest or rape.

AN OVERVIEW OF EARLY U.S. LEGAL HISTORY ON ABORTION

Roots in the British Legal System

The U.S. legal system has its origins in the British legal system. Until England broke away from the Roman Catholic Church during the 16th century, it observed the church's laws. Henry de Bracton (c. 1210–1268), the father of English common law, was the first to mention abortion in English common law. (English common law was based on judicial precedents, or court decisions and opinions, rather than on written laws.) Greatly influenced by church law and theologians, Bracton wrote in *De Legibus et Consuetudinibus Angliae* (c. 1235), "If there be anyone who strikes a pregnant woman or gives her a poison whereby he causes an abortion, if the foetus be already formed or animated, and especially if it be animated, he commits homicide."

When the English jurist Sir Edward Coke (1552–1634) wrote *The Institutes of the Laws of England* (1628) 400 years later, the law had changed. "If a woman be quick with child," Coke wrote, "and by a potion or otherwise killeth it in her womb; or if a man beat her, whereby the child dieth in her body, and she is delivered of a dead child, this is a great misprision [misdemeanor], but no murder; but if the child be born alive, and dieth of the potion, battery, or other cause, this is murder." The term *quickening* refers to the first time the mother feels the fetus moving in the womb, generally between the 16th and 18th weeks of pregnancy.

A century later the English jurist and professor William Blackstone (1723–1780) upheld in *Commentaries on the Laws of England* (1765–1769) Coke's interpretation that it was a serious misdemeanor if the child was killed in the womb and murder if it was killed after birth. Despite the observations of Coke and Blackstone, abortion was not a criminal offense in England between 1327 and 1803.

After 1803, however, British law prohibited abortion. The first written statute in England against abortion was the Miscarriage of Women Act of 1803 (also known as Lord Ellenborough's Act), which affirmed punishment for the administration of drugs to induce abortion. The punishment for abortion before quickening included exile, whipping, or imprisonment. The punishment for abortion after quickening was death. However, after the death penalty was abolished in 1837, abortion both before and after quickening was considered a felony with similar punishments. (Britain legalized abortion through 24 weeks of gestation in 1968.)

The First Abortion Laws in the United States

In 1821 Connecticut passed the first abortion law in the United States. Although it was patterned after the British 1803 Miscarriage of Women Act, which addressed all forms of abortion, the Connecticut statute addressed post-quickening abortion only, declaring it a felony.

In 1828 New York passed a statute with two provisions. The first provision imposed a second-degree manslaughter penalty for a post-quickening abortion. A pre-quickening abortion was considered a misdemeanor. The second provision contained an exception clause permitting "therapeutic" abortion if "necessary to preserve the life of such a mother or shall have been advised by two physicians to be necessary for such a purpose." This New York law served as a model for many state statutes prohibiting abortion.

Despite state statutes regulating abortion, the sale of abortion-inducing drugs continued during the first half of the 19th century. Newspapers regularly advertised "monthly pills" and new methods to relieve "obstructions of the womb."

In 1871 the *New York Times* called abortion "The Evil of the Age" (August 23, 1871). The newspaper asserted, "The enormous amount of medical malpractice [a euphemism for abortion] that exists and flourishes, almost unchecked, in the City of New York, is a theme for most serious consideration. Thousands of human beings are thus murdered before they have seen the light of this world."

The American Medical Association

The American Medical Association (AMA), founded in 1847, initially campaigned against abortion. At that time women did not regularly turn to physicians for questions on childbirth and "women problems"; instead, they were more likely to rely on midwives and pharmacists. In some instances the people they sought help from were "quacks," people with no medical training, but who advertised their expertise and "services" to women. The AMA was concerned about the dangers that abortions posed, and it argued that abortion providers violated the Hippocratic Oath.

The simplest solution to this difficult situation was to make abortion illegal. Physicians saw this as an opportunity to drive the quacks out of the field and to bolster their own professional image. In addition, medical science had recently recognized that life existed in the fetus before quickening, and many physicians were morally offended by the act of aborting a live fetus.

The AMA was not motivated to criminalize abortion for moral or professional reasons alone. Physicians were swept up by the growing anti-immigrant sentiments of the time. There were concerns that, because of the uncontrolled use of abortion, the proportion of "good Anglo-Saxon stock" was diminishing in the face of increasing immigration, which was predominantly Catholic at the time.

Antiabortion Laws

Intense lobbying by the AMA produced the most important proliferation of antiabortion legislation in U.S. history between 1860 to 1880. States and territories enacted more than 40 antiabortion statutes. Of these, 13 outlawed abortion for the first time and 21 revised old antiabortion laws by making them more stringent. In 1873 Congress passed the Comstock Law (named after its chief supporter, the American morals crusader Anthony Comstock [1844–1915]). Primarily intended to ban the dissemination of pornography and birth control devices, this legislation also prohibited the use of abortion devices.

Abortion continued despite the laws that banned it. Frederick Joseph Taussig (1872–1943), a gynecologist and professor at Washington University Medical School in St. Louis, Missouri, noted in *Abortion, Spontaneous, and Induced* (1936) that during the early 20th century as many as one out of three pregnancies was terminated. (Other forms of birth control were either unreliable or difficult to obtain.) Wealthy women generally found physicians who lent their own interpretations to the allowable exceptions for therapeutic (medically necessary) abortions. Poor women, however, usually had to resort to self-induced or illegal abortions, which resulted in countless mutilations and deaths.

In 1934 Congress held hearings to amend the Comstock Law to allow doctors to provide birth control information and prescribe contraceptive devices. However, support was strong for the law; defenders of the law held that allowing doctors to provide birth control information was tantamount to the government supporting population control. The Comstock Law remained in effect for nearly four more decades. On January 8, 1971, President Richard M. Nixon (1913–1994) signed a law overturning the 98-year-old federal anti-contraception law.

CHANGING ATTITUDES IN THE 20TH CENTURY

Over time, advances in medicine enabled most women to carry their pregnancies to term uneventfully. As a result, doctors became hard-pressed to diagnose life-threatening complications so that they might prescribe therapeutic abortions. In 1959 the American Law Institute proposed a revised Model Penal Code that gave physicians guidelines to follow. The code proposed that physicians be permitted to terminate a pregnancy if one of the following conditions was met:

- The pregnancy threatened the life of the mother or would critically impair the mother's physical or mental condition.
- The child would be born with a grave physical or mental defect.
- The pregnancy resulted from rape or incest.

The need for the abortion had to be approved by two physicians. The inclusion of the mother's mental condition became a factor for doctors because the definition of health was beginning to include mental health at that time.

By the 1960s all 50 states and the District of Columbia allowed therapeutic abortions to save the life of the mother. Colorado and New Mexico also permitted abortions to prevent serious irreparable harm to the mother. Alabama, Massachusetts, Oregon, and the District of Columbia allowed abortions simply to protect the health of the mother.

Thalidomide and Rubella

No sooner were these laws adopted than their restrictions were tested by events that occurred during the early 1960s. In 1962 Sherri Finkbine of Arizona found out that thalidomide, a drug she had been taking to treat morning sickness during her pregnancy, may have caused deformities in the child she was carrying. European women who had used the drug were reported to be delivering severely deformed babies. Finkbine decided, on her physician's advice, to have a legal abortion.

After Finkbine publicized her dilemma to warn others of the effects of thalidomide, the hospital refused to perform the abortion for fear of criminal liability. An appeal to the Arizona Supreme Court was unsuccessful, so the Finkbines flew to Sweden, where the abortion was performed. The Swedish doctor confirmed that the embryo was deformed.

During the early 1960s a rubella (German measles) epidemic swept the United States. Many pregnant women who had contracted rubella obtained legal abortions because they thought their fetuses might have birth defects. Many others could not have abortions (legal or illegal), either because of legal restrictions or a lack of funds. Consequently, many women delivered children with an increased risk of disabilities.

In 1967 the AMA called for the liberalization of abortion laws and in 1970 urged that abortion be limited only by the "sound clinical judgment" of a physician.

Women Speak Out

The thalidomide and rubella episodes stimulated interest in the issue of abortion and created empathy for the pregnant women who had found themselves in those difficult situations. Furthermore, the 1960s were a period of change—a time when many people questioned accepted beliefs. Americans were discussing human sexuality more openly, which made it easier to talk about abortion. Many sought to put a stop to the deaths and mutilations caused by unqualified abortionists.

The Laws Begin to Change

Increased interest in the abortion issue caused many states to reform their laws. In 1967 California, Colorado, and North Carolina became the first states to liberalize their statutes. By 1973 a total of 13 states had enacted this type of legislation.

In 1970 Alaska, Hawaii, New York, and Washington chose the radical alternative of legalizing all abortions performed by a physician up to a legally determined time in the pregnancy. Alaska, Hawaii, and Washington also established state residency requirements and shorter periods during which women could have an abortion on demand. By one vote, New York passed the most liberal law of the four states. It permitted abortion for any reason up to 24 weeks of pregnancy. Beyond that point, abortions could only be performed to save a mother's life.

In 1972 the American Bar Association approved the Uniform Abortion Act as a model for all state statutes. It was based on the New York law. That same year the President's Commission on Population Growth and the American Future, headed by the philanthropist John D. Rockefeller III (1906–1978), released its final report, which recommended that "present state laws restricting abortion be liberalized along the lines of the New York statute."

Meanwhile, as legislatures continued to reexamine their state abortion laws, state and federal courts were beginning to declare some states' abortion laws unconstitutional because they were vague and interfered with a woman's right to privacy. Many thousands of women traveled to states where abortion had become legal to obtain an abortion. According to John W. Klotz, in *A Christian View of Abortion* (1973), the New York State Department of Health reported that 278,122 legal abortions were performed between July 1, 1970, and December 31, 1971. Furthermore, the department noted that 40% of the women who had these abortions were from out of state. Many states watched to see what would happen in Alaska, Hawaii, New York, and Washington, and awaited legal clarification from the U.S. Supreme Court. This arrived on January 22, 1973, in the historic *Roe v. Wade* decision. The landmark ruling eliminated all prohibitions on abortion during the first trimester, while permitting the states to implement "reasonable" regulations that would allow abortions in specific cases during the second and third trimesters. Over the next three decades a number of other significant Supreme Court rulings on abortion followed, addressing issues such as public funding for abortion, parental notification in cases involving minors, and rules governing protests outside health clinics that provide abortion, among others. The *Roe v. Wade* decision, along with other important Supreme Court rulings on abortion, is discussed in Chapter 2. *Roe v. Wade* is also the topic of Chapter 10.

CHAPTER 2
U.S. SUPREME COURT DECISIONS

Abortion is an emotional and divisive issue. Generally speaking, people who identify as pro-choice believe that women should be able to control their own bodies and reproductive decisions. They believe that abortion is about reproductive choice and a constitutional right to privacy. By contrast, those who identify as pro-life for the most part believe that fetuses have a right to life and that no one should have the legal right to destroy a fetus after it is conceived.

The issue of abortion affects not only women in their reproductive years but also potential fathers and other family members, as well as those involved in the debate on moral, ethical, philosophical, and legal grounds. Thus, abortion is a national issue. In the United States it is governed by federal law.

The federal court system consists of three major types of courts: district courts, circuit courts of appeals, and the U.S. Supreme Court. There is at least one district court in each state; they serve as trial courts for lawsuits pertaining to federal law that arise in that state. Circuit courts of appeals reconsider rulings from the district courts. Federal lawsuits that have passed through the district courts and the circuit courts of appeals may then be appealed to the Supreme Court, which is the ultimate authority on interpreting federal law.

State laws can modify federal laws somewhat, but state abortion laws that contradict federal law cannot be enforced. The Supreme Court, as the highest federal court in the country, is the ultimate battleground in the debate over abortion.

ROE V. WADE

On January 22, 1973, the U.S. Supreme Court issued a landmark decision in the now famous *Roe v. Wade* (410 U.S. 113) legal battle. This ruling made it legal for a woman and her doctor to choose abortion without restrictions during the earlier months of pregnancy and with restrictions during the later months. The lawsuit was filed on behalf of Norma McCorvey (1947–), who used the alias Jane Roe. Her attorneys alleged that the abortion law in Texas (the state in which she lived) violated her constitutional rights and the rights of other women. The defendant was Henry Menasco Wade (1914–2001), the district attorney of Dallas County, Texas.

Now, more than four decades and dozens of court decisions later, the essential tenet of the *Roe v. Wade* decision—that abortion is a constitutional liberty—remains the law of the land. However, several court decisions have permitted placing restrictions and preconditions on a woman's right to an abortion. This chapter examines the major steps in the Supreme Court's interpretation of the *Roe v. Wade* decision from 1973 to November 2015. Table 2.1 presents a chronology and brief summary of key abortion cases. The citations, such as 410 U.S. 113, refer to the volume (first number) and page (last number) of the *United States Reports* that contain the final, official judicial decisions of the Supreme Court.

Table 2.1 shows that as of 2015 the last Supreme Court decision on abortion was *Gonzales v. Carhart* (550 U.S. 124 [2007]), which ruled that the Partial-Birth Abortion Ban Act of 2003 was constitutional. In November 2015 the Supreme Court announced that it would hear a new case with potentially major ramifications for the future legality of the *Roe v. Wade* decision. The case *Whole Woman's Health v. Cole* (No. 15-274) emerged as a legal challenge to a 2013 Texas law known as HB 2, which imposed significant restrictions on abortion providers throughout the state. Scott Lemieux explains in "The US Supreme Court May Make Abortion the Deciding Factor in 2016" (Guardian.com, November 16, 2015) that a possible decision to uphold HB 2 in the nation's highest court could severely limit a woman's access to abortion services throughout the country. The court was expected to deliver a ruling on the case in June 2016.

TABLE 2.1

Chronology of key Supreme Court decisions on abortion, 1973–2015

Roe v. Wade—1973, 410 U.S. 113

Found abortion legal and established the trimester approach of unrestricted abortion in the first trimester, reasonably regulated abortion in relation to the woman's health in the second trimester, and permitted states to prohibit abortion in the third trimester, except when necessary to preserve the woman's life or health.

Doe v. Bolton—1973, 410 U.S. 179

Held unconstitutional Georgia's statute requiring performance of abortions in hospitals, approval by hospital abortion committee, confirmation by two consulting physicians, and restriction to state residents.

Bigelow v. Virginia—1975, 421 U.S. 809

Made invalid the application of a Virginia statute that prohibited the advertisement of abortion services.

Connecticut v. Menillo—1975, 423 U.S. 9

Ruled that states may require that abortions must be performed by physicians. This case was an appeal of a conviction of a nonphysician for performing abortions.

Planned Parenthood of Central Missouri v. Danforth—1976, 428 U.S. 52

Ruled that a state may not require the written permission of a spouse or the consent of a parent, in the case of a minor, for an abortion. Further ruled that the state could not prohibit the use of saline injection abortions, and found the provision requiring the physician to preserve the life of the fetus "unconstitutionally overbroad."

Maher v. Roe—1977, 432 U.S. 464; **Beal v. Doe**—432 U.S. 438; **Poelker v. Doe**—432 U.S. 519

Ruled that, although the state could not ban abortion, it was under no legal obligation to fund nontherapeutic abortions or provide the public facilities for such abortions.

Colautti v. Franklin—1979, 439 U.S. 379

Overturned a Pennsylvania law that required physicians to try to save the fetus even if the fetus was less than six months developed and not yet viable.

Bellotti v. Baird—1979, 443 U.S. 622

Found that a statute requiring a minor to get her parents' consent or to obtain judicial approval following parental notification unconstitutionally burdened the minor's right to an abortion.

Harris v. McRae—1980, 448 U.S. 297

Found that the Hyde Amendment did not impinge on a woman's freedom to terminate a pregnancy but, rather, encouraged alternatives deemed to be in the public interest. This ruling also permitted use of federal Medicaid funds only for abortions necessary to save the life of the pregnant woman.

Williams v. Zbaraz—1980, 448 U.S. 358

Ruled that states do not have to pay for medically necessary abortions for women on Medicaid (as in **Harris v. McRae**). This case was a challenge to a version of the Hyde Amendment in Illinois.

H.L. v. Matheson—1981, 450 U.S. 398

Upheld a Utah statute requiring a physician to notify a minor's parents of their daughter's intention to obtain an abortion.

Planned Parenthood of Kansas City, Missouri v. Ashcroft—1983, 462 U.S. 476

Found unconstitutional that all abortions after 12 weeks of pregnancy be performed in a hospital, but upheld a provision requiring pathology reports for every abortion, the presence of a second physician for abortions performed after viability, and parental consent or judicial bypass for minors.

City of Akron v. Akron Center for Reproductive Health, Inc.—1983, 462 U.S. 416

Held unconstitutional the following requirements: that all abortions after the first trimester be performed in a hospital, parental consent or judicial order be required for all minors under 15 years of age, specific information designed to dissuade a woman from abortion be presented, a 24-hour waiting period be observed, and methods for the disposal of fetal tissue be established.

Simopoulos v. Virginia—1983, 462 U.S. 506

Upheld Virginia hospitalization requirement that included outpatient clinics. This case was an appeal of a criminal conviction of a physician for violating a Virginia law that requires all post-first-trimester abortions to be performed in hospitals. Virginia law provides for licensing of freestanding ambulatory surgical facilities as "hospitals." If Dr. Simopoulos's clinic had been licensed, criminal prosecution could have been avoided. The Virginia law is constitutional and not as restrictive as the laws struck down in **City of Akron v. Akron Center for Reproductive Health, Inc.** (1983) and **Planned Parenthood of Kansas City, Missouri v. Ashcroft** (1983)

Thornburgh v. American College of Obstetricians and Gynecologists—1986, 476 U.S. 747

Ruled that the information required under "informed consent," public reports, and disclosure of detailed information about abortions performed were not reasonably related to protecting a woman's health.

Webster v. Reproductive Health Services—1989, 492 U.S. 490

Upheld the Missouri law stating that "the life of each human being begins at conception." Also ruled that the state had the right to require physicians to perform viability tests on any fetus believed to be 20 or more weeks old, to forbid the use of public employees and facilities to perform abortions not necessary to save a woman's life, and to prohibit the use of public funds, employees, or facilities to counsel a woman to have an abortion not necessary to save her life.

Hodgson v. Minnesota—1990, 497 U.S. 417

Upheld a law requiring minors to notify both parents of an abortion decision because there was a provision for judicial bypass within the law.

Ohio v. Akron Center for Reproductive Health, Inc.—1990, 497 U.S. 502

Upheld ruling requiring one-parent notification plus judicial bypass. Also upheld a requirement that the physician personally notify the parent and ruled that states need not guarantee absolute anonymity to the minor seeking bypass.

Rust v. Sullivan—1991, 500 U.S. 173

Prohibited clinics that used Title X funds from counseling regarding abortion or giving abortion referrals.

Planned Parenthood of Southeastern Pennsylvania v. Casey—1992, 505 U.S. 833

Stopping just short of overturning **Roe v. Wade**, this ruling dropped the trimester framework and adopted an "undue burden" standard. Specifically, it upheld informed consent, a 24-hour waiting period, parental consent, and reporting and recordkeeping requirements. It rejected a requirement for spousal consent.

Indeed, at the state level there has been much judicial activity since the *Gonzales v. Carhart* ruling. In *Who Decides? The Status of Women's Reproductive Rights in the United States* (January 2015, http://www.prochoiceamerica.org/assets/download-files/2015-who-decides.pdf), NARAL Pro-Choice America (NARAL) identifies 27 legislative

TABLE 2.1

Chronology of key Supreme Court decisions on abortion, 1973–2013 [CONTINUED]

Bray v. Alexandria Clinic—1993, 506 U.S. 263

Found that the antiabortion protests outside of clinics could not be interpreted as a violation of the Civil Rights Act. Women seeking abortions were not a class of persons qualifying for protection under the law and the protesters' behavior did not show class-based discriminatory ill will against women.

National Organization for Women v. Scheidler—1994, 510 U.S. 249

Ruled that the Racketeer Influenced and Corrupt Organizations Act did not have to include an economic motive and could be used to prosecute the protest activities of antiabortion groups and any other groups that seek to prevent the operation of legitimate businesses.

Madsen v. Women's Health Center—1994, 512 U.S. 753

Upheld an injunction forbidding antiabortion protesters from entering a 36-foot fixed buffer zone in front of an abortion clinic, and upheld noise restrictions, which prevented the use of bullhorns and shouting. The court did not uphold the injunction preventing protesters from approaching patients and staff workers in a 300-foot buffer zone around clinics and staff residences or the prohibition against nonthreatening posters and signs in the 36-foot buffer zone.

Schenck v. Pro-Choice Network of Western New York—1997, 519 U.S. 357

Upheld an injunction forbidding antiabortion protesters from entering a 15-foot fixed buffer zone in front of an abortion clinic. Also upheld the provision of "cease and desist," whereby two protesters at a time could perform "sidewalk counseling." However, the protesters had to stop counseling and leave the buffer zone on request. The court did not uphold the injunction preventing protesters from coming within a 15-foot floating buffer zone of people entering or leaving an abortion clinic.

Hill v. Colorado—2000, 530 U.S. 703

Ruled that a Colorado statute does not violate the First Amendment by forbidding anyone from knowingly approaching closer than within eight feet of another person who is within 100 feet of the entrance of a health care facility, without that person's consent, to give them a leaflet, display a sign, or engage in protest, education, or counseling. It was found not to violate the First Amendment because it does not regulate speech on the basis of content or viewpoint.

Stenberg v. Carhart—2000, 530 U.S. 914

Upheld by a narrow margin (5–4) the Eighth Circuit Court of Appeals' decision that made Nebraska's ban on "partial-birth" abortion invalid. The court ruled on two components of Nebraska's ban, including the lack of a health exception and the undue burden on a woman's right to abortion created by broad language of the ban.

Scheidler v. NOW—2003, 537 U.S. 393

Held that antiabortion groups could not be sued for extortion under racketeering laws intended to combat organized crime. Ruled that the Partial-Birth Abortion Ban Act of 2003 was unconstitutional in three ways: it places an undue burden on women seeking abortions, its language is vague, and it lacks a required exception for medical actions needed to preserve the woman's health.

Scheidler v. NOW—2006, 547 U.S. 9

Ruled 8–0 that the physical violence that occurred outside of abortion clinics was not punishable under the Hobbs Act. This ruling appears to have ended a case that was fought for 20 years.

Ayotte v. Planned Parenthood of Northern New England—2006, 546 U.S. 320

Let stand a New Hampshire parental notification law that requires a 48-hour prior notification of parents before an abortion is performed on their minor child, even if the delay puts the health of the child at risk. The high court ruled that lower court decisions of unconstitutionality of the law were in error, and it returned the case to lower courts and to the state legislature to consider other remedies for the lack of a health exception.

Gonzales v. Carhart—2007, 550 U.S. 124

Ruled that the Partial-Birth Abortion Ban Act of 2003 is constitutional. This is the first time the U.S. Supreme Court has upheld an abortion restriction without requiring an exception to protect the health of the mother, and it is the first time the high court has approved a ban on a specific medical procedure. The Partial-Birth Abortion Ban Act disallows abortion by the intact dilation and extraction (IDX or intact D&X) procedure, which is generally used for abortions at 21 weeks or more of pregnancy.

SOURCE: Created by Barbara Wexler for Gale, © 2015

measures enacted by 16 states in 2014 as being antichoice. In addition, the organization suggests that "if *Roe v. Wade* were overturned, it would open the door for anti-choice lawmakers in state and federal governments to enact and enforce laws banning abortion." According to the organization, 13 states had near-total criminal bans on abortion care in 2014. In four of those states (Louisiana, Mississippi, North Dakota, and South Dakota) near-total criminal bans would automatically become law in the event of *Roe*'s repeal.

History of *Roe v. Wade*

Texas's abortion law had been in place since 1857, and permitted abortion only when the mother's life was endangered. Norma McCorvey, a pregnant single woman, challenged the constitutionality of this law in 1969, using the pseudonym Jane Roe to protect her privacy. In a 7–2 decision in *Roe v. Wade*, the Supreme Court found that a law that prohibited abortion, except to save the life of the mother and without regard for the state of the pregnancy, violated the due process clause of the Fifth Amendment, which guarantees that no level of government can arbitrarily or unfairly deprive individuals of their basic constitutional rights to life, liberty, and property. The 14th Amendment takes this guarantee one step further by ensuring protection against such infringements (taking away of rights) by state governments. The high court said the 14th Amendment protects the right to privacy against state action, including a woman's right to terminate her pregnancy. The court based this right to privacy on the 1942 case *Skinner v. Oklahoma* (316 U.S. 535), which struck down a state law that called for sterilizing people who had been convicted two or more times of "felonies involving moral turpitude" (immoral acts).

In the *Roe v. Wade* decision, however, the court noted that, although the right to abortion is guaranteed, the state has legitimate interests in protecting the health of the pregnant woman and the potentiality of human life. The weight given to each of these interests changes as the pregnancy develops.

The court divided a normal pregnancy into three-month stages (trimesters):

- First trimester—during approximately the first three months the decision to abort must be left up to the woman and her physician.
- Second trimester—after the first trimester of pregnancy the state may regulate the abortion procedure in ways necessary to promote the mother's health.
- Third trimester—after the fetus is viable (able to survive outside the womb) the state, to protect the potential life of the fetus, may regulate and even forbid abortion, except where necessary to preserve the life or health of the mother.

Doe v. Bolton Expands *Roe v. Wade*

On the same day that the Supreme Court decided *Roe v. Wade*, it expanded the ruling with *Doe v. Bolton* (410 U.S. 179 [1973]), a lawsuit brought against the attorney general of Georgia by a pregnant woman using the pseudonym Mary Doe and 23 others. Doe had applied for a therapeutic (medically necessary) abortion under Georgia law and was turned down. While reiterating its *Roe v. Wade* ruling that states may not prevent abortion by making it a crime, the high court also observed that states are not allowed to make abortions hard to obtain by imposing complicated procedural conditions. The court found unconstitutional the following state requirements:

- All abortions must take place in hospitals that are accredited by the Joint Commission on Accreditation of Hospitals.
- Abortions must be approved by a hospital abortion committee.
- Two consulting physicians must confirm the judgment of the performing physician.

GOVERNMENT SUPPORT OR NONSUPPORT OF ABORTION

Public Funding of Nontherapeutic Abortions

On June 20, 1977, the Supreme Court ruled on three cases concerning women who were too poor to afford an abortion. One case involved the Connecticut Welfare Department, which had limited state Medicaid benefits for first-trimester abortions to those that were medically necessary. A woman using the pseudonym Susan Roe challenged the regulations and sued Edward Maher, the Connecticut commissioner of social services. In *Maher v. Roe* (432 U.S. 464), the court held that the 14th Amendment does not require a state participating in Medicaid to pay for expenses resulting from abortions not considered medically necessary simply because it pays childbirth expenses. The court observed that a state may choose to favor childbirth over abortion and is not obligated to explain its choice to do so.

The second case was similar to *Maher v. Roe*. A Pennsylvania law restricted Medicaid-funded abortions, allowing them only in situations deemed medically necessary by a physician. In *Beal v. Doe* (432 U.S. 438), the Supreme Court found that states could exclude nontherapeutic abortions from coverage under their Medicaid programs.

The third case involved a St. Louis, Missouri, policy that prohibited nontherapeutic abortions in the city's two publicly run hospitals. In *Poelker v. Doe* (432 U.S. 519), the high court ruled that St. Louis could refuse to provide nontherapeutic abortions in its publicly financed hospitals even though it provided facilities for childbirth. Because the policy did not deny women the right to have an abortion, it was consistent with the U.S. Constitution. In summary, the Supreme Court found with these three cases that although the state cannot ban abortions, it is under no legal obligation to fund nontherapeutic abortions or to provide public facilities for such abortions.

Abortion Funding Restrictions of the Hyde Amendment: Constitutional or Unconstitutional?

The Hyde Amendment was first passed by Congress in 1976 and excludes abortion from the comprehensive health care services provided to low-income individuals by the federal government through Medicaid. *Maher v. Roe*, *Beal v. Doe*, and *Poelker v. Doe* did not address the issue of whether a federal law such as the Hyde Amendment, or state laws with similar provisions, were constitutional. Because most federal funding for abortion was through Medicaid, cutting federal monies mostly affected the poor. Not surprisingly, the issue of the constitutionality of the Hyde Amendment soon made its way into the nation's courts.

In 1980, in a 5–4 decision, the U.S. Supreme Court held in *Harris v. McRae* (448 U.S. 297) that the Hyde Amendment is constitutional. The court ruled that the funding restrictions of the Hyde Amendment do not infringe on a woman's right to terminate her pregnancy as held in *Roe v. Wade*. The court stated, "It simply does not follow that a woman's freedom of choice carries with it a constitutional entitlement to the financial resources to avail herself of the full range of protected choices.... Although government may not place obstacles in the path of a woman's exercise of her freedom of choice, it need not remove those not of its own creation."

PUBLIC FUNDING OF THERAPEUTIC ABORTIONS. In *Harris v. McRae*, the high court further ruled that a state that participates in the Medicaid program is not required to fund therapeutic abortions if federal reimbursement has been withdrawn under the Hyde Amendment. The same day the Supreme Court, in three related cases—*Williams v. Zbaraz*, *Miller v. Zbaraz*, and *United States v. Zbaraz* (448 U.S. 358)—held that an Illinois law, with similar funding restrictions as the Hyde Amendment, did not violate the 14th Amendment.

FEDERALLY FUNDED CLINICS CANNOT COUNSEL ABOUT ABORTION AS AN OPTION. In 1988 the U.S. Department of Health and Human Services issued regulations stating that organizations that accepted federal funds for purposes of promoting family planning could not discuss abortion as a family planning option. The regulations were challenged in court as exceeding what federal law authorized the agency to do, as well as being an unconstitutional violation of the First and Fifth Amendment rights of organizations receiving federal family planning funds. In May 1991 the U.S. Supreme Court ruled on these issues in *Rust v. Sullivan* (500 U.S. 173). The court found that the regulations were both constitutional and within the bounds set by federal law on family planning funding.

STATE RESTRICTIONS ON ABORTION

Most abortion legislation takes place at the state level. Since *Roe v. Wade*, abortion laws generally have been modified by placing restrictions on the ability to obtain an abortion. Over the years many states have passed statutes that stretch the limits of the law, mainly in the areas of informed consent, waiting periods, spousal or parental consent, parental notice, and place of abortions, as well as fetal viability (the ability of a fetus to survive outside the uterus) and the disposal of the fetus. State laws such as these often result in court battles that rise to the level of the U.S. Supreme Court.

Table 2.2 shows the 13 states that had near-total abortion bans in 2015. According to NARAL, in "What Is Choice?" (2015, http://www.prochoiceamerica.org/what-is-choice/maps-and-charts/map.jsp?mapID=26), these bans contradicted federal law in place at that time, so they were considered unconstitutional and unenforceable.

Informed Consent and Spousal/Parental Consent

Planned Parenthood of Central Missouri v. Danforth (428 U.S. 52 [1976]) was the first case heard before the U.S. Supreme Court that confronted *Roe v. Wade* and *Doe v. Bolton*. Two Missouri-licensed physicians challenged several restrictions of the Missouri Code, which required the following:

- A woman must sign a written consent to the abortion and certify that "her consent is informed and freely given and is not the result of coercion."
- A woman must get a written consent from her husband for the abortion.
- The attending physician must exercise professional care to preserve the fetus's life and health, failing which he or she will be held guilty of manslaughter and liable for damages.
- An unmarried woman under the age of 18 years must get the written consent of a parent or person in the place of a parent to permit abortion.

The Supreme Court ruled in *Planned Parenthood of Central Missouri v. Danforth* that during the first 12 weeks of pregnancy an abortion was a matter of interest only to the woman and her physician. The state cannot "delegate to a spouse a veto power which the state itself is absolutely and totally prohibited from exercising during the first trimester of pregnancy," as ruled in *Roe v. Wade*. Similarly, the court struck down the parental consent requirement. The court found that the provision requiring the physician to preserve the life and health of the fetus was "unconstitutionally overbroad," especially because it covered the first three months of pregnancy, when the fetus is not able to survive outside the womb. In addition, the majority ruled that the state could not prohibit the use of any safe abortion method.

PARENTAL CONSENT. In 1979 a Massachusetts law required parental consent for an abortion performed on an unmarried woman under the age of 18 years. However, if either or both of the parents refused, a judge of the superior court could rule on the issue. The *Bellotti v. Baird* (443 U.S. 622 [1979]) case asked whether the law unconstitutionally restricted the right of a minor to have an abortion. In an 8–1 ruling, the U.S. Supreme Court observed, "A child, merely on account of his minority, is not beyond the protection of the Constitution." The court declared that the Massachusetts statute was unconstitutional on two grounds: "First, it permits judicial authorization for an abortion to be withheld from a minor who is found by the superior court to be mature and fully competent to make this decision independently. Second, it requires parental consultation or notification in every instance, whether or not in the pregnant minor's best interests, without affording her an opportunity to receive an independent judicial determination that she is mature enough to consent or that an abortion would be in her best interests."

Parental Notification

Two years later the U.S. Supreme Court ruled again on whether a minor, who was fully dependent on her parents, had to inform her parents of her decision to have an abortion (i.e., to notify them, not to obtain their consent). Referring to *Bellotti v. Baird*, the court noted in *H. L. v. Matheson* (450 U.S. 398 [1981]), "A statute setting out a mere requirement of parental notice when possible does not violate the constitutional rights of an immature, dependent minor.... Whether or not to bear a child... is a grave decision, and a girl of tender years, under emotional stress, may be ill-equipped to make it without mature advice and emotional support."

Similarly, in *Ohio v. Akron Center for Reproductive Health, Inc.* (497 U.S. 502 [1990]) the Supreme Court upheld a 1985 Ohio statute that required a physician

TABLE 2.2

State near-total abortion bans, 2015

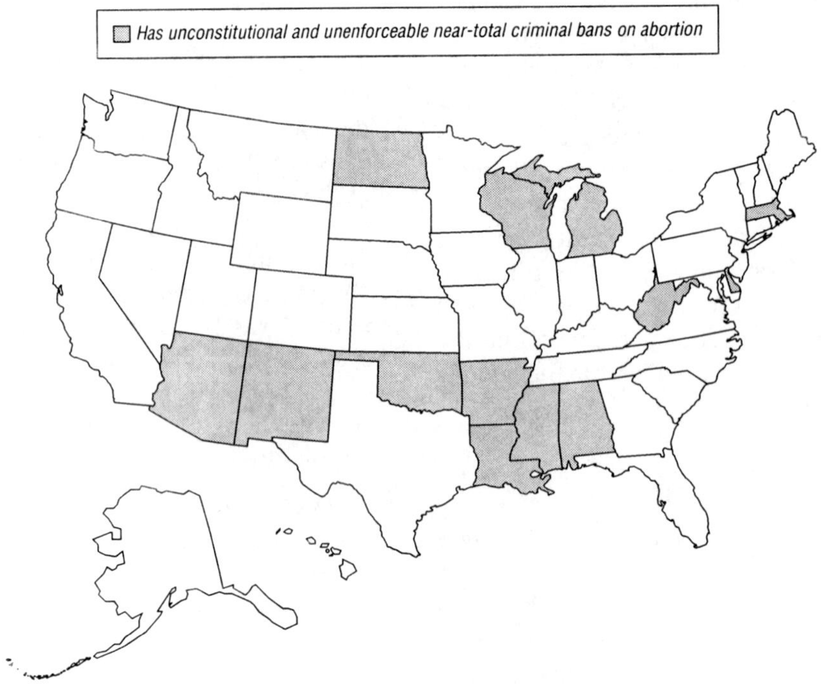

State	Has life exception	Has limited health exception	Has health exception	Has rape/incest exception	Without exception
Alabama	✓		✓		
Alaska					
Arizona	✓				
Arkansas					
California					
Colorado			✓*		
Connecticut					
Delaware	✓	✓		✓	
District of Columbia					
Florida					
Georgia					
Hawaii					
Idaho					
Illinois					
Indiana					
Iowa					
Kansas					
Kentucky					
Louisiana	✓			✓	
Maine					
Maryland					
Massachusetts					✓
Michigan	✓	✓			
Minnesota					
Mississippi	✓			✓	
Missouri					
Montana					
Nebraska					
Nevada					
New Hampshire					
New Jersey					
New Mexico	✓	✓		✓	
New York					
North Carolina					
North Dakota	✓	✓			
Ohio					
Oklahoma	✓				
Oregon					
Pennsylvania					
Rhode Island					

TABLE 2.2

State near-total abortion bans, 2015 [CONTINUED]

State	Has life exception	Has limited health exception	Has health exception	Has rape/incest exception	Without exception
South Carolina					
South Dakota					
Tennessee					
Texas					
Utah					
Vermont					
Virginia					
Washington					
West Virginia	✓				
Wisconsin	✓				
Wyoming					
Totals	11	4	2	4	1

*Law contains a full health exception, but requires approval from a three-physician panel.
Notes: 13 states have unconstitutional and unenforceable near-total criminal bans on abortion: AL, AR, AZ, DE, LA, MA, MI, MS, ND, NM, OK, WI, WV.

SOURCE: "Near-Total Abortion Bans," in *What Is Choice?* NARAL Pro-Choice America and NARAL Pro-Choice America Foundation, 2015, http://www.prochoiceamerica.org/what-is-choice/maps-and-charts/map.jsp?mapID=26 (accessed September 21, 2015)

performing an abortion on a minor to give 24-hour prior notice to at least one parent or guardian. The law provided the minor with a way to bypass her parents (called a judicial bypass) by asking the juvenile court to issue an order that would authorize her to give her own consent. In upholding this part of the statute, the Supreme Court also ruled that states need not guarantee absolute anonymity to a minor seeking judicial bypass.

In 1981 Minnesota passed a law (Subdivision 2 of Minn. Stat. 144.343) that required a minor to inform both parents 48 hours before having an abortion, even if the parents were no longer married and one parent had little or nothing to do with the minor's upbringing. Subdivision 2 was mandatory except in cases of parental abuse or neglect. The law also created a judicial bypass procedure. Subdivision 6 allowed a minor who did not want to inform either parent to go to court, be supplied with counsel, and be judged whether she was mature enough to make the decision alone or if an abortion was in her best interest.

The Supreme Court upheld the Minnesota law in *Hodgson v. Minnesota* (497 U.S. 417 [1990]) because it provided a provision for judicial bypass. The high court ruled that "the constitutional objection to the two-parent notice requirement is removed by the judicial bypass option provided in Subdivision 6 of the Minnesota statute."

In 2003 Planned Parenthood of Northern New England sought a ruling against a 2003 New Hampshire law that required written parental notification 48 hours before any abortion was provided to a minor unless "the attending abortion provider certifies in the pregnant minor's medical record that the abortion is necessary to prevent the minor's death and there is insufficient time to provide the required notice." There was also a provision for judicial bypass within the law. In *Planned Parenthood of Northern New England et al. v. Peter Heed, Attorney General of the State of New Hampshire* (No. 04-1161), the district court found the law unconstitutional because it lacked an explicit exception to protect the health of the pregnant minor and because the exception for abortions necessary to prevent the minor's death was too narrow. An appeals court upheld this ruling in 2004.

The U.S. Supreme Court heard this case in November 2005 and ruled in January 2006. In *Ayotte v. Planned Parenthood of Northern New England* (546 U.S. 320), the high court ruled that it would be unconstitutional to apply the New Hampshire law in such a manner that women who risked serious and irreversible damage to their health were denied an abortion. The court did not, however, agree that the entire law was unconstitutional and returned the case to the lower courts and state legislature to reconsider whether there might be other remedies for the lack of a health exception. The New Hampshire legislature repealed the law in 2007.

NARAL indicates that 30 states had laws requiring parental consent in 2015. (See Table 2.3.) Three of these state laws (in California, Montana, and New Mexico) contradicted federal law, so they were considered unconstitutional and unenforceable. That same year another 19 states required parental notification before a minor had an abortion.

Place Restriction, Fetal Development and Viability Discussion, and Fetal Disposal

In 1975 the U.S. Supreme Court ruled in *Connecticut v. Menillo* (423 U.S. 9) that a state may require that abortions be performed only by physicians. Such restrictions continued in 1978, when the city of Akron, Ohio, enacted the ordinance Regulations of Abortions, which determined how abortions should be performed in the city. Among the restrictions on abortions were the following:

- All abortions performed after the first trimester of pregnancy had to be done in a hospital.

TABLE 2.3

State restrictions on minors' access to abortions, 2015

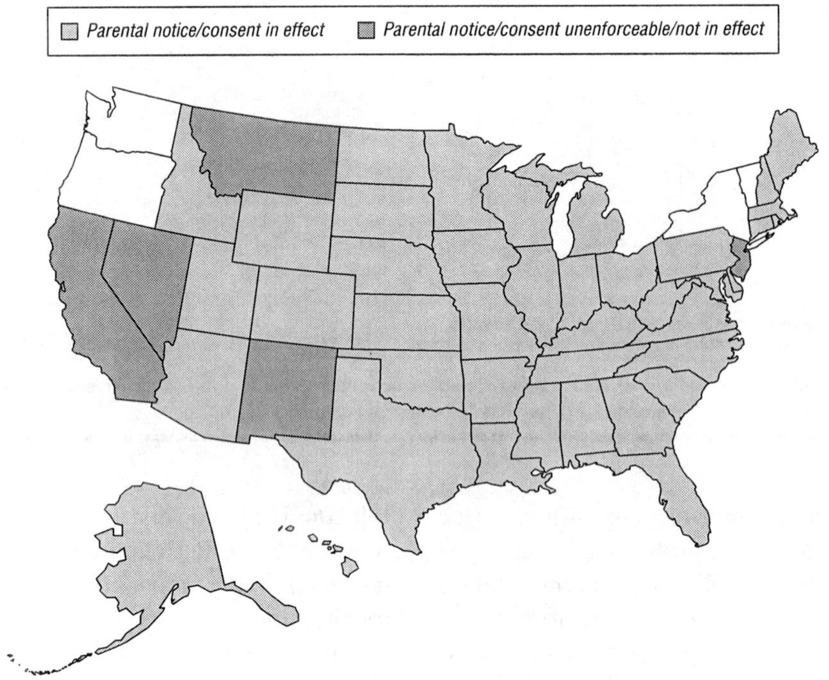

State	State mandates: Parental consent	State mandates: Parental notice	Consent/notice required from: One parent	Consent/notice required from: Two parents	Law is unconstitutional and unenforceable and/or not in effect
Alabama	✓		✓		
Alaska		✓	✓		
Arizona	✓		✓		
Arkansas	✓		✓		
California	✓		✓		✓
Colorado		✓		✓	
Connecticut					
Delaware		✓	✓		
District of Columbia					
Florida		✓	✓		
Georgia		✓	✓		
Hawaii					
Idaho	✓		✓		
Illinois		✓	✓		
Indiana	✓		✓		
Iowa		✓	✓		
Kansas	✓		✓		
Kentucky	✓		✓		
Louisiana	✓		✓		
Maine	✓		✓		
Maryland		✓	✓		
Massachusetts	✓			✓*	
Michigan	✓		✓		
Minnesota		✓		✓	
Mississippi	✓			✓	
Missouri	✓		✓		
Montana	✓		✓		✓
Nebraska	✓		✓		
Nevada		✓	✓		✓
New Hampshire		✓	✓		
New Jersey		✓	✓		✓
New Mexico	✓		✓		✓
New York					
North Carolina	✓		✓		
North Dakota	✓			✓	
Ohio	✓		✓		
Oklahoma	✓	✓	✓		
Oregon					
Pennsylvania	✓				

TABLE 2.3

State restrictions on minors' access to abortions, 2015 [CONTINUED]

State	State mandates: Parental consent	State mandates: Parental notice	Consent/notice required from: One parent	Consent/notice required from: Two parents	Law is unconstitutional and unenforceable and/or not in effect
Rhode Island	✓		✓		
South Carolina	✓		✓		
South Dakota		✓	✓		
Tennessee	✓		✓		
Texas	✓	✓	✓		
Utah	✓	✓	✓		
Vermont					
Virginia	✓	✓	✓		
Washington					
West Virginia		✓	✓		
Wisconsin	✓		✓		
Wyoming	✓	✓	✓		
Totals	30	19	39	5	5

*This statute requires two-parent consent, but a court has issued an order that the law be enforced as requiring the consent of one parent.
30 states restrict young women's access to abortion by requiring parental consent: AL, AR, AZ, CA, ID, IN, KS, KY, LA, MA, ME, MI, MO, MS, MT, NC, ND, NE, NM, OH, OK, PA, RI, SC, TN, TX, UT, VA, WI, WY.
3 of these laws are unconstitutional and unenforceable: CA, MT, NM.
19 states restrict young women's access to abortion by requiring parental notice: AK, CO, DE, FL, GA, IA, IL, MD, MN, NH, NJ, NV, OK, SD, TX, UT, VA, WV, WY.
2 of these laws are unconstitutional and unenforceable and/or not in effect: NJ, NV.
Notes: Some states allow additional exceptions to these restrictions not included in this chart.

SOURCE: "Restrictions on Young Women's Access to Abortion," in *What Is Choice?* NARAL Pro-Choice America and NARAL Pro-Choice America Foundation, 2015, http://www.prochoiceamerica.org/what-is-choice/maps-and-charts/map.jsp?mapID=12 (accessed September 21, 2015)

- The attending physician must inform the patient of the status of her pregnancy; the development of the fetus; the date of possible fetal viability; the physical and emotional complications that may result from an abortion; and the availability of agencies to provide her with assistance and information regarding birth control, childbirth, and adoption. The physician must also tell the patient about the particular risks associated with her pregnancy and the abortion method to be used.
- Physicians performing abortions must ensure that fetal remains were disposed of in a "humane and sanitary manner."

Violation of any provision constituted a criminal misdemeanor. Many antiabortion groups considered the Akron ordinance model legislation to be followed by other communities wishing to regulate abortion within their jurisdictions.

After mixed rulings in the federal district court and in the federal court of appeals, the case was argued before the Supreme Court. In a 6–3 decision in *City of Akron v. Akron Center for Reproductive Health, Inc.* (462 U.S. 416 [1983]), the Supreme Court struck down many aspects of Akron's ordinance.

Noting the significant medical improvements in abortion procedures and the concurrent sharp decrease in the number of deaths resulting from late-term abortions, the high court ruled that it was not necessary that all second trimester abortions be performed in a hospital. The court also ruled that the provision regarding the information the physician must give the woman before abortion was unconstitutional: "By insisting upon recitation of a lengthy and inflexible list of information, Akron unreasonably has placed 'obstacles in the path of the doctor upon whom [the woman is] entitled to rely for advice in connection with her decision.'"

Finally, the Supreme Court invalidated the provision requiring a "humane and sanitary" disposal of the fetal remains. Although Akron claimed the purpose of this provision was to prevent the disposal of aborted fetuses in garbage piles, the city was not clear that this alone was the reason for the provision. The high court agreed with the appellate court that the provision suggested a possible regulation on "some sort of 'decent burial' of an embryo at the earliest stages of formation." The court concluded that this unclear provision was "fatal" where a physician could be criminally held liable for disposing of the fetal remains.

A case in 1983 further challenged such restrictions on abortion. The case of *Planned Parenthood of Kansas City, Missouri v. Ashcroft* (462 U.S. 476) concerned a Missouri law requiring the following:

- All abortions after the first trimester must be performed in a hospital.
- Minors must have parental consent or judicial authorization for their abortions.
- Two doctors must be present at the abortion.
- A pathologist's report must be obtained for every abortion.

The court found the hospitalization requirement to be unconstitutional for the same reasons stated in *City of*

Akron v. Akron Center for Reproductive Health, Inc., but found the other restrictions constitutional.

Late-Term Abortions

STATE PARTIAL-BIRTH ABORTION LAWS. Table 2.4 shows the 32 states with laws banning partial-birth abortions. The status of each law as of September 2015 is shown in the column to the right of each state. The term *partial-birth abortion* is favored by those who oppose the procedure and is the common name for the medical procedure known as intact dilation and extraction (intact D&X), which can be used to end pregnancies in the second or third trimester, generally after 20 weeks of gestation. Karen Pazol et al. of the Centers for Disease Control and Prevention report in "Abortion Surveillance—United States, 2011" (*Morbidity and Mortality Weekly Report*, vol. 63, no. 11, November 28, 2014) that 730,322 abortions were performed in 2011. Of these abortions, only 1.4% were performed after 21 weeks or later of pregnancy.

TABLE 2.4

State bans on "partial-birth" abortion, September 2015

		Definition		Exceptions		
State	Status of law	Mirrors federal definition	State definition	Broad health	Narrow health	Life only
Alabama	a		a			a
Alaska	a		a			a
Arizona	c	c				c
Arkansas	c	c				c
Florida	a		a	c, d		a
Georgia	c, d		c, d			
Idaho	a		a			a
Illinois	a		a			a
Indiana	e		e			e
Iowa	a		a			a
Kansas	c	c				c
Kentucky	a		a			a
Louisiana	c	c				c
Michigan	c	c				c
Mississippi	e		e			e
Missouri	b	b				b
Montana	d, e		d, e			d, e
Nebraska	a		a			a
New Hampshire	c	c				c
New Jersey	a		a			a
New Mexico	c, d		c, d		c, d	
North Dakota	c	c				c
Ohio	c	c			c	
Oklahoma	e		e			e
Rhode Island	a		a			a
South Carolina	e		e			e
South Dakota	e		e			e
Tennessee	e		e			e
Utah	c	c				c
Virginia	c	c				c
West Virginia	a		a			a
Wisconsin	a		a			a
Total	**19**	**10**	**9**	**1**	**2**	**16**

[a]Enforcement permanently enjoined by court order; policy not in effect.
[b]This law is temporarily enjoined pending a final decision in the courts.
[c]Policy is currently in effect.
[d]Law applies post-viability only.
[e]This policy is presumably unenforceable under the terms set out in *Stenberg v. Carhart*; however, it has not been challenged in court.

SOURCE: "Bans on 'Partial-Birth' Abortion," in *State Policies in Brief: Bans on "Partial-Birth" Abortion*, Guttmacher Institute, September 1, 2015, http://www.guttmacher.org/statecenter/spibs/spib_BPBA.pdf (accessed September 21, 2015)

Nebraska's partial-birth abortion law was the first to reach the U.S. Supreme Court, in *Stenberg v. Carhart* (530 U.S. 914 [2000]). Although the term *partial-birth abortion* generally refers to the intact D&X procedure, the legal definition varies among states. This phrase was defined in the Nebraska statute as "an abortion procedure in which the person performing the abortion partially delivers vaginally a living unborn child before killing the unborn child and completing the delivery. For purposes of this subdivision, the term *partially delivers vaginally a living unborn child before killing the unborn child* means deliberately and intentionally delivering into the vagina a living unborn child, or a substantial portion thereof, for the purpose of performing a procedure that the person performing such procedure knows will kill the unborn child and does kill the unborn child."

Attorneys challenging this and similar laws as unconstitutional had three arguments:

- These bans are deceptive measures designed to outlaw virtually every type of abortion procedure.
- These laws are unconstitutional because they have no exceptions for women's health, and criminalize doctors for providing the safest medical care.
- These laws are unconstitutional because they unduly burden a woman's right to choose, thus violating standards set in *Roe v. Wade* and *Planned Parenthood of Southeastern Pennsylvania v. Casey* (505 U.S. 833 [1992]).

The court ruled on the last two points: the lack of a health exception (allowing an abortion when "necessary, in appropriate medical judgment, for the preservation of the life or health of the mother") and the undue burden on a woman's right to abortion (created by the broad language of the ban, which made it unclear which methods of abortion were banned). For the majority, Justice Stephen Breyer (1938–) wrote, "Taking account of these virtually irreconcilable points of view, aware that constitutional law must govern a society whose different members sincerely hold directly opposing views, and considering the matter in light of the Constitution's guarantees of fundamental individual liberty, this Court, in the course of a generation, has determined and then redetermined that the Constitution offers basic protection to the woman's right to choose."

For the minority, Justice Clarence Thomas (1948–) wrote:

> *Casey* itself noted that States may "express profound respect for the life of the unborn".... States may, without a doubt, express this profound respect by prohibiting a procedure that approaches infanticide, and thereby dehumanizes the fetus and trivializes human life. The AMA [in the American Medical Association

> Board of Trustees "Factsheet" on H.R. 1122, June 1997] has recognized that this procedure is "ethically different from other destructive abortion techniques because the fetus, normally twenty weeks or longer in gestation, is killed outside the womb. The 'partial birth' gives the fetus an autonomy which separates it from the right of the woman to choose treatments for her own body."

FEDERAL PARTIAL-BIRTH ABORTION LAWS. In 1995 Congress passed the Partial-Birth Abortion Ban Act, which was vetoed by President Bill Clinton (1946–) in 1996. In 1997 Congress once again passed the Partial-Birth Abortion Ban Act, which was vetoed by President Clinton that same year. Congress then passed the Partial-Birth Abortion Ban Act of 2003. The act imposed civil and criminal penalties on physicians who knowingly performed the intact D&X abortion procedure, which was called intact D&E in the act and in subsequent court rulings because it is a variation of the dilation and evacuation (D&E) procedure. In November 2003 President George W. Bush (1946–) signed it into law, becoming the first U.S. president to ever place a federal ban on abortion. However, within hours of Bush's signing the bill, a federal judge in Nebraska granted a temporary restraining order, making the law ineffective until its constitutionality—according to the 2000 *Stenberg v. Carhart* decision—could be determined.

Lawsuits challenging the constitutionality of the Partial-Birth Abortion Ban Act of 2003 were brought in three states: California, Nebraska, and New York. In 2004 federal judges in all three states ruled the legislation to be unconstitutional. The federal judge in California, the first to render a decision, ruled that the Partial-Birth Abortion Ban Act of 2003 was unconstitutional in three ways: it placed an undue burden on women seeking abortions, its language was vague, and it lacked an exception for medical actions needed to preserve the woman's health. In July 2005 a federal appeals court in St. Louis upheld the Nebraska ruling, this was then appealed to the U.S. Supreme Court.

THE PARTIAL-BIRTH ABORTION BAN ACT OF 2003 IS DECLARED CONSTITUTIONAL. The constitutionality of the 2003 Partial-Birth Abortion Ban Act was heard in the Supreme Court as *Gonzales v. Carhart*. In April 2007 the high court ruled in a 5–4 decision that the law was constitutional.

Justice Anthony M. Kennedy (1936–) delivered the opinion of the court. He was joined in this opinion by Chief Justice John G. Roberts Jr. (1955–) and Justices Samuel A. Alito Jr. (1950–), Antonin Scalia (1936–), and Thomas. The long opinion includes the following: "The Act's ban on abortions that involve partial delivery of a living fetus furthers the Government's objectives. No one would dispute that, for many, D&E is a procedure itself laden with the power to devalue human life. Congress could nonetheless conclude that the type of abortion proscribed by the Act requires specific regulation because it implicates additional ethical and moral concerns that justify a special prohibition. Congress determined that the abortion methods it proscribed had a 'disturbing similarity to the killing of a newborn infant.'"

This decision opened the door to reviving state bans on late-term abortion procedures that had previously been blocked by the courts. Those who applauded the high court's decision in upholding the federal Partial-Birth Abortion Ban Act not only expected state late-term abortion bans to be revived but also saw the possibility of adding more restrictions on late-term abortion procedures.

Justice Ruth Bader Ginsburg's (1933–) dissenting opinion, which was joined by Justices John Paul Stevens (1920–), David H. Souter (1939–), and Breyer, stated in part: "Today's decision is alarming.... It tolerates, indeed applauds, federal intervention to ban nationwide a procedure found necessary and proper in certain cases by the American College of Obstetricians and Gynecologists (ACOG). It blurs the line, firmly drawn in *Casey*, between previability and postviability abortions. And, for the first time since *Roe*, the Court blesses a prohibition with no exception safeguarding a woman's health."

Ginsburg ended her dissent with the following concern about a future attack on the *Roe v. Wade* decision and a woman's right to choose abortion: "In sum, the notion that the Partial-Birth Abortion Ban Act furthers any legitimate governmental interest is, quite simply, irrational. The court's defense of the statute provides no saving explanation. In candor, the Act, and the court's defense of it, cannot be understood as anything other than an effort to chip away at a right declared again and again by this Court—and with increasing comprehension of its centrality to women's lives."

Based on the court's ruling, 10 states (Alabama, Arizona, Florida, Kansas, Louisiana, Mississippi, North Carolina, Oklahoma, Texas, and Virginia) enacted laws requiring physicians to perform an ultrasound (a method that produces images of internal body structures) prior to an abortion. Some of the new laws require women to look at the ultrasound image of the fetus and listen to the fetal heartbeat before undergoing an abortion.

LATER-TERM ABORTIONS. The majority of states restrict later-term abortions. The exact meaning of "later-term" varies from one state to another. Table 2.5 shows state policies on later-term abortions and that the threshold for later-term ranges from viability to the third trimester. In the wake of the *Gonzalez v. Carhart* decision a number of states enacted restrictions that, in the opinion of the Guttmacher Institute, violate the standards established by the Supreme Court because they place limits on abortions even before a fetus is viable. As of November 2015, these policies had not been considered by the Supreme Court.

TABLE 2.5

State policies on later-term abortions, September 2015

State	State restrictions on later abortion: Limit on abortion after viability	State restrictions on later abortion: Limit on abortion at a specific gestational age	Exceptions: Life and health	Exceptions: Life and physical health	Exceptions: Life	When a later abortion is performed a second physician must: Attend	When a later abortion is performed a second physician must: Approve
Alabama		20 weeks postfertilization[c]		X		Postviability	Postviability
Arizona	X	[b]	X			Postviability	
Arkansas		20 weeks postfertilization[c]		X[f]		Postviability	
California	X		X				
Connecticut	X		X				
Delaware	X		X				[b]
Florida		24 weeks LMP	X			Postviability	X
Georgia	X	[d]		X[g]			
Hawaii	X		X				
Idaho	X	[b]			X		Postviability
Illinois	X		X			X	
Indiana		20 weeks postfertilization[c]		X		X	
Iowa		3rd trimester LMP	X				
Kansas[e]		22 weeks LMP[c]		X			Postviability
Kentucky	X		X				
Louisiana		20 weeks postfertilization[c]		X[g]		Postviability	
Maine	X		X				
Maryland	X		X[g]				
Massachusetts		24 weeks post-implantation	X				
Michigan	X				X		
Minnesota	X		X			X	
Mississippi		20 weeks LMP[c]		X			
Missouri	X			X		X	
Montana	X		X[h]				X
Nebraska		20 weeks postfertilization[c]		X			
Nevada		24 weeks postfertilization	X				
New York		24 weeks postfertilization			X	X	
North Carolina		20 weeks LMP	X				
North Dakota		20 weeks postfertilization[c]		X			
Ohio	X		X			X	X
Oklahoma[e]		20 weeks postfertilization[c]		X		Postviability	
Pennsylvania		24 weeks LMP	X[h]			X	X
Rhode Island		24 weeks LMP			X		
South Carolina		3rd trimester postfertilization	X[i]				X
South Dakota		24 weeks LMP	X				
Tennessee	X		X				
Texas		20 weeks postfertilization[c]		X[g]			
Utah	X		X[f, g, h]				
Virginia		3rd trimester LMP	X				X
Washington	X		X				
West Virginia		22 weeks LMP[c]		X[g]			
Wisconsin	X	[a]	X				
Wyoming	X		X				
Total	**21**	**22**	**26**	**13**	**4**	**13**	**9**

LMP (last menstrual period) = calculates the beginning of pregnancy from the woman's last menstrual period.
States that do not explicitly enumerate the manner in which gestational age should be determined are labeled as 'LMP' in keeping with standard medical practice.
Postfertilization = calculates the beginning of pregnancy from the date of conception; 20 weeks postfertilization is equivalent to 22 weeks LMP.
Post-implantation = calculates the beginning of pregnancy from the date of implantation; 24 weeks implantation is equivalent to 27 weeks LMP.
[a]New law scheduled to take effect early in 2016.
[b]Enforcement permanently enjoined by a court order; policy not in effect.
[c]Based on the assertion that the fetus can feel pain at 18 or 20 weeks postfertilization.
[d]A new Georgia law that would ban abortion at 20 weeks postfertilization is only being enforced against postviability abortions.
[e]A new law would ban the most commonly used method of abortion in the second trimester, thereby essentially banning abortion as early as 14 weeks LMP. The Kansas law is blocked pending the resolution of a court case. The Oklahoma law is scheduled to take effect later in 2015.
[f]Also permitted in case of rape or incest.
[g]Also permitted in case of fetal abnormality; in Georgia, Louisiana, Texas, Utah and West Virginia the law applies to a lethal abnormality.
[h]The exception permits abortions when the woman suffers from a "substantial and irreversible impairment of a major bodily function."
[i]If done for mental health reasons, must have the certification of an independent psychiatrist.

SOURCE: "Later Abortion Policies," in *State Policies in Brief: State Policies on Later Abortion*, Guttmacher Institute, September 1, 2015, http://www.guttmacher.org/statecenter/spibs/spib_PLTA.pdf (accessed September 1, 2015)

PROTESTERS AT ABORTION CLINICS

In the four decades since the *Roe v. Wade* decision, reproductive health clinics and health care providers across the United States and Canada have been under attack by antiabortion protesters. Physicians and clinic workers have been shot; clinics have been bombed, burned down, invaded, and blockaded; and patients have been abused and intimidated. In 1993 the protests turned deadly for the first time when the physician David Gunn (1946–1993) was fatally shot by

Michael Griffin (1961–), an antiabortion protester, in Pensacola, Florida.

The year before, in 1992, the U.S. Supreme Court heard *Bray v. Alexandria Clinic* (506 U.S. 263 [1993]), a case in which antiabortion protesters challenged an injunction (ban) against their activities, which included blocking access to health care facilities in the District of Columbia. The injunction being challenged was based on an 1871 civil rights statute that provided protection against private conspiracies, such as the Ku Klux Klan preventing African Americans from exercising their freedoms. In this case it was argued that antiabortion activists were preventing women from exercising their freedoms. The high court found that antiabortion protests outside an abortion clinic were not in violation of the Civil Rights Act because "women seeking abortions" were not a "class of persons of the equal protection of the laws, or of equal privileges and immunities under the laws" and protesters did not show class-based discrimination toward women.

To help prevent clinic violence, Congress overwhelmingly passed the Freedom of Access to Clinic Entrances (FACE) Act of 1994, which was signed into law by President Clinton. FACE is designed to protect those providing and those receiving reproductive health care services. It forbids the use of "force," "threat of force," or "physical obstruction" to prevent someone from providing or receiving reproductive health services. There are criminal and civil penalties for those who break the law. Although the law has had an effect on certain types of clinic violence (see Chapter 6), it has not eliminated it.

Other Supreme Court cases provide for the constitutionality of buffer zones between protesters and patients and clinic employees. For instance, in *Madsen v. Women's Health Center* (512 U.S. 753 [1994]), the court upheld an injunction that forbade protesters from entering a 36-foot (11-m) buffer zone in front of an abortion clinic and upheld noise restrictions. However, the court did not uphold an injunction that prevented protesters from getting within 300 feet (91.4 m) of a clinic or staff residence to approach clinic staff and patients. Also, nonthreatening posters within the 36-foot buffer zone were allowed.

In its 1997 *Schenck v. Pro-Choice Network of Western New York* (519 U.S. 357) ruling, the court upheld an injunction that forbade antiabortion protesters from entering a 15-foot (4.6-m) fixed buffer zone in front of an abortion clinic. The protesters had argued that their right to free speech was being violated, but the high court ruled that their free speech was ensured because they could be heard from a distance. Also, the court allowed "cease and desist" counseling. This meant that as many as two protesters at a time could perform "sidewalk counseling" within the buffer zone, but if the counselors were asked to stop (to "cease and desist"), they had to honor that request and leave the buffer zone. The court did not uphold the injunction preventing protesters from coming within a 15-foot floating buffer zone of people entering or leaving an abortion clinic. A floating buffer zone around a person moves as the person moves.

In 2000 in *Hill v. Colorado* (530 U.S. 703), the court ruled that a Colorado statute does not violate the First Amendment (free speech) and the right to a free press. The statute forbids anyone to knowingly come closer than 8 feet (2.4 m) to anyone who is within 100 feet (30.5 m) of the entrance of a health care facility without that person's consent, for the purpose of giving the person a leaflet, offering education or counseling, displaying a sign, or otherwise engaging in protest. The court concluded that the statute "is a regulation of the places where some speech may occur."

National Organization for Women v. Scheidler: A 20-Year-Long Case

In 2003 the 17-year-old *National Organization for Women v. Scheidler* case was decided, but the case would not be over until 2006. The parties to the case were the National Organization for Women (NOW) and Joseph Scheidler of the Pro-Life Action League.

In June 1986 NOW and two abortion clinics in Delaware filed a complaint in federal court against Scheidler and the Pro-Life Action League, alleging violations of the Sherman and Clayton antitrust laws that are intended to prevent the formation of monopolies. In 1989 NOW added charges that individuals and organizations that oppose legal abortion violated the Racketeer Influenced and Corrupt Organizations (RICO) Act by engaging in a nationwide conspiracy to shut down abortion clinics through "a pattern of racketeering activity" that included acts of extortion in violation of the Hobbs Act.

In 1991 the case was dismissed on the grounds that the RICO law requires the defendants to have an economic motive for their crimes, and an appeal by NOW was unsuccessful. In 1992 NOW asked the Supreme Court for a ruling on the use of the RICO statute. In 1994 the high court ruled in favor of NOW, allowing it to use federal antiracketeering laws against antiabortion activists who organize others for terrorist activities, such as bombing and forcefully blocking abortion clinics. RICO cannot be used against those engaging in peaceful protests.

After many delays, the *NOW v. Scheidler* trial took place in 1998. The jury found the defendants guilty of racketeering and engaging in a nationwide conspiracy to deny women access to medical facilities. In 2002, however, Scheidler asked the Supreme Court to review the decision. In February 2003 the Supreme Court decided 8–1 in *Scheidler v. NOW* (537 U.S. 393) that the RICO statute was used improperly against Scheidler and other antiabortion activists, meaning that these groups could not be sued for extortion under racketeering laws that are intended to combat organized crime. Thus, the prior guilty verdict against Scheidler and his codefendants was overturned.

NOW claimed that the 2003 decision did not address the question of whether physical violence outside of clinics might still be punished under the Hobbs Act. In February 2006 the Supreme Court ruled 8–0 (Justice Alito did not take part in the case) on this issue in favor of Scheidler in *Scheidler v. NOW* (547 U.S. 9), stating that the charge of extortion could not be applied to pro-life demonstrations outside abortion facilities. Physical violence outside of clinics was not covered under the Hobbs Act.

Antiabortion advocates (and others such as labor union supporters) hailed the decision as one that supported the right of people to protest for social change. Pro-choice advocates saw the ruling as a statement that the Supreme Court was no longer going to protect abortion clinics and women attending those clinics against the violence of antiabortion protesters. In the article "Supreme Court Rules against NOW, Clinics in Anti-abortion Violence Case" (MsMagazine.com, February 28, 2006), Kim Gandy, the president of NOW, lamented this decision, "Without strong protections against clinic assaults, the legal right to abortion could become meaningless. If women are too terrified to walk into clinics and healthcare providers are too terrified to keep their doors open, then we will have lost the fight for reproductive freedom even with *Roe v. Wade* still on the books."

RULINGS ON THE FETUS

Saving a "Viable Fetus"

In January 1979 the issue of the legal identity of the fetus first reached the U.S. Supreme Court. In *Colautti v. Franklin* (439 U.S. 379), the plaintiff (the person who brings an action in a court of law) challenged the provisions of a Pennsylvania law that gave the state the power to protect an unborn child beginning in the sixth month of pregnancy.

This law required physicians performing abortions to save the fetus if they had grounds to believe that the fetus "may be viable." The Supreme Court held that the provisions of the law were "void for vagueness" because the meanings of the terms *viable* and *may be viable* were unclear and because these provisions interfered with the physicians' proper exercise of judgment. The court also found the law unconstitutional because it could impose criminal liability on physicians if they were thought to have failed to take proper action.

"FETAL PAIN" LAWS. In June 2013 the U.S. House of Representatives passed the Pain-Capable Unborn Child Protection Act. Written by Representative Trent Franks (1957–; R-Arizona), the bill prohibited doctors from performing an abortion if they believe the fetus is 20 weeks or more past conception, with exceptions under certain circumstances. The bill was based in part on the notion that at 20 weeks a fetus can feel pain. However, in the most exhaustive review of scientific evidence performed to date, "Fetal Pain: A Systematic Multidisciplinary Review of the Evidence" (*Journal of the American Medical Association*, vol. 294, no. 8, August 2005), Susan J. Lee et al. explain that that the fetus does not have the capacity to feel pain before 29 or 30 weeks. In September 2015 the act failed to pass the U.S. Senate, after Republicans were unable to organize the 60 votes needed to overcome a Democratic filibuster and bring the act to a vote.

Ruling That Life Begins at Conception

In 1986 Missouri passed legislation amending a number of laws concerning unborn children and abortion. It placed several restrictions on abortion. The new law:

- Declared that life begins at conception.
- Required physicians to perform tests to determine the viability of fetuses after 20 weeks of gestational age.
- Forbade the use of public employees and facilities for abortions not necessary to save the mother's life.
- Prohibited the use of public funds, employees, or facilities for the purpose of counseling a woman to have an abortion not necessary to save her life.

Lower courts struck down these restrictions, but the Supreme Court did not. In 1989 the court upheld the Missouri law in *Webster v. Reproductive Health Services* (492 U.S. 490). This ruling was the first case in which a majority of the justices generally opposed abortion, and it revealed the court's willingness to adopt a more lenient attitude toward state limitations on abortions.

Writing for the 5–4 majority, Chief Justice William H. Rehnquist (1924–2005), who was joined by Justices Byron R. White (1917–2002) and Kennedy, found nothing wrong with the preamble of the Missouri law, which stated that "the life of each human being begins at conception." The court observed that *Roe v. Wade* "implies no limitation on a State's authority to make a value judgment favoring childbirth over abortion.... The preamble can be read simply to express that sort of value judgment." The court chose not to rule on the constitutionality of the law's preamble because it considered the preamble to be merely an abstract proposition.

Relying on *Maher v. Roe*, *Poelker v. Doe*, and *Harris v. McRae*, the court ruled that "a government's decision to favor childbirth over abortion through the allocation of public funds does not violate *Roe v. Wade*." In addition, "Missouri's decision to use public facilities and employees to encourage childbirth over abortion places no governmental obstacle in the path of a woman who chooses to terminate her pregnancy, but leaves her with the same choices as if the State had decided not to operate any hospitals at all."

Perhaps the most controversial aspect of the Missouri law was the requirement that a physician had to determine the viability of the fetus if the physician thought the fetus might be 20 or more weeks old. There was no debate over whether a fetus is viable at 20 weeks, because the earliest that a fetus is viable is at 21 to 22 weeks of gestational life. However, there could be a four-week error in estimating gestational age. The court ruled that the testing for fetal viability was constitutional because it furthered Missouri's interest in protecting potential human life.

Chief Justice Rehnquist thought the "rigid" trimester system outlined in *Roe v. Wade* was no longer useful, if it ever was. He felt the *Roe v. Wade* framework, which contains specific elements such as trimesters and viability, was not consistent with the concept of a constitution that deals in general principles.

Although they came close, the majority did not overturn *Roe v. Wade*. While respecting the preamble of the Missouri law, Rehnquist concluded that although the state's interest had been moved back well into the second trimester of pregnancy, *Webster* did not revisit the *Roe v. Wade* ruling.

Scalia, however, believed *Roe v. Wade* should have been overturned in this case because most of the justices thought the *Roe v. Wade* decision was wrong. He stated, "It thus appears that the mansion of constitutionalized abortion law, constructed overnight in *Roe v. Wade*, must be disassembled doorjamb by doorjamb, and never entirely brought down, no matter how wrong it may be."

Justice Harry A. Blackmun (1908–1999), who wrote the *Roe v. Wade* decision, was equally angry but for the opposite reason. In a dissent joined by Justices William J. Brennan Jr. (1906–1997) and Thurgood Marshall (1908–1993), Blackmun observed that "*Roe v. Wade*... and the fundamental constitutional right of women to decide whether to terminate a pregnancy, survive but are not secure."

Although *Webster* did not overturn *Roe v. Wade*, it did mark a significant change in the legal landscape that was related to abortion. It gave the states more latitude in placing restrictions on abortion and weakened the viability and trimester framework that had previously been used to help determine the legality of terminating a pregnancy.

CASEY SUPERSEDES, BUT DOES NOT OVERTURN, *ROE*

From the Trimester Framework to Undue Burden

Pennsylvania has a long history of trying to pass restrictive abortion statutes, which began with the Abortion Control Act of 1974. In 1989, having seen how in *Webster* a more conservative Supreme Court seemed ready to overturn decisions made by an earlier, more liberal court, the Pennsylvania legislature passed a new Abortion Control Act, which was an amended version of the 1974 abortion law.

Before the Abortion Control Act took effect, five abortion clinics and one physician (representing himself and a group of physicians who provided abortion services) sued the state of Pennsylvania, which was represented by Governor Robert P. Casey (1932–2000). The resulting case was *Planned Parenthood of Southeastern Pennsylvania v. Casey.*

The Supreme Court ruling on *Casey* was a 5–4 split decision, with the majority opinion written by Justices Sandra Day O'Connor (1930–), Kennedy, and Souter and joined in part by Justices Stevens and Blackmun. The majority reaffirmed the essential holding in *Roe v. Wade*, "A recognition of a woman's right to choose to have an abortion before fetal viability and to obtain it without undue interference from the State." After viability the state may prohibit abortion, but only if it provides exceptions for pregnancies that may endanger the woman's life or health.

In addition, the court rejected the trimester framework, which had strictly limited the state from regulating abortion during early pregnancy, and replaced it with the undue burden standard. Under the undue burden standard states may restrict the abortion process throughout pregnancy as long as they do not have "the purpose or effect of placing a substantial obstacle in the path of a woman seeking an abortion of a nonviable fetus."

The justices upheld Pennsylvania's proposed restrictions—a 24-hour waiting period, informed consent, parental consent, and reporting and recordkeeping requirements—except for the spousal-consent requirement. Chief Justice Rehnquist and Justices Thomas, White, and Scalia agreed with the provisions upheld by the majority decision, but they felt the decision did not go far enough. They proposed that requiring spousal consent was a rational attempt to encourage communication between spouses and should be upheld. Furthermore, they felt that a woman's liberty to abort her unborn child is not a right protected by the Constitution and that the *Roe v. Wade* decision was a mistake.

Stevens, however, wrote an opinion supporting the *Roe v. Wade* decision and rejecting the 24-hour waiting period and the "biased" informed-consent provision (which required pro-life information to be given to the woman seeking an abortion). Blackmun rejected all the provisions of the Pennsylvania law and reaffirmed the constitutionality of the *Roe v. Wade* decision.

THE BASIS FOR MAINTAINING *ROE V. WADE*. The justices who wrote the majority opinion explained that they upheld *Roe v. Wade*'s essential holding because their duty is "to define the liberty of all," not to impose their own moral standards: "These matters, involving the most intimate and personal choices a person may make in a lifetime, choices central to personal dignity and autonomy, are central to the liberty protected by the Fourteenth Amendment. At the heart of liberty is the right to define one's own concept of existence, of meaning, of the universe, and of the mystery of human life. Beliefs about these matters could not define the attributes of personhood were they formed under compulsion of the State."

The justices also maintained:

> Though abortion is conduct, it does not follow that the State is entitled to proscribe it in all instances. That is because the liberty of the woman is at stake in a sense unique to the human condition, and so, unique to the law. The mother who carries a child to full term is subject to anxieties, to physical constraints, to pain that only she must bear. That these sacrifices have from the beginning of the human race been endured by woman with a pride that ennobles her in the eyes of others and gives to the infant a bond of love cannot alone be grounds for the State to insist she make the sacrifice. Her suffering is too intimate and personal for the State to insist, without more, upon its own vision of the woman's role, however dominant that vision has been in the course of our history and our culture. The destiny of the woman must be shaped to a large extent on her own conception of her spiritual imperatives and her place in society.

The court also upheld the right to abortion because of its obligation to follow precedent. Under the doctrine of stare decisis (literally, to stand by things decided), which requires courts to reach consistent conclusions in cases that raise the same factual and legal issues, a majority of the court could not justify overthrowing the findings of *Roe v. Wade*.

CHAPTER 3

ABORTION: A MAJOR POLITICAL ISSUE

A DEFINITION OF POLITICS

Merriam-Webster (November 2015, http://www.merriam-webster.com/dictionary/politics) defines *politics* as "the art or science concerned with guiding or influencing governmental policy." This chapter examines those who make the policy (the laws)—Congress and state legislatures—and those who rule on the constitutionality of those laws—the state-level federal courts and the U.S. Supreme Court—to examine key factors in the politics of abortion.

JUDICIAL APPOINTMENTS AND POLITICS

When the president and most of the U.S. Senate are of the same political party, and when they are in agreement about the direction public policy should take, confirmation of a judicial nominee is relatively easy. The opposition party, however, is sometimes able to use procedural practices, such as filibusters (prolonged speeches), to delay or prevent the confirmation vote. When the president and the Senate are at odds, confirmation of a judge has the potential to be contentious.

Federal judges are appointed for life, so each appointment has a long-lasting influence on the court system and on the lives of Americans. Because the judges are appointed by the president, the nominees usually hold political views that are similar to the president's. Thus, if a president is opposed to abortion, it is likely that he will appoint federal judges who are known to be conservative on this issue.

Jeffrey A. Segal, the coauthor of *Advice and Consent: The Politics of Judicial Appointments* (2005), notes that "most justices appointed by conservative presidents cast a high percentage of conservative votes.... Likewise, most justices appointed by liberal presidents cast a higher percentage of left-of-center votes than their colleagues seated by more conservative presidents."

However, Lee Epstein, Segal's coauthor, adds, "During the first four years of justices' tenure, their voting behavior correlates at a rather high level with their appointing president's ideology, but for justices with ten or more years of service, that relationship drops precipitously. In other words, liberal presidents appoint liberal justices who continue to take liberal positions for a while, and the same holds true for conservatives. But as new issues come to the Court, or as the justice for whatever reason makes adjustments in his or her political outlook, the president's influence wanes."

Given their prominent role in interpreting the country's laws, federal judges have had a tremendous impact on the issue of abortion. This is demonstrated by the numerous U.S. Supreme Court rulings that have dealt with this topic since the 1970s (see Chapter 2). When President George W. Bush (1946–) nominated new justices in 2005 and 2006, people on both sides of the abortion issue were interested in their opinions on the issue. The same was true when President Barack Obama (1961–) nominated new justices in 2009 and 2010.

Bush's Supreme Court Nominees

In 2004 a bipartisan (two-party) group of seven moderate Senate Democrats and seven moderate Senate Republicans (called the Gang of 14) advised President Bush about acceptable Supreme Court nominees to replace retiring Justice Sandra Day O'Connor (1930–). In July 2005 President Bush nominated John G. Roberts Jr. (1955–) to replace O'Connor. However, in September 2005—before Roberts could be confirmed by the Senate—Chief Justice William H. Rehnquist (1924–2005) died. Bush took this opportunity to renominate Roberts, this time for the chief justice position, and Roberts was confirmed in September 2005. In November 2005 Bush nominated Samuel A. Alito Jr. (1950–) to replace O'Connor. Alito was confirmed in January 2006.

Obama's Supreme Court Nominees

On May 1, 2009, President Obama announced Justice David H. Souter's (1939–) retirement at the end of his term in June 2009. Although Souter was appointed by President George H. W. Bush (1924–), a Republican conservative, he had liberal leanings and wrote (with Justices Anthony M. Kennedy [1936–] and O'Connor) in the 1992 decision of *Planned Parenthood of Southeastern Pennsylvania v. Casey* (505 U.S. 833) that "the essential holding of *Roe v. Wade* should be retained and once again reaffirmed."

On May 26, 2009, Obama announced his choice for Souter's replacement: federal appeals court judge Sonia Sotomayor (1954–). Her views on abortion and *Roe v. Wade* (410 U.S. 113 [1973]) were largely unknown at the time of her nomination, and her related decisions revealed only that she based her judicial decisions on constitutional law. Nonetheless, Robert Barnes and Michael D. Shear report in "White House Tries to Quell Abortion Rights Supporters' Fears about Sotomayor" (WashingtonPost.com, May 29, 2009) that a few days after Sotomayor's nomination Robert Gibbs (1971–), the White House press secretary, assured pro-choice supporters that Sotomayor believed in "constitutional protections for a woman's right to [abortion]." She was officially confirmed by the Senate in August 2009.

In April 2010 Justice John Paul Stevens (1920–), at that time the longest-serving justice on the Supreme Court, announced that he would retire in June 2010. Nominated by President Gerald R. Ford (1913–2006), a Republican, Stevens was considered a liberal member of the high court and was a supporter of abortion rights. Obama nominated the U.S. solicitor general Elena Kagan (1960–) as Stevens's replacement. The Office of the Solicitor General is within the U.S. Department of Justice; it supervises and conducts the legal proceedings in the Supreme Court in which the U.S. government is either the plaintiff or the defendant. The solicitor general personally argues most of these cases.

As the senior domestic policy adviser to President Bill Clinton (1946–), Kagan recommended in 1997 that Clinton support a ban on late-term abortions if it included an exception for the health of the mother. As explained by Eleanor Clift in "Context Matters" (Newsweek.com, May 13, 2010), this apparent pro-life stance was not as it seemed. Clift quotes Karen O'Connor of the Women and Politics Institute at the American University, who noted that Kagan was simply "trying to get as much as possible for women in a hostile [political] environment." Clift describes Kagan as a "consensus seeker" and a "pragmatic politician." Kagan was officially confirmed by the Senate in August 2010.

Should Potential Judges' Positions on Abortion Be a Key Issue in Their Nominations?

During Roberts's nomination, the Senate Republican Policy Committee stated that judicial nominees should not be coerced to reveal their positions on particular issues. According to Denis Steven Rutkus of the Congressional Research Service (CRS), in *Proper Scope of Questioning of Supreme Court Nominees: The Current Debate* (September 1, 2005, http://congressionalresearch.com), the committee noted that "no judicial nominee should be compelled to answer any question that would force him or her to prejudge or signal future conclusions regarding any case or issue." Furthermore, the committee suggested that this practice turns "judicial nominees into mere 'candidates' who must make political promises in order to be confirmed."

The public disagreed with the Senate Republican Policy Committee, as shown by a 2005 Quinnipiac University national poll. The poll asked whether senators should support or oppose Roberts's nomination based on his qualifications alone, or whether they should also consider his views on controversial issues such as abortion. In the press release "Supreme Court Nominee Should Speak Up on Abortion, U.S. Voters Tell Quinnipiac University National Poll" (July 27, 2005, http://www.quinnipiac.edu/news-and-events/quinnipiac-university-poll/national/release-detail?ReleaseID=820), the university notes that 56% of respondents thought that senators should consider Roberts's views on controversial issues such as abortion when deciding whether or not to confirm his appointment, whereas 36% thought that he should be judged on his qualifications alone. Quinnipiac pollsters also asked if Roberts should reveal his position on abortion during his Senate confirmation hearings. Sixty-one percent of respondents said Roberts should reveal his position, whereas 32% of respondents said he should not. The poll found that respondents were split on whether Roberts should be confirmed if he refused to speak publicly about his views on the subject, with 43% saying such a refusal would justify voting against his confirmation, compared with 47% who said this would not justify denying his confirmation.

In May 2009 Quinnipiac University asked a similar question about Sotomayor's nomination. In the press release "U.S. Voters Approve 2–1 of Obama's Sotomayor Pick, Quinnipiac University National Poll Finds; Legal Skill More Important Than Diversity, Most Say" (May 29, 2009, http://www.quinnipiac.edu/news-and-events/quinnipiac-university-poll/national/release-detail?ReleaseID=1306) the university indicates that 47% of respondents said senators should only consider Sotomayor's qualifications, whereas 43% thought her views on controversial issues such as abortion should be considered—a much lower percentage than with the Roberts nomination. A majority of Republicans (58%) thought senators should consider Sotomayor's views, in contrast with the position of the Senate Republican Policy Committee in 2005, whereas only 32% of Democrats felt this way. A larger percentage of Democrats (56%) than Republicans (33%) thought that only Sotomayor's qualifications should be considered.

In May 2010 Quinnipiac University asked a similar question about Kagan's nomination. The university reports in the press release "Obama Approval Tips Positive for First Time This Year, Quinnipiac University National Poll Finds; More Voters Approve of Kagan Supreme Court Pick" (May 26, 2010, https://www.quinnipiac.edu/news-and-events/quinnipiac-university-poll/national/release-detail?ReleaseID=1458) that respondents were evenly split: 43% said Kagan's views on controversial issues such as abortion should be considered by senators, whereas 43% said her qualifications should be all that mattered. The percentage of respondents believing that qualifications were all that mattered was down from 2009, but the percentage of those who thought that views on controversial issues should be considered remained the same.

WHAT ROBERTS, ALITO, SOTOMAYOR, AND KAGAN SAID AS CANDIDATES AND HOW THEY SUBSEQUENTLY VOTED. During his Senate confirmation hearings, Roberts would not say whether he would reverse the long-standing *Roe v. Wade* decision legalizing abortion, but he did say he believed the U.S. Constitution provided a right to privacy, which is a key foundational point of *Roe v. Wade*. Alito said during his Senate confirmation hearings that he would approach any Supreme Court case on abortion with an open mind. Both were confirmed, and in November 2006 both were involved in ruling on the constitutionality of the Partial-Birth Abortion Ban Act of 2003 in *Gonzales v. Carhart* (550 U.S. 124 [2007]). Roberts and Alito voted with Justices Antonin Scalia (1936–), Kennedy, and Clarence Thomas (1948–) that the act was constitutional—this majority thus overturned many previous lower court rulings that the act was unconstitutional. Chapter 2 contains a detailed discussion of this Supreme Court decision.

During her Senate confirmation hearings, Sotomayor did not reveal her opinion about abortion. By contrast, Kagan made clear during the hearings that any restrictions on abortion must take into account the life and health of the mother. As of November 2015, *Gonzales v. Carhart* was the most recent decision the Supreme Court had rendered related to abortion, so Justices Sotomayor and Kagan had not yet had an opportunity to vote on an abortion-related issue in the high court.

STATE GOVERNMENTS AND LEGISLATURES ON ABORTION

The 1973 *Roe v. Wade* decision catalyzed the pro-life movement. Following the landmark decision, pro-life groups (called antiabortion or antichoice groups by their opponents) supported constitutional amendments to overturn the *Roe v. Wade* ruling, but none was passed. A constitutional amendment requires two-thirds approval of each house of Congress and ratification by three-quarters of the state legislatures. Since then, antiabortion groups have attempted to limit aspects of the *Roe v. Wade* decision by influencing the appointment of lower-court and Supreme Court judges and also by advocating laws that restrict the circumstances under which abortions can be performed. Pro-choice groups suggest that antichoice legislative measures—such as recognizing the embryo and fetus as a person for legal purposes, mandating a waiting period, counseling requirements, and restricting minors' access to abortion—are attempts to chip away at the *Roe v. Wade* decision.

NARAL Pro-Choice America (NARAL) is a prominent advocacy group devoted to protecting a woman's right to choose to have an abortion. NARAL tracks state legislation that it considers to be antichoice. Figure 3.1 shows that between 1995 and 2014 state governments enacted 835 such measures. According to NARAL, 27 antichoice measures were enacted in 16 states in 2014. (See Figure 3.2.) NARAL reports in *Who Decides? The Status of Women's Reproductive Rights in the United States* (January 2015, http://www.prochoiceamerica.org/assets/download-files/2015-who-decides.pdf) that in 2014 Louisiana enacted the most antichoice legislation, with four measures, and that Alabama, Florida, Indiana, Kansas, Missouri, Oklahoma, South Dakota, and Virginia each enacted two antichoice measures. In contrast, 373 pro-choice measures were enacted between 2004 and 2014. In 2014, 17 states and the District of Columbia enacted 22 pro-choice measures. California enacted the most pro-choice legislation in 2015, with three measures.

Figure 3.3 shows the choice positions of state governments in 2015. To be considered either pro-choice or antichoice in this analysis, most of the legislature and the governor of the state must hold the position in question. NARAL rated 13 states and the District of Columbia as having pro-choice governments in 2015 and 28 as having antichoice governments. Figure 3.4 shows each governor's position on choice. Table 3.1 shows each state legislature's (as well as Congress's) position on choice.

State restrictions on abortion are varied and numerous. Table 3.2 shows an overview of state abortion laws in 2015. The most common restrictions in effect were parental notification or consent requirements for minors, state-mandated counseling, waiting periods before receiving an abortion, and limitations on public funding.

HOMICIDE LAWS AND FETUSES

According to the National Conference of State Legislatures, in "Fetal Homicide Laws" (http://www.ncsl.org/research/health/fetal-homicide-state-laws.aspx), as of

FIGURE 3.1

Cumulative number of antichoice measures enacted, 1995–2014

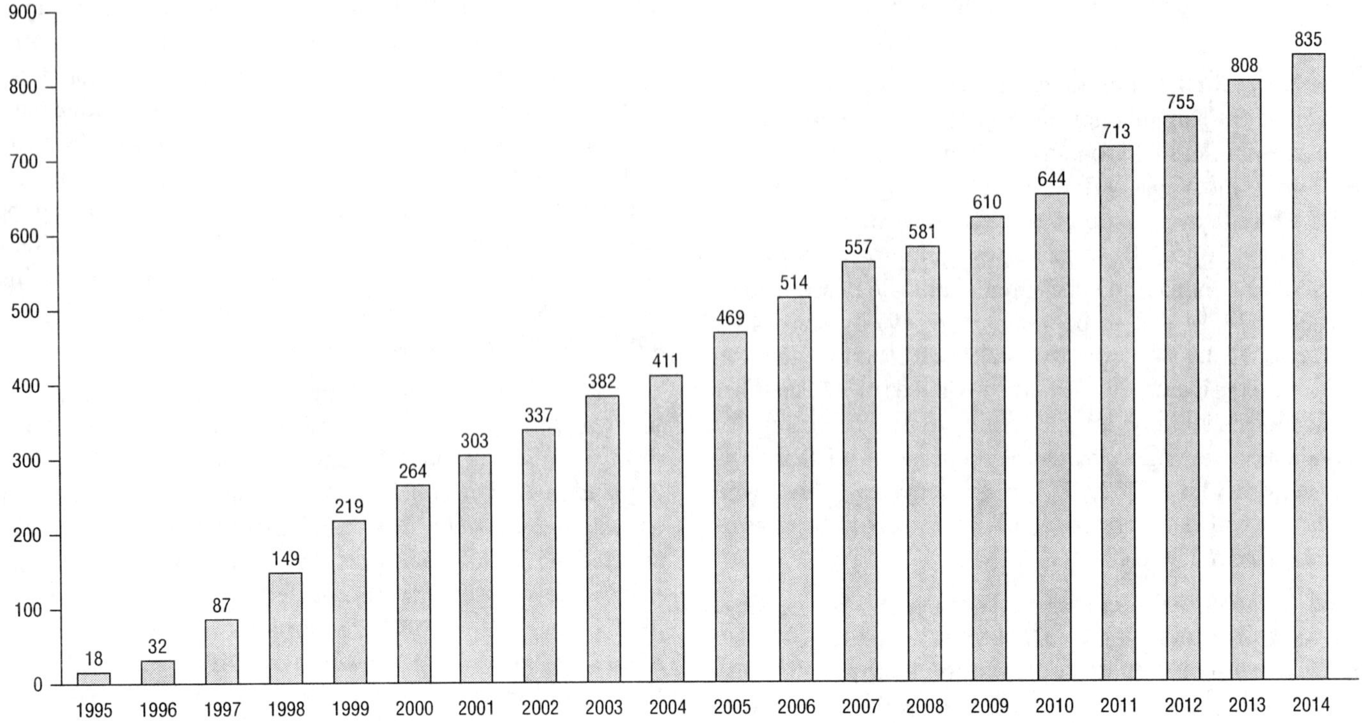

Note: Chart includes only state measures not local ordinances.

SOURCE: "Cumulative Number of Anti-Choice Statewide Measures Enacted since 1994," in *Who Decides? The Status of Women's Reproductive Rights in the United States*, 24th edition, NARAL Pro-Choice America and NARAL Pro-Choice America Foundation, 2015, http://www.prochoiceamerica.org/assets/download-files/2015-who-decides.pdf (accessed November 9, 2015)

March 2015, 38 states had homicide laws that recognize unborn fetuses as victims at some point before birth. The Unborn Victims of Violence Act of 2004 covers unborn victims of federal and military crimes; it does not, however, override existing state laws. The legislation indicates that anyone who causes the death or bodily injury of a fetus is "guilty of a separate offense" and that "the punishment for that separate offense is the same as the punishment provided for that conduct under Federal law had that injury or death occurred to the unborn child's mother." The law makes exceptions for legal medical procedures, including abortion, and acts on behalf of a pregnant woman. However, opponents of the law consider it a sneak attack on abortion rights because, in effect, it considers a fetus to be a person. They also state that pro-life groups are attempting to label the fetus as a person to change public perception about the nature of abortion.

FEDERAL FUNDING AND ABORTION

The federal government established the Medicaid program in 1965 to pay for medical care for the nation's needy through a federal-state cost-sharing arrangement. During the administration of President Richard M. Nixon (1913–1994), the U.S. Department of Health, Education, and Welfare (HEW; now called the U.S. Department of Health and Human Services) reimbursed states for abortions for poor women. Following the *Roe v. Wade* decision in 1973, the HEW considered abortion to be a medical procedure funded by Medicaid, so a cost-sharing arrangement went into effect.

Rachel K. Jones and Kathryn Kooistra indicate in "Abortion Incidence and Access to Services in the United States, 2008" (*Perspectives on Sexual and Reproductive Health*, vol. 43, no. 1, March 2011) that after *Roe v. Wade* the number of abortions increased rapidly, with approximately 1 million abortions performed in 1975. Antiabortion supporters were angered by what they considered to be a mass slaughter partially financed with tax dollars, and they responded by lobbying their senators and representatives to end this practice.

The Hyde Amendment

In 1976 Representative Henry J. Hyde (1924–2007; R-IL) introduced an abortion rider to the HEW-Labor appropriations bill. The rider, and related measures implemented

FIGURE 3.2

States that enacted antichoice measures in 2014

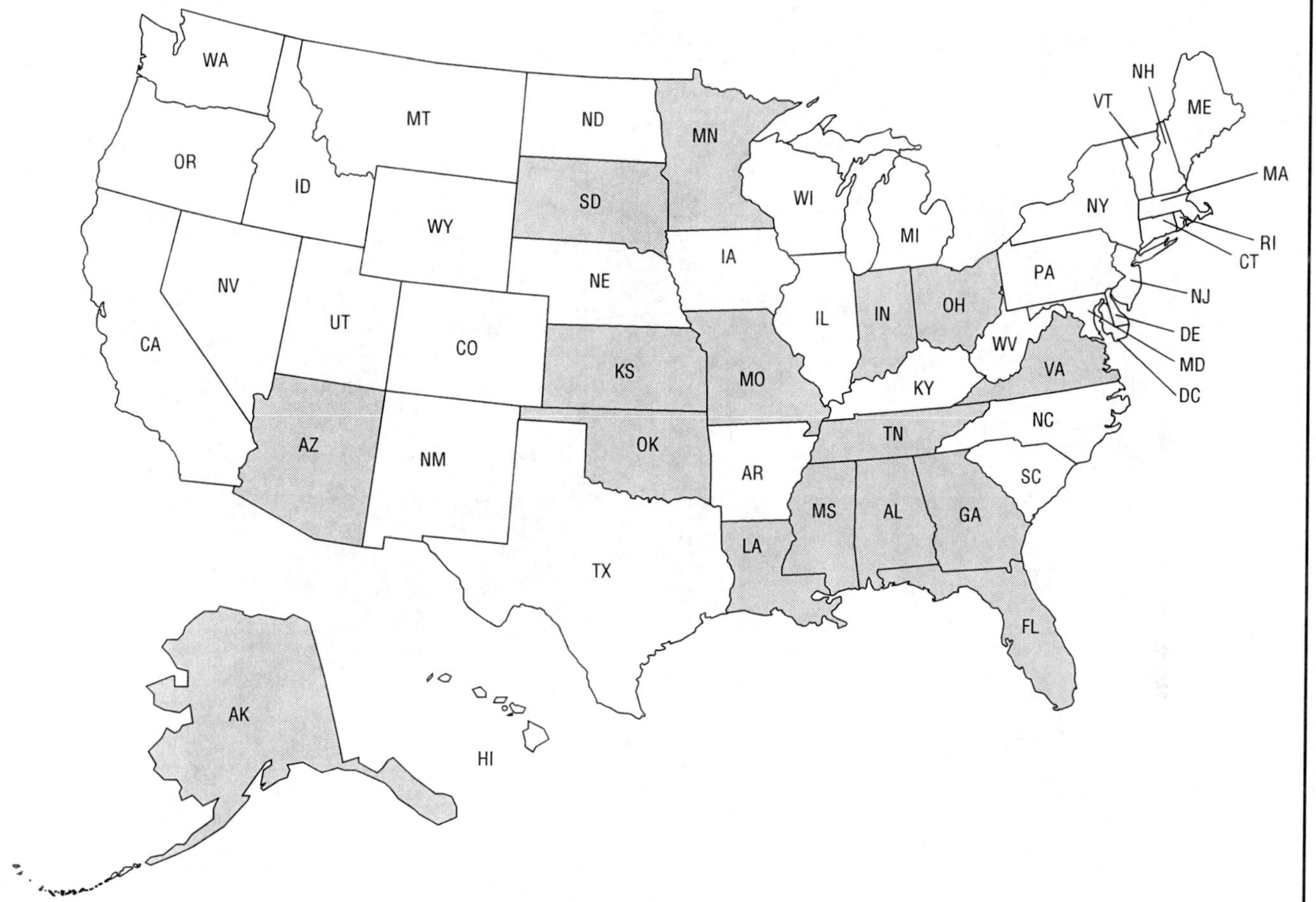

SOURCE: "States That Enacted Anti-Choice Measures in 2014," in *Who Decides? The Status of Women's Reproductive Rights in the United States*, 24th edition, NARAL Pro-Choice America and NARAL Pro-Choice America Foundation, 2015, http://www.prochoiceamerica.org/assets/download-files/2015-who-decides.pdf (accessed November 9, 2015)

in later years, came to be known as the Hyde Amendment. Hyde originally proposed that no federal funding could be used for abortion. Following considerable debate, Congress settled on a compromise, which stated that none of the funds contained in the appropriations bill would be used to perform abortions except:

- For victims of rape or incest if the occurrence was reported promptly to the proper authorities
- If justified to save the mother's life
- In instances where two doctors determined that "severe and long-lasting physical health damage to the mother" may result

The Departments of Labor and Health, Education, and Welfare Appropriations Act, which included the abortion provision, became law in September 1976 and went into effect in August 1977. In 1979 the physical health provision of the Hyde Amendment was removed, and in 1981 the rape and incest provision was removed. Thus, federal funding could be used for abortion services only to save the mother's life. In 1980 the Supreme Court ruled in *Harris v. McRae* (448 U.S. 297) that the Hyde Amendment and its restrictions were constitutional (see Chapter 2). In 1993 Congress rewrote the Hyde Amendment to once again include federal funding of abortions for pregnancies that resulted from rape or incest, and that form of the amendment was still in force as of November 2015. The Patient Protection and Affordable Care Act of 2010 (also known as the Affordable Care Act [ACA]), which focused on reform of the private health insurance market, maintains the Hyde Amendment restrictions.

STATE FUNDING AND ABORTION

Medicaid, a federal assistance program for low-income people, is implemented by the states using federal funds and guidelines. Thus, as of November 2015 states must at a minimum cover the cost of abortions for Medicaid beneficiaries when their pregnancies result from

FIGURE 3.3

Pro-choice and antichoice state governments, 2015

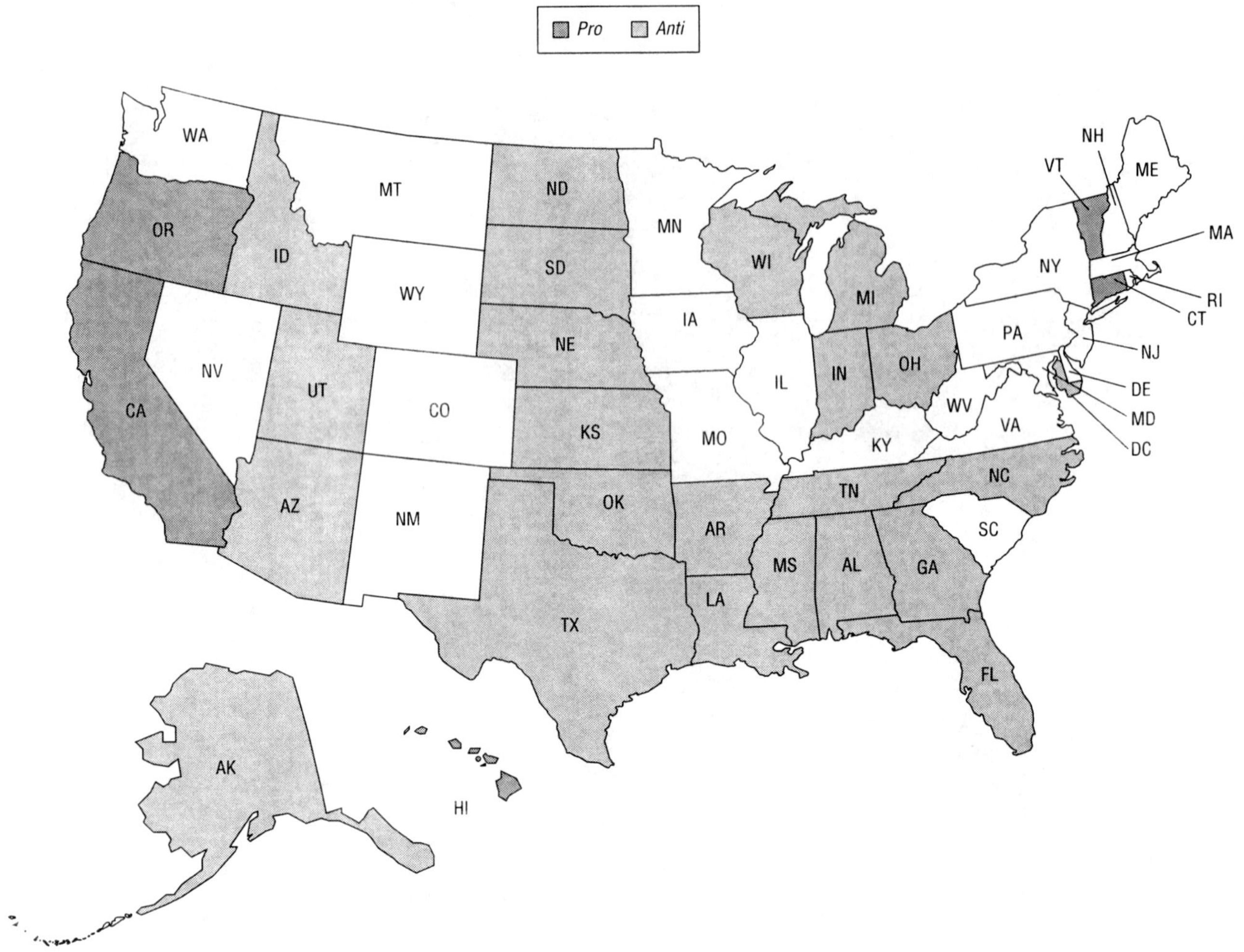

SOURCE: "Pro-Choice and Anti-Choice State Governments," in *Who Decides? The Status of Women's Reproductive Rights in the United States*, 24th edition, NARAL Pro-Choice America and NARAL Pro-Choice America Foundation, 2015, http://www.prochoiceamerica.org/assets/download-files/2015-who-decides.pdf (accessed November 9, 2015)

rape or incest, or if the continued pregnancy endangers the life of the mother.

As of September 2015, 32 states and the District of Columbia only paid for abortions under Medicaid in cases of life endangerment, rape, and incest. (See Table 3.3.) In addition, six of those states allowed funding in situations involving fetal impairment or threats to the mother's long-term health. South Dakota, in violation of federal law, provided Medicaid funding for abortion only if a woman's life was in danger. In the remaining 17 states, Medicaid would pay for most medically necessary abortions. In many states this policy was the result of a court order rather than a voluntary decision by the legislature.

Abortion Funding and Managed Care

In 1996, for the first time since the *Roe v. Wade* decision, congressional elections resulted in a pro-life majority in both the House of Representatives and the Senate. Pro-life lawmakers pointed out that because states were increasingly contracting with managed-care organizations to provide Medicaid recipients with health services, the Hyde Amendment had to be revised. Representative Hyde sought to forbid health plans from offering abortion coverage when they contracted with states under Medicaid. He claimed that in cases where states used their own funds to pay for abortions beyond the federally mandated cases of rape, incest, and life endangerment, purchasing a health plan using a "co-mingling" of federal and state monies presented the possibility of an indirect federal abortion subsidy.

Hyde's proposed change was met with opposition from pro-choice Democrats. They protested that the new law would negatively affect privately insured women whose insurance companies contracted with the states. It would also affect Medicaid recipients in those states where

FIGURE 3.4

Choice positions of state governors, 2015

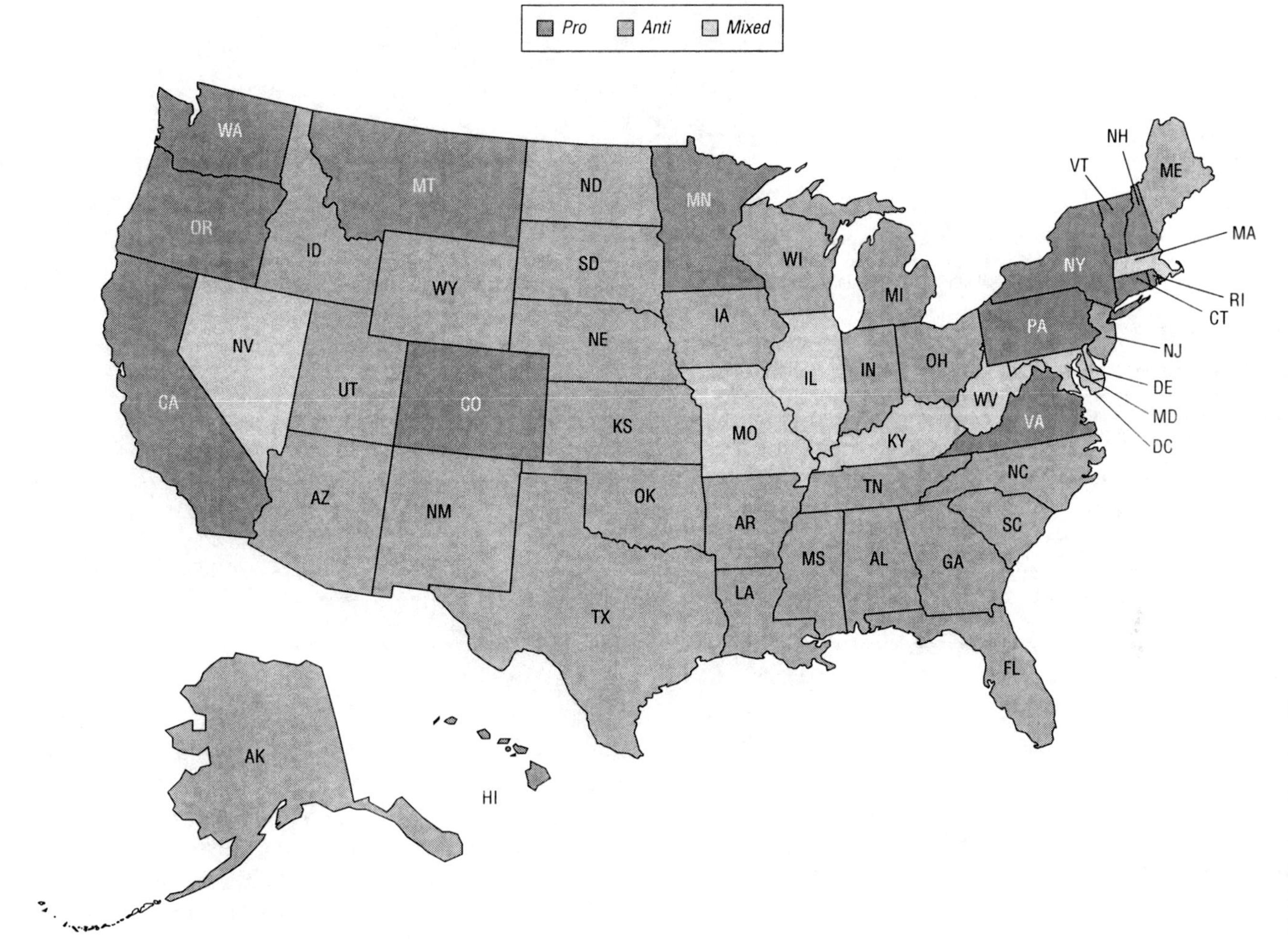

SOURCE: "Choice Positions of Executives," in *Who Decides? The Status of Women's Reproductive Rights in the United States*, 24th edition, NARAL Pro-Choice America and NARAL Pro-Choice America Foundation, 2015, http://www.prochoiceamerica.org/assets/download-files/2015-who-decides.pdf (accessed November 9, 2015)

abortions were subsidized. The revised version eventually passed with the provision that federal funds would not be used to purchase managed-care packages that included coverage of abortion. States that covered abortion with their own funds would be able to continue doing so under a separate program. In November 1997 President Clinton signed the Departments of Labor, Health and Human Services, and Education, and Related Agencies Appropriations Act of 1998 with this abortion provision.

Abortion Funding and the State Children's Health Insurance Program

In August 1997 the Balanced Budget Act amended the Social Security Act by adding Title XXI (State Children's Health Insurance Program [CHIP]) to allocate funds to states to provide child health assistance to uninsured, low-income children who are not eligible for Medicaid. Under CHIP state funds may be used for abortion only to save the life of the mother or if the pregnancy resulted from rape or incest.

The Impact of the Patient Protection and Affordable Care Act

The landmark 2010 health care reform legislation, the ACA, did not alter federal abortion policy. Under the law, health plans are not required to cover abortions as part of their health benefits. They can opt to cover no abortions, only those abortions permitted by the Hyde Amendment (rape, incest, and life endangerment), or abortions beyond those allowed by Hyde.

The ACA specifies that an insurance exchange be available in every state, which residents can use to shop for different health insurance policies. Within the exchanges, ACA requires that there be at least one plan that covers

TABLE 3.1

Choice positions of the federal and state legislatures, 2015

U.S. Congress

The choice composition of the U.S. Senate is:
- 37 pro-choice senators
- 9 mixed-choice senators
- 54 anti-choice senators

The choice composition of the U.S. House is:
- 166 pro-choice members
- 22 mixed-choice members
- 246 anti-choice members

State legislatures

Legislatures that are anti-choice outnumber pro-choice legislatures:
- 8 states and the District of Columbia have pro-choice legislatures (both the house and senate are pro-choice): CA, CT, DC (city council), HI, MD, MA, NJ, OR, VT.
- 25 states have anti-choice legislatures (both the house and senate are anti-choice): AL, AK, AR, AZ, FL, ID, IN, KS, KY, LA, MI, MS, MO, NE, NC, ND, OH, OK, SD, TN, TX, UT, VA, WV, WI.

Choice composition of state senates*:
- 12 states and the District of Columbia have a pro-choice senate: CA, CT, DC (city council), HI, IL, IA, MD, MA, MN, NJ, NM, OR, VT.
- 10 states have a mixed-choice senate: CO, DE, ME, MT, NV, NH, PA, SC, WA, WY.
- 28 states have an anti-choice senate: AL, AK, AZ, AR, FL, GA, ID, IN, KS, KY, LA, MI, MS, MO, NE, NY, NC, ND, OH, OK, RI, SD, TN, TX, UT, VA, WV, WI.

Choice composition of state houses:
- 12 states have a pro-choice house: CA, CO, CT, HI, ME, MD, MA, NJ, NY, OR, VT, WA.
- 7 states have a mixed-choice house: DE, GA, IL, NV, NH, NM, RI.
- 30 states have an anti-choice house: AL, AK, AZ, AR, FL, ID, IN, IA, KS, KY, LA, MI, MN, MS, MO, MT, NC, ND, OH, OK, PA, SC, SD, TN, TX, UT, VA, WV, WI, WY.

*The terms "house" and "senate" include the equivalent bodies in states that have different titles for their state legislative bodies. Nebraska has a unicameral body that is counted as a senate, and the District of Columbia's city council—for this purpose—is counted as a senate.

SOURCE: "Choice Positions of Legislatures," in *Who Decides? The Status of Women's Reproductive Rights in the United States*, 24th edition, NARAL Pro-Choice America and NARAL Pro-Choice America Foundation, 2015, http://www.prochoiceamerica.org/assets/download-files/2015-who-decides.pdf (accessed November 9, 2015)

abortions beyond those permitted under the Hyde Amendment, and at least one that only covers abortions permitted under the Hyde Amendment.

The ACA offers conscience protections for providers. The law stipulates that health care providers and health care facilities may not be discriminated against because of their willingness, or unwillingness, to cover, provide, pay for, or refer for abortions.

ABORTION SERVICES FOR MILITARY PERSONNEL

According to David F. Burrelli of the CRS, in *Abortion Services and Military Medical Facilities* (April 24, 2002, http://digital.library.unt.edu/govdocs/crs/permalink/meta-crs-2404:1), before 1970 the U.S. armed forces did not have an official policy regarding the provision of abortion. Military medical facilities followed the laws in the states in which they were located, and it was up to individual physicians whether to offer abortion services.

In 1970 the U.S. Department of Defense (DOD) issued an order that abortions in the military should be performed only when medically necessary or when the mental health of the mother was in danger. After the 1973 Supreme Court decision in *Roe v. Wade*, the DOD funded abortions for women eligible for military health care. To perform an abortion, Burrelli explains, two physicians had to satisfy the stipulation of medical necessity or risk to mental health and funding had to comply with state regulations.

By 1981 abortion was allowed only to save the life of the mother. In 1988 the DOD began banning all abortions at military medical facilities overseas, even if the woman was willing to pay for the procedure herself. Burrelli notes that in 1993 President Clinton issued a memorandum to "permit abortion services to be provided [at U.S. military facilities], if paid for entirely with non-DOD funds." However, in 1996, after Republicans took control of Congress, the National Defense Authorization Act established a policy where the military would only permit privately funded abortions in overseas facilities in cases of rape or incest. The military continued to permit, and pay for, abortions that were necessary because the mother's life was in danger.

The National Defense Authorization Act of 2013 adjusted the military's policy on funding for abortions at overseas facilities. Under the act, the military would now pay for abortions overseas that were medically necessary or that were the result of rape or incest. As of November 2015, abortions that did not meet these standards remained unavailable at overseas military facilities, even if paid for with private funds. According to NARAL, in the fact sheet "Lift the Ban on Privately Funded Abortion Services for Military Women" (January 1, 2015, http://www.prochoiceamerica.org/media/fact-sheets/abortion-private-ban-military-women.pdf), this means that many women in the U.S. armed forces seeking an abortion have two options. One is to get an abortion at a private facility overseas. However, depending on where the woman is stationed, adequate medical services may be difficult or impossible to access. The other option is

TABLE 3.2

Overview of state abortion laws, 2015

State	Must be performed by a licensed physician	Must be performed in a hospital if at:	Second physician must participate if at:	Prohibited except in cases of life or health endangerment if at:	"Partial-birth" abortion banned	Public funding of abortion: Funds all or most medically necessary abortions	Public funding of abortion: Funds limited to life endangerment, rape and incest	Private insurance coverage limited
AL	X	Viability	Viability	20 weeks[a]	▼		X	
AK	X				▼	X		
AZ	X	Viability	Viability	Viability	X	X		X
AR	X		Viability	20 weeks[b]	X		X	
CA				Viability		X		
CO							X	
CT		Viability		Viability		X		
DE	X			Viability			X	
DC							X	
FL	X	Viability	24 weeks	24 weeks	▼		X	
GA	X			Viability	Postviability		X	
HI	X			Viability		X		
ID	X	Viability	3rd trimester	Viability	▼		X	X
IL			Viability	Viability	▼	X		
IN	X	20 weeks	20 weeks	20 weeks[a]	X		X[a]	X
IA	X			3rd trimester	▼		X	
KS	X		Viability	20 weeks[a]	X		X	X
KY	X	2nd trimester		Viability	▼		X	X
LA	X		Viability	20 weeks[a]	X		X	
ME	X			Viability			X	
MD	X			Viability[d]		X		
MA	X			24 weeks		X		
MI	X			Viability[c]	X		X	X
MN	X	20 weeks	24 weeks	24 weeks		X		
MS	X[f]			20 weeks[a]	X		X[d]	
MO	X	Viability	Viability	Viability	▼		X	X
MT			Viability	Viability[a]	Postviability	X		
NE	X			20 weeks[a]	▼		X	X
NV	X	24 weeks		24 weeks			X	
NH					X		X	
NJ	X[e]	14 weeks			▼	X		
NM	X				Postviability	X		
NY			24 weeks	24 weeks[c]		X		
NC	X	20 weeks		20 weeks			X	
ND	X			20 weeks[a]	X		X	X
OH	X	Viability	Viability	Viability[a]	X		X	
OK	X	2nd trimester	Viability	20 weeks[a]	X		X	X
OR						X		
PA	X	Viability	Viability	24 weeks[a]			X	
RI				24 weeks[c]	▼		X	▼
SC	X	3rd trimester	3rd trimester	3rd trimester	X		X	
SD	X	24 weeks		24 weeks	X		Life only	
TN	X			Viability	X		X	
TX	X			20 weeks[a]			X	
UT	X	90 days		Viability[b, d]	X		X[a]	X
VT						X		
VA	X	2nd trimester	Viability	3rd trimester	X		X[d]	
WA				Viability		X		
WV				20 weeks[a]	▼	X		
WI	X	Viability		Viability	▼		X[a]	
WY	X			Viability			X	
Total	**38**	**20**	**18**	**43**	**19**	**17**	**32 + DC**	**11**

to return to the United States for an abortion, but this requires permission from a commanding officer that may not be forthcoming.

ABORTION SERVICES FOR INCARCERATED WOMEN

In "Advocating for Pregnant Women in Prison: The Role of the Correctional Nurse" (*Journal of Forensic Nursing*, vol. 9, no. 2, April–June 2013), Ginette G. Ferszt, Joyce E. Hickey, and Kimberly Seleyman report that the incidence of pregnancy among incarcerated women in U.S. jails and prisons ranges from 6% to 10%. Although no data exist on the percentage of unwanted pregnancies among incarcerated women, the Guttmacher Institute reports in "Facts on Induced Abortion in the United States" (July 2014, http://www.guttmacher.org/pubs/fb_induced_abortion.pdf) that 21% of all pregnancies (not including miscarriages) in the general population of U.S. women are terminated by abortion. It is reasonable to assume that a similar percentage of pregnant, incarcerated women would choose to terminate their pregnancies.

TABLE 3.2

Overview of state abortion laws, 2015 [CONTINUED]

State	Providers may refuse to participate		Mandated counseling includes information on:			Waiting period (in hours) after counseling	Parental involvement required for minors
	Individual	Institution	Breast cancer link	Fetal pain	Negative psychological effects		
AL						48	Consent
AK	X	Private	X	X			Notice
AZ	X	X				24	Consent
AR	X	X		X[h]		48	Consent
CA	X	Religious					▼
CO							Notice
CT	X						
DE	X	X				▼	Notice[j]
DC							
FL	X	X				24	Notice
GA	X	X		X		24	Notice
HI	X	X					
ID	X	X				24	Consent
IL	X	Private					Notice
IN	X	Private		X		18	Consent
IA	X	Private					Notice
KS	X	X	X	X	X	24	Consent
KY	X	X				24	Consent
LA	X	X		X	X	24	Consent
ME	X	X					
MD	X	X					Notice
MA	X	X				▼	Consent
MI	X	X			X	24	▼
MN	X	Private		X[h]		24	Notice[i]
MS	X	X	X			24	Consent[i]
MO	X	X		X[h]		72	Consent
MT	X	Private				▼	Notice
NE	X	X			X	24	Consent
NV	X	Private					▼
NH							Notice
NJ	X	Private					▼
NM	X	X					▼
NY	X						
NC	X	X			X	72	Consent
ND	X	X				24	Consent[i]
OH	X	X				24	Consent
OK	X	Private	X	X[h]		24	Consent and notice
OR	X	Private					
PA	X	Private				24	Consent
RI	X						Consent
SC	X	Private				24	Consent
SD	X	X		X	X	72[k]	Notice
TN	X	X				48	Consent
TX	X	Private	X	X	X	24	Consent and notice
UT	X	Private		X[h]	X	72[k]	Consent and notice
VT							
VA	X	X				24	Consent and notice
WA	X	X					
WV					X	24	Notice[j]
WI	X	X				24	Consent[j]
WY	X	Private					Consent and notice
Total	**45**	**42**	**5**	**12**	**9**	**28**	**38**

▼Permanently enjoined; law not in effect.
[a]Exception in case of threat to the woman's physical health.
[b]Exception in case of rape or incest.
[c]Exception in case of life endangerment only.
[d]Exception in case of fetal abnormality.
[e]Only applies to surgical abortion.
[f]Law limits abortion provision to OB/GYNs.
[g]Enforcement temporarily enjoined by court order; policy not in effect.
[h]Fetal pain information is given only to women who are at least 20 weeks gestation; in Missouri at 22 weeks gestation.
[i]Both parents must consent to the abortion.
[j]Specified health professionals may waive parental involvement in certain circumstances.
[k]In South Dakota, the waiting period excludes weekends or annual holidays and in Utah the waiting period is waived in cases of rape, incest, fetal defect or if the patient is younger than 15.

SOURCE: "Overview of State Abortion Law," in *State Policies in Brief: An Overview of Abortion Laws*, Guttmacher Institute, September 1, 2015, http://www.guttmacher.org/statecenter/spibs/spib_OAL.pdf (accessed September 21, 2015)

Carolyn B. Sufrin, Mitchell D. Creinin, and Judy C. Chang state in "Incarcerated Women and Abortion Provision: A Survey of Correctional Health Providers" (*Perspectives on Sexual and Reproductive Health*, vol. 41, no. 1, March 2009) that "the Eighth Amendment, which prohibits cruel and unusual punishment, guarantees all

TABLE 3.3

State funding of abortion under Medicaid, September 2015

State	Generally follows the federal standard, funds in cases of: Life endangerment, rape and incest	Other exceptions	Funds all or most medically necessary abortions
Alabama	X		
Alaska			Court order[c]
Arizona			Court order
Arkansas	X		
California			Court order
Colorado	X		
Connecticut			Court order
Delaware	X		
Dist. of Columbia	X		
Florida	X		
Georgia	X		
Hawaii			Voluntarily
Idaho	X		
Illinois			Court order
Indiana	X	Physical health	
Iowa[a]	X	Fetal impairment	
Kansas	X		
Kentucky	X		
Louisiana	X		
Maine	X		
Maryland			Voluntarily
Massachusetts			Court order
Michigan	X		
Minnesota			Court order
Mississippi	X	Fetal impairment	
Missouri	X		
Montana			Court order
Nebraska	X		
Nevada	X		
New Hampshire	X		
New Jersey			Court order
New Mexico			Court order
New York			Voluntarily
North Carolina	X		
North Dakota	X		
Ohio	X		
Oklahoma	X		
Oregon			Court order
Pennsylvania	X		
Rhode Island	X		
South Carolina	X		
South Dakota	[b]		
Tennessee	X		
Texas	X		
Utah	X	Physical health	
Vermont			Court order
Virginia	X	Fetal impairment	
Washington			Voluntarily
West Virginia			Court order
Wisconsin	X	Physical health	
Wyoming	X		
Total	**32 + DC**		**17**

[a]The Iowa governor must approve any abortion paid for by the Medicaid program.
[b]State only pays for abortions when necessary to protect the woman's life.
[c]A law that defines medically necessary is temporarily blocked by a court.

SOURCE: "State Funding of Abortion under Medicaid," in *State Policies in Brief: State Funding of Abortion under Medicaid*, Guttmacher Institute, September 1, 2015, http://www.guttmacher.org/statecenter/spibs/spib_SFAM.pdf (accessed September 21, 2015)

prisoners the right to health care; the Fourteenth Amendment, which prohibits states from depriving a person privacy without due process of the law, protects women's right to choose abortion regardless of incarceration. Nevertheless... the thicket of abortion politics can limit prisoners' access to health services." The researchers find that, in 2006 and 2007, abortion was more likely to be available from correctional health providers in states with predominantly Democratic legislatures (78% of facilities provided such services) than in states with bipartisan legislatures (72%) or Republican-dominated legislatures (50%). In "Sufferings Peculiarly Their Own: The Thirteenth Amendment, in Defense of Incarcerated Women's Reproductive Rights" (*Berkeley Journal of African-American Law & Policy*, vol. 15, no. 1, 2013), Alexandria Gutierrez asserts that the 13th Amendment's protection against involuntary servitude and slavery also protects abortion rights. She opines, "To refuse an incarcerated woman the right to an abortion, to force her to labor in prison, is to deprive her of her Thirteenth Amendment right to be free from 'slavery'—her criminal conviction notwithstanding." Nevertheless, Gutierrez observes that the status of incarcerated women's abortion rights is shaky, with the courts split on whether policies preventing inmates from terminating their pregnancies are unconstitutional.

AVOIDING ABORTION: FUNDING FOR FAMILY PLANNING AND CONTRACEPTION THROUGH TITLE X

In 1970 Congress enacted Title X (Family Planning Program) of the Public Health Service Act, which provides federal assistance to family planning clinics for contraception, infertility, and basic gynecologic services. The law specifically prohibits abortion as a method of family planning and forbids the use of any program monies to perform or advocate abortion. The program is intended to primarily benefit low-income women and adolescents.

The Guttmacher Institute is an organization that studies family planning and advocates for what it considers to be good family planning policy, including legal access to abortion. The institute explains in "Publicly Funded Family Planning Services in the United States" (July 2015, http://www.guttmacher.org/pubs/fb_contraceptive_serv.pdf) that more than 4,100 family planning centers across the United States received Title X funding in 2010. In *Title X Family Planning Annual Report: 2014 National Summary* (August 2015, http://www.hhs.gov/opa/pdfs/title-x-fpar-2014-national.pdf), the U.S. Department of Health and Human Services (HHS) indicates that of women using Title X–funded clinics in 2014, 82% were 20 years and older and 54% were white. Approximately 69% had incomes at or below the federal poverty level ($23,850 per year for a family of four). The HHS indicates that of the 3.8 million women using Title X–supported clinics in 2014, nearly 3.2 million (84%) used some form of birth control.

Guidelines instituted during the administration of President Jimmy Carter (1924–) indicated that federally funded clinics could not advise a pregnant woman to have an abortion and that a clinic could not pay for the abortion should a woman choose to have one. However, the clinics "are to" inform her in a "nondirective" manner that her options include keeping the baby, giving the child up for adoption, or ending the pregnancy by having an abortion. In September 1986 the administration of President Ronald Reagan (1911–2004) changed the wording in the guidelines from "are to"—which implied a mandatory requirement—to "may"—which was subject to individual judgment. Should the woman want an abortion, the federally funded agency had to provide her with a list of abortion clinics that operated without federal funding.

Confidential Family Planning Services for Adolescents

The HHS notes in *Title X Family Planning Annual Report: 2014 National Summary* that in 2014 teens made up 18% of family planning clients in Title X–funded clinics nationally. The law requires Title X–funded clinics to encourage parental participation in teenage reproductive health decisions, but under federal law clinics have to respect a teenager's wish not to involve his or her parents. Courts have recognized the importance of confidential services for teenagers. In *Planned Parenthood Association of Utah v. Matheson* (582 F. Supp. 1001, 1009 [D.C. Utah 1983]), a district federal court prohibited a "blanket parental notification requirement" for minors seeking contraceptives. The court observed that adolescents who seek contraceptives are usually already sexually active. Therefore, these same adolescents would continue engaging in sexual activity even if they could not obtain contraceptives, thereby exposing themselves to "the health risks of early pregnancy and venereal disease."

Laws vary among the states about whether minors can consent to their own health care. Table 3.4 shows that 21 states plus the District of Columbia allowed minors to consent to contraceptive health care services in September 2015. Some other states allowed minors to give consent only if their health was in danger or if they were married, a parent, or were pregnant or had been pregnant. As with a variety of issues, state laws and federal law are not always the same. However, the Guttmacher Institute points out in "State Policies in Brief: Minors' Access to Contraceptive Services" (September 1, 2015, http://www.guttmacher.org/statecenter/spibs/spib_MACS.pdf) that since the 1980s state laws have come to more closely reflect federal law, which has upheld a minor's right to privacy in obtaining contraceptives.

Title X–Funded Clinics and the Gag Rule

Besides funding family planning clinics run by state and local governments, Title X also awards grants to private nonprofit groups, such as the Planned Parenthood Federation of America, that offer family planning services. However, clinics that receive Title X funds must abide by Title X program guidelines. In 1988 the HHS, acting on President Reagan's recommendation, issued guidelines reaffirming that Congress intended Title X funds "to be used only to support preventive family planning services."

Furthermore, the Reagan administration prohibited counselors at federally funded clinics from discussing abortion as an alternative in an unintended pregnancy and from referring pregnant women to abortion providers even if patients asked for such assistance and it was paid for with private funds. This prohibition against discussing abortion in Title X–funded clinics became known as the gag rule.

Following the issuance of these guidelines, 36 state health departments and 78 national organizations openly opposed the gag rule because they said it violated the clinics' First Amendment right to free speech and infringed on the doctor-patient relationship. In a 5–4 decision in *Rust v. Sullivan* (500 U.S. 173 [1991]), the Supreme Court upheld the gag rule.

The American Medical Association attacked the ruling, not only because it interfered with the doctor-patient relationship but also because it exposed doctors to the risk of medical malpractice lawsuits for not informing women with high-risk pregnancies about all available options. Pregnancy can be a risk to the health of a woman with diabetes, cancer, acquired immunodeficiency syndrome (AIDS), hypertension, renal (kidney) disease, sickle cell anemia, malnutrition, or other serious illnesses. Some of these diseases particularly affect African American women who, because of their greater rates of poverty, are more likely than white women to use federally funded clinics for health care.

Some federally funded clinics, including Planned Parenthood, chose, at the risk of having to close, to turn down federal support rather than comply with the gag rule. William R. Archer Jr. (1928–), the deputy assistant secretary of the HHS, responded that if clinics did not comply, the HHS would simply find other clinics to replace them. However, in some parts of the country there were no other existing health care providers ready to step in, leaving women who depended on subsidized health care with no source for prenatal care and contraceptive services.

Those in Congress who opposed *Rust v. Sullivan* fought to overturn the Title X gag rule by placing a rider blocking it on an HHS appropriations bill. In November 1991, when President George H. W. Bush received the appropriations bill, he vetoed it because of the rider.

Supporters of the bill tried to garner the two-thirds majority in Congress needed to overturn the presidential veto but failed. In August 1992 a federal appeals court ruled that the HHS could move forward with implementation of the regulations. However, on January 22, 1993, two days after President Clinton took the oath of office and on the 20th anniversary of *Roe v. Wade*, Clinton repealed the gag rule.

TABLE 3.4

State policies on minors' access to contraceptive services, September 2015

State	Explicitly allows all minors to consent to services[a]	Explicitly affirms certain minors may consent to services[a]: Health	Married	Parent	Pregnant or ever pregnant	Other	No explicit policy[a]
Alabama			X[b]	X[b]	X[b]	High school graduate[b] or 14 years[b]	
Alaska	X						
Arizona	X						
Arkansas	X						
California	X						
Colorado	X						
Connecticut			X[c]				
Delaware						12 years[d]	
Dist. of Columbia	X						
Florida		X	X	X	X		
Georgia	X						
Hawaii						14 years[d]	
Idaho	X						
Illinois		X	X	X	X	Referral	
Indiana			X[c]				
Iowa	X						
Kansas						Mature minor	
Kentucky	X[d]						
Louisiana			X[c]				
Maine		X	X	X			
Maryland	X[d]						
Massachusetts	X[e]						
Michigan			X[c]				
Minnesota	X[d]						
Mississippi			X	X		Referral	
Missouri			X[c]				
Montana	X[d]						
Nebraska			X[c]				
Nevada			X[c]	X[b]		Mature minor[b]	
New Hampshire						Mature minor[b]	
New Jersey			X[b]		X[b]		
New Mexico	X						
New York	X[e]						
North Carolina	X						
North Dakota							X
Ohio							X
Oklahoma			X[d]		X[d]		
Oregon	X[d]						
Pennsylvania			X[b]		X[b]	High school graduate[b] or 14 years[b]	
Rhode Island							X
South Carolina			X[c]			16 years or mature minor	
South Dakota			X[c]				
Tennessee	X						
Texas			X[c]			f	
Utah			X[c]			f	
Vermont			X[c]				
Virginia	X						
Washington	X						
West Virginia			X[c]			Mature minor	
Wisconsin							X
Wyoming	X[e]						
Total	**21 + DC**	**3**	**21**	**6**	**6**	**11**	**4**

[a]US Supreme Court rulings have extended privacy rights to include a minor's decision to obtain contraceptives.
[b]State policy does not specifically address contraceptive services but applies to medical care in general.
[c]State law confers the rights and responsibilities of adulthood to minors who are married.
[d]Physician may, but is not required to, inform the minor's parents.
[e]The state funds a statewide program that gives minors access to confidential contraceptive care.
[f]State funds may not be used to provide minors with confidential contraceptive services.

SOURCE: "Minors' Access to Contraceptive Services," in *State Policies in Brief: Minors' Access to Contraceptive Services*, Guttmacher Institute, September 1, 2015, http://www.guttmacher.org/statecenter/spibs/spib_MACS.pdf (accessed September 21 2015)

In 2000 Title X regulations were adopted that mandated that pregnant women at Title X–funded clinics be told all their legal medical options—including termination of pregnancy—in a factual and accurate manner, without encouraging abortion. The clinics could provide a referral for abortion services if requested, but the clinics could not provide abortion services themselves. These regulations were still in effect as of November 2015.

The Adequacy of Title X Funding

Although the authorizing law for the Title X family planning program expired on September 30, 1985, annual

TABLE 3.5

Funding for the Office of Family Planning, fiscal years 1971–2015

Fiscal year	Title X appropriated funds
2015	$286,479,000
2014	$286,400,000
2013	$278,349,286[a]
2012	$297,400,000[b]
2011	299,400,000
2010	317,491,000
2009	307,491,000
2008	299,981,000
2007	283,146,000
2006	283,103,000
2005	285,977,000
2004	278,348,000
2003	273,350,000
2002	265,000,000
2001	253,932,000
2000	238,885,000
1999	215,000,000
1998	203,452,000
1997	198,452,000
1996	192,592,000
1995	193,349,000
1994	180,918,000
1993	173,418,000
1992	149,585,000
1991	144,311,000
1990	139,135,000
1989	138,320,000
1988	139,663,000
1987	142,500,000
1986	136,372,000
1985	142,500,000
1984	140,000,000
1983	124,088,000
1982	124,176,000
1981	161,671,000
1980	162,000,000
1979	135,000,000
1978	135,000,000
1977	113,000,000
1976	100,615,000
1975	100,615,000
1974	100,615,000
1973	100,615,000
1972	61,815,000
1971	6,000,000

[a]Revised fiscal year 13 annualized CR level.
[b]Congress imposed a 0.19% rescission, resulting in a net appropriation of $296,838,000.
CR = Continuing Resolution.

SOURCE: "Funding History," in *Title X Funding History*, U.S. Department of Health and Human Services, Office of Population Affairs, Office of Family Planning, 2015, http://www.hhs.gov/opa/about-opa-and-initiatives/funding-history/ (accessed September 21, 2015)

appropriations legislation has continued its funding. During the Reagan (1981–1989) and George H. W. Bush (1989–1993) administrations, funding was less than it was in fiscal year (FY) 1980. (See Table 3.5.) Funding rose dramatically during the Clinton administration (1993–2001) and continued to rise during the George W. Bush (2001–2009) and Obama (2009–) administrations. However, after peaking at $317.5 million in FY 2010, funding decreased in each of the next three fiscal years, before rising slightly in FYs 2014 and 2015. The National Family Planning and Reproductive Health Association explains in "Title X Budget & Appropriations" (2015, http://www.nationalfamilyplanning.org/title-x_budget-appropriations?) that Title X funding was cut in response to pressure to reduce the federal deficit and that in FY 2015 the program was funded at $286.5 million.

Attempts to "Defund" Title X

Each year antiabortion lawmakers try to "defund," or eliminate, federal monies from the Title X program. Although the law prohibits Title X funds from being used for abortion, opponents of Title X argue that organizations such as Planned Parenthood, which provides abortions, should not receive Title X funds. Critics feel that instead of preventing teen pregnancy by providing adolescents with contraceptives, more efforts should be made in encouraging abstinence before marriage. In 2011 the House of Representatives did vote to eliminate all funding for Title X, but this was not enacted into law.

In 2015 conservative lawmakers again launched a campaign to eliminate the Title X program. Tara Culp-Ressler reports in "House Republicans Propose Stripping Family Planning Services from Millions of Low-Income Women" (ThinkProgress.org, June 17, 2015) that in June of that year Republicans in the House of Representatives crafted a budget proposal that called for the termination of all funding for Title X. Opposition to the program intensified a month later, following the release of two undercover videos that showed Planned Parenthood employees discussing the sale of organs harvested from aborted fetuses for the purpose of medical research. In "Congress Bears down on Planned Parenthood after Second Video" (Politico.com, July 21, 2015), Rachael Bade and Jake Sherman indicate that Republican lawmakers pointed to the videos, which had been released by the antiabortion organization Center for Medical Progress, as evidence that Planned Parenthood was illegally profiting from the sale of fetal tissue. Republicans in both the House of Representatives and the Senate proceeded to launch formal inquiries into the allegations, while proposing amendments to the federal budget aimed at ending all funding for Planned Parenthood.

However, Dave Levitan notes in "Unspinning the Planned Parenthood Video" (FactCheck.org, July 21, 2015) that the videos soon proved to have been heavily edited, distorting the meaning and intent of what the Planned Parenthood employees had said. According to Levitan, the full video footage showed employees repeatedly stating that sales of fetal tissue were merely intended to cover expenses and that the organization earned no profits from the transactions. Even after the unedited footage was released, conservative legislators continued to pursue efforts to defund the organization. The videos also prompted condemnation from several leading Republican candidates for the 2016 presidential election, notably Carly Fiorina (1954–), whose denunciation of Planned Parenthood earned energetic applause during the second Republican primary debate in September 2015. "This is about the character of our nation," Fiorina told the audience, as quoted by Jeremy W. Peters in

"Carly Fiorina Offers Republicans a Pathway to Reach Women" (NYTimes.com, September 17, 2015). Sarah Kliff notes in "Carly Fiorina Is Wrong about the Planned Parenthood Tapes" (Vox.com, September 17, 2015) that Fiorina also referred to images of a "fully formed fetus," its "legs kicking" while doctors discuss the need to "keep it alive to harvest its brain." According to Kliff, no such footage actually appeared in the videos.

On September 29, 2015, Cecile Richards (1958–), the president of Planned Parenthood, appeared at a congressional committee hearing. In her testimony, Richards asserted that Planned Parenthood only donated fetal tissue at the request of the women who received the abortions and that the organization did not profit from their sale. Furthermore, Julie Mack explains in "The Pro-Life Case for Supporting Planned Parenthood" (MLive.com, October 10, 2015) that only 12% of the 2.6 million people who use Planned Parenthood annually receive abortions from the organization and that abortion services are not financed with federal funds. Mack notes that the majority of Planned Parenthood clients use the organization for contraception and other medical services related to reproductive health. Defunding the organization, Mack asserts, would inevitably lead to a steep rise in the number of unintended pregnancies, resulting in an overall increase in the abortion rate. In "Planned Parenthood Will No Longer Accept Reimbursement for Fetal Tissue" (NPR.org, October 13, 2015), Brakkton Booker reports that in October 2015 Planned Parenthood announced it would no longer accept any financial compensation for the donation of fetal tissue for medical research, in an effort to distance itself from the controversy surrounding the videos.

Abstinence-Only Education

Title X–funded clinics offer adolescents abstinence counseling and education. However, in December 2004 the House of Representatives Committee on Government Reform reported in *The Content of Federally Funded Abstinence-Only Education Programs* (http://spot.colorado.edu/~tooley/HenryWaxman.pdf) that "over 80% of the abstinence-only curricula... contain false, misleading, or distorted information about reproductive health." Moreover, the committee noted, the government appropriated twice as much on abstinence-only education in FY 2005 (about $170 million) than in FY 2001 for an educational program that did not teach basic facts about contraception.

Most studies find that abstinence-only education does not help teens abstain from sex and provides teens with erroneous information. However, John B. Jemmott III, Loretta S. Jemmott, and Geoffrey T. Fong suggest that one type of abstinence-only program may work. In "Efficacy of a Theory-Based Abstinence-Only Intervention over 24 Months: A Randomized Controlled Trial with Young Adolescents" (*Archives of Pediatric Adolescent Medicine*, vol. 164, no. 2, February 2010), the researchers report that an eight-hour abstinence-only intervention reduced sexual initiation and sexual intercourse among African American sixth and seventh graders for two years after the intervention. This abstinence-only sex education course was different from its predecessors in that it did not advocate abstinence until marriage, portray sex negatively, or suggest that condoms were ineffective. Nonetheless, the American Academy of Pediatrics states in "Sexuality, Contraception, and the Media" (*Pediatrics*, vol. 126, no. 3, September 2010) that "federal money should be spent on comprehensive sex education programs but not on abstinence-only programs, which have been found to be ineffective."

In his FY 2010 budget President Obama eliminated funding for abstinence-only education. The FY 2011 budget allocated no funds for abstinence-only education but focused on a broader, more comprehensive teen pregnancy prevention program to be managed by the newly created Office of Adolescent Health. As part of the negotiations surrounding the passage of the ACA, Congress reinstated funding for one abstinence-only program (Title V) for five years. The ACA also established the Personal Responsibility Education Program (PREP). Managed by the Administration on Children, Youth, and Families, PREP's purpose was to educate adolescents about both abstinence and contraception.

The National Campaign to Prevent Teen and Unplanned Pregnancy reports in the press release "Congress Passes Bill That Includes Two Year Extension of Funding for the Personal Responsibility Education Program" (https://thenationalcampaign.org/press-release/congress-passes-bill-includes-two-year-extension-funding-personal-responsibility) that in April 2015 overwhelming majorities in both the House of Representatives and the Senate voted to extend the State Abstinence Education Grant Program through FY 2017. Part of the Medicare Access and CHIP Reauthorization Act of 2015, the extension also raised annual funding for the programs from $50 million to $75 million.

INTERNATIONAL U.S. AID FOR FAMILY PLANNING AND CONTRACEPTION

Foreign Assistance Act

In 1961 Congress passed the Foreign Assistance Act (FAA), which reorganized U.S. foreign assistance programs and mandated the creation of the U.S. Agency for International Development (USAID) to administer them. USAID offered direct support to the developing nations of the world.

The FAA had few restrictions on how assistance was to be provided and contained only general guidelines on the factors to consider before providing assistance. In 1973 Congress amended the FAA with the Helms

Amendment, which forbid the use of U.S. foreign aid funding "to pay for the performance of abortions as a method of family planning or to motivate or coerce any person to practice abortions."

The Mexico City Policy/Global Gag Rule

At the United Nations (UN) population conference in Mexico City, Mexico, in 1984, President Reagan announced that the United States would no longer support overseas private family planning groups that, with their own funds, performed or promoted abortion. He indicated that the United States would provide monies to organizations that advocated only "natural" or noncontraceptive methods of family planning.

When the International Planned Parenthood Federation (IPPF) refused to implement the Reagan family planning restriction at its affiliates in developing countries, the administration withdrew U.S. funds from the IPPF. The IPPF took USAID to court and lost. In June 1991 the Supreme Court upheld the policy by refusing to hear the case *Planned Parenthood Federation of America v. Agency for International Development* (cert. denied, 498 U.S. 933). Although the Reagan restriction was never enacted into law, it was enforced as an executive order for almost a decade.

In 1985 the Reagan administration also withheld $10 million in aid from the UN Fund for Population Activities (now called the UN Population Fund, but the UNFPA acronym is still used). The UNFPA is dedicated to limiting the world's population increase. The Reagan administration charged the UNFPA with helping the government of China to carry out forced abortions and sterilizations. The $10 million was roughly equal to the UNFPA's annual spending in China. Funding for the UNFPA has been debated in Congress every year since 1985.

The Reagan administration's Mexico City Policy was retained by the administration of George H. W. Bush. However, when President Clinton took office in January 1993, he revoked the Mexico City Policy (which had also become known as the global gag rule) and restored the U.S. contribution to the UNFPA.

Since 1994 antiabortion advocates have introduced abortion-related clauses to a number of foreign aid measures. These lawmakers, led by Representative Christopher H. Smith (1953–; R-NJ), have sought to restrict U.S. aid to family planning groups that provide legal abortion services or advocate abortion rights in their countries.

For the first time, the global gag rule was written into law in the omnibus appropriations bill for FY 2000. (An omnibus appropriations bill authorizes the government to spend money on a variety of things.) In exchange for the release by Congress of $926 million in dues owed the UN, President Clinton agreed to restrictions on the $385 million appropriated for international family planning. Private organizations that performed or promoted abortion could not receive U.S. funds, as was the case under the Mexico City Policy.

On January 22, 2001, the first day of President George W. Bush's presidency and the 28th anniversary of *Roe v. Wade*, he issued a memorandum reinstating the Mexico City Policy.

Although the reinstated global gag rule was identical to the one implemented two decades earlier, the trend in abortion law worldwide had been toward making laws less restrictive. In 2014 approximately 74% of the world's population lived in countries where abortion was legal for a range of reasons or without restriction. (See Table 3.6.) About 26% lived in countries where abortion was either prohibited or only available to save a woman's life.

In September 2003 President Bush issued an executive order preventing the U.S. Department of State from giving family planning grants to international groups that provide abortion-related counseling, effectively extending the global gag rule, which previously applied only to USAID. However, the new order exempted agencies in Africa and the Caribbean that would benefit from President Bush's five-year, $15 billion global AIDS initiative.

In April 2005 the Senate passed an amendment to the Foreign Affairs Authorization Act brought forward by Senators Barbara Boxer (1940–; D-CA) and Olympia J. Snowe (1947–; R-ME) that would repeal the global gag rule. In a House-Senate conference committee meeting during which House-Senate differences in the act were being negotiated, the Boxer-Snowe amendment was dropped. In November 2005 President Bush signed the act without the amendment. In 2007 another Boxer-Snowe amendment to repeal the global gag rule passed in the Senate. However, the bill was dropped and never passed into law due to the threat of a presidential veto during budget negotiations.

When President Obama took office in January 2009, one of his first acts was to repeal the global gag rule and restore funding to international health groups that perform or promote abortions. Obama's commitment to funding international family planning and reproductive health programs that include access to contraception and abortion counseling and services continued through his FY 2016 budget.

NONMARITAL CHILDBEARING, WELFARE REFORM, AND ABORTION

In 1995, as Congress worked to overhaul the nation's welfare system, the legislators were split on issues concerning teen pregnancy and abortion. Some believed that discontinuing federal cash assistance to the needy would help discourage nonmarital childbearing. According to Lisa

TABLE 3.6

Countries, by restrictiveness of abortion law, 2014

I. To save the women's life or prohibited altogether. Countries printed in bold make an explicit exception to save the woman's life. (See also Note I.)			II. To preserve health (also to save the woman's life). Countries printed in bold recognize an exception to preserve the woman's mental health. (See also Note II.)			III. Socioeconomic grounds (also to save the woman's life and health)	IV. Without restriction as to reason (See also Note IV.)		
Afghanistan	**Iran**–F	Philippines	**Algeria**	**Jamaica**	**Saint Kitts & Nevis**	Barbados–PA/R/I/F	Albania–PA	Fmr. Yugoslav Rep.	Russian Fed.
Andorra	Iraq	San Marino	Argentina–R	Jordan	**Saint Lucia**–R/I	Belize–F	Armenia–PA	Macedonia–PA	Serbia–PA
Angola	**Ireland**	Sao Tome & Principe	Bahamas	Kenya	**Samoa**	Cyprus–R/F	Australia–♦	Georgia–PA	Singapore***
Antigua & Barbuda	**Kiribati**	Senegal	Benin–R/I/F	Kuwait–SA/PA/F	Saudi Arabia–SA/PA	Fiji–R/I/F/PA	Austria*	Germany*	Slovak Rep.–PA
Bangladesh	Laos	**Solomon Islands**	Bolivia–R/I	Lesotho–R/I/F	**Seychelles**–R/I/F/+	Finland–R/I/F/+	Azerbaijan	Greece–PA	Slovenia–PA
Bhutan–R/I/+	**Lebanon**	**Somalia**	**Botswana**–R/I/F	**Liberia**–R/I/F	**Sierra Leone**	Great Britain–F	Bahrain	Guyana†	South Africa
Brazil–R/+	**Libya**	**South Sudan**	Burkina Faso–R/I/F	Liechtenstein–+	**Swaziland**–R/I/F	Hong Kong–R/I/F	Belarus	Hungary	Spain*–PA
Brunei Darussalam	Madagascar	**Sri Lanka**	Burundi	**Malaysia**	**Thailand**–R/F	Iceland–R/I/F/+	Belgium*	Italy§	Sweden**
Central African Rep.	**Malawi**	**Sudan**–R	Cameroon–R	Maldives–SA	Togo–R/I/F	India–PA/R/F	Bosnia-	Kazakhstan	Switzerland
Chile–x	**Mali**–R/I	Suriname	Chad–F	**Mauritius**–R/F/PA	**Trinidad & Tobago**	Japan–SA/R	Herzegovina–PA	Kosovo‡–PA/S	Tajikistan
Congo (Brazzaville)	Malta–x	**Syria**–SA/PA	**Colombia**–R/I/F	Monaco–R/I/F/xx	Vanuatu	Saint Vincent &	Bulgaria	Kyrgyzstan	Tunisia∞
Côte d'Ivoire	Marshall Islands–U	**Tanzania**	Comoros	Morocco–SA	Zimbabwe–R/I/F/xx	Grenadines–R/I/F	Cambodia*–PA	Latvia–PA	Turkey‡–SA/PA
Dem. Rep. of Congo	Mauritania	**Timor-Leste**–PA	Costa Rica	Mozambique		Taiwan–SA/PA/I/F	Canada°	Lithuania–PA	Turkmenistan
Dominica	**Mexico**–R/F/♦	Tonga	Djibouti	**Namibia**–R/I/F		Zambia–F	Cape Verde	Luxembourg*	Ukraine
Dominican Republic	Micronesia–U	**Tuvalu**	Ecuador–R_1	**Nauru**			China°–S	Moldova–PA	United States^–PA/♦
Egypt	**Myanmar**	**Uganda**	Equatorial Guinea–SA/PA	**New Zealand**–I/F			Croatia–PA	Mongolia∞	Uruguay–PA
El Salvador–x	Nicaragua–x	**United Arab**	Eritrea	Niger–F			Cuba–PA	Montenegro–PA/S	Uzbekistan
Gabon	**Nigeria**	**Emirates**–SA/PA	Ethiopia–R/I/F/+	**Northern Ireland**			Czech Rep.–PA	Nepal–S	Vietnam°
Guatemala	**Oman**	**Venezuela**	**Gambia**	Pakistan			Dem. People's Rep.	Netherlands^	
Guinea-Bissau	Palau–U	**West Bank & Gaza Strip**	**Ghana**–R/I/F/+	Peru			of Korea°	Norway–PA	
Haiti	**Panama**–PA/R/F	**Yemen**	Grenada	Poland–PA/R/I/F			Denmark–PA	Portugal‡–PA	
Honduras	**Papua New Guinea**		Guinea–R/I/F	Qatar–F			Estonia	Puerto Rico^	
Indonesia–SA/R/F	**Paraguay**		**Israel**–R/I/F/+	Rep. of Korea–SA/R/I/+			France*	Romania*	
				Rwanda–R/I/+					

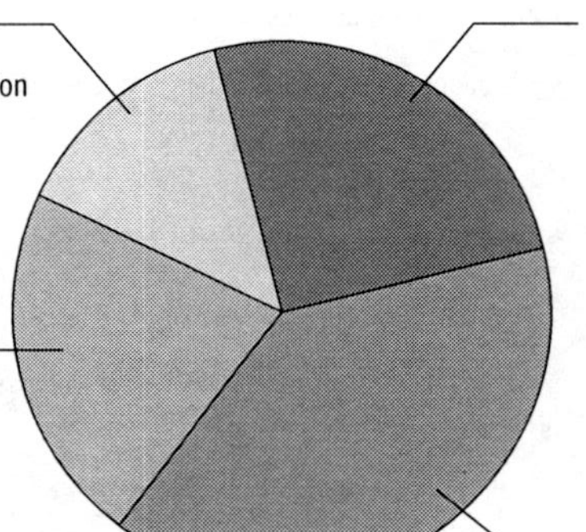

TABLE 3.6

Countries, by restrictiveness of abortion law, 2014 [CONTINUED]

A note on terminology:

"Countries" listed on the table include independent states and, where populations exceed one million, semi-autonomous regions, territories and jurisdictions of special status. The table therefore includes Hong Kong, Northern Ireland, Puerto Rico, Taiwan, and the West Bank and Gaza Strip.

Note I: Laws that make no explicit exception to save a woman's life are normally interpreted to permit life-saving abortions on grounds of the general criminal law defense of "necessity." In this situation, although laws do not expressly permit abortion, the procedure could be performed on the rationale that it is necessary to preserve the life of the woman.

Note II: According to the World Health Organization, "health" is "a state of complete physical, mental and social well-being and not merely the absence of disease or infirmity." Laws in this category that do not make an explicit exception to protect a woman's mental health should be interpreted to allow abortion on such grounds.

Note IV: Gestational limits key.

All Countries in Category IV have gestational limits of 12 weeks unless otherwise indicated. Gestational limits are calculated from the first day of the last menstrual period, which is considered to occur two weeks prior to conception. Where laws specify that gestational age limits are calculated from the date of conception, these limits have been extended by two weeks.

†Gestational limit of 8 weeks
‡Gestational limit of 10 weeks
§Gestational limit of 90 days
∞Gestational limit of three months
*Gestational limit of 14 weeks
**Gestational limit of 18 weeks
***Gestational limit of 24 weeks
^Law does not limit pre-viability abortion
°Law does not indicate gestational limit; regulatory mechanisms vary

Indications:

R Abortion permitted in cases of rape
R_1 Abortion permitted in the case of rape of a woman with a mental disability
I Abortion permitted in cases of incest
F Abortion permitted in cases of fetal impairment
SA Spousal authorization required
PA Parental authorization/notification required
\+ Abortion permitted on additional enumerated grounds relating to such factors as the woman's age or capacity to care for a child
S Sex selective abortion prohibited
x Legislation eliminated all exceptions to prohibition on abortion; availability of defense of necessity highly unlikely
xx Legislation explicitly permits abortion only to protect the physical health of the woman
U Law unclear
♦ Federal system in which abortion law is determined at state level; classification reflects legal status of abortion for largest group of people

SOURCE: Adapted from "Categories of Abortion Laws from Most to Least Restrictive," in *The World's Abortion Laws 2014*, Center for Reproductive Rights, July 2014, http://www.reproductiverights.org/sites/crr.civicactions.net/files/documents/AbortionMap2014.PDF (accessed September 21, 2015)

Kaeser of the Guttmacher Institute, in "Washington Memo" (August 7, 1996), these members regarded out-of-wedlock births, especially among adolescents, as "both a central cause of welfare dependency and a direct result of the 'culture' it creates." Others feared that limiting welfare cash benefits would lead poor women to choose abortion.

In 1996 the 60-year-old federal cash assistance program, Aid to Families with Dependent Children, was eliminated, and President Clinton signed the Personal Responsibility and Work Opportunity Reconciliation Act of 1996 into law. This new welfare law created the Temporary Assistance for Needy Families (TANF) program. TANF provides assistance and work opportunities to needy families by granting states federal funds and wide flexibility to implement their own welfare programs.

The new welfare reform law outlined specific provisions for reducing nonmarital and teen pregnancies. It allowed states to spend a portion of their TANF funds on "pre-pregnancy family services," but prohibited funding of other medical services, such as abortions.

Although most nonmarital births were to women not on welfare, Congress used the welfare reform law to stress the issue of "illegitimacy." To encourage the states to develop effective solutions for reducing out-of-wedlock births, the act provided for a performance incentive called "Bonus to Reward Decrease in Illegitimacy Ratio." Under the new law the federal government awarded up to $100 million annually each year between 1996 and 2003 to a maximum of five states that reduced nonmarital births while decreasing their abortion rates below 1995 levels.

The "Bonus to Reward Decrease in Illegitimacy Ratio" program ended on October 1, 2003 (the end of the federal government's fiscal year). This may account for some of the rise in the birth rate among unmarried women in that year. Joyce A. Martin et al. of the Centers for Disease Control and Prevention note in "Births: Final Data for 2013" (*National Vital Statistics Reports*, vol. 64, no. 1, January 2015) that the birth rate among unmarried women peaked in 2007 and 2008, when it topped 51.8 per 1,000 women, before gradually declining to 44.3 per 1,000 by 2013. (See Table 3.7.)

A Changing Pattern of Nonmarital Childbearing

Table 3.8 shows the changing pattern of childbearing in unmarried women over the past three decades. The birth rate for older unmarried women has increased, whereas the birth rate for younger unmarried women has decreased. Reflecting these trends, the birth rate for unmarried women aged 15 to 29 years declined in 2013. In particular, the rate of 24 births per 1,000 unmarried women aged 15 to 19 years was only 52% of that age group's 1994 birth rate peak of 45.8. The birth rate for women aged 30 to 34 years was essentially unchanged in 2013, while the birth rate among women aged 35 to 39 years increased.

TABLE 3.7

Number, rate, and percentage of births to unmarried women, and birth rate for married women, 1980, 1985, 1990, 1995, and 2000–13

	Births to unmarried women			Birth rate for
Year	Number	Rate[a]	Percent[b]	married women[c]
2013	1,595,873	44.3	40.6	86.9
2012	1,609,619	45.3	40.7	86.0
2011	1,607,773	46.0	40.7	85.1
2010	1,633,471	47.5	40.8	84.3
2009	1,693,658	49.9	41.0	85.6
2008	1,726,566	51.8	40.6	86.9
2007	1,715,047	51.8	39.7	89.1
2006	1,641,946	50.3	38.5	88.7
2005	1,527,034	47.2	36.9	87.9
2004	1,470,189	46.0	35.8	88.1
2003	1,415,995	44.7	34.6	88.4
2002	1,365,966	43.6	34.0	86.9
2001	1,349,249	43.7	33.5	86.6
2000	1,347,043	44.1	33.2	87.4
1995	1,253,976	44.3	32.2	82.6
1990	1,165,384	43.8	28.0	93.2
1985	828,174	32.8	22.0	93.3
1980	665,747	29.4	18.4	97.0

[a]Births to unmarried women per 1,000 unmarried women aged 15–44.
[b]Percentage of all births to unmarried women.
[c]Births to married women per 1,000 married women aged 15–44.
Note: Rates for 2001–2009 have been revised, using revised intercensal population estimates based on the 2010 census.

SOURCE: Joyce A. Martin et al., "Table B. Births and Birth Rates for Unmarried and Married Women: United States, 1980, 1985, 1990, 1995, and 2000–2013," in "Births: Final Data for 2013," *National Vital Statistics Report*, vol. 64, no. 1, January 15, 2015, http://www.cdc.gov/nchs/data/nvsr/nvsr64/nvsr64_01.pdf (accessed September 21, 2015)

Economic issues are of high concern with unmarried teenage mothers because they have not yet entered the workforce and established a stable career and, in many cases, have not yet completed their schooling. Health issues also are of concern because low birth weight and preterm babies are born in higher percentages to women at either end of their childbearing years. (See Table 3.9.) Unmarried teens have a high percentage of low birth weight babies and are less likely than older women to be able to economically support a child and provide appropriate health care.

ABORTION AND THE 2014 MIDTERM ELECTIONS

By 2014 Democrats had gained an advantage among the American public on the issue of reproductive rights. According to the Pew Research Center, in "As Midterms Near, GOP Leads on Key Issues, Democrats Have a More Positive Image" (October 23, 2014, http://www.people-press.org/2014/10/23/as-midterms-near-gop-leads-on-key-issues-democrats-have-a-more-positive-image), nearly half (46%) of Americans favored the Democrats on the issue of abortion and contraception, compared with 37% who favored Republicans. Despite this edge, Republicans held a distinct advantage on a range of other issues, including national security and the economy, leading to sweeping Republican victories in the 2014 midterm elections.

TABLE 3.8

Birth rates for unmarried women, by age and race/ethnicity, 1970, 1975, and 1980–2013

[Rates are births to unmarried women per 1,000 unmarried women. Populations estimated as of July 1 for all years.]

	Age of mother (years)								
		15–19							
Year and race and Hispanic origin	15–44[a]	Total	15–17	18–19	20–24	25–29	30–34	35–39	40–44[b]
All races[c]									
2013[d]	44.3	24.0	11.9	42.1	63.1	66.7	56.6	31.8	8.3
2012[d]	45.3	26.7	13.7	45.8	64.7	67.2	56.3	30.9	8.5
2011[d]	46.0	28.4	14.9	48.2	66.7	67.8	56.2	29.9	8.2
2010[d]	47.5	31.1	16.8	52.0	70.0	69.2	56.3	29.6	8.0
2009[d]	49.9	34.0	18.8	56.3	74.4	73.0	57.1	29.7	7.8
2008[d]	51.8	35.9	20.1	59.7	78.1	75.7	58.8	30.2	7.5
2007[d]	51.8	36.5	20.4	61.9	79.8	76.9	58.0	28.7	6.8
2006[d]	50.3	35.5	20.1	60.3	79.1	75.4	55.3	26.8	6.5
2005[d]	47.2	33.9	19.4	57.0	74.5	71.5	50.4	24.5	6.2
2004[d]	46.0	34.2	19.9	56.6	72.3	69.1	47.3	23.5	6.0
2003[d]	44.7	34.3	20.1	56.6	71.0	66.2	44.2	22.3	5.8
2002[d]	43.6	35.1	20.7	58.1	70.0	62.0	41.3	20.9	5.4
2001[d]	43.7	36.8	21.8	60.2	70.8	59.6	40.3	20.4	5.3
2000[d]	44.1	39.0	23.9	62.2	72.2	58.5	39.3	19.7	5.0
1999[d]	43.3	39.7	25.0	62.3	70.8	56.9	38.1	19.0	4.6
1998[d]	43.3	40.9	26.5	63.6	70.4	55.4	38.1	18.7	4.6
1997[d]	42.9	41.4	27.7	63.9	68.9	53.4	37.9	18.7	4.6
1996[d]	43.8	42.2	28.5	64.9	68.9	54.5	40.2	19.9	4.8
1995[d]	44.3	43.8	30.1	66.5	68.7	54.3	38.9	19.3	4.7
1994[d]	46.2	45.8	31.7	69.1	70.9	57.4	39.6	19.7	4.7
1993[d]	44.8	44.0	30.3	66.2	68.5	55.9	38.0	18.9	4.4
1992[d]	44.9	44.2	30.2	66.7	67.9	55.6	37.6	18.8	4.1
1991[d]	45.0	44.6	30.8	65.4	67.8	56.0	37.9	17.9	3.8
1990[d]	43.8	42.5	29.6	60.7	65.1	56.0	37.6	17.3	3.6
1989[d]	41.6	40.1	28.7	56.0	61.2	52.8	34.9	16.0	3.4
1988[d]	38.5	36.4	26.4	51.5	56.0	48.5	32.0	15.0	3.2
1987[d]	36.0	33.8	24.5	48.9	52.6	44.5	29.6	13.5	2.9
1986[d]	34.2	32.3	22.8	48.0	49.3	42.2	27.2	12.2	2.7
1985[d]	32.8	31.4	22.4	45.9	46.5	39.9	25.2	11.6	2.5
1984[d, e]	31.0	30.0	21.9	42.5	43.0	37.1	23.3	10.9	2.5
1983[d, e]	30.3	29.5	22.0	40.7	41.8	35.5	22.4	10.2	2.6
1982[d, e]	30.0	28.7	21.5	39.6	41.5	35.1	21.9	10.0	2.7
1981[d, e]	29.5	27.9	20.9	39.0	41.1	34.5	20.8	9.8	2.6
1980[d, e]	29.4	27.6	20.6	39.0	40.9	34.0	21.1	9.7	2.6
1980[e, f]	28.4	27.5	20.7	38.7	39.7	31.4	18.5	8.4	2.3
1975[e, f]	24.5	23.9	19.3	32.5	31.2	27.5	17.9	9.1	2.6
1970[f, g]	26.4	22.4	17.1	32.9	38.4	37.0	27.1	13.6	3.5
White total									
2013[d]	40.8	21.9	10.8	38.6	56.9	62.5	56.2	32.3	7.7
2012[d]	42.1	24.1	12.4	41.4	58.3	63.2	56.3	31.5	8.5
2011[d]	42.7	25.5	13.4	43.4	60.1	63.8	56.2	30.6	8.3
2010[d]	44.5	27.9	15.1	46.9	63.4	65.8	56.8	30.7	8.1
2009[d]	46.6	30.4	16.7	50.5	67.3	69.7	57.7	30.6	7.8
2008[d]	48.4	31.9	17.8	53.3	70.9	73.1	60.0	31.1	7.3
2007[d]	48.3	32.3	17.9	55.1	72.6	74.3	59.5	29.1	6.5
2006[d]	46.4	31.1	17.3	53.3	71.7	72.4	55.5	26.6	6.3
2005[d]	43.2	29.7	16.7	50.3	67.0	67.7	49.8	23.9	5.9
2004[d]	41.8	29.9	17.0	49.9	64.5	65.0	46.2	22.8	5.6
2003[d]	40.5	29.9	17.1	50.0	63.2	61.7	42.3	21.3	5.5
2002[d]	39.0	30.3	17.5	50.8	61.6	57.5	38.8	19.5	5.1
2001[d]	38.4	31.2	18.1	51.9	61.5	54.9	37.2	18.6	4.9
2000[d]	38.2	32.7	19.7	53.1	61.7	52.9	35.9	17.9	4.5
1999[d]	37.4	33.2	20.6	52.9	60.2	50.8	34.9	17.4	4.1
1998[d]	36.9	33.6	21.5	53.1	59.5	48.6	34.1	16.9	4.1
1997[d]	36.3	33.6	22.0	52.9	57.9	47.0	33.6	16.6	3.9
1996[d]	37.0	34.0	22.3	53.5	57.9	48.1	35.4	17.7	4.3
1995[d]	37.0	35.0	23.3	54.7	57.2	47.4	33.7	16.8	4.2
1994[d]	37.8	35.8	23.9	55.8	57.5	48.6	33.8	17.2	4.3
1993[d]	35.6	33.3	21.9	52.0	53.8	46.0	31.9	16.3	3.9
1992[d]	35.0	32.7	21.4	51.2	52.4	44.8	31.3	16.1	3.6
1991[d]	34.5	32.7	21.7	49.4	51.4	44.3	30.9	15.2	3.2
1990[d]	32.9	30.6	20.4	44.9	48.2	43.0	29.9	14.5	3.2
1989[d]	30.2	28.0	19.3	40.2	43.8	39.1	26.8	13.1	2.9
1988[d]	27.4	25.3	17.6	36.8	39.2	35.4	24.2	12.1	2.7
1987[d]	25.3	23.2	16.2	34.5	36.6	32.0	22.3	10.7	2.4
1986[d]	23.9	21.8	14.9	33.5	34.2	30.5	20.1	9.7	2.2

TABLE 3.8

Birth rates for unmarried women, by age and race/ethnicity, 1970, 1975, and 1980–2013 [CONTINUED]

[Rates are births to unmarried women per 1,000 unmarried women. Populations estimated as of July 1 for all years.]

Year and race and Hispanic origin	Age of mother (years)								
	15–44[a]	15–19			20–24	25–29	30–34	35–39	40–44[b]
		Total	15–17	18–19					
1985[d]	22.5	20.8	14.5	31.2	31.7	28.5	18.4	9.0	2.0
1984[d, e]	20.6	19.3	13.7	27.9	28.5	25.5	16.8	8.4	2.0
1983[d, e]	19.8	18.7	13.6	26.4	27.1	23.8	15.9	7.8	2.0
1982[d, e]	19.3	18.0	13.1	25.3	26.5	23.1	15.3	7.4	2.1
1981[d, e]	18.6	17.2	12.6	24.6	25.8	22.3	14.2	7.2	1.9
1980[d, e]	18.1	16.5	12.0	24.1	25.1	21.5	14.1	7.1	1.8
Non-Hispanic white									
2013[d]	31.7	16.2	7.0	29.8	45.6	47.6	40.9	22.6	6.1
2012[d]	32.1	17.8	8.0	32.1	46.6	47.8	40.2	21.8	6.1
2011[d]	32.3	18.8	8.6	33.6	47.8	47.8	39.2	20.7	6.0
2010[d]	32.9	20.3	9.5	36.0	49.5	48.0	38.7	20.2	5.8
2009[d]	33.6	21.8	10.4	38.1	51.4	49.3	37.9	20.0	5.5
2008[d]	34.3	22.5	10.8	39.7	52.9	50.8	38.4	20.4	5.2
2007[d]	33.8	22.6	10.9	40.7	53.4	50.7	37.2	19.2	4.6
2006[d]	32.4	21.6	10.7	38.9	52.6	49.1	35.1	17.9	4.5
2005[d]	30.4	20.9	10.3	37.4	49.9	46.0	31.7	16.2	4.3
2004[d]	29.6	21.3	10.7	37.4	48.6	44.2	30.0	15.7	4.2
2003[d]	28.8	21.5	11.0	37.8	47.6	41.5	28.0	14.8	4.1
2002[d]	27.9	22.1	11.4	38.8	46.3	38.9	26.2	13.6	3.7
2001[d]	27.8	23.1	12.1	40.3	46.4	37.8	25.4	13.2	3.6
2000[d]	28.0	24.7	13.6	42.1	47.0	36.9	24.8	12.9	3.3
1999[d]	27.9	25.6	14.6	42.7	46.3	36.2	24.8	13.0	3.1
1998[d]	27.9	26.2	15.5	43.1	46.3	35.4	25.0	13.1	3.1
1997[d]	27.5	26.4	16.2	43.3	44.8	34.4	24.9	12.7	2.9
1996[d]	28.2	27.0	16.9	43.9	44.5	35.0	26.4	13.8	3.3
1995[d]	28.1	27.7	17.6	44.6	43.9	34.4	25.1	12.9	3.2
1994[d]	28.4	28.1	17.9	45.0	43.8	34.7	24.6	12.8	3.1
1993[d]	—	—	—	—	—	—	—	—	—
1992[d]	—	—	—	—	—	—	—	—	—
1991[d]	—	—	—	—	—	—	—	—	—
1990[d, h]	24.4	25.0	16.2	37.0	36.4	30.3	20.5	6.1	—
Black total									
2013[d]	61.7	38.5	19.0	66.2	100.7	92.3	60.6	31.1	8.4
2012[d]	62.6	43.4	22.0	73.2	103.5	91.2	59.6	29.7	8.1
2011[d]	63.7	46.7	24.7	77.4	106.9	92.4	59.1	28.9	7.8
2010[d]	65.3	50.8	27.6	83.6	112.6	92.5	58.6	27.8	7.8
2009[d]	68.7	55.9	31.1	91.3	119.5	95.6	60.3	28.4	7.6
2008[d]	71.0	59.7	33.9	98.4	124.0	97.0	61.1	28.5	7.6
2007[d]	71.4	61.3	34.8	103.6	125.3	99.1	59.9	28.0	7.4
2006[d]	70.7	61.1	35.4	103.3	125.5	98.0	58.4	27.3	7.2
2005[d]	67.2	58.7	34.4	97.9	120.4	94.7	53.9	25.9	7.1
2004[d]	66.8	60.1	36.1	98.0	119.6	92.5	52.0	25.7	6.8
2003[d]	65.9	61.0	37.4	98.0	117.8	91.3	51.2	25.2	6.5
2002[d]	66.1	64.0	39.4	102.8	119.0	86.3	50.2	24.9	6.3
2001[d]	68.0	69.4	43.5	109.1	122.5	84.4	51.2	25.4	6.3
2000[d]	70.5	75.0	48.3	115.0	129.0	85.9	50.2	25.4	6.3
1999[d]	69.7	76.5	50.0	115.8	126.8	85.5	49.0	24.2	5.8
1998[d]	71.6	81.5	55.0	121.5	127.8	86.5	50.5	24.3	6.0
1997[d]	71.5	84.5	59.0	124.8	124.2	81.4	51.0	24.3	6.5
1996[d]	72.8	87.5	62.6	127.2	122.6	81.2	53.4	25.2	6.1
1995[d]	74.5	91.2	67.4	129.2	124.6	82.3	53.3	25.3	6.0
1994[d]	80.8	99.3	73.9	139.6	135.2	91.3	56.5	26.0	5.9
1993[d]	83.0	101.2	75.9	140.0	139.9	92.8	56.7	25.7	5.8
1992[d]	85.7	104.8	77.2	146.4	142.6	96.8	57.3	25.6	5.4
1991[d]	89.0	107.8	79.9	147.7	146.4	100.0	59.8	25.5	5.4
1990[d]	90.5	106.0	78.8	143.7	144.8	105.3	61.5	25.5	5.1
1989[d]	90.7	104.5	78.9	140.9	142.4	102.9	60.5	24.9	5.0
1988[d]	86.5	96.1	73.5	130.5	133.6	97.2	57.4	24.1	5.0
1987[d]	82.6	90.9	69.9	123.0	126.1	91.6	53.1	22.4	4.7
1986[d]	79.0	88.5	67.0	121.1	118.0	84.6	50.0	20.6	4.4
1985[d]	77.0	87.6	66.8	117.9	113.1	79.3	47.5	20.4	4.3
1984[d, e]	75.2	86.1	66.5	113.6	107.9	77.8	43.8	19.4	4.3
1983[d, e]	76.2	85.5	66.8	111.9	107.2	79.7	43.8	19.4	4.8
1982[d, e]	77.9	85.1	66.3	112.7	109.3	82.7	44.1	19.5	5.2
1981[d, e]	79.4	85.0	65.9	114.2	110.7	83.1	45.5	19.6	5.6
1980[d, e]	81.1	87.9	68.8	118.2	112.3	81.4	46.7	19.0	5.5

Besides taking control of both the House of Representatives and the Senate, Republicans also won key electoral battles at the state level. In "The Fight for Abortion Rights Just Got a Whole Lot Harder" (MotherJones.com, November

TABLE 3.8

Birth rates for unmarried women, by age and race/ethnicity, 1970, 1975, and 1980–2013 [CONTINUED]

[Rates are births to unmarried women per 1,000 unmarried women. Populations estimated as of July 1 for all years.]

Year and race and Hispanic origin	Age of mother (years)								
		15–19							
	15–44[a]	Total	15–17	18–19	20–24	25–29	30–34	35–39	40–44[b]
Asian or Pacific Islander total									
2013[d]	21.8	7.2	3.5	12.6	20.7	31.5	44.1	31.5	12.6
2012[d]	22.9	8.1	3.9	14.2	22.0	35.2	43.6	30.1	12.1
2011[d]	22.4	8.6	4.4	14.8	22.3	35.1	42.3	27.0	9.9
2010[d]	22.3	9.2	4.8	15.4	23.2	35.0	40.0	26.6	9.9
2009[d]	23.6	10.6	5.9	17.1	25.3	36.2	39.2	27.3	9.9
2008[d]	23.9	11.4	6.3	18.4	26.4	33.5	37.9	30.3	10.8
2007[d]	23.9	11.9	6.7	19.2	27.1	32.3	36.9	28.8	9.9
2006[d]	23.4	12.0	7.3	18.9	26.8	30.5	37.6	29.7	9.4
2005[d]	22.8	11.9	6.8	19.3	25.8	31.4	36.8	24.6	9.3
2004[d]	22.1	12.3	7.3	19.4	24.8	30.7	35.8	20.7	8.6
2003[d]	21.1	12.3	7.1	19.6	24.2	29.0	31.8	19.8	7.9
2002[d]	20.6	13.0	7.3	21.0	24.4	26.7	29.4	19.1	6.9
2001[d]	20.5	14.2	8.5	22.4	23.9	25.7	28.7	19.5	6.3
2000[d]	20.9	15.2	9.6	23.2	24.2	25.4	29.7	18.4	6.9
Hispanic[i]									
2013[d]	69.9	37.6	21.1	63.0	93.1	112.0	100.1	56.8	16.8
2012[d]	72.6	41.8	24.5	68.5	96.5	113.2	103.9	57.6	16.5
2011[d]	75.1	44.7	27.0	71.7	100.6	116.2	106.0	58.0	16.2
2010[d]	80.6	50.0	30.8	79.8	110.5	123.9	105.8	61.7	16.3
2009[d]	89.4	56.7	35.3	90.9	125.4	139.4	112.4	63.7	17.1
2008[d]	97.3	62.4	39.4	101.1	141.0	151.1	121.6	66.9	16.2
2007[d]	102.1	65.4	40.6	109.2	153.8	161.1	127.0	64.9	14.9
2006[d]	101.5	65.9	40.5	110.2	155.1	160.7	122.9	61.3	14.8
2005[d]	96.2	63.7	40.3	103.9	142.5	151.2	116.7	58.1	14.1
2004[d]	92.7	64.2	41.2	102.9	133.4	142.5	108.8	56.0	13.7
2003[d]	89.9	63.5	41.1	101.2	130.2	135.6	98.7	54.0	13.2
2002[d]	87.0	63.9	41.9	100.7	127.2	125.1	91.0	52.4	12.8
2001[d]	86.8	65.5	43.4	101.1	129.8	121.0	91.4	49.6	12.2
2000[d]	87.2	68.5	47.0	102.2	130.5	121.6	89.4	46.1	12.2
1999[d]	84.9	68.6	48.7	99.9	126.1	119.6	84.2	42.4	11.2
1998[d]	82.8	69.3	49.8	101.2	120.6	115.9	78.2	38.8	12.0
1997[d]	83.2	69.2	50.7	100.6	122.8	114.8	78.8	40.5	12.1
1996[d]	86.2	69.3	49.7	102.3	131.6	122.0	84.6	41.2	12.3
1995[d]	88.8	73.2	52.8	108.6	135.8	122.3	84.1	42.2	12.1
1994[d]	95.8	77.7	55.7	115.4	144.5	131.7	91.2	47.4	13.9
1993[d]	91.4	71.1	49.6	108.8	134.3	130.4	87.8	47.1	14.1
1992[d]	92.8	70.3	49.2	106.6	138.2	133.4	89.9	47.8	14.6
1991[d]	92.5	71.0	49.5	107.5	134.2	135.1	88.2	47.6	14.1
1990[d, h]	89.6	65.9	45.9	98.9	129.8	131.7	88.1	50.8	13.7

— Data not available.
[a]Rates computed by relating total births to unmarried mothers, regardless of age of mother, to unmarried women aged 15–44.
[b]Beginning in 1997, birth rates computed by relating births to unmarried women aged 40 and over to unmarried women aged 40–44.
[c]Includes races other than white, black, and Asian or Pacific Islander.
[d]Data for states in which marital status was not reported have been inferred and included with data from the remaining states.
[e]Based on 100% of births in selected states and a 50% sample of births in all other states; see reference 11.
[f]Births to unmarried women are estimated for the United States from data for registration areas in which marital status of mother was reported.
[g]Based on a 50% sample of births.
[h]Rates based on data for 48 states and the District of Columbia (DC), which reported Hispanic origin on the birth certificate. Rates for age group 35–39 are based on births to unmarried women aged 35–44.
[i]Includes all persons of Hispanic origin of any race.
Notes: Race and Hispanic origin are reported separately on birth certificates. Persons of Hispanic origin may be of any race. Race categories are consistent with 1977 Office of Management and Budget standards. Forty-four states and DC reported multiple-race data for 2013 that were bridged to single-race categories for comparability with other states. Multiple-race reporting areas vary for 2003–2013. Rates cannot be computed for unmarried non-Hispanic black women or for American Indian or Alaska Native women because the necessary populations are not available.

SOURCE: Joyce A. Martin et al., "Table 16. Birth Rates for Unmarried Women, by Age of Mother: United States, 1970, 1975, and 1980–2013, and by Age and Race and Hispanic Origin of Mother: United States, 1980–2013," in "Births: Final Data for 2013," *National Vital Statistics Report*, vol. 64, no. 1, January 15, 2015, http://www.cdc.gov/nchs/data/nvsr/nvsr64/nvsr64_01.pdf (accessed September 21, 2015)

6, 2014), Molly Redden indicates that by November 2014 Republicans had majorities in 67 of 99 state legislative bodies, up from 57 prior to the election. According to Redden, these victories delivered a significant blow to pro-choice advocates, because most antiabortion legislation originated at the state level. Republican control over a number of state legislatures, notably in Washington and Nevada, effectively derailed ongoing efforts to expand access to abortion and contraception within those states, while also threatening funding for sex education programs.

TABLE 3.9

Preterm and low birthweight births by age, race, and Hispanic origin of mother, 2013

Age (years) and race and Hispanic origin of mother	Preterm[a]							Low birthweight[b]						
	Percent			Number				Percent			Number			
	Total	Early[c]	Late[d]	Total	Early[c]	Late[d]	Unknown	Total	Very[e]	Moderately[f]	Total	Very[e]	Moderately[f]	Unknown
All races[g]														
All ages	11.39	3.40	7.99	447,361	133,503	313,858	3,680	8.02	1.41	6.61	315,099	55,458	259,641	4,449
Under 15	21.11	8.71	12.40	652	269	383	10	12.29	3.01	9.29	380	93	287	7
15–19	12.98	4.23	8.75	35,411	11,545	23,866	296	9.31	1.62	7.69	25,406	4,427	20,979	304
15	17.35	6.20	11.15	1,631	583	1,048	22	10.23	1.98	8.25	963	186	777	10
16	14.97	4.92	10.04	3,368	1,108	2,260	32	9.61	1.66	7.95	2,163	373	1,790	28
17	13.42	4.49	8.94	5,747	1,921	3,826	51	9.22	1.61	7.61	3,945	689	3,256	52
18	12.93	4.31	8.62	9,839	3,280	6,559	68	9.45	1.72	7.74	7,191	1,306	5,885	77
19	12.15	3.81	8.34	14,826	4,653	10,173	123	9.13	1.54	7.60	11,144	1,873	9,271	137
20–24	11.30	3.42	7.88	101,254	30,640	70,614	941	8.25	1.42	6.83	73,906	12,690	61,216	1,038
25–29	10.48	3.05	7.43	117,337	34,118	83,219	1,084	7.34	1.26	6.08	82,174	14,107	68,067	1,284
30–34	10.80	3.16	7.64	111,942	32,783	79,159	800	7.50	1.34	6.17	77,721	13,850	63,871	1,144
35–39	12.70	3.73	8.96	61,379	18,039	43,340	404	8.67	1.59	7.08	41,923	7,704	34,219	529
40–44	15.89	4.99	10.90	17,380	5,457	11,923	129	10.97	2.11	8.86	11,991	2,302	9,689	130
45–54	24.60	7.99	16.60	2,006	652	1,354	16	19.59	3.49	16.09	1,598	285	1,313	13
Non-Hispanic white[h]														
All ages	10.17	2.87	7.31	216,449	60,976	155,473	1,569	6.98	1.11	5.87	148,390	23,600	124,790	1,916
Under 15	21.07	8.99	12.08	150	64	86	5	12.06	3.51	8.56	86	25	61	4
15–19	11.78	3.71	8.07	12,697	3,997	8,700	99	8.19	1.45	6.74	8,827	1,560	7,267	120
15	14.94	5.39	9.55	402	145	257	8	8.47	2.01	6.46	228	54	174	6
16	14.22	4.68	9.54	1,002	330	672	7	8.56	1.66	6.90	603	117	486	11
17	11.99	4.05	7.94	1,844	623	1,221	12	8.14	1.43	6.71	1,251	220	1,031	20
18	11.88	3.81	8.08	3,621	1,160	2,461	23	8.55	1.54	7.01	2,604	468	2,136	35
19	11.17	3.33	7.83	5,828	1,739	4,089	49	7.93	1.34	6.59	4,141	701	3,440	48
20–24	10.09	2.87	7.21	43,490	12,385	31,105	402	7.11	1.10	6.00	30,636	4,752	25,884	370
25–29	9.45	2.61	6.85	60,243	16,601	43,642	455	6.48	1.01	5.46	41,271	6,455	34,816	528
30–34	9.70	2.71	6.99	60,204	16,822	43,382	375	6.56	1.04	5.52	40,666	6,423	34,243	597
35–39	11.31	3.09	8.22	30,423	8,301	22,122	173	7.60	1.21	6.39	20,443	3,265	17,178	238
40–44	14.45	4.37	10.08	8,214	2,485	5,729	53	9.96	1.75	8.21	5,661	993	4,668	54
45–54	23.20	7.24	15.96	1,028	321	707	7	18.05	2.86	15.18	800	127	673	5
Non-Hispanic black[h]														
All ages	16.27	5.90	10.36	94,869	34,421	60,448	639	13.08	2.90	10.18	76,195	16,890	59,305	1,243
Under 15	25.07	10.95	14.12	261	114	147	2	14.79	3.55	11.24	154	37	117	2
15–19	16.59	6.14	10.44	10,281	3,808	6,473	86	13.44	2.53	10.90	8,324	1,570	6,754	120
15	21.47	7.74	13.73	555	200	355	9	13.39	2.20	11.19	347	57	290	2
16	18.29	7.08	11.20	986	382	604	9	13.14	2.39	10.75	708	129	579	14
17	17.62	6.58	11.05	1,680	627	1,053	15	13.05	2.47	10.58	1,243	235	1,008	20
18	16.30	6.32	9.97	2,737	1,062	1,675	18	13.48	2.76	10.71	2,262	464	1,798	26
19	15.62	5.55	10.07	4,323	1,537	2,786	35	13.61	2.48	11.13	3,764	685	3,079	58
20–24	15.29	5.45	9.84	28,360	10,105	18,255	217	12.89	2.64	10.24	23,872	4,895	18,977	400
25–29	15.48	5.56	9.93	23,804	8,543	15,261	145	12.32	2.71	9.61	18,924	4,167	14,757	333
30–34	16.73	6.17	10.56	18,822	6,938	11,884	115	13.11	3.24	9.87	14,735	3,638	11,097	248
35–39	18.80	6.90	11.90	10,057	3,693	6,364	53	14.30	3.72	10.58	7,641	1,988	5,653	116
40–44	21.36	8.03	13.33	2,955	1,111	1,844	18	16.31	3.95	12.36	2,255	546	1,709	24
45–54	29.64	9.82	19.82	329	109	220	3	26.06	4.40	21.65	290	49	241	—
Hispanic[i]														
All ages	11.31	3.18	8.13	101,839	28,601	73,238	629	7.09	1.21	5.87	63,832	10,933	52,899	564
Under 15	17.84	6.44	11.40	216	78	138	3	10.72	2.31	8.41	130	28	102	1
15–19	11.79	3.49	8.30	10,952	3,241	7,711	90	7.91	1.22	6.69	7,348	1,135	6,213	49
15	15.78	5.45	10.34	597	206	391	5	9.19	1.72	7.47	348	65	283	2
16	13.37	3.88	9.49	1,236	359	877	13	8.43	1.30	7.13	780	120	660	2
17	12.10	3.58	8.53	1,973	583	1,390	20	7.98	1.24	6.74	1,302	203	1,099	9
18	11.83	3.53	8.30	3,068	916	2,152	22	7.99	1.25	6.74	2,073	324	1,749	13
19	10.84	3.13	7.71	4,078	1,177	2,901	30	7.56	1.12	6.44	2,845	423	2,422	23
20–24	10.38	2.85	7.52	24,646	6,774	17,872	168	6.75	1.05	5.69	16,031	2,503	13,528	150
25–29	10.37	2.81	7.56	25,304	6,852	18,452	171	6.39	1.06	5.32	15,587	2,597	12,990	171
30–34	11.41	3.17	8.24	22,400	6,216	16,184	118	6.96	1.29	5.67	13,666	2,529	11,137	111
35–39	13.60	4.00	9.61	13,959	4,099	9,860	60	8.19	1.58	6.61	8,400	1,620	6,780	58
40–44	16.53	5.04	11.49	4,046	1,233	2,813	19	9.98	1.95	8.04	2,443	476	1,967	22
45–54	23.58	8.06	15.52	316	108	208	—	16.97	3.36	13.60	227	45	182	2

TABLE 3.9

Preterm and low birthweight births by age, race, and Hispanic origin of mother, 2013 [CONTINUED]

— Quantity zero.
[a]Less than 37 completed weeks of gestation.
[b]Less than 2,500 grams.
[c]Less than 34 completed weeks of gestation.
[d]34–36 completed weeks of gestation.
[e]Less than 1,500 grams.
[f]1,500–2,499 grams.
[g]Includes races other than white and black and origin not stated.
[h]Race and Hispanic origin are reported separately on birth certificates. Persons of Hispanic origin may be of any race. Race categories are consistent with 1977 Office of Management and Budget standards. Forty-four states and the District of Columbia reported multiple-race data for 2013 that were bridged to single-race categories for comparability with other states.
[i]Includes all persons of Hispanic origin of any race.

SOURCE: Joyce A. Martin et al., "Table 25. Preterm and Low Birthweight Births, by Age and Race and Hispanic Origin of Mother: United States, 2013," in "Births: Final Data for 2013, " *National Vital Statistics Report*, vol. 64, no. 1, January 15, 2015, http://www.cdc.gov/nchs/data/nvsr/nvsr64/nvsr64_01.pdf (accessed September 21, 2015)

CHAPTER 4

ABORTION IN THE UNITED STATES: A STATISTICAL STUDY

WHO COLLECTS ABORTION DATA?

There are two major sources for abortion statistics. The Centers for Disease Control and Prevention (CDC) collects abortion statistics for the U.S. government. The Guttmacher Institute, a private organization that studies reproductive health issues and strongly supports the position that abortion is an acceptable option, conducts periodic surveys of abortions that are performed in the United States and throughout the world.

The CDC compiles abortion information collected by state health departments, hospitals, and other medical facilities. These data come from 52 reporting areas: the 50 states, the District of Columbia, and New York City. By contrast, the Guttmacher Institute directly contacts all known abortion providers for its periodic surveys and follows up its inquiries by letter and telephone. Thus, the Guttmacher Institute data are considered to be the most accurate data available.

The number of abortions reported to the CDC by the individual states is generally lower than that collected by the Guttmacher Institute. The CDC believes that the number of abortions performed in physicians' offices is probably underreported more often than are those done in hospitals and other medical facilities. Because most abortions in physicians' offices are performed early in pregnancy, the CDC's early abortion counts are likely less than the actual numbers.

HOW MANY ABORTIONS?

CDC Data

The CDC began its abortion surveillance in 1969, two years after Colorado became the first state to liberalize its abortion statute. As of November 2015, the most recent CDC survey data of legally induced abortions were compiled in "Abortion Surveillance—United States, 2011" (*Morbidity and Mortality Weekly Report*, vol. 63, no. 11, November 28, 2014) by Karen Pazol et al. In 2011, 730,322 abortions were reported. Overall, between 2002 and 2011, the total number of reported abortions decreased 14%, the abortion rate decreased 14%, and the abortion ratio decreased 12%. (See Figure 4.1.).

The overall abortion rate refers to the number of abortions performed per 1,000 women aged 15 to 44 years (the primary childbearing years). In 2011 the abortion rate was 13.9. (See Table 4.1.) The abortion ratio is the number of legal abortions for every 1,000 live births in a given year. In 2011 the abortion ratio was 219 abortions per 1,000 live births, or about one abortion for every four births.

Guttmacher Institute Data

The Guttmacher Institute started collecting data on abortion in 1973, the year of the *Roe v. Wade* (410 U.S. 113) ruling. Because the Guttmacher Institute directly surveys abortion providers, its abortion counts and rates are generally higher than those reported by the CDC. According to the Guttmacher Institute, the abortion rate for women aged 15 to 44 years was 21.1 abortions per 1,000 women in 2001 and 16.9 abortions per 1,000 women in 2011. (See Figure 4.2.) By contrast, the CDC calculated the annual abortion rate for women in the same age group as 16.2 abortions per 1,000 women in 2002 and as 13.9 abortions per 1,000 women in 2011. (See Table 4.1.)

CHARACTERISTICS OF WOMEN SEEKING ABORTION

According to Pazol et al., nearly half (46.7%) of the women who had abortions in 2011 were younger than 25 years of age. (See Table 4.2.) More than half were white (54.9%), and nearly two-thirds were in the first two months of pregnancy (65.9%). (See Table 4.3 and Table 4.4.) As Table 4.5 shows, the vast majority (85.5%) of women who received abortions in 2011 were not married.

FIGURE 4.1

Number, ratio, and rate of reported abortions, 2002–11

[Data are for 46 reporting areas; excludes Alaska, California, Louisiana, Maryland, New Hampshire, and West Virginia]

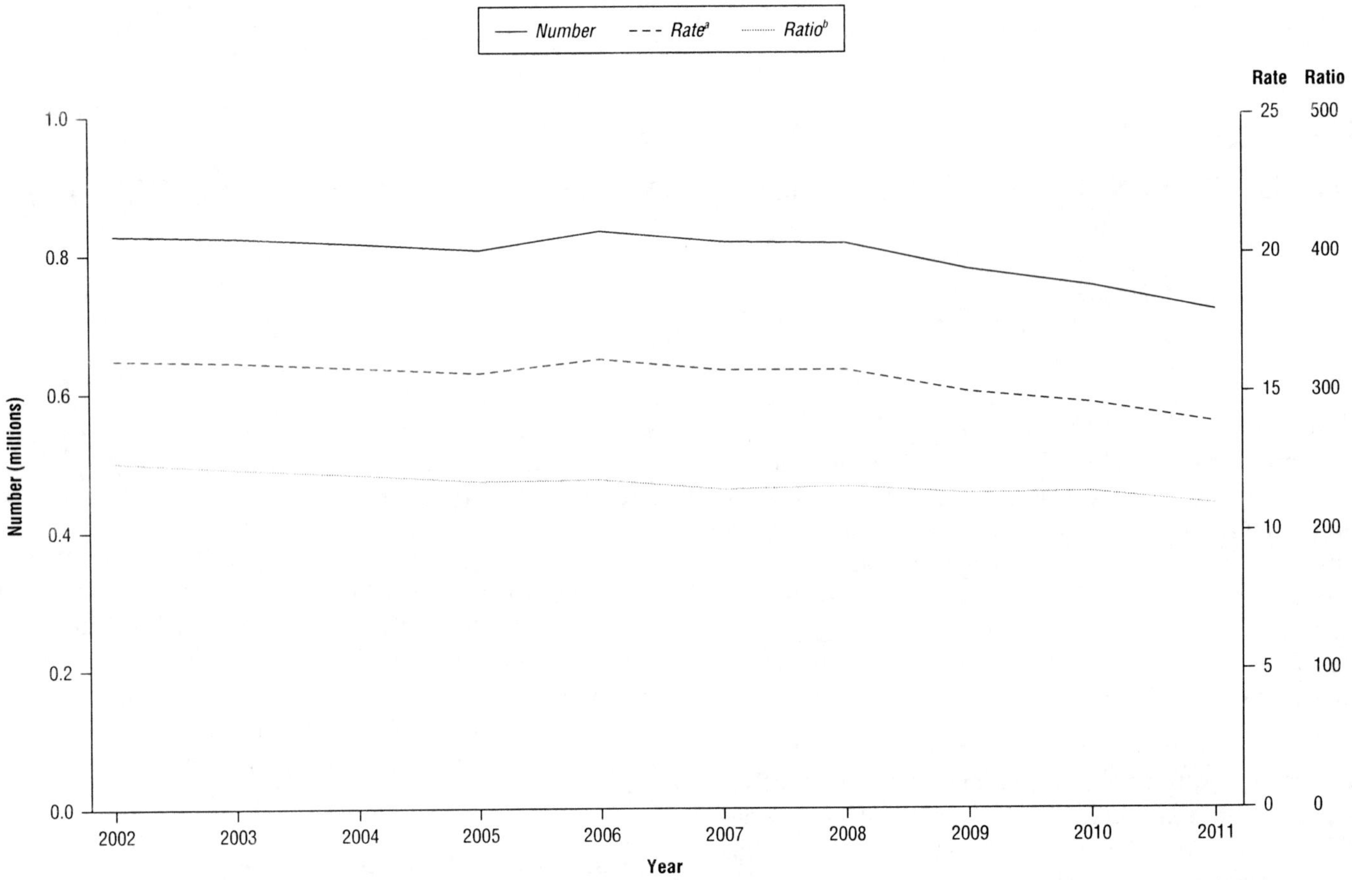

[a]Number of abortions per 1,000 women aged 15–44 years.
[b]Number of abortions per 1,000 live births.

SOURCE: Karen Pazol et al., "Figure 1. Number, Rate, and Ratio of Abortions Performed, by Year—Selected Reporting Areas, United States, 2002–2011," in "Abortion Surveillance—United States, 2011," *MMWR*, vol. 63, no. 11, November 28, 2014, http://www.cdc.gov/mmwr/pdf/ss/ss6311.pdf (accessed September 21, 2015)

The Age of the Woman and of the Pregnancy

According to Pazol et al., women in the 20- to 24-year-old age group obtained the greatest proportion of abortions in 2011—one-third (32.9%) of the total. (See Table 4.2.) One-quarter of abortions (24.9%) were obtained by those aged 25 to 29 years, while 13.4% were obtained by women aged 15 to 19 years. Women younger than 15 years obtained less than 1% of abortions. Women aged 30 to 34 years had 15.8% of abortions in 2011, and women 35 years and older had 12.5%.

Pazol et al. indicate that although teenagers younger than 15 years of age obtained less than 1% of all abortions in 2011, their abortion ratio (the number of abortions per 1,000 live births) was 839, by far the highest of any age group. (See Figure 4.3 and Table 4.6.) Put simply, although the total number of abortions obtained by this age group was small, the high ratio indicates that nearly as many adolescents aged 14 years and younger obtained abortions in 2011 as gave birth. Nationwide, there were 2,728 abortions within this age group in 2011.

In 2011 the abortion ratio was lowest for women aged 30 to 34 years (132 per 1,000 live births). (See Table 4.6.) Women aged 35 to 39 years and 25 to 29 years had the second- and third-lowest ratios of abortions to live births (164 and 178 per 1,000 live births, respectively).

In 2011 most abortions (65.9%) were early abortions—obtained during the first eight weeks of pregnancy. (See Table 4.4.) Figure 4.4 shows that older women were more likely to obtain an early abortion than younger women.

Race and Ethnicity

In 2011, 54.9% of women in the United States who had an abortion were white, 37.3% were African American, and

7.8% were of other races. (See Table 4.3.) However, the abortion ratio for African American women (381 per 1,000 live births) was more than three times the ratio for white women (126 per 1,000 live births). Similarly, the abortion rate for African American women (25.8 per 1,000 women) was more than three times the rate for white women (7.8 per 1,000 women).

TABLE 4.1

Number, rate, and ratio of reported abortions, selected states, 2002–11

	All reporting areas[a]	Continuously reporting areas[b]			
Year	No.	No.	%[c]	Rate[d]	Ratio[e]
2002	854,122	828,027	96.9	16.2	250
2003	848,163	824,230	97.2	16.1	245
2004	839,226	815,969	97.2	15.9	241
2005	820,151	805,725	98.2	15.7	236
2006	852,385[f]	832,692	97.7	16.2	237
2007	827,609	817,222	98.7	15.8	230
2008	825,564	815,006	98.7	15.8	232
2009	789,217[g]	777,340	98.5	15.0	227
2010	765,651	753,065	98.4	14.6	228
2011	730,322	717,903	98.3	13.9	219

[a]Excludes states that did not report abortion numbers to CDC: Alaska (2002), California (2002–2011), Delaware (2009), Louisiana (2005), Maryland (2007– 2011), New Hampshire (2002–2011), and West Virginia (2003–2004).
[b]Only includes areas that reported abortion counts every year during the period of analysis (2002–2011).
[c]Abortions from areas that reported every year during 2002–2011 as a percentage of all reported abortions.
[d]Number of abortions per 1,000 women aged 15–44 years.
[e]Number of abortions per 1,000 live births.
[f]This number is greater than reported in the 2006 report because of numbers subsequently provided by Louisiana.
[g]This number is greater than reported in the 2009 report because of numbers subsequently provided by Delaware.

SOURCE: Karen Pazol et al., "Table 1. Number, Rate, and Ratio of Reported Abortions—Selected Reporting Areas, United States, 2002–2011," in "Abortion Surveillance—United States, 2011," *MMWR*, vol. 63, no. 11, November 28, 2014, http://www.cdc.gov/mmwr/pdf/ss/ss6311.pdf (accessed September 21, 2015)

The abortion ratio for Hispanic women in 2011 was lower than that for non-Hispanic women (198 per 1,000 versus 210 per 1,000 live births). (See Table 4.7.) Conversely, the abortion rate for Hispanic women was higher than that for non-Hispanic women (15.8 per 1,000 women versus 13 per 1,000 women).

Table 4.8 shows that in 2013 Hispanic women had the highest fertility rate at 72.9 births per 1,000 people. By contrast, non-Hispanic African Americans had a fertility rate of 64.6, and non-Hispanic whites had a fertility rate of 58.7.

Marital Status

Pazol et al. report that in 2011, as in past years, unmarried women (divorced, widowed, or never married) accounted for the greatest proportion of those who had an abortion (85.7%). (See Table 4.9.) Married women made up only 14.3% of those who had an abortion in 2011.

IMPACT OF CONTRACEPTIVE USE ON UNINTENDED PREGNANCY AND ABORTION

Nathalie Bajos et al. examine in "Contraception at the Time of Abortion: High-Risk Time or High-Risk Women?" (*Human Reproduction*, vol. 21, no. 11, November 2006) the contraceptive use of women who had an abortion compared with women who had not had an

FIGURE 4.2

Number of abortions per 1,000 women aged 15–44, 1973–2011

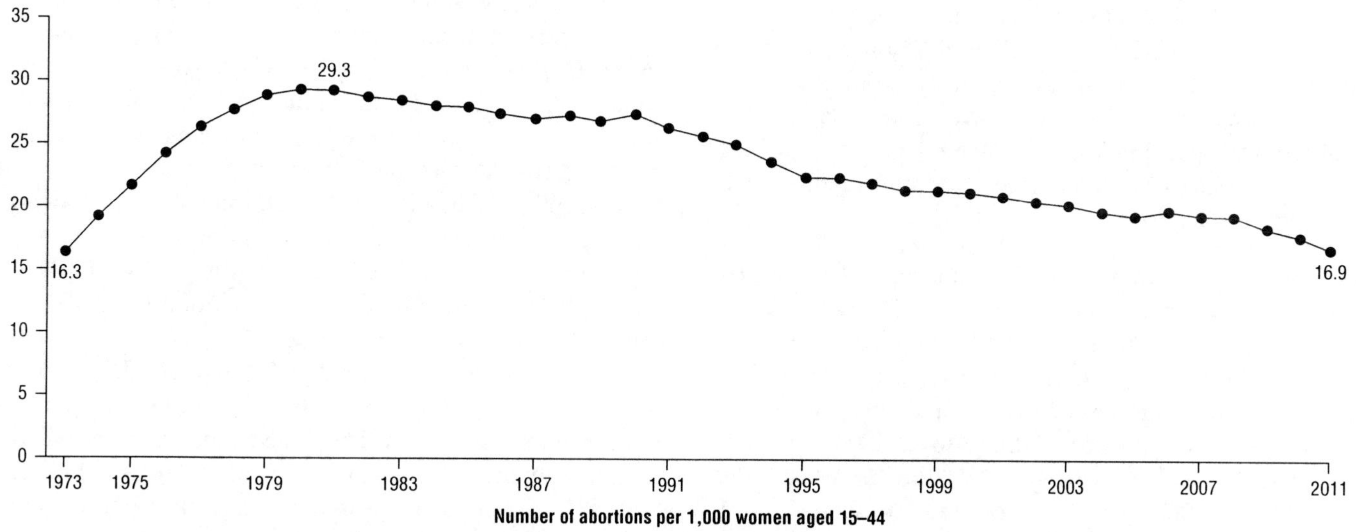

SOURCE: "In 2011, the U.S. Abortion Rate Reached Its Lowest Level since 1973," in *Fact Sheet: Induced Abortion in the United States*, Guttmacher Institute, July 2014, http://www.guttmacher.org/pubs/fb_induced_abortion.html (accessed September 21, 2015)

TABLE 4.2

Abortions by age group and year, 2002–11

Age (yrs)	Year: 2002	2003	2004	2005	2006	2007	2008	2009	2010	2011	% change: 2002 to 2006	2007 to 2011	2010 to 2011	2002 to 2011
% of abortions														
<15	0.6	0.6	0.6	0.6	0.5	0.5	0.5	0.5	0.5	0.4	−16.7	−20.0	−20.0	−33.3
15–19	16.9	16.7	16.6	16.5	16.5	16.5	16.1	15.5	14.6	13.4	−2.4	−18.8	−8.2	−20.7
20–24	33.4	33.5	33.1	32.8	32.7	32.6	32.7	32.6	32.8	32.9	−2.1	0.9	0.3	−1.5
25–29	22.6	22.7	23.1	23.5	24.1	24.2	24.4	24.4	24.5	24.9	6.6	2.9	1.6	10.2
30–34	14.9	14.9	14.8	14.6	14.2	14.1	14.4	14.8	15.3	15.8	−4.7	12.1	3.3	6.0
35–39	8.4	8.4	8.5	8.8	8.9	8.9	8.8	8.9	8.9	8.9	6.0	0.0	0.0	6.0
≥40	3.2	3.2	3.2	3.2	3.2	3.2	3.1	3.3	3.4	3.6	0.0	12.5	5.9	12.5
Abortion rate[a]														
<15	1.4	1.4	1.3	1.3	1.2	1.2	1.2	1.1	1.0	0.9	−14.3	−25.0	−10.0	−35.7
15–19	16.0	15.7	15.1	14.5	14.7	14.4	14.0	12.9	11.8	10.6	−8.1	−26.4	−10.2	−33.8
20–24	31.9	31.3	30.3	29.4	30.1	29.6	29.7	28.0	27.0	25.2	−5.6	−14.9	−6.7	−21.0
25–29	23.4	23.2	22.8	22.3	22.9	22.1	22.1	21.0	20.4	19.6	−2.1	−11.3	−3.9	−16.2
30–34	13.9	13.9	13.8	13.7	14.0	13.8	14.0	13.5	13.4	12.8	0.7	−7.2	−4.5	−7.9
35–39	7.4	7.5	7.6	7.8	8.0	7.9	8.0	7.7	7.7	7.5	8.1	−5.1	−2.6	1.4
≥40	2.6	2.6	2.6	2.6	2.7	2.7	2.7	2.8	2.8	2.8	3.8	3.7	0.0	7.7
Abortion ratio[b]														
<15	771	848	790	776	765	784	813	841	862	849	−0.8	8.3	−1.5	10.1
15–19	375	381	372	364	357	344	345	335	339	332	−4.8	−3.5	−2.1	−11.5
20–24	308	305	297	288	285	280	289	287	296	290	−7.5	3.6	−2.0	−5.8
25–29	202	197	194	190	192	186	190	186	186	180	−5.0	−3.2	−3.2	−10.9
30–34	150	146	144	142	143	139	142	139	138	133	−4.7	−4.3	−3.6	−11.3
35–39	183	177	173	172	174	171	175	173	172	165	−4.9	−3.5	−4.1	−9.8
≥40	317	299	292	285	285	280	274	276	275	275	−10.1	−1.8	0.0	−13.2
Total (no.)	**726,052**	**725,196**	**713,348**	**701,294**	**721,476**	**713,299**	**716,664**	**685,284**	**664,761**	**632,627**	—	—	—	—

[a]Number of abortions obtained by women in a given age group per 1,000 women in that same age group. Adolescents aged 13–14 years were used as the denominator for the group of adolescents aged <15 years, and women aged 40–44 years were used as the denominator for the group of women aged ≥40 years. For each state, abortions for women of unknown age were distributed according to the distribution of abortions among women of known age for that state.
[b]Number of abortions obtained by women in a given age group per 1,000 live births to women in that same age group. For each state, abortions for women of unknown age were distributed according to the distribution of abortions among women of known age for that state.
Notes: Data from 43 reporting areas; by year, these reporting areas represent 97%–98% of all abortions reported to CDC by age during 2002–2011. Excludes nine reporting areas (Alaska, California, Florida, Louisiana, Maryland, New Hampshire, West Virginia, Vermont, and Wyoming) that did not report, did not report by age, or did not meet reporting standards for ≥1 year.

SOURCE: Karen Pazol et al., "Table 4. Reported Abortions, by Known Age Group and Year—Selected Reporting Areas, United States, 2002–2011," in "Abortion Surveillance—United States, 2011," *MMWR*, vol. 63, no. 11, November 28, 2014, http://www.cdc.gov/mmwr/pdf/ss/ss6311.pdf (accessed September 21, 2015)

abortion. Bajos et al. find that women who had an abortion were less likely to use contraception than women who had not had an abortion. In addition, they were much less likely to have used birth control pills or an intrauterine device (IUD) for contraception before their abortion than women who had not had an abortion. Conversely, women who had an abortion were more likely than women who had not had an abortion to use condoms and natural methods of birth control. These are less effective contraceptive methods than birth control pills or IUDs.

In "Family Planning and the Burden of Unintended Pregnancies" (*Epidemiology Review*, vol. 32, June 22, 2010), Amy O. Tsui, Raegan McDonald-Mosley, and Anne E. Burke report that countries with the highest use of "modern" contraceptive methods generally have the lowest abortion rates. Gilda Sedgh et al. assert in "Induced Abortion: Incidence and Trends Worldwide from 1995 to 2008" (*Lancet*, vol. 379, no. 9816, February 2012) that "there is a positive correlation between unmet need for contraception and abortion levels," and they observe that the decline in the global abortion rate stalled between 2003 and 2008 in part because contraceptive use plateaued worldwide.

According to Gina M. Secura et al., in "Provision of No-Cost, Long-Acting Contraception and Teenage Pregnancy" (*New England Journal of Medicine*, vol. 371, no. 14, October 2, 2014), access to contraception can play a significant role in reducing both pregnancy and abortion rates among teens. The researchers examine the results of the Contraceptive CHOICE Project, an initiative that provided free long-acting, reversible contraception to 1,404 teenage girls over a three-year period. According to Secura et al., CHOICE participants between the ages of 18 and 19 years reported an abortion rate of 11.6 per 1,000 teens over the course of the study, compared with a rate of 23.7 abortions per 1,000 teens among 18- to 19-year-old girls nationwide during the same period. This discrepancy was even more dramatic among African American girls aged 18 to 19 years, with CHOICE participants in that age group reporting a rate of 9.4 abortions per 1,000 teens, compared with a rate of 34.5 abortions per 1,000 teens among African American girls aged 18 to 19 years nationwide.

TABLE 4.3

Percentage, rate, and ratio of reported abortions, by race, selected states, 2011

	White		Black		Other		Total abortions reported by known race	
State/area[a]	No.	(%)[b]	No.	(%)	No.	(%)	No.	% all reported abortions[c]
Alabama	3,625	(38.2)	5,558	(58.6)	300	(3.2)	9,483	(99.6)
Alaska	939	(62.2)	101	(6.7)	470	(31.1)	1,510	(92.8)
Arkansas	2,159	(53.6)	1,527	(37.9)	342	(8.5)	4,028	(99.9)
Colorado	6,777	(70.2)	718	(7.4)	2,153	(22.3)	9,648	(92.1)
Delaware	1,943	(52.6)	—[d]	—	—	—	3,696	(97.4)
District of Columbia[e]	618	(22.5)	1,544	(56.2)	584	(21.3)	2,746	(99.2)
Idaho	1,244	(92.1)	16	(1.2)	90	(6.7)	1,350	(93.8)
Indiana	5,612	(64.6)	2,734	(31.5)	346	(4.0)	8,692	(95.4)
Iowa	3,749	(77.9)	594	(12.3)	472	(9.8)	4,815	(100.0)
Kansas	5,101	(65.8)	1,738	(22.4)	917	(11.8)	7,756	(99.6)
Louisiana	3,105	(38.1)	4,727	(57.9)	327	(4.0)	8,159	(91.1)
Michigan	10,661	(47.4)	10,912	(48.5)	920	(4.1)	22,493	(96.3)
Minnesota	6,478	(59.8)	2,566	(23.7)	1,783	(16.5)	10,827	(97.8)
Mississippi	414	(19.1)	1,378	(63.5)	379	(17.5)	2,171	(97.6)
Missouri	3,076	(53.6)	2,369	(41.3)	298	(5.2)	5,743	(99.5)
Montana	1,935	(90.1)	23	(1.1)	189	(8.8)	2,147	(100.0)
New Jersey[f]	9,430	(36.1)	11,298	(43.2)	5,418	(20.7)	26,146	(98.4)
New York State	17,865	(68.1)	7,760	(29.6)	605	(2.3)	26,230	(85.1)
North Carolina	10,081	(42.8)	12,435	(52.8)	1,051	(4.5)	23,567	(90.0)
North Dakota	962	(78.7)	39	(3.2)	221	(18.1)	1,222	(98.0)
Ohio	13,340	(57.4)	9,178	(39.5)	720	(3.1)	23,238	(93.8)
Oklahoma	3,897	(72.0)	962	(17.8)	557	(10.3)	5,416	(100.0)
Oregon	7,726	(84.5)	517	(5.7)	895	(9.8)	9,138	(95.5)
Pennsylvania	18,931	(52.3)	14,899	(41.1)	2,389	(6.6)	36,219	(99.8)
Rhode Island	2,994	(77.5)	652	(16.9)	216	(5.6)	3,862	(92.7)
South Carolina	3,591	(56.3)	2,537	(39.8)	249	(3.9)	6,377	(100.0)
South Dakota	450	(76.8)	51	(8.7)	85	(14.5)	586	(98.2)
Tennessee	7,400	(47.3)	7,799	(49.9)	431	(2.8)	15,630	(97.0)
Utah	2,486	(84.8)	81	(2.8)	366	(12.5)	2,933	(86.6)
Virginia	12,070	(49.3)	10,777	(44.0)	1,643	(6.7)	24,490	(96.4)
West Virginia	1,603	(87.3)	213	(11.6)	21	(1.1)	1,837	(100.0)
Wisconsin[g]	4,799	(70.5)	1,590	(23.4)	419	(6.2)	6,808	(97.0)
Total	**175,061**	**(54.9)**	**117,293**[h]	**(37.3)**	**24,856**[h]	**(7.8)**	**318,963**	**(95.3)**[i]
Rate[j]	**7.8**		**25.8**		**15.5**		**11.2**	
Ratio[k]	**126**		**381**		**247**		**177**	

[a]Data from 32 reporting areas; excludes 20 areas (Arizona, California, Connecticut, Florida, Georgia, Hawaii, Illinois, Kentucky, Maine, Maryland, Massachusetts, Nebraska, Nevada, New Hampshire, New Mexico, New York City, Texas, Vermont, Washington, and Wyoming) that did not report, did not report by race, or did not meet reporting standards.
[b]Percentages for the individual component categories might not add to 100 because of rounding.
[c]Calculated as the number of abortions reported by known race, divided by the sum of abortions reported by known and unknown race.
[d]Cell details not displayed because of small numbers (N = 1–4).
[e]Because reporting is not mandatory, information could not be obtained for all abortions performed in the District of Columbia.
[f]Data from hospitals and licensed ambulatory care facilities only; because reporting is not mandatory for private physicians and women's centers, information could not be obtained for all abortions performed in New Jersey.
[g]Includes residents only.
[h]Small numbers removed from individual cells have been subtracted from the column total so that the missing number cannot be back-calculated.
[i]Percentage based on a total of 334,645 abortions reported among the areas that met reporting standards for race.
[j]Number of abortions obtained by women in a given racial group per 1,000 women in that same group. For each state, abortions for women of unknown race were distributed according to the distribution of abortions among women of known race for that state.
[k]Number of abortions obtained by women in a given racial group per 1,000 live births to women in that same racial group. For each state, abortions for women of unknown race were distributed according to the distribution of abortions among women of known race for that state.

SOURCE: Karen Pazol et al., "Table 13. Reported Abortions, by Known Race of Women Who Obtained an Abortion and Reporting Area of Occurrence—Selected Reporting Areas, United States, 2011," in "Abortion Surveillance—United States, 2011," *MMWR*, vol. 63, no. 11, November 28, 2014, http://www.cdc.gov/mmwr/pdf/ss/ss6311.pdf (accessed September 21, 2015)

OUT-OF-STATE VERSUS IN-STATE ABORTIONS

Many women travel out of state for abortions because of a lack of providers in their area or to avoid restrictive laws, such as required parental notification and consent, waiting periods, and required counseling that involves more than one visit to the provider. (See Chapters 2 and 10.) Table 4.10 lists the states that required a waiting period before an abortion can be obtained or that required biased counseling in 2015. Biased counseling is what pro-choice organizations call counseling that they feel is intended to encourage a woman to change her mind and not have an abortion.

Theodore J. Joyce et al. of the Guttmacher Institute find in *The Impact of State Mandatory Counseling and Waiting Period Laws on Abortion: A Literature Review* (April 2009, http://www.guttmacher.org/pubs/MandatoryCounseling.pdf) that if the counseling was delivered over

TABLE 4.4

Percentage of reported abortions by weeks of gestation, selected states, 2002–11

Weeks of gestation	Year										% change			
	2002	2003	2004	2005	2006	2007	2008	2009	2010	2011	2002 to 2006	2007 to 2011	2010 to 2011	2002 to 2011
≤13 weeks' gestation (%)	**91.4**	**91.1**	**91.5**	**91.5**	**91.6**	**91.6**	**91.5**	**91.9**	**91.9**	**91.6**	**0.2**	**0.0**	**−0.3**	**0.2**
≤6–8	62.2	62.0	63.2	63.5	63.7	64.0	64.4	65.5	66.0	65.9	2.4	3.0	−0.2	5.9
9–13	29.2	29.1	28.3	28.0	27.9	27.6	27.1	26.4	25.9	25.7	−4.5	−6.9	−0.8	−12.0
>13 weeks' gestation (%)	**8.6**	**8.9**	**8.5**	**8.4**	**8.3**	**8.4**	**8.5**	**8.2**	**8.2**	**8.5**	**−3.5**	**1.2**	**3.7**	**−1.2**
14–15	3.0	3.2	3.3	3.2	3.3	3.3	3.4	3.3	3.3	3.4	10.0	3.0	3.0	13.3
16–17	2.1	2.1	1.9	1.9	1.8	1.9	1.9	1.8	1.8	1.8	−14.3	−5.3	0.0	−14.3
18–20	2.1	2.1	1.9	1.9	1.9	1.9	1.9	1.8	1.8	1.9	−9.5	0.0	5.6	−9.5
≥21	1.4	1.5	1.4	1.4	1.3	1.3	1.3	1.3	1.3	1.4	−7.1	7.7	7.7	0.0
Total (no.)	**530,874**	**534,077**	**526,832**	**515,519**	**529,476**	**523,073**	**525,466**	**501,500**	**490,946**	**464,518**	—	—	—	—

Notes: Data from 31 reporting areas; by year, these reporting areas represent 78%–83% of the abortions reported to CDC (Centers for Disease Control) by gestational age during 2002–2011. Excludes 21 areas (Alaska, California, Connecticut, Delaware, District of Columbia, Florida, Illinois, Louisiana, Maryland, Massachusetts, Mississippi, Nebraska, Nevada, New Hampshire, New York State, Pennsylvania, Rhode Island, Vermont, West Virginia, Wisconsin, and Wyoming) that did not report, did not report by gestational age, or did not meet reporting standards for ≥1 year.

SOURCE: Karen Pazol et al., "Table 8. Reported Abortions, by Known Weeks of Gestation and Year—Selected Reporting Areas, United States, 2002–2011," in "Abortion Surveillance—United States, 2011," *MMWR*, vol. 63, no. 11, November 28, 2014, http://www.cdc.gov/mmwr/pdf/ss/ss6311.pdf (accessed September 21, 2015)

the Internet, by mail, or by telephone it had no measurable impact on a woman's choice but might postpone the abortion. If the counseling required an additional in-person visit before the procedure, it, too, had no impact on choice but placed extra burdens on women such as the costs of child care, time off from work, or extra travel.

Table 4.11 presents abortion data on the state of residence of women who obtained an abortion in 2011. It also shows the number of abortions that occurred in each state that year, and the percentage of abortions in each state that were obtained by women who resided in another state. In 2011 the largest reported numbers of abortions occurred in New York (111,296), Florida (77,166), and Texas (72,332). The fewest abortions in 2011 were performed in South Dakota (597), North Dakota (1,247), and Vermont (1,355). It should be noted that some jurisdictions did not report abortion information to the CDC in 2011.

As Table 4.11 shows, some states reported that a high percentage of the abortions performed there were obtained by women from another state. States with the highest percentages of abortions obtained by out-of-state residents included the District of Columbia (53.6%), Kansas (50.6%), and North Dakota (32.4%). The states with the lowest percentages of abortions obtained by out-of-state residents in 2011 were Alaska (0.7%), Arizona (1%), and Hawaii (1.2%).

ABORTION PROVIDERS

Rachel K. Jones and Jenna Jerman of the Guttmacher Institute report in "Abortion Incidence and Service Availability in the United States, 2011" (*Perspectives on Sexual and Reproductive Health*, vol. 46, no. 1, March 2014) that 89% of all U.S. counties had no abortion providers in 2011. Thirty-eight percent of women of childbearing age (aged 15 to 44 years) lived in counties with no known providers. The states with the highest percentage of women in counties with no abortion providers were Wyoming (100%), Mississippi (91%), West Virginia (90%), Arkansas (78%), Virginia (78%), South Dakota (77%), Kansas (74%), Kentucky (74%), Missouri (74%), North Dakota (73%), and South Carolina (72%). For many women in rural areas, obtaining an abortion entailed traveling hundreds of miles from their residence.

Jones and Jerman report that of the 1,720 providers in 2011, 49% were clinics, 35% were hospitals, and 17% were physicians' offices. However, 94% of abortions were performed in clinics, 4% were performed in hospitals, and 1% were performed in physicians' offices.

Medical Training

"Abortion Training in United States Obstetrics and Gynecology Residency Programs" (*Obstetrics and Gynecology*, vol. 108, no. 2, August 2006) details the most recent comprehensive study to show the availability of abortion medical training in the United States as of November 2015. In the article, Katherine L. Eastwood et al. report the results of a questionnaire they sent to the directors of physician residency programs in the United States to try and determine the availability of abortion training.

TABLE 4.5

Reported abortions, by marital status and state, 2011

State/area	Married No.	Married (%)[a]	Unmarried No.	Unmarried (%)	Total abortions reported by known marital status No.	% of all reported abortions[b]
Alabama	1,006	(10.6)	8,507	(89.4)	9,513	(99.9)
Alaska	320	(20.3)	1,257	(79.7)	1,577	(96.9)
Arizona	2,342	(16.8)	11,616	(83.2)	13,958	(96.9)
Arkansas	386	(9.6)	3,632	(90.4)	4,018	(99.6)
Colorado	1,895	(19.3)	7,908	(80.7)	9,803	(93.6)
Delaware	437	(11.5)	3,357	(88.5)	3,794	(100.0)
District of Columbia[c]	200	(7.3)	2,542	(92.7)	2,742	(99.1)
Hawaii	475	(18.0)	2,167	(82.0)	2,642	(98.9)
Idaho	226	(15.7)	1,209	(84.3)	1,435	(99.7)
Illinois[d]	4,538	(12.2)	32,596	(87.8)	37,134	(97.9)
Indiana	1,279	(14.2)	7,748	(85.8)	9,027	(99.1)
Iowa	816	(17.0)	3,990	(83.0)	4,806	(99.8)
Kansas	1,128	(14.5)	6,645	(85.5)	7,773	(99.8)
Kentucky	559	(14.1)	3,398	(85.9)	3,957	(100.0)
Louisiana	810	(9.6)	7,657	(90.4)	8,467	(94.6)
Michigan	2,355	(10.1)	20,929	(89.9)	23,284	(99.6)
Minnesota	1,608	(14.8)	9,271	(85.2)	10,879	(98.3)
Mississippi	179	(8.1)	2,043	(91.9)	2,222	(99.9)
Missouri	918	(16.0)	4,813	(84.0)	5,731	(99.3)
Montana	335	(15.8)	1,789	(84.2)	2,124	(98.9)
New Jersey[e]	3,194	(12.1)	23,176	(87.9)	26,370	(99.3)
New Mexico	573	(14.7)	3,326	(85.3)	3,899	(95.5)
North Carolina	4,710	(19.0)	20,019	(81.0)	24,729	(94.4)
North Dakota	159	(12.8)	1,084	(87.2)	1,243	(99.7)
Ohio	3,313	(13.8)	20,625	(86.2)	23,938	(96.7)
Oklahoma	790	(14.6)	4,626	(85.4)	5,416	(100.0)
Oregon	1,729	(19.4)	7,165	(80.6)	8,894	(93.0)
Pennsylvania	4,322	(11.9)	31,952	(88.1)	36,274	(100.0)
Rhode Island	501	(13.6)	3,191	(86.4)	3,692	(88.6)
South Carolina	818	(12.8)	5,559	(87.2)	6,377	(100.0)
South Dakota	96	(16.1)	501	(83.9)	597	(100.0)
Tennessee	2,213	(14.6)	12,911	(85.4)	15,124	(93.9)
Texas	11,893	(16.4)	60,435	(83.6)	72,328	(100.0)
Utah	1,081	(35.1)	2,003	(64.9)	3,084	(91.1)
Virginia	3,992	(16.4)	20,365	(83.6)	24,357	(95.8)
West Virginia	321	(17.5)	1,516	(82.5)	1,837	(100.0)
Wisconsin	1,038	(14.4)	6,193	(85.6)	7,231	(99.8)
Total	**62,555**	**(14.5)**	**367,721**	**(85.5)**	**430,276**	
Abortion ratio[g]	**43**		**373**		**176**	**(97.9)[f]**

[a]Percentages for the individual component categories might not add to 100 because of rounding.
[b]Calculated as the number of abortions reported by known marital status divided by the sum of abortions reported by known and unknown marital status.
[c]Because reporting is not mandatory, information could not be obtained for all abortions performed in the District of Columbia.
[d]Includes residents only.
[e]Data from hospitals and licensed ambulatory care facilities only; because reporting is not mandatory for private physicians and women's centers, information could not be obtained for all abortions performed in New Jersey.
[f]Percentage based on a total of 439,439 abortions reported among the areas that met reporting standards for marital status.
[g]Number of abortions obtained by women by marital status per 1,000 live births to women of the same marital status. For each state, abortions for women of unknown marital status were distributed according to the distribution of abortions among women of known marital status for that state.
Notes: Data from 37 reporting areas; excludes 15 areas (California, Connecticut, Florida, Georgia, Maine, Maryland, Massachusetts, Nebraska, Nevada, New Hampshire, New York City, New York State, Vermont, Washington, and Wyoming) that did not report, did not report by marital status, or did not meet reporting standards.

SOURCE: Karen Pazol et al., "Table 17. Reported Abortions, by Known Marital Status and Reporting Area of Occurrence—Selected Reporting Areas, United States, 2011," in "Abortion Surveillance—United States, 2011," *MMWR*, vol. 63, no. 11, November 28, 2014, http://www.cdc.gov/mmwr/pdf/ss/ss6311.pdf (accessed September 21, 2015)

Eastwood et al. find that larger residency programs were more likely than smaller residency programs to include abortion techniques in routine physician training, rather than include it as optional training. Nearly three-quarters of large programs included routine training in abortion techniques, whereas slightly less than half of medium and small programs did. Only 8% to 14% of all programs excluded abortion training altogether. Catholic-affiliated (12%) and Protestant-affiliated (33%) programs were less likely than other types of programs (nonreligious, 55%; Jewish, 58%; and other programs, 89%) to offer routine training in abortion techniques.

Eastwood et al. note that physicians' training in abortion techniques is extremely important because abortion is one of the most common medical procedures performed in the United States. They state, "Women seeking such care [abortions], the majority of whom are poor, require access to treatment by well-qualified

FIGURE 4.3

Percentage, rate, and ratio of reported abortions, by age group, selected states, 2011

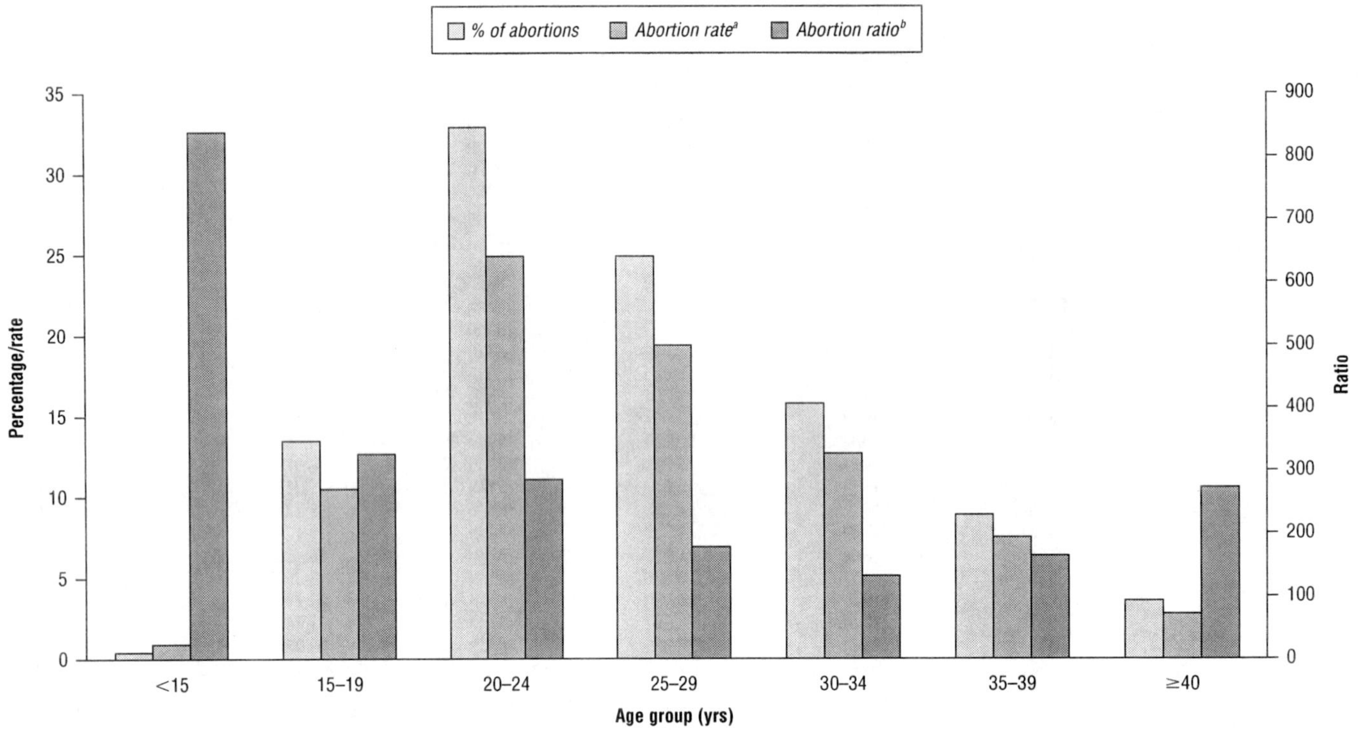

[a]Number of abortions per 1,000 women aged 15–44 years.
[b]Number of abortions per 1,000 live births.
Notes: Data are for 46 areas; excludes California, Florida, Maryland, New Hampshire, Vermont, and Wyoming.

SOURCE: Karen Pazol et al., "Figure 2. Percentage of Total Abortions, Abortion Rate, and Abortion Ratio, by Age Group of Women Who Obtained an Abortion—Selected Reporting Areas, United States, 2011," in "Abortion Surveillance—United States, 2011," *MMWR*, vol. 63, no. 11, November 28, 2014, http://www.cdc.gov/mmwr/pdf/ss/ss6311.pdf (accessed September 21, 2015)

providers, and if complications arise, need appropriate and compassionate care. Continued abortion provision necessitates ongoing training of new providers, a task that can largely be accomplished by educating residents in obstetrics and gynecology in various techniques of elective abortion and the management of complications associated with the various procedures used."

In "Abortion Education and Training" (*Committee Opinion*, no. 612, November 2014), the American College of Obstetricians and Gynecologists' Committee on Health Care for Underserved Women states:

> Access to safe abortion services is a key component of women's health care. Safe, accessible abortion care requires sufficient numbers of trained health care providers who offer the service. However, the number of abortion providers in the United States has not met the level of need. In the United States, 94% of abortions are provided in facilities outside of the traditional learning environment of the medical trainee, requiring concentrated efforts to integrate abortion training into medical school and residency curricula. Legal, regulatory, and other restrictions form barriers to education and training in abortion care. As a result, educators may encounter multiple obstacles to integrating appropriate training.

SURVEY OF FAMILY PLANNING SPECIALISTS. Jenna Turk et al. report in "Barriers to D&E Practice among Family Planning Subspecialists" (*Contraception*, vol. 88, no. 4, October 2013) the results of a survey of physicians who had completed a fellowship in family planning. The survey was intended to find out more about the physicians and to determine whether they face any specific obstacles to practice. The researchers were particularly interested in dilation and extraction procedures (D&E), which account for nearly 9% of all abortions, and more than 95% of second-trimester abortions, in the United States each year.

Turk et al. find that most of the fellowship physicians were young women working in the northeastern and western United States. Almost all of the survey respondents currently performed D&E abortions, with an average of 200 such procedures annually. Respondents working in more abortion-restrictive parts of the country were four times more likely to report a personal obstacle, such as a concern for their personal safety, while those who worked

TABLE 4.6

Reported abortions, by age group and state, 2011

State/area	<15 No.	<15 (%)[a]	15–19 No.	15–19 (%)	20–24 No.	20–24 (%)	25–29 No.	25–29 (%)	30–34 No.	30–34 (%)	35–39 No.	35–39 (%)	≥40 No.	≥40 (%)	Total abortions reported by known age No.	% of all reported abortions[b]
Alaska	7	(0.4)	272	(16.8)	561	(34.7)	398	(24.6)	205	(12.7)	132	(8.2)	42	(2.6)	1,617	(99.4)
Alabama	66	(0.7)	1,406	(14.8)	3,340	(35.1)	2,361	(24.8)	1,410	(14.8)	719	(7.6)	218	(2.3)	9,520	(100.0)
Arkansas	32	(0.8)	583	(14.5)	1,337	(33.2)	1,003	(24.9)	625	(15.5)	331	(8.2)	121	(3.0)	4,032	(100.0)
Arizona	52	(0.4)	1,818	(12.6)	4,651	(32.3)	3,619	(25.1)	2,297	(16.0)	1,386	(9.6)	578	(4.0)	14,401	(100.0)
Colorado	47	(0.4)	1,444	(13.8)	3,429	(32.8)	2,636	(25.2)	1,525	(14.6)	951	(9.1)	426	(4.1)	10,458	(99.8)
Connecticut	49	(0.4)	1,779	(14.4)	4,150	(33.7)	3,128	(25.4)	1,760	(14.3)	1,039	(8.4)	419	(3.4)	12,324	(97.7)
District of Columbia[c]	17	(0.6)	429	(15.5)	938	(33.9)	656	(23.7)	446	(16.1)	226	(8.2)	56	(2.0)	2,768	(100.0)
Delaware	23	(0.6)	569	(15.0)	1,287	(33.9)	944	(24.9)	572	(15.1)	280	(7.4)	119	(3.1)	3,794	(100.0)
Georgia	220	(0.7)	4,116	(12.6)	10,212	(31.2)	8,268	(25.2)	5,637	(17.2)	3,240	(9.9)	1,077	(3.3)	32,770	(100.0)
Hawaii	10	(0.4)	446	(16.7)	878	(32.9)	615	(23.0)	386	(14.5)	231	(8.7)	104	(3.9)	2,670	(100.0)
Iowa	20	(0.4)	715	(14.8)	1,663	(34.5)	1,147	(23.8)	679	(14.1)	381	(7.9)	210	(4.4)	4,815	(100.0)
Idaho	6	(0.4)	207	(14.4)	475	(33.0)	329	(22.9)	252	(17.5)	115	(8.0)	55	(3.8)	1,439	(99.9)
Illinois[d]	185	(0.5)	5,702	(15.1)	11,867	(31.5)	9,099	(24.1)	6,143	(16.3)	3,390	(9.0)	1,295	(3.4)	37,681	(99.4)
Indiana	46	(0.5)	1,195	(13.2)	3,063	(33.7)	2,191	(24.1)	1,459	(16.1)	815	(9.0)	309	(3.4)	9,078	(99.6)
Kansas	31	(0.4)	982	(12.6)	2,606	(33.5)	1,994	(25.6)	1,238	(15.9)	673	(8.6)	264	(3.4)	7,788	(100.0)
Kentucky	22	(0.6)	567	(14.3)	1,295	(32.7)	929	(23.5)	607	(15.3)	384	(9.7)	153	(3.9)	3,957	(100.0)
Louisiana	72	(0.8)	1,242	(13.9)	3,079	(34.4)	2,330	(26.1)	1,290	(14.4)	683	(7.6)	242	(2.7)	8,938	(99.8)
Massachusetts	37	(0.2)	2,576	(12.4)	6,958	(33.6)	5,214	(25.2)	3,195	(15.4)	1,895	(9.2)	827	(4.0)	20,702	(100.0)
Maine	10	(0.6)	254	(14.4)	616	(35.0)	415	(23.6)	260	(14.8)	155	(8.8)	52	(3.0)	1,762	(99.4)
Michigan	103	(0.4)	3,563	(15.3)	8,257	(35.4)	5,411	(23.2)	3,377	(14.5)	1,901	(8.2)	710	(3.0)	23,322	(99.8)
Minnesota	31	(0.3)	1,378	(12.4)	3,653	(33.0)	2,828	(25.5)	1,764	(15.9)	956	(8.6)	460	(4.2)	11,070	(100.0)
Missouri	31	(0.5)	830	(14.4)	2,097	(36.3)	1,344	(23.3)	840	(14.6)	454	(7.9)	175	(3.0)	5,771	(100.0)
Mississippi	22	(1.0)	289	(13.0)	801	(36.1)	584	(26.3)	336	(15.1)	146	(6.6)	42	(1.9)	2,220	(99.8)
Montana	6	(0.3)	356	(16.6)	730	(34.0)	507	(23.6)	297	(13.8)	159	(7.4)	92	(4.3)	2,147	(100.0)
North Carolina	135	(0.5)	3,186	(12.8)	8,457	(33.9)	6,178	(24.7)	3,987	(16.0)	2,210	(8.8)	825	(3.3)	24,978	(95.4)
North Dakota	—[e]	—	172	(13.8)	475	(38.1)	316	(25.3)	158	(12.7)	87	(7.0)	—	—	1,247	(100.0)
Nebraska	10	(0.4)	358	(15.1)	784	(33.1)	591	(24.9)	355	(15.0)	195	(8.2)	79	(3.3)	2,372	(100.0)
New Jersey[f]	116	(0.4)	3,651	(13.7)	8,502	(32.0)	6,454	(24.3)	4,409	(16.6)	2,417	(9.1)	1,009	(3.8)	26,558	(100.0)
New Mexico	31	(0.8)	604	(16.1)	1,276	(33.9)	877	(23.3)	543	(14.4)	287	(7.6)	145	(3.9)	3,763	(92.2)
Nevada	15	(0.2)	870	(12.1)	2,164	(30.0)	1,711	(23.7)	1,204	(16.7)	691	(9.6)	551	(7.6)	7,206	(100.0)
New York	437	(0.4)	16,014	(14.4)	35,040	(31.5)	27,279	(24.6)	18,101	(16.3)	10,207	(9.0)	4,022	(3.6)	111,100	(99.8)
New York City	317	(0.4)	10,985	(13.6)	24,266	(30.2)	20,126	(25.0)	13,809	(17.2)	7,903	(9.8)	3,077	(3.8)	80,483	(100.0)
New York State	120	(0.4)	5,029	(16.4)	10,774	(35.2)	7,153	(23.4)	4,292	(14.0)	2,304	(7.5)	945	(3.1)	30,617	(99.4)
Ohio	125	(0.5)	3,499	(14.3)	8,545	(34.8)	6,014	(24.5)	3,640	(14.8)	1,949	(7.9)	778	(3.2)	24,550	(99.1)
Oklahoma	35	(0.6)	755	(14.0)	1,869	(34.7)	1,343	(24.9)	752	(13.9)	469	(8.7)	169	(3.1)	5,392	(99.6)
Oregon	23	(0.2)	1,300	(13.7)	3,047	(32.1)	2,327	(24.5)	1,548	(16.3)	874	(9.2)	383	(4.0)	9,502	(99.3)
Pennsylvania	161	(0.4)	5,022	(13.8)	12,691	(35.0)	8,902	(24.5)	5,238	(14.4)	3,054	(8.4)	1,210	(3.3)	36,278	(100.0)
Rhode Island	21	(0.5)	630	(15.1)	1,473	(35.4)	978	(23.5)	584	(14.0)	351	(8.4)	128	(3.1)	4,165	(100.0)
South Carolina	29	(0.5)	924	(14.5)	2,166	(34.0)	1,558	(24.4)	938	(14.7)	551	(8.6)	213	(3.3)	6,379	(100.0)
South Dakota	—	—	95	(15.9)	209	(35.0)	138	(23.1)	84	(14.1)	50	(8.4)	—	—	597	(100.0)
Tennessee	62	(0.4)	2,056	(12.8)	5,446	(34.0)	4,112	(25.7)	2,503	(15.6)	1,367	(8.5)	462	(2.9)	16,008	(99.3)
Texas	176	(0.2)	7,548	(10.4)	23,363	(32.3)	19,139	(26.5)	12,141	(16.8)	6,866	(9.5)	3,059	(4.2)	72,292	(99.9)
Utah	18	(0.5)	454	(13.5)	1,056	(31.5)	833	(24.8)	562	(16.7)	296	(8.8)	138	(4.1)	3,357	(99.1)
Virginia	76	(0.3)	2,845	(11.3)	8,270	(32.8)	6,501	(25.8)	4,175	(16.6)	2,415	(9.6)	902	(3.6)	25,184	(99.1)
Washington	70	(0.3)	2,987	(14.8)	6,514	(32.3)	4,919	(24.4)	3,123	(15.5)	1,766	(8.7)	812	(4.0)	20,191	(99.8)
Wisconsin	28	(0.4)	900	(12.8)	2,409	(34.3)	1,829	(26.1)	1,020	(14.5)	583	(8.3)	250	(3.6)	7,019	(100.0)
West Virginia	12	(0.7)	297	(16.2)	614	(33.4)	425	(23.1)	285	(15.5)	160	(8.7)	44	(2.4)	1,837	(100.0)
Total	**2,728**	**(0.4)**	**86,885**	**(13.5)**	**212,313**	**(32.9)**	**160,374**	**(24.9)**	**101,950**	**(15.8)**	**57,487**	**(8.9)**	**23,282**	**(3.6)**	**645,019**	**(99.5)[g]**
Abortion rate[h]	**0.9**		**10.5**		**24.9**		**19.4**		**12.7**		**7.5**		**2.8**		**13.1**	
Abortion ratio[i]	**839**		**326**		**285**		**178**		**132**		**164**		**273**		**207**	

in hospitals were more likely to cite institutional barriers such as lack of support from colleagues and coworkers.

HOW MUCH DOES AN ABORTION COST?

Abortion fees vary depending on the stage of pregnancy, where the abortion is performed, the type of procedure that is employed, and the anesthetic that is used. There may be other costs if the abortion cannot be done locally. Such expenses might include travel costs, costs for overnight stays, and lost wages.

In "Early Abortion Options" (April 2, 2014, http://www.ourbodiesourselves.org/health-info/early-abortion-options), Our Bodies Ourselves, a nonprofit organization dedicated to promoting education related to female reproductive health and sexuality, breaks down average costs related to abortion procedures. Nationwide, abortions involving medication range anywhere from $300 and $800, whereas aspiration abortions (a type of surgical abortion) performed during the first trimester typically range from $300 to $950. The Planned Parenthood Federation of America

TABLE 4.6

Reported abortions, by age group and state, 2011 [CONTINUED]

[a]Percentages for the individual component categories might not add to 100 because of rounding.
[b]Calculated as the number of abortions reported by known age divided by the sum of abortions reported by known and unknown age.
[c]Because reporting is not mandatory, information could not be obtained for all abortions performed in the District of Columbia.
[d]Includes residents only.
[e]Cell details not displayed because of small numbers (population = 1–4).
[f]Data from hospitals and licensed ambulatory care facilities only; because reporting is not mandatory for private physicians and women's centers, information could not be obtained for all abortions performed in New Jersey.
[g]Percentage based on a total of 648,169 abortions reported among the areas that met reporting standards for age.
[h]Number of abortions obtained by women in a given age group per 1,000 women in that same age group. Women aged 13–14 years were used as the denominator for the group of women aged <15 years, and women aged 40–44 years were used as the denominator for the group of women aged ≥40 years. Women aged 15–44 years were used as the denominator for the overall rate. For each state, abortions for women of unknown age were distributed according to the distribution of abortions among women of known age for that state.
[i]Number of abortions obtained by women in a given age group per 1,000 live births to women in that same age group. For each state, abortions for women of unknown age were distributed according to the distribution of abortions among women of known age for that state.
Notes: Data from 46 reporting areas; excludes six states (California, Florida, Maryland, New Hampshire, Vermont, and Wyoming) that did not report, did not report by age, or did not meet reporting standards.

SOURCE: Karen Pazol et al., "Table 3. Reported Abortions, by Known Age Group and Reporting Area of Occurrence—Selected Reporting Areas, United States, 2011," in "Abortion Surveillance—United States, 2011," *MMWR*, vol. 63, no. 11, November 28, 2014, http://www.cdc.gov/mmwr/pdf/ss/ss6311.pdf (accessed September 21, 2015)

FIGURE 4.4

Percentage of reported abortions, by age group and weeks of gestation, selected states, 2011

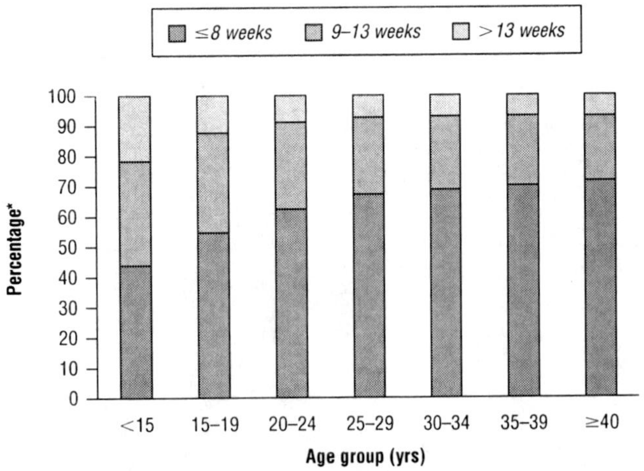

*Based on the total number of abortions reported with known weeks of gestation.
Notes: Data from 38 reporting areas; excludes 14 reporting areas (California, Connecticut, Florida, Illinois, Kentucky, Maryland, Massachusetts, Mississippi, Nebraska, New Hampshire, Pennsylvania, Vermont, Wisconsin, and Wyoming) that did not report, did not report by age or gestational age, or did not meet reporting standards.

SOURCE: Karen Pazol et al., "Figure 3. Percentage Distribution of Gestational Ages at Time of Abortion, by Age of Woman—Selected Reporting Areas, United States, 2011," in "Abortion Surveillance—United States, 2011," *MMWR*, vol. 63, no. 11, November 28, 2014, http://www.cdc.gov/mmwr/pdf/ss/ss6311.pdf (accessed September 21, 2015)

reports in "In-Clinic Abortion Procedures" (2014, https://www.plannedparenthood.org/learn/abortion/in-clinic-abortion-procedures) that aspiration abortions can cost up to $1,500 during the first trimester, and generally become more expensive during the second trimester or later.

ABORTION METHODS

Abortion may be performed using surgical or medication methods. Surgical abortions are performed in a few ways, depending on the length of the pregnancy, and have been available in the United States for decades. Early medication abortions, which are performed with the drugs mifepristone and misoprostol, have been available in the United States only since the U.S. Food and Drug Administration (FDA) approved mifepristone in 2000. Mifepristone is the drug that terminates the pregnancy and misoprostol helps evacuate the uterus. The type of abortion a woman obtains depends on her choice of method, her health, and the gestational age of the fetus.

Percentages of Methods Used

The CDC has collected data since 1973 on the types of procedures that are used each year to perform abortions and has determined that there has been a shift in the proportion of which procedures are used. From 1973 to 1991 the percentage of abortions performed by curettage (gentle scraping with a spoonlike instrument, which includes dilation of the cervix and evacuation of the uterus by aspiration) increased from 88.4% to 99%. The percentage then dropped slightly during the late 1990s, falling to 87.1% in 2005. The 2005 decline brought the percentage of curettage performed below the 1973 level for the first time. Table 4.12 shows that the percentage of abortions performed by curettage dropped further to 79.6% in 2011. Conversely, the proportion of early medication abortions has risen dramatically since the approval of mifepristone by the FDA in 2000, to 20% in 2011.

Very few abortions are performed by intrauterine instillation (induction), which involves injecting a salt solution to cause uterine contractions, which then expel the fetus. The percentage of abortions performed this way declined sharply from 10.3% in 1973 to 0.8% in 2005.

TABLE 4.7

Percentage, rate, and ratio of reported abortions, by ethnicity, selected states, 2002–11

	Year										% change			
Ethnicity	**2002**	**2003**	**2004**	**2005**	**2006**	**2007**	**2008**	**2009**	**2010**	**2011**	**2002 to 2006**	**2007 to 2011**	**2010 to 2011**	**2002 to 2011**
% of abortions														
Hispanic	21.7	21.9	22.3	22.0	22.8	22.6	23.0	22.6	22.8	22.0	5.1	−2.7	−3.5	1.4
Non-Hispanic	78.3	78.1	77.7	78.0	77.2	77.4	77.0	77.4	77.2	78.0	−1.4	0.8	1.0	−0.4
Abortion rate[a]														
Hispanic	23.9	23.2	22.4	21.3	21.9	20.7	20.2	18.7	17.8	15.8	−8.4	−23.7	−11.2	−33.9
Non-Hispanic	15.2	15.1	14.7	14.6	14.9	14.7	14.5	14.2	13.7	13.0	−2.0	−11.6	−5.1	−14.5
Abortion ratio[b]														
Hispanic	245	238	228	217	219	208	210	204	210	198	−10.6	−4.8	−5.7	−19.2
Non-Hispanic	247	242	235	233	230	224	223	222	220	210	−6.9	−6.3	−4.5	−15.0
Total (no.)	**357,680**	**353,736**	**337,014**	**336,711**	**350,764**	**344,801**	**340,302**	**333,088**	**321,495**	**301,888**	—	—	—	—

[a]Number of abortions obtained by women in a given ethnic group per 1,000 women in that same ethnic group. For each state, abortions for women of unknown ethnicity were distributed according to the distribution of abortions among women of known ethnicity for that state.
[b]Number of abortions obtained by women in a given ethnic group per 1,000 live births to women in that same ethnic group. For each state, abortions for women of unknown ethnicity were distributed according to the distribution of abortions among women of known ethnicity for that state.
Notes: Data from 19 reporting areas; by year, these reporting areas represent 57%–65% of the abortions reported by ethnicity during 2002–2011. Excludes 33 areas (Alaska, Arizona, California, Connecticut, Florida, Georgia, Hawaii, Illinois, Indiana, Iowa, Kentucky, Louisiana, Maine, Maryland, Massachusetts, Michigan, Montana, Nebraska, Nevada, New Hampshire, New Mexico, New York State, North Carolina, North Dakota, Oklahoma, Pennsylvania, Rhode Island, South Dakota, Vermont, Virginia, Washington, West Virginia, and Wyoming) that did not report, did not report by ethnicity, or did not meet reporting standards for ≥1 year.

SOURCE: Karen Pazol et al., "Table 16. Reported Abortions, by Known Ethnicity of Women Who Obtained an Abortion and Year—Selected Reporting Areas, United States, 2002–2011," in "Abortion Surveillance—United States, 2011," *MMWR*, vol. 63, no. 11, November 28, 2014, http://www.cdc.gov/mmwr/pdf/ss/ss6311.pdf (accessed September 21, 2015)

TABLE 4.8

Birth rates and fertility rates by Hispanic origin and race of mother, 2013

		Hispanic						Non-Hispanic		
Characteristic	**All origins**[a]	**Total**	**Mexican**	**Puerto Rican**	**Cuban**	**Central and South American**	**Other and unknown Hispanic**	**Total**[b]	**White**	**Black**
						Number				
Births	3,932,181	901,033	545,202	68,302	18,854	131,305	137,370	3,003,556	2,129,196	583,834
						Rate				
Birth rate[c]	12.4	16.7	—	—	—	[c]	—	11.6	10.7	14.4
Fertility rate[c]	62.5	72.9	—	—	—	[c]	—	59.9	58.7	64.6
Total fertility rate[c]	1,857.5	2,149.0	—	—	—	[c]	—	1,784.0	1,751.0	1,881.5
Sex ratio[d]	1,049	1,043	1,044	1,039	1,066	1,039	1,039	1,051	1,054	1,031
All births						Percent				
Births to mothers under age 20	7.0	10.5	11.1	11.8	4.6	5.8	12.4	6.0	5.1	10.8
4th and higher-order births[e]	12.0	16.0	18.0	12.8	5.6	13.5	13.1	10.8	9.8	15.8
Births to unmarried mothers	40.6	53.2	51.9	64.6	50.1	50.1	56.1	36.8	29.3	71.5
Mothers born in the 50 states and DC	77.7	49.4	48.4	73.1	49.5	17.2	72.4	86.1	93.8	85.6
						Mean				
Age of mother (years) at first birth	26.0	24.0	23.4	23.9	26.7	26.4	23.7	26.5	26.8	23.9

— Data not available.
[a]Includes origin not stated.
[b]Includes races other than white and black.
[c]For Central and South American population, includes other and unknown Hispanic.
[d]Male births per 1,000 female births.
[e]Based on live-birth order.
Notes: Birth rates are births per 1,000 population. Fertility rates are computed by relating total births, regardless of age of mother, to women aged 15–44. Total fertility rates are sums of birth rates for 5-year age groups multiplied by 5. Populations estimated as of July 1. Mean age at first birth is the arithmetic average of the age of mothers at the time of birth, computed directly from the frequency of first births by age of mother. Race and Hispanic origin are reported separately on birth certificates. Race categories are consistent with 1977 Office of Management and Budget standards. Forty-four states and the District of Columbia (DC) reported multiple-race data for 2013 that were bridged to single-race categories for comparability with other states. Persons of Hispanic origin may be of any race. In this table, Hispanic women are classified only by place or origin; non-Hispanic women are classified by race. This table will be updated to include rates for specified Hispanic origin groups when 2013 population data for these groups available.

SOURCE: Joyce A. Martin et al., "Table 14. Selected Demographic Characteristics of Births, by Hispanic Origin of Mother, and by Race for Mothers of Non-Hispanic Origin: United States, 2013," in "Births: Final Data for 2013," *National Vital Statistics Report*, vol. 64, no. 1, January 15, 2015, http://www.cdc.gov/nchs/data/nvsr/nvsr64/nvsr64_01.pdf (accessed September 21, 2015)

TABLE 4.9

Reported abortions by race, age, and marital status, selected states, 2011

Characteristic	White No.	White (%)[a]	Black No.	Black (%)	Other No.	Other (%)	Total No.	Total (%)
Age group (yrs)[b]								
<15	542	(0.4)	654	(0.6)	59	(0.3)	1,255	(0.5)
15–19	20,780	(13.8)	14,860	(14.6)	2,525	(11.5)	38,165	(13.9)
15	1,087	(0.7)	1,014	(1.0)	146	(0.7)	2,247	(0.8)
16	2,069	(1.4)	1,598	(1.6)	220	(1.0)	3,887	(1.4)
17	3,331	(2.2)	2,476	(2.4)	387	(1.8)	6,194	(2.3)
18	6,208	(4.1)	4,209	(4.1)	782	(3.6)	11,199	(4.1)
19	8,085	(5.4)	5,563	(5.5)	990	(4.5)	14,638	(5.3)
20–24	51,350	(34.1)	35,723	(35.1)	6,452	(29.4)	93,525	(34.1)
25–29	36,560	(24.3)	25,499	(25.0)	5,376	(24.5)	67,435	(24.6)
30–34	22,347	(14.8)	15,559	(15.3)	3,886	(17.7)	41,792	(15.2)
35–39	13,169	(8.7)	7,333	(7.2)	2,565	(11.7)	23,067	(8.4)
≥40	5,793	(3.8)	2,213	(2.2)	1,084	(4.9)	9,090	(3.3)
Marital status[c]								
Married	21,593	(16.6)	7,166	(7.7)	6,069	(28.8)	34,828	(14.3)
Unmarried	108,615	(83.4)	85,401	(92.3)	15,006	(71.2)	209,022	(85.7)

[a]Percentages for the individual component categories might not add to 100 because of rounding.
[b]Data from 30 reporting areas; excludes 22 areas (Arizona, California, Connecticut, Florida, Georgia, Hawaii, Illinois, Kentucky, Maine, Maryland, Massachusetts, Nebraska, Nevada, New Hampshire, New Mexico, New York City, Pennsylvania, Texas, Vermont, Washington, Wisconsin, and Wyoming) that did not report, did not report by race or age, or did not meet reporting standards.
[c]Data from 29 reporting areas; excludes 23 areas (Arizona, California, Connecticut, Florida, Georgia, Hawaii, Illinois, Kentucky, Maine, Maryland, Massachusetts, Nebraska, Nevada, New Hampshire, New Mexico, New York City, New York State, Pennsylvania, Texas, Vermont, Washington, Wisconsin, and Wyoming) that did not report, did not report by race or marital status, or did not meet reporting standards.

SOURCE: Karen Pazol et al., "Table 20. Reported Abortions, by Known Race, Age Group, and Marital Status of Women Who Obtained an Abortion—Selected Reporting Areas, United States, 2011," in "Abortion Surveillance—United States, 2011," *MMWR*, vol. 63, no. 11, November 28, 2014, http://www.cdc.gov/mmwr/pdf/ss/ss6311.pdf (accessed September 21, 2015)

Table 4.12 shows that less than 0.1% of abortions were performed by intrauterine instillation in 2011.

DEATHS FROM ABORTION

As Table 4.13 shows, the fatality rate from abortion procedures dropped from 2.09 deaths per 100,000 reported legal induced abortions for the period 1973 to 1977 to a low of 0.52 deaths per 100,000 for the 1993 to 1997 period. Between 2003 and 2010 the rate was 0.7 deaths per 100,000 abortions. Although induced abortion–related deaths are rare, medical and surgical abortions are procedures that entail some risk. In general, early abortions are safer than later abortions, and abortions performed at or before eight weeks of pregnancy are considered to be the safest.

TABLE 4.10

Mandatory state waiting periods and biased counseling for abortion, 2015

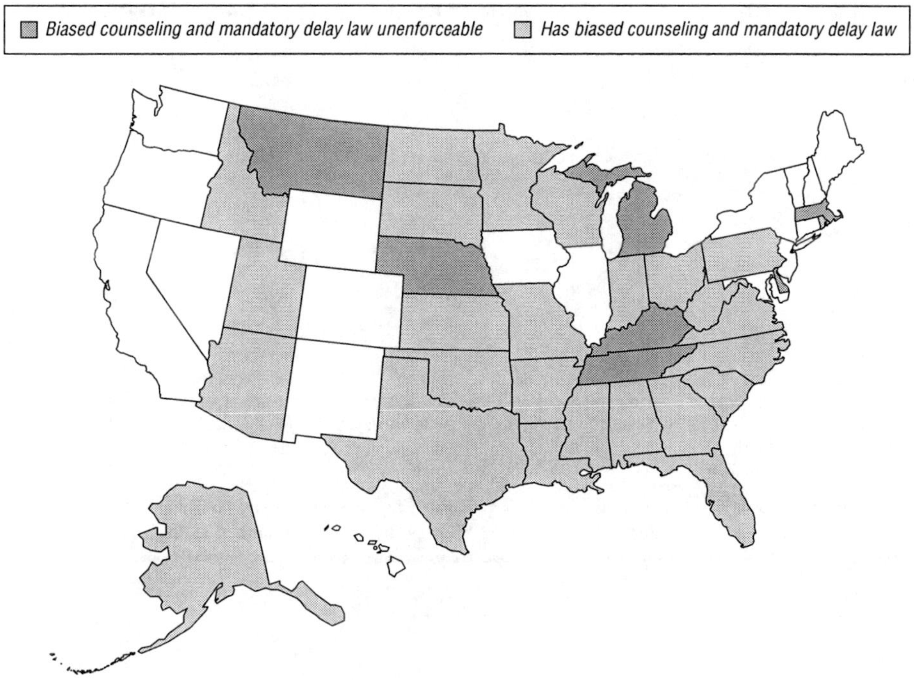

State	State subjects women seeking abortion to: Biased counseling	Mandatory delay	Law fully or partially unenforceable: Fully unenforceable	Partially unenforceable
Alabama	✓	✓		
Alaska	✓			
Arizona	✓	✓		
Arkansas	✓	✓		
California				
Colorado				
Connecticut				
Delaware	✓	✓[a]		✓
District of Columbia				
Florida	✓			
Georgia	✓	✓		
Hawaii				
Idaho	✓	✓		
Illinois				
Indiana	✓	✓		
Iowa				
Kansas	✓	✓		✓
Kentucky	✓[b]	✓		
Louisiana	✓	✓		
Maine				
Maryland				
Massachusetts	✓	✓[a]		✓
Michigan	✓	✓		✓
Minnesota	✓	✓		
Mississippi	✓	✓		
Missouri	✓	✓		
Montana	✓	✓	✓	
Nebraska	✓	✓		
Nevada				
New Hampshire				
New Jersey				
New Mexico				
New York				
North Carolina	✓	✓		
North Dakota	✓	✓		
Ohio	✓	✓		
Oklahoma	✓	✓		
Oregon				

TABLE 4.10

Mandatory state waiting periods and biased counseling for abortion, 2015 [CONTINUED]

	State subjects women seeking abortion to:		Law fully or partially unenforceable	
State	**Biased counseling**	**Mandatory delay**	**Fully unenforceable**	**Partially unenforceable**
Pennsylvania	✓	✓		
Rhode Island	✓			
South Carolina	✓	✓		
South Dakota	✓	✓		✓
Tennessee	✓	✓	✓	
Texas	✓	✓		
Utah	✓	✓		
Vermont				
Virginia	✓	✓		
Washington				
West Virginia	✓	✓		
Wisconsin	✓	✓		
Wyoming				
Totals:	**33**	**30**	**2**	**5**

[a]The law is unconstitutional & unenforceable only with respect to the mandatory delay.
[b]The law is unconstitutional & unenforceable only with respect to the in-person receipt of the state-mandated information and materials provision.
Notes: 33 states have laws subjecting women seeking abortions to biased counseling and/or mandatory delays: AK, AL, AR, AZ, DE, FL, GA, ID, IN, KS, KY, LA, MA, MI, MN, MO, MS, MT, NC, ND, NE, OH, OK, PA, RI, SC, SD, TN, TX, UT, VA, WI, WV.
7 of these laws are fully or partially unconstitutional and unenforceable: DE, KY, MA, MI, MT, SD, TN.

SOURCE: "Biased Counseling and Mandatory Delay," in *What Is Choice*, NARAL Pro-Choice America and NARAL Pro-Choice America Foundation, 2015, http://www.prochoiceamerica.org/what-is-choice/maps-and-charts/map.jsp?mapID=14 (accessed September 21, 2015)

TABLE 4.11

Number, rate, and ratio of reported abortions by state, and percentage of reported abortions obtained by out-of-state residents, 2011

	Residence			Occurrence			% obtained by out-of-state residents[a]
State/area	**No.**	**Rate**	**Ratio**	**No.**	**Rate**	**Ratio**	
Alabama	8,949	9.3	151	9,523	9.9	160	16.1
Alaska	1,789	12.3	156	1,627	11.2	142	0.7
Arizona	13,814	10.9	161	14,401	11.3	168	1.0
Arkansas	4,429	7.8	114	4,033	7.1	104	12.6
California[b]	—	—	—	—	—	—	—
Colorado	9,284	8.9	143	10,474	10.1	161	11.3
Connecticut	12,502	18.2	335	12,615	18.4	338	2.9
Delaware	3,483	19.5	309	3,794	21.2	337	17.4
District of Columbia[c]	1,569	9.4	169	2,768	16.7	298	53.6
Florida[d]	—	—	—	77,166	21.6	362	—
Georgia	29,757	14.3	225	32,770	15.8	247	10.4
Hawaii	2,650	10.1	140	2,671	10.1	141	1.2
Idaho	2,021	6.5	91	1,440	4.7	65	4.7
Illinois	38,702	14.8	240	41,324	15.8	256	7.6
Indiana	10,157	7.9	121	9,112	7.1	109	5.2
Iowa[e]	4,246	7.3	111	4,815	8.3	126	16
Kansas	4,222	7.6	107	7,788	14.0	196	50.6
Kentucky	5,514	6.4	100	3,957	4.6	71	11
Louisiana[e]	8,162	8.8	132	8,955	9.6	145	5.0
Maine	1,660	6.9	131	1,773	7.4	140	2.7
Maryland[b]	—	—	—	—	—	—	—
Massachusetts[e]	16,394	12.2	224	20,703	15.4	283	4.3
Michigan	23,177	12.2	203	23,366	12.3	205	2.3
Minnesota	10,582	10.1	155	11,070	10.6	162	8.3
Mississippi	5,578	9.2	140	2,224	3.7	56	2.0
Missouri	11,419	9.7	150	5,772	4.9	76	8.1
Montana	1,919	10.6	159	2,147	11.9	178	12.7
Nebraska	2,275	6.4	88	2,372	6.6	92	9.7
Nevada	6,654	12.1	189	7,206	13.1	204	5.7
New Hampshire[b]	—	—	—	—	—	—	—
New Jersey[f]	26,800	15.5	253	26,558	15.4	251	5.2
New Mexico	4,391	11.0	161	4,083	10.2	150	7.7
New York	107,596	26.7	446	111,296	27.6	461	3.8
New York City	—	—	—	80,485	42.2	674	8.2
New York State	—	—	—	30,811	14.5	253	6.4
North Carolina	22,731	11.6	189	26,192	13.4	218	15.5
North Dakota	955	7.3	100	1,247	9.5	131	32.4
Ohio	24,108	10.9	175	24,764	11.2	180	6.1
Oklahoma	5,407	7.3	103	5,416	7.3	104	10.6
Oregon	8,921	11.7	198	9,567	12.6	212	9.7
Pennsylvania	36,529	15.0	255	36,280	14.9	253	5.0
Rhode Island	3,454	16.2	315	4,165	19.6	380	19.5
South Carolina	10,547	11.4	184	6,379	6.9	111	4.2
South Dakota	757	4.9	64	597	3.9	50	14.7
Tennessee	13,114	10.3	165	16,115	12.6	202	24.2
Texas	70,214	13.0	186	72,332	13.4	192	3.1
Utah	3,226	5.3	63	3,386	5.5	66	9.0
Vermont	1,286	11.0	212	1,355	11.5	223	5.9
Virginia	25,215	15.2	246	25,413	15.3	248	7.0
Washington	20,081	14.7	231	20,225	14.8	233	4.9
West Virginia	2,193	6.4	106	1,837	5.4	89	11.5
Wisconsin	8,168	7.5	120	7,249	6.6	107	3.2
Wyoming	619	5.8	84	—[g]	—[h]	—[h]	—[h]
Canada	170	NA	NA	NA	NA	NA	NA
Mexico	525	NA	NA	NA	NA	NA	NA
Other country or territory	128	NA	NA	NA	NA	NA	NA
Total known	**640,879**	**NA**	**NA**	**NA**	**NA**	**NA**	**NA**
Percentage reported by known residence	**87.8**	**NA**	**NA**	**NA**	**NA**	**NA**	**NA**
Total unknown residence	**89,443**	**NA**	**NA**	**NA**	**NA**	**NA**	**NA**
Out of state, exact residence not-stated	4,666	NA	NA	NA	NA	NA	NA
No residence information provided	84,777	NA	NA	NA	NA	NA	NA
Percentage reported by unknown residence	**12.2**	**NA**	**NA**	**NA**	**NA**	**NA**	**NA**
Total	**730,322**	**NA**	**NA**	**NA**	**NA**	**NA**	**NA**

TABLE 4.11

Number, rate, and ratio of reported abortions by state, and percentage of reported abortions obtained by out-of-state residents, 2011 [CONTINUED]

NA = not applicable.
[a]Additional details on the state in which abortions were provided, cross-tabulated by the state of maternal residence, are available at http://www.cdc.gov/reproductivehealth/data_stats/Abortion.htm.
[b]State did not report; because numbers for this state are available only from other states where residents obtained abortions, meaningful statistics cannot be reported.
[c]Because reporting is not mandatory, a complete count of abortions performed in the District of Columbia could not be obtained.
[d]State reported by occurrence only; because abortion counts by residence for this state are available only from other states where residents obtained abortions, meaningful statistics cannot be reported.
[e]State reported abortion numbers for both in-state and out-of-state residents; for out-of-state residents, the state or area of residence was not provided.
[f]Data from hospitals and licensed ambulatory care facilities only; because reporting is not mandatory for private physicians and women's centers, a complete count of abortions performed in New Jersey could not be obtained.
[g]Total abortion count ≤20.
[h]Abortion rates and ratios and percentage of abortions obtained by out-of-state residents were not calculated for Wyoming because results based on a small number of abortions are unstable.
Notes: Number of abortions per 1,000 women aged 15–44 years. Number of abortions per 1,000 live births.

SOURCE: Karen Pazol et al., "Table 2. Number, Rate, and Ratio of Reported Abortions, by Reporting Area of Residence and Occurrence and by Percentage of Abortions Obtained by Out-of-State Residents—United States, 2011," in "Abortion Surveillance—United States, 2011," *MMWR*, vol. 63, no. 11, November 28, 2014, http://www.cdc.gov/mmwr/pdf/ss/ss6311.pdf (accessed September 21, 2015)

TABLE 4.12

Number and percentage of reported abortions by known method, selected states, 2011

State/area	Curettage[a]: Curettage, ≤13 weeks' gestation No.	(%)[d]	Curettage[a]: Curettage, >13 weeks' gestation No.	(%)	Curettage[a]: Curettage unknown gestational age No.	(%)	Medical: Medical, ≤8 weeks' gestation No.	(%)	Medical: Medical, >8 weeks' gestation No.	(%)	Medical: Medical, unknown gestational age No.	(%)	Intrauterine instillation[b] No.	(%)	Other[c] No.	(%)	Total abortions reported by known method type No.	% of all reported abortions[e]
Alabama[f]	6,786	(71.6)	908	(9.6)	—[g]	—	NA	NA	NA	NA	NA	NA	—	—	1,773	(18.7)	9,483	(99.6)
Alaska	1,238	(78.0)	18	(1.1)	—	—	313	(19.7)	14	(0.9)	—	—	0	(0.0)	—	—	1,588	(97.6)
Arizona	7,943	(55.2)	1,092	(7.6)	5	(0.0)	5,116	(35.6)	217	(1.5)	9	(0.1)	0	(0.0)	7	(0.0)	14,389	(99.9)
Arkansas	2,737	(67.9)	536	(13.3)	0	(0.0)	713	(17.7)	46	(1.1)	0	(0.0)	—	—	—	—	4,033	(100.0)
Colorado	5,416	(51.7)	622	(5.9)	—	—	3,690	(35.2)	180	(1.7)	103	(1.0)	—	—	362	(3.5)	10,474	(100.0)
Connecticut[h]	NA	NA	NA	NA	8,859	(70.2)	NA	NA	NA	NA	3,756	(29.8)	0	(0.0)	0	(0.0)	12,615	(100.0)
Delaware	2,169	(58.2)	148	(4.0)	10	(0.3)	1,323	(35.5)	58	(1.6)	12	(0.3)	7	(0.2)	0	(0.0)	3,727	(98.2)
District of Columbia[i]	1,381	(50.6)	530	(19.4)	0	(0.0)	801	(29.3)	19	(0.7)	0	(0.0)	0	(0.0)	0	(0.0)	2,731	(98.7)
Georgia	24,985	(76.2)	3,796	(11.6)	0	(0.0)	3,712	(11.3)	265	(0.8)	0	(0.0)	0	(0.0)	10	(0.0)	32,768	(100.0)
Hawaii[f]	2,218	(83.1)	308	(11.5)	7	(0.3)	NA	NA	NA	NA	NA	NA	0	(0.0)	136	(5.1)	2,669	(99.9)
Idaho	929	(64.5)	—	—	—	—	484	(33.6)	—	—	—	—	—	—	8	(0.6)	1,440	(100.0)
Indiana	7,309	(80.2)	135	(1.5)	0	(0.0)	1,549	(17.0)	78	(0.9)	0	(0.0)	0	(0.0)	37	(0.4)	9,108	(100.0)
Iowa	2,010	(41.7)	60	(1.2)	5	(0.1)	2,317	(48.1)	78	(1.6)	7	(0.1)	0	(0.0)	338	(7.0)	4,815	(100.0)
Kansas	5,482	(70.4)	680	(8.7)	0	(0.0)	1,611	(20.7)	12	(0.2)	0	(0.0)	—	—	—	—	7,788	(100.0)
Kentucky	2,541	(64.2)	414	(10.5)	0	(0.0)	998	(25.2)	—	—	0	(0.0)	0	(0.0)	—	—	3,955	(99.9)
Louisiana[f]	5,589	(66.9)	848	(10.1)	19	(0.2)	NA	NA	NA	NA	NA	NA	0	(0.0)	1,904	(22.8)	8,360	(93.4)
Maine	1,390	(78.6)	20	(1.1)	—	—	333	(18.8)	24	(1.4)	—	—	0	(0.0)	0	(0.0)	1,768	(99.7)
Massachusetts[h]	NA	NA	NA	NA	15,470	(74.7)	NA	NA	NA	NA	5,071	(24.5)	—	—	—	—	20,703	(100.0)
Michigan	18,028	(77.3)	2,135	(9.1)	14	(0.1)	3,068	(13.1)	120	(0.5)	—	—	—	—	23	(0.1)	23,337[j]	(99.9)
Minnesota	7,905	(71.4)	973	(8.8)	0	(0.0)	2,024	(18.3)	151	(1.4)	0	(0.0)	7	(0.1)	10	(0.1)	11,070	(100.0)
Mississippi	1,621	(72.9)	74	(3.3)	529	(23.8)	0	(0.0)	0	(0.0)	0	(0.0)	0	(0.0)	0	(0.0)	2,224	(100.0)
Missouri	3,351	(62.5)	616	(11.5)	—	—	1,330	(24.8)	56	(1.0)	—	—	0	(0.0)	—	—	5,359	(92.8)
Montana	1,197	(55.8)	135	(6.3)	0	(0.0)	809	(37.7)	5	(0.2)	0	(0.0)	—	—	—	—	2,147	(100.0)
Nebraska	924	(39.0)	111	(4.7)	444	(18.7)	529	(22.3)	5	(0.2)	359	(15.1)	0	(0.0)	0	(0.0)	2,372	(100.0)
Nevada	5,673	(79.8)	598	(8.4)	106	(1.5)	656	(9.2)	36	(0.5)	—	—	—	—	27	(0.4)	7,108	(98.6)
New Jersey[k]	20,843	(78.5)	4,090	(15.4)	306	(1.2)	1,261	(4.7)	36	(0.1)	—	—	—	—	13	(0.0)	26,557	(100.0)
New Mexico	2,500	(69.9)	348	(9.7)	118	(3.3)	339	(9.5)	42	(1.2)	107	(3.0)	0	(0.0)	120	(3.4)	3,574	(87.5)
New York	79,794	(72.2)	11,112	(10.1)	3,204	(2.9)	13,023	(11.8)	1,986	(1.8)	1,065	(1.0)	40	(0.0)	291	(0.3)	110,515	(99.3)
New York City	61,319	(76.2)	8,608	(10.7)	104	(0.1)	9,872	(12.3)	467	(0.6)	23	(0.0)	15	(0.0)	73	(0.1)	80,481	(100.0)
New York State	18,475	(61.5)	2,504	(8.3)	3,100	(10.3)	3,151	(10.5)	1,519	(5.1)	1,042	(3.5)	25	(0.1)	218	(0.7)	30,034	(97.5)
North Carolina	17,122	(66.3)	1,821	(7.0)	891	(3.4)	5,506	(21.3)	129	(0.5)	352	(1.4)	—	—	—	—	25,833	(98.6)
North Dakota	1,005	(80.6)	45	(3.6)	0	(0.0)	193	(15.5)	0	(0.0)	—	—	—	—	0	(0.0)	1,247	(100.0)
Ohio	19,787	(82.7)	2,944	(12.3)	140	(0.6)	1,170	(4.9)	57	(0.2)	7	(0.0)	20	(0.1)	386	(1.6)	23,934[j]	(96.6)
Oklahoma	3,357	(62.0)	435	(8.0)	0	(0.0)	1,613	(29.8)	11	(0.2)	0	(0.0)	0	(0.0)	0	(0.0)	5,416	(100.0)
Oregon	6,132	(64.2)	803	(8.4)	217	(2.3)	2,169	(22.7)	109	(1.1)	72	(0.8)	0	(0.0)	43	(0.5)	9,545	(99.8)
Pennsylvania	23,942	(66.0)	4,532	(12.5)	0	(0.0)	7,438	(20.5)	351	(1.0)	0	(0.0)	5	(0.0)	9	(0.0)	36,277	(100.0)
Rhode Island	2,774	(66.7)	294	(7.1)	32	(0.8)	1,026	(24.7)	27	(0.6)	6	(0.1)	—	—	—	—	4,161	(99.9)
South Carolina	3,784	(59.4)	72	(1.1)	0	(0.0)	2,397	(37.6)	117	(1.8)	0	(0.0)	—	—	—	—	6,374	(99.9)
South Dakota	382	(64.0)	—	—	0	(0.0)	197	(33.0)	17	(2.8)	0	(0.0)	—	—	—	—	597	(100.0)
Tennessee[f]	10,230	(64.1)	561	(3.5)	100	(0.6)	NA	NA	NA	NA	NA	NA	0	(0.0)	5,060	(31.7)	15,951	(99.0)
Texas	49,886	(69.0)	3,506	(4.8)	—	—	18,550	(25.6)	343	(0.5)	0	(0.0)	—	—	40	(0.1)	72,332	(100.0)
Utah	1,911	(56.5)	216	(6.4)	20	(0.6)	1,134	(33.5)	46	(1.4)	57	(1.7)	—	—	—	—	3,385	(100.0)
Virginia	20,219	(79.7)	338	(1.3)	119	(0.5)	4,532	(17.9)	87	(0.3)	46	(0.2)	10	(0.0)	32	(0.1)	25,383	(99.9)
Washington	13,214	(65.4)	1,769	(8.7)	25	(0.1)	4,998	(24.7)	146	(0.7)	22	(0.1)	38	(0.2)	7	(0.0)	20,219	(100.0)
West Virginia	1,477	(80.4)	105	(5.7)	—	—	241	(13.1)	13	(0.7)	0	(0.0)	0	(0.0)	—	—	1,837	(100.0)

TABLE 4.12

Number and percentage of reported abortions by known method, selected states, 2011 [CONTINUED]

State/area	Curettage[a]						Medical										Total abortions reported by known method type	
	Curettage, ≤13 weeks' gestation		Curettage, >13 weeks' gestation		Curettage unknown gestational age		Medical, ≤8 weeks' gestation		Medical, >8 weeks' gestation		Medical, unknown gestational age		Intrauterine instillation[b]		Other[c]			
	No.	(%)[d]	No.	(%)	No.	(%)	No.	(%)	No.	(%)	No.	(%)	No.	(%)	No.	(%)	No.	% of all reported abortions[e]
Total	424,641	(70.9)	51,051	(8.5)	—[l]	—	107,704	(18.0)	5,428	(0.9)	—[m]	—	161	(0.0)	10,814	(1.8)	599,168[n]	(99.3)[o]
Total among states with medical abortion on their reporting form[p]	399,669	(71.0)	48,435	(8.6)	—	—	107,704	(19.1)	5,428	(0.9)	—	—	159	(0.0)	1,941	(0.3)	562,705[n]	(99.4)[q]

NA = not available.

[a]Includes aspiration curettage, suction curettage, manual vacuum aspiration, menstrual extraction, sharp curettage, and dilation and evacuation procedures.

[b]Intrauterine instillations reported at ≤12 weeks' gestation are not presented with abortions reported by known method type.

[c]Includes hysterotomy/hysterectomy and procedures reported as "other."

[d]Percentages for the individual component categories might not add to 100 because of rounding and because some areas report more than one method for each abortion.

[e]Calculated as the number of abortions reported by known method type divided by the sum of abortions reported by known and unknown method type.

[f]Numbers for medical abortion are not presented because medical abortion was not included as a separate category on the reporting form.

[g]Cells details not displayed because of small numbers (population = 1–4).

[h]Numbers for curettage procedures at ≤13 weeks versus >13 weeks and for medical abortion at ≤8 weeks versus >8 weeks are not presented because gestational age data were not provided or were provided in incompatible categories.

[i]Because reporting is not mandatory, information could not be obtained for all abortions performed in the District of Columbia.

[j]Because more than one method was reported for some abortions, the sum of the individual methods exceeds the total number of abortions reported by known method type. "Other" methods might have been used concomitantly with specified method types to aid in the completion of the abortion.

[k]Data from hospitals and licensed ambulatory care facilities only; because reporting is not mandatory for private physicians and women's centers, information could not be obtained for all abortions performed in New Jersey.

[l]Curettage abortions reported without a gestational age were distributed among the curettage categories according to the distribution of abortions performed by curettage at known gestational age.

[m]Medical abortions reported without a gestational age were distributed among the medical abortion categories according to the distribution of medical abortions at known gestational age.

[n]Because some states reported more than one method for some abortions, the sum of the individual methods exceeds the total number of abortions reported by known method type.

[o]Percentage based on a total of 603,228 abortions reported among the areas that met reporting standards for method type.

[p]Excludes four states (Alabama, Hawaii, Louisiana, and Tennessee) that have been included in the total for all areas reporting by method type because these states did not include medical abortion as a separate category on their reporting form.

[q]Percentage based on a total of 565,964 abortions reported among the areas that met reporting standards for method type and included medical abortion on their reporting form.

Notes: Data from 44 reporting areas; excludes eight reporting areas (California, Florida, Illinois, Maryland, New Hampshire, Vermont, Wisconsin, and Wyoming) that did not report, did not report by method type, or did not meet reporting standards. Because four reporting areas did not include medical abortion as a separate category on their reporting form (Alabama, Hawaii, Louisiana, and Tennessee), numbers and percentages including this method are based on 40 reporting areas.

SOURCE: Karen Pazol et al., "Table 11. Reported Abortions, by Known Method Type and Reporting Area of Occurrence—Selected Reporting Areas, United States, 2011," in "Abortion Surveillance—United States, 2011," *MMWR*, vol. 63, no. 11, November 28, 2014, http://www.cdc.gov/mmwr/pdf/ss/ss6311.pdf (accessed September 21, 2015)

TABLE 4.13

Number of reported deaths and fatality rates for abortion-related deaths, by type of abortion, 1973–2010

	Type of abortion				
	Induced				
Year	Legal[a]	Ilegal[b]	Unknown[c]	Total	Case-fatality rate per 100,000 legal abortions
1973–1977					2.09
1973	25	19	3	47	
1974	26	6	1	33	
1975	29	4	1	34	
1976	11	2	1	14	
1977	17	4	0	21	
1978–1982					0.78
1978	9	7	0	16	
1979	22	0	0	22	
1980	9	1	2	12	
1981	8	1	0	9	
1982	11	1	0	12	
1983–1987					0.66
1983	11	1	0	12	
1984	12	0	0	12	
1985	11	1	1	13	
1986	11	0	2	13	
1987	7	2	0	9	
1988–1992					0.74
1988	16	0	0	16	
1989	12	1	0	13	
1990	9	0	0	9	
1991	11	1	0	12	
1992	10	0	0	10	
1993–1997					0.52
1993	6	1	2	9	
1994	10	2	0	12	
1995	4	0	0	4	
1996	9	0	0	9	
1997	7	0	0	7	
1998–2002					0.63
1998	9	0	0	9	
1999	4	0	0	4	
2000	11	0	0	11	
2001	7	1	0	8	
2002	10	0	0	10	
2003–2010					0.70
2003	10	0	0	10	
2004	7	1	0	8	
2005	7	0	0	7	
2006	7	0	0	7	
2007	6	0	0	6	
2008	12	0	0	12	
2009	8	0	0	8	
2010	10	0	0	10	
Total	**421**	**56**	**13**	**490**	0.82

TABLE 4.13

Number of reported deaths and fatality rates for abortion-related deaths, by type of abortion, 1973–2010 [CONTINUED]

CDC = Centers for Disease Control and Prevention.
[a]An abortion is defined as "legal" if it was performed by a licensed clinician.
[b]An abortion is defined as "illegal" if it was performed by any person other than a licensed clinician.
[c]Unknown whether abortion was induced or spontaneous.
Notes: Number of legal induced abortion-related deaths per 100,000 reported legal induced abortions. Because a substantial number of legal induced abortions occurred outside reporting areas that provided data to CDC, national case-fatality rates (i.e., number of legal induced abortion-related deaths per 100,000 reported legal induced abortions in the United States) were calculated with denominator data from a more complete source (14). Case-fatality rates were computed for consecutive 5-year periods during 1973–2002 and then during a 8-year period during 2003–2010, because rates based on ≤20 cases are highly variable (35).
Certain numbers might differ from those in reports published previously because additional information has been supplied to CDC subsequent to publication.

SOURCE: Karen Pazol et al., "Table 25. Number of Deaths and Case-Fatality Rates for Abortion-Related Deaths Reported to CDC, by Type of Abortion—United States, 1973–2010," in "Abortion Surveillance—United States, 2011," *MMWR*, vol. 63, no. 11, November 28, 2014, http://www.cdc.gov/mmwr/pdf/ss/ss6311.pdf (accessed September 21, 2015)

CHAPTER 5
TEEN PREGNANCY AND ABORTION

TEEN PREGNANCY

Teen pregnancy is a serious concern in the United States. The Centers for Disease Control and Prevention (CDC) reports in "About Teen Pregnancy" (May 19, 2015, http://www.cdc.gov/teenpregnancy/about/index.htm) that in 2013 there were 273,105 babies born to women aged 15 to 19 years. The birth rate was 26.5 per 1,000 teens—a record low for U.S. teens and a 10% decrease from 2012. As Figure 5.1 shows, aside from a slight increase between 2005 and 2008, teen birth rates in the United States have fallen steadily since the early 1990s.

A Decline in Teen Pregnancy

Teen pregnancy rates have been in decline since the 1990s. In *Teen Pregnancy* (May 2014, http://www.childtrends.org/wp-content/uploads/2012/07/14_Teen_Pregnancy.pdf), Child Trends, a leading youth advocacy research group, reports that in 1990 the overall teen pregnancy rate was 116.9 pregnancies for every 1,000 women aged 15 to 19 years. (See Figure 5.2.) By 2010 the rate had fallen to 57.4. The decline was most dramatic among African American women aged 15 to 19 years, with the pregnancy rate falling from 223.8 per 1,000 women in 1990 to 99.5 per 1,000 in 2010.

Explaining the Decline in Teen Pregnancy Rates

John S. Santelli and Andrea J. Melnikas analyze in "Teen Fertility in Transition: Recent and Historic Trends in the United States" (*Annual Review of Public Health*, vol. 31, April 21, 2010) data from multiple sources to examine changes in teen fertility and determine why teen pregnancy rates fell beginning in the 1990s, and why birth rates rose unexpectedly in 2006 and 2007. The researchers conclude that "improved condom and contraceptive use explains most of the declines in teen pregnancy both historically and between 1991 and 2005; likewise, declines in contraceptive use appear to explain rising teen fertility in 2006 and 2007." Santelli and Melnikas note that "shifts in sexuality education may also provide an explanation for deterioration of contraceptive use after 2003 and the rise in birth rates after 2005." They add, "The federal funding rules for abstinence programs require a focus on failure rates of condoms and contraception; this approach may be undermining teen contraceptive use."

Legislation enacted in December 2009 ended the requirement that federally funded family planning education for adolescents have abstinence-only promotion as their exclusive purpose. Although the direct impact of this move away from abstinence-only sex education programs on teen pregnancy remained unclear at the close of 2015, teen pregnancy rates continued their steady decline during these years. According to Teresa Wiltz of the Pew Charitable Trusts, in "Racial and Ethnic Disparities Persist in Teen Pregnancy Rates" (March 3, 2015, http://www.pewtrusts.org/en/research-and-analysis/blogs/stateline/2015/3/03/racial-and-ethnic-disparities-persist-in-teen-pregnancy-rates), teen pregnancy rates fell across all racial and ethnic groups between 2012 and 2013. The largest percentage decline occurred among non-Hispanic African Americans (11%) and Native Americans or Alaskan Natives (11%), followed by Hispanics (10%), Asians or Pacific Islanders (10%), and non-Hispanic whites (9%).

Variations in Teen Pregnancy Rates and Outcomes

Teen pregnancy rates and the outcomes of pregnancy—live birth, spontaneous fetal loss (miscarriage), or induced abortion—vary by age, race, and ethnicity. Figure 5.3 shows that in 2009 non-Hispanic white teenagers became pregnant at a much lower rate, compared with others of comparable age. Among non-Hispanic white teenagers who did become pregnant, well over half of the pregnancies ended with a live birth. This was also the case for Hispanic teenagers, although this group also experienced the highest rates of spontaneous fetal loss. Non-Hispanic African Americans aged 15 to 19 years were the only group where fewer than half of all pregnancies ended with a live birth.

Most Teen Pregnancies Are Unintended

According to the CDC, in *U.S. Teen Pregnancy Outcomes by Age, Race and Hispanic Ethnicity* (2013, http://www.cdc.gov/teenpregnancy/pdf/teen-pregnancy-rates-2013.pdf), among women who were teenagers when they conceived their child, 77% reported that their teenage pregnancy was unintended. More than half (58%) of the respondents described their pregnancy as "mistimed," meaning they became pregnant earlier than they would have liked. About half (51%) said their pregnancy occurred two or more years before they wanted to become pregnant.

FIGURE 5.1

Teen pregnancy, abortion, and birth rates, 1976–2012

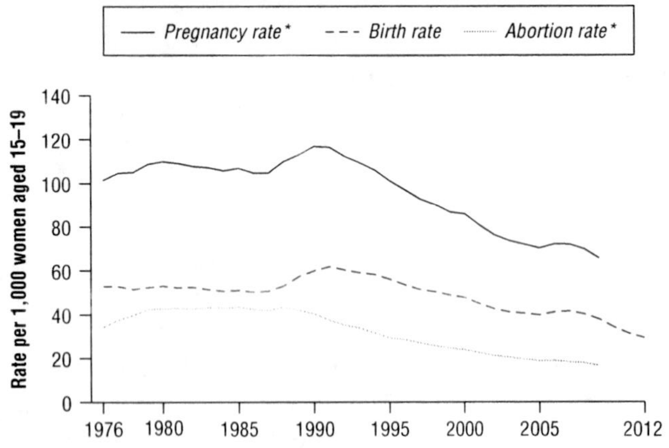

*Data not available for 2010–2012.

SOURCE: Sally C. Curtin et al., "Figure 3. Pregnancy, Birth, and Abortion Rates for Teenagers Aged 15–19: United States, 1976–2009, and Birth Rate, 2010–2012," in "Pregnancy Rates for U.S. Women Continue to Drop," *NCHS Data Brief*, no. 136, December 2013, http://www.cdc.gov/nchs/data/databriefs/db136.pdf (accessed September 22, 2015)

The CDC explains the implications of unintended teen pregnancies: "If U.S. teenagers had only births that they intended to have (and unintended births to teens were postponed until after age 20), then the U.S. teen birth rate in 2008 would have been just 22.8% of 40.2, or 9.2 per 1,000. If this happened, teen births would drop from 11% of all births in the United States to just 4% of all births."

Life Consequences of Teen Pregnancy

In "Teenage Pregnancy" (*Pediatric and Adolescent Gynecology*, vol. 22, August 2012), Ramiro Molina Cartes and Electra González Araya report that the consequences of pregnancy for teenagers can be very negative. They often include incomplete education; larger families; difficulties in maternal role; abandonment by their partner; fewer possibilities of having a stable, qualified, and well-paid job; and greater difficulty in improving their socioeconomic level.

FIGURE 5.2

Teen pregnancy rates by race and ethnicity, 1990–2010

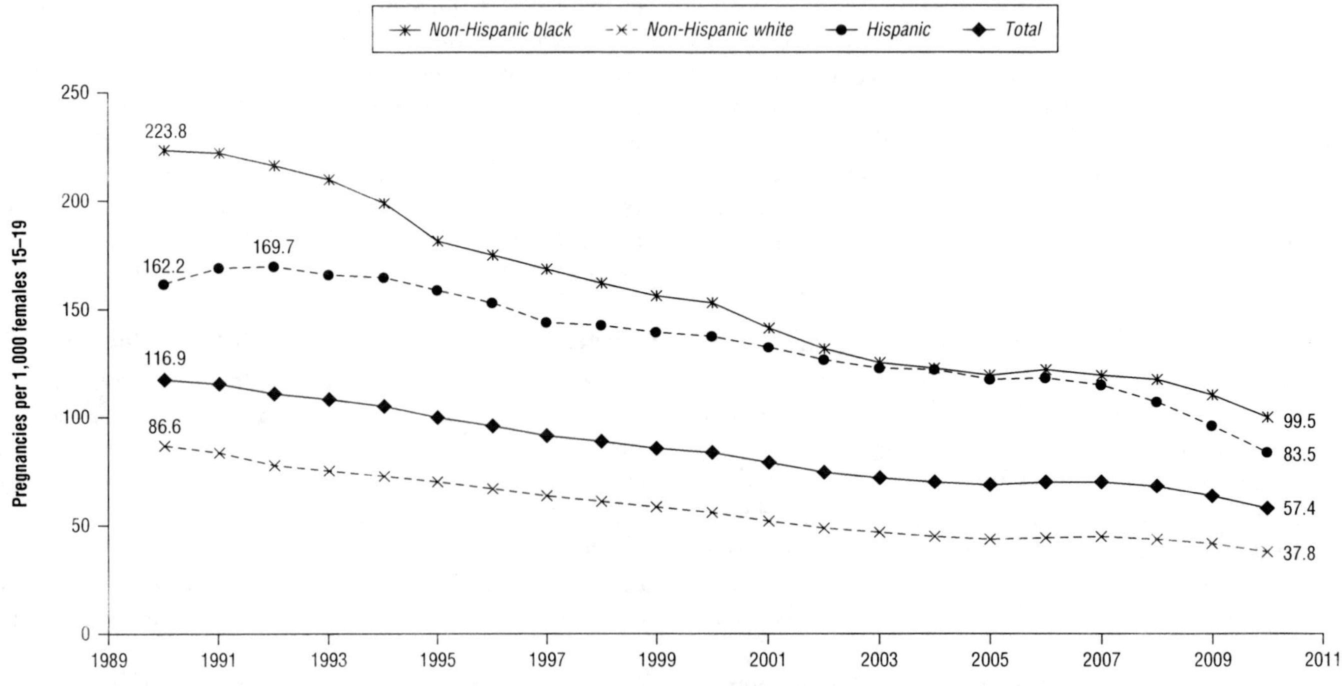

SOURCE: "Figure 2. Pregnancy Rates for Females (15–19), Selected Years 1990–2010," in *Teen Pregnancy*, Child Trends, May 2014, http://www.childtrends.org/wp-content/uploads/2012/07/14_Teen_Pregnancy.pdf (accessed September 22, 2015)

Amanda Y. Black, Nathalie A. Fleming, and Ellen S. Rome point out in "Pregnancy in Adolescents" (*Adolescent Medicine: State of the Art Reviews*, vol. 23, no. 1, April 2012) that the children of teenage mothers are often premature and have lower birth weights, which increases the risk of infant death, blindness, deafness, chronic respiratory problems, mental retardation, mental illness, cerebral palsy, and other disabilities. Children of teenage mothers are more likely to suffer abuse and neglect and to perform poorly in school. Sons of teen mothers are twice as likely to end up in prison than are the sons of older mothers and the daughters of teenage mothers are three times more likely to become teen mothers themselves than are the daughters of older mothers.

FIGURE 5.3

Teen pregnancy rates by outcome and race/ethnicity, 1990 and 2009

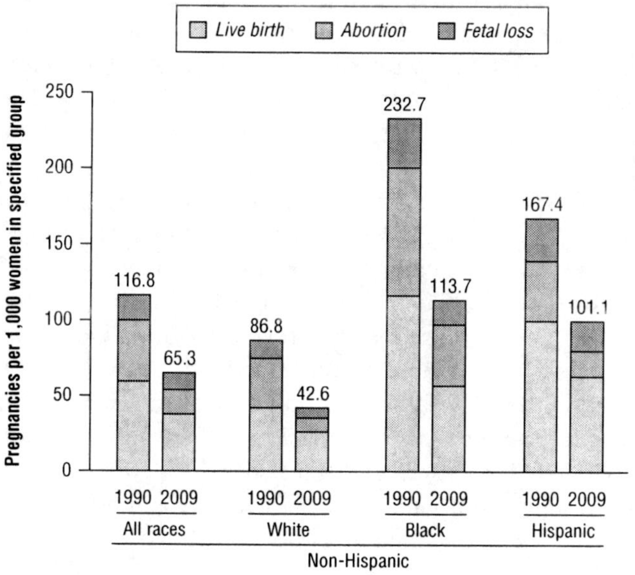

SOURCE: "Pregnancy, Birth, Abortion, and Fetal Loss Rates for Teenagers 15–19 Years by Race and Hispanic Origin: United States, 1990 and 2009," in *NCHS Data on Teen Pregnancy*, Centers for Disease Control and Prevention, National Center for Health Statistics, April 2014, http://www.cdc.gov/nchs/data/factsheets/factsheet_teenage_pregnancy.pdf (accessed September 22, 2015)

PREVENTING TEEN PREGNANCY

In "Youth Risk Behavior Surveillance—United States, 2013" (*Morbidity and Mortality Weekly Report*, vol. 63, no. 4, June 13, 2014), Laura Kann et al. indicate that in 2013 only 3.1% of female high school students and 8.3% of male high school students reported having their first sexual intercourse before the age of 13 years. (See Table 5.1.) Kann et al. also report the percentage of ninth through 12th graders who had ever had sexual intercourse by the time they were surveyed in 2013: 46% of high school girls and 47.5% of high school boys.

Sex and Abstinence-Only Education: Priorities Shown by Funding

What methods may be used to prevent teen pregnancy from occurring? What is the role of sex education and the availability of contraception? Countries such as France, Germany, and the Netherlands try to prevent teenage pregnancy through education about sexuality and contraception, while between 1996 and 2009 the United States placed more emphasis on preventing teenage sex by encouraging abstinence.

The 1996 federal welfare reform law, the Personal Responsibility and Work Opportunity Reconciliation Act

TABLE 5.1

Percentage of high school students who ever had sexual intercourse and who had sexual intercourse for the first time before age 13, by sex, race/ethnicity, and grade, 2013

	Ever had sexual intercourse			Had first sexual intercourse before age 13 years		
	Female	Male	Total	Female	Male	Total
Category	%	%	%	%	%	%
Race/ethnicity						
White*	45.3	42.2	43.7	2.1	4.4	3.3
Black*	53.4	68.4	60.6	4.9	24.0	14.0
Hispanic	46.9	51.7	49.2	3.8	9.2	6.4
Grade						
9	28.1	32.0	30.0	2.9	8.7	5.8
10	41.7	41.1	41.4	3.2	8.7	6.0
11	53.9	54.3	54.1	3.3	8.0	5.6
12	62.8	65.4	64.1	2.5	7.4	4.9
Total	**46.0**	**47.5**	**46.8**	**3.1**	**8.3**	**5.6**

*Non-Hispanic.

SOURCE: Laura Kann et al., "Table 63. Percentage of High School Students Who Ever Had Sexual Intercourse and Who Had Sexual Intercourse for the First Time before Age 13 Years, by Sex, Race/Ethnicity, and Grade—United States, Youth Risk Behavior Survey, 2013," in "Youth Risk Behavior Surveillance—United States, 2013," *MMWR*, vol. 63, no. 4, June 13, 2014, http://www.cdc.gov/mmwr/pdf/ss/ss6304.pdf (accessed September 22, 2015)

(Title V, Section 510), provided an annual $50 million allocation over a five-year period (1998 to 2002) to states for abstinence education programs. The purpose of these programs was "to enable the State to provide abstinence education, and at the option of the State, where appropriate, mentoring, counseling, and adult supervision to promote abstinence from sexual activity, with a focus on those groups which are most likely to bear children out-of-wedlock." Funded programs were prohibited from teaching birth control or the health benefits of condoms and contraception, because abstinence-only proponents believed that such instruction contradicted their message. However, students requesting contraceptive information could be given referrals. In addition, the law included an incentive provision, allotting $50 million to be distributed to the top-five states that reduced their nonmarital births without increasing abortions during the previous two years. Congress then passed the Welfare Reform Extension Act of 2003, the Welfare Reform Extension Act of 2004, and the Welfare Reform Extension Act of 2005, which reauthorized and funded the Title V abstinence-only education program in those years and through 2009.

In his fiscal year (FY) 2010 budget, President Barack Obama (1961–) eliminated funding for abstinence-only education and reallocated $178 million for teen pregnancy prevention. Sharon Jayson reports in "Obama Budget Shifts Money from Abstinence-Only Sex Education: It's a Major Reversal from Bush's Policies" (USAToday.com, May 12, 2009) that about three-fourths of the funding would be used for community-based programs that were shown to delay teens' first intercourse, increase contraceptive use for sexually active teens, and reduce teen pregnancy. The other one-fourth would be used for "innovative" programs.

Ultimately, in March 2010 the federal government committed to fund Title V abstinence-only education at $50 million annually for five additional years as part of the health care reform package passed that year. However, this was in addition to funding for nonabstinence-focused teen pregnancy prevention programs. These funding priorities continued during the next several years of the Obama administration. For example, the Sexuality Information and Education Council of the United States explains in "The President's FY 2016 Budget Shows Strong Support for Effective Adolescent Sexual Health Promotion Programs" (February 3, 2015, http://www.siecus.org/index.cfm?fuseaction=Feature.showFeature&FeatureID=2395) that for FY 2016 Obama proposed a $105 million allocation for the Teen Pregnancy Prevention Initiative, which was intended to support evidence-based approaches to preventing teen pregnancy. Another $75 million was proposed for the Personal Responsibility Education Program (PREP). PREP was created through the 2010 health care reform legislation and was designed to teach adolescents about abstinence and contraception. Table 5.2 provides a

TABLE 5.2

Federal funding for teenage pregnancy prevention programs, fiscal years 1998–2015

[Millions of dollars]

Fiscal year	Teen pregnancy prevention (TPP) program	Evaluation funds for TPP program	Personal responsibility education program (PREP)	Title V abstinence education block grant	Community-based abstinence education (CBAE) program	Evaluation funds for CBAE program	Competitive abstinence-only grants	Adolescent family life (AFL) program—"care" component	Adolescent family life (AFL) program—"prevention" component
1998	—	—	—	$50.0	—	—	—	$7.7	$9.0
1999	—	—	—	50.0	—	—	—	8.7	9.0
2000	—	—	—	50.0	—	—	—	10.2	9.1
2001	—	—	—	50.0	$20.0	—	—	15.3	9.1
2002	—	—	—	50.0	40.0	—	—	18.7	10.2
2003	—	—	—	50.0	54.6	—	—	20.7	10.2
2004	—	—	—	50.0	70.0	$4.5	—	20.5	10.2
2005	—	—	—	50.0	99.2	4.5	—	17.6	13.1
2006	—	—	—	50.0	108.8	4.5	—	17.6	13.1
2007	—	—	—	50.0	108.9	4.5	—	17.6	13.1
2008	—	—	—	50.0	108.9	4.5	—	16.7	13.1
2009	—	—	—	37.5	94.7	4.5	—	16.7	13.1
2010	$110.0	$4.5	$75.0	50.0	0.0	0.0	—	16.7	0.0
2011	104.8	4.4	75.0	50.0	0.0	0.0	—	12.4	0.0
2012	104.8	8.5	75.0	50.0	0.0	0.0	$5.0	0.0	0.0
2013	98.4	8.5	71.2	47.5	0.0	0.0	4.7	0.0	0.0
2014	101.0	8.5	69.6	46.4	0.0	0.0	5.0	0.0	0.0
2015	101.0	6.8	75.0	50.0	0.0	0.0	5.0	0.0	0.0
Total	**$620.0**	**$41.2**	**$440.8**	**$881.4**	**$705.1**	**$27.0**	**$19.7**	**$217.1**	**$132.3**

Note: These data reflect appropriations after all rescissions and post-sequester for fiscal year 2013 and fiscal year 2014. Dashes indicate that program was not yet authorized.

SOURCE: Carmen Solomon-Frears, "Table A-1. Federal Teen Pregnancy Prevention Program Funding, FY1998–FY2015," in *Pregnancy Prevention: Statistics and Programs*, Congressional Research Service, June 23, 2015, https://www.fas.org/sgp/crs/misc/RS20301.pdf (accessed September 23, 2015)

breakdown of federal funding for teen pregnancy prevention programs between FYs 1998 and 2015.

Meanwhile, in April 2015 majorities in both the U.S. Senate and the U.S. House of Representatives voted to extend the State Abstinence Education Grant Program through FY 2017. Besides extending the program for two more years, Congress voted to increase the annual funding for abstinence-only education from $50 million to $75 million.

Positions of Medical Societies on Abstinence-Only Education

In 2006, in response to research demonstrating that abstinence-only programs did not delay the age at which teenagers engaged in first sexual intercourse, provided misinformation and withheld needed information about contraception and protection from sexually transmitted infections (STIs), and was ethically problematic in its coercive nature, the Society for Adolescent Medicine (SAM) published "Abstinence-Only Education Policies and Programs: A Position Paper of the Society for Adolescent Medicine" (*Journal of Adolescent Health*, vol. 38, no. 1, January 2006). SAM documents the problems with abstinence-only sex education and states that it "supports a comprehensive approach to sexual risk reduction including abstinence as well as correct and consistent use of condoms and contraception among teens who choose to be sexually active.... Efforts to promote abstinence should be provided within health education programs that provide adolescents with complete and accurate information about sexual health, including information about concepts of healthy sexuality, sexual orientation and tolerance, personal responsibility, risks of HIV and other STIs and unwanted pregnancy, access to reproductive health care, and benefits and risks of condoms and other contraceptive methods."

SAM suggests that "government policy regarding sexual and reproductive health education should be science-based" and that "current U.S. federal law and guidelines regarding abstinence-only funding are ethically flawed and interfere with fundamental human rights." Furthermore, SAM calls for the repeal of abstinence-only funding laws and the institution of funding that supports "comprehensive medically accurate sexuality education." SAM (now the Society for Adolescent Health and Medicine) continued to support this position as of November 2015.

Other medical societies that have taken positions against abstinence-only education include the American Academy of Pediatrics (AAP), which states in "Sexuality, Contraception, and the Media" (*Pediatrics*, vol. 126, no. 3, September 2010), "It is unwise to promote 'abstinence-only' sex education when it has been shown to be ineffective and when the media have become such an important source of information about 'nonabstinence.'" In addition, the American Public Health Association (APHA), in "Abstinence and U.S. Abstinence Only Education Policies: Ethical and Human Rights Concerns" (November 8, 2006, http://www.apha.org), asserts that "significant ethical and human rights concerns arise when abstinence is presented to adolescents as the sole choice, or when health information regarding other choices is limited or misrepresented. In previous policy statements, APHA has strongly supported sexual and reproductive rights, comprehensive health and sexuality education in schools extending from kindergarten through high school, and adolescent access to confidential reproductive health care."

Public Opinion on the Need for Sex Education

A July 2015 survey conducted by the National Campaign to Prevent Teen and Unplanned Pregnancy finds that a large majority (83%) of U.S. adults supported the federally funded Teen Pregnancy Prevention Program (TPPP), which promotes contraception and other initiatives aimed at curbing teen pregnancy. (See Figure 5.4.) TPPP enjoyed strong bipartisan support, with 92% of Democrats and 75% of Republicans nationwide endorsing the program. Non-Hispanic African Americans expressed the highest level of support for TPPP in 2015, at 88%; support among non-Hispanic whites was 83%, while 81% of Hispanics supported the program. Geographically, support for TPPP was strongest in the West, where 86% of adults surveyed endorsed the program, followed by the South (84%), the north-central United States (82%), and the Northeast (79%).

State Sex Education Policy

As of September 2015, 22 states and the District of Columbia mandated sex education in public schools, and 33 states and the District of Columbia mandated human immunodeficiency virus (HIV) education. (See Table 5.3.) Of these, only 13 states required that the information within these courses be medically accurate. In 25 states, when sex education was provided, it was required that abstinence be stressed, while another 12 states required that it be covered but not necessarily stressed. (See Table 5.4.) Only 18 states and the District of Columbia required that sex education programs cover contraception, whereas 20 states required that HIV programs cover the use of condoms. No state required that contraception be stressed in either sex education classes or HIV prevention classes.

Parental consent requirements or "opt-out" clauses, which allow parents to remove students from instruction the parents find objectionable, may restrict the information adolescents receive. As of September 2015, three states required parental consent for students to participate in sex education or HIV education classes and 35 states and the District of Columbia permitted parents to remove their children from instruction. (See Table 5.3.)

FIGURE 5.4

Percentage of adults who support the Teen Pregnancy Prevention Program and Title X funding for contraception and pregnancy prevention, by race/ethnicity, political affiliation, and geographical location, 2015

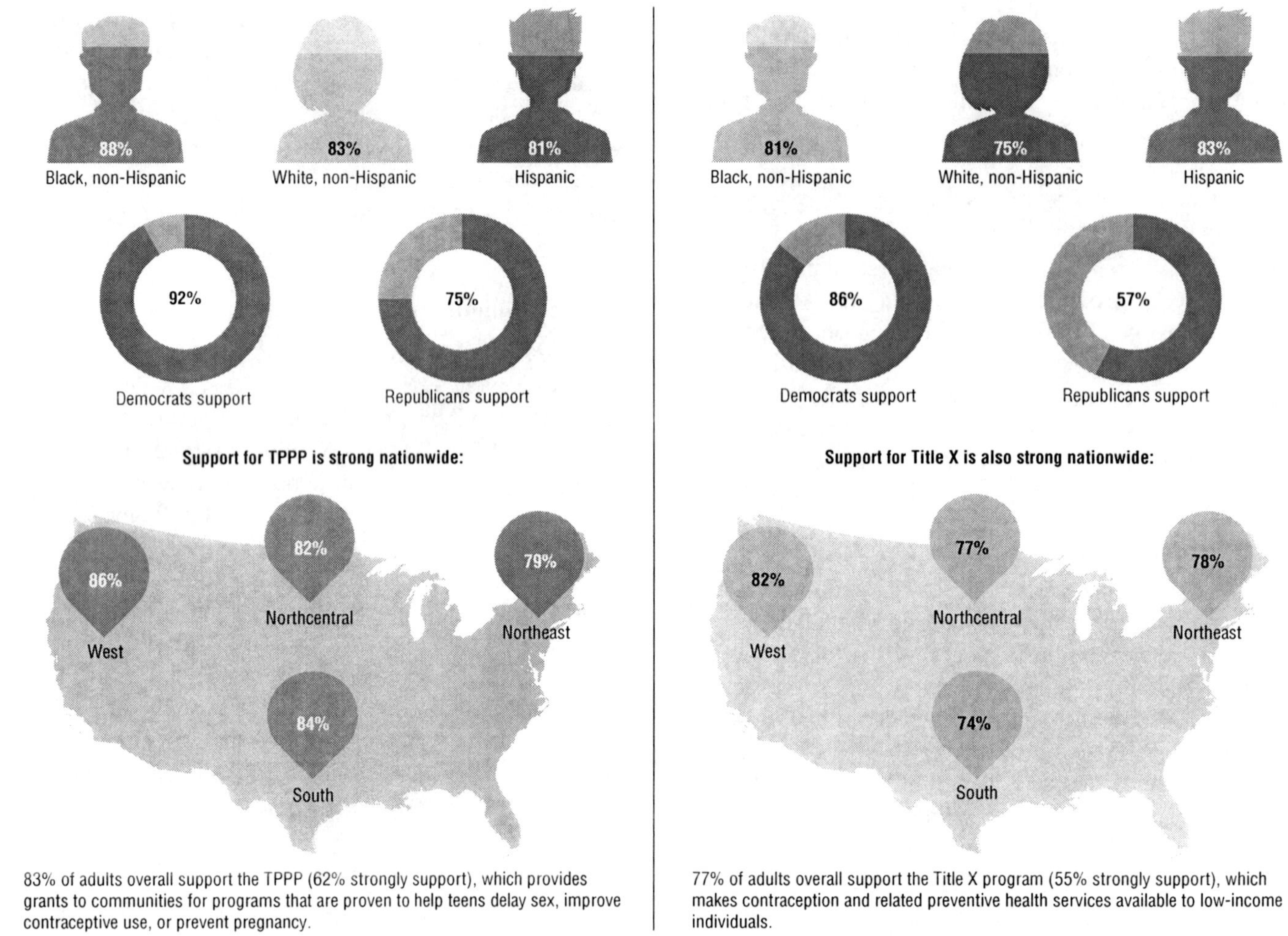

TPPP = Teen Pregnancy Prevention Program.

SOURCE: Adapted from *Survey Says: Don't Mess with Success*, The National Campaign to Prevent Teen and Unplanned Pregnancy, July 2015, http://thenationalcampaign.org/sites/default/files/resource-primary-download/surverysays_21_ letter.pdf (accessed September 22, 2015)

Characteristics of Effective Sex Education Programs

In *What Works 2011–2012: Curriculum-Based Programs That Prevent Teen Pregnancy* (October 2011, https://thenationalcampaign.org/sites/default/files/resource-primary-download/WhatWorks.pdf), Katy Suellentrop of the National Campaign to Prevent Teen and Unplanned Pregnancy provides an overview of the characteristics of sex education programs that can "help delay sex, improve contraceptive use, and/or prevent teen pregnancy." Suellentrop lists specific programs that have been shown to be effective, describes their effects, and provides other information that is specific to each program. Suellentrop also lists general characteristics of effective sex education programs and notes that they:

- Convince teens that not having sex or that using contraception consistently and carefully is the *right* thing to do, as opposed to simply laying out the pros and cons of different sexual choices. That is, there is a clear message.
- Last a sufficient length of time (i.e., more than a few weeks)
- Select leaders who believe in the program and provide them with adequate training
- Actively engage participants and have them personalize the information
- Address peer pressure
- Teach communication skills
- Reflect the age, sexual experience, and culture of young people in the program

TABLE 5.3

State sex and sexually transmitted infections/human immunodeficiency virus general requirements education policy, September 2015

State	Sex education[a] mandated	HIV education mandated	When provided, sex or HIV education must: Be medically accurate	Be age appropriate	Be culturally appropriate and unbiased	Cannot promote religion	Parental role: Notice	Consent	Optout
Alabama		X		X					X
Arizona				X			HIV	Sex	HIV
Arkansas									
California		X	X	X	X	X	X		X
Colorado			X	X	X		X		X
Connecticut		X							X
Delaware	X	X							
Dist. of Columbia	X	X		X			X		X
Florida				X					X
Georgia	X	X					X		X
Hawaii			X	X					
Idaho									X
Illinois[b]		X	X	X					X
Indiana		X							
Iowa	X	X	X	X	X		X		X
Kentucky	X	X							
Louisiana				X		X	X		X
Maine	X	X	X	X					X
Maryland	X	X							X
Massachusetts							X		X
Michigan		X	X[c]	X			X		X
Minnesota	X	X							X
Mississippi[d]	X			X			X		X
Missouri		X		X			X		X
Montana	X	X							
Nevada	X	X		X			X	X	
New Hampshire		X							X
New Jersey	X	X	X	X	X		X		X
New Mexico	X	X							X
New York		X		HIV					HIV
North Carolina	X	X	X	X					
North Dakota	X								
Ohio	X	X							X
Oklahoma		X					X		X
Oregon	X	X	X	X	X		X		X
Pennsylvania		X		HIV			X		HIV
Rhode Island	X	X	X	X	X				X
South Carolina	X	X		X			X		X
Tennessee	X[e]	X		HIV					X
Texas				X			X		X
Utah[f]	X	X	X		X		X	X	
Vermont	X	X		X					X
Virginia				X			X		X
Washington		X	X	X	X		X		X
West Virginia	X	X					X		X
Wisconsin		X					X		X
Total	**22 + DC**	**33 + DC**	**13**	**26 + DC**	**8**	**2**	**22 + DC**	**3**	**35 + DC**

[a]Sex education typically includes discussion of sexually transmitted infections (STIs).
[b]Sex education is not mandatory, but health education is required and it includes medically accurate information on abstinence.
[c]Sex education "shall not be medically inaccurate."
[d]Localities may include topics such as contraception or STIs only with permission from the State Department of Education.
[e]Sex education is required if the pregnancy rate for 15–17 teen women is at least 19.5 or higher.
[f]State also prohibits teachers from responding to students' spontaneous questions in ways that conflict with the law's requirements.
Note: HIV = Human Immunodeficiency Virus.

SOURCE: "General Requirements: Sex and HIV Education," in *State Polices in Brief: Sex and HIV Education*, Guttmacher Institute, September 1, 2015, http://www.guttmacher.org/statecenter/spibs/spib_SE.pdf (accessed September 22, 2015)

Media Influences on Teenage Sex

In September 2010 the AAP published "Sexuality, Contraception, and the Media," a policy statement that reviews the literature on the prevalence of sex in the media and its effect on teen sexual attitudes, values, beliefs, and practices. The AAP notes that American youth spend more than seven hours per day using, watching, and listening to a variety of media, including watching television and movies, listening to music, reading magazines, and visiting various Internet sites. It observes that all media are filled with sexual messages and images and that many of those messages and images are unrealistic. For example, the AAP states that "75% of prime-time programs contain sexual content, yet only 14% of sexual incidents mention any risks or responsibilities of sexual activity." In another example, results of studies show that college students who watched

TABLE 5.4

State sex and sexually transmitted infections/human immunodeficiency virus content requirements education policy, September 2015

	When provided, sex education must								When provided, HIV education must	
	Include information on:					Include life skills for:			Include information on:	
State	Contraception	Abstinence	Importance of sex only within marriage	Sexual orientation	Negative outcomes of teen sex	Avoiding coercion	Healthy decision-making	Family commu-nication	Condoms	Abstinence
Alabama	X	Stress	X	Negative	X	X			X	Stress
Arizona		Stress		[a]	X	X				Stress
Arkansas		Stress	X			X				Stress
California	X	Cover		Inclusive			X	X	X	Cover
Colorado	X	Cover		Inclusive		X	X	X	X	Cover
Delaware	X	Stress		Inclusive		X	X		X	Stress
Dist. of Columbia	X					X				
Florida		Stress	X		X					Stress
Georgia		Stress	X		X					Cover
Hawaii	X	Cover							X	Stress
Illinois	X	Stress	X		X	X			X	Stress
Indiana		Stress	X							Stress
Iowa				Inclusive						
Kentucky		Cover			X		X			Cover
Louisiana		Stress	X							Stress
Maine	X	Stress					X	X	X	Stress
Maryland	X	Cover				X	X		X	Cover
Michigan		Stress	X		X	X	X			Stress
Minnesota		Cover					X			Cover
Mississippi[b]	[c]	Stress	X		X	X				Stress
Missouri		Stress	X		X	X	X			Stress
Montana		Cover								Cover
New Hampshire										Cover
New Jersey	X	Stress		Inclusive			X		X	Stress
New Mexico	X	Cover		Inclusive		X	X	X	X	Stress
New York									X	Stress
North Carolina	X	Stress	X			X	X	X	X	Stress
North Dakota		Cover								
Ohio		Stress	X		X					Stress
Oklahoma		Stress		[a]					X	Cover
Oregon	X	Stress		Inclusive		X	X	X	X	Stress
Pennsylvania										Stress
Rhode Island	X	Stress		Inclusive		X	X		X	Stress
South Carolina	X	Stress	X	Negative						Stress
Tennessee		Stress	X		X	X	X	X		Stress
Texas		Stress	X	Negative	X	X	X		X	Stress
Utah[d]		Stress	X	Negative		X	X	X		Stress
Vermont	X	Cover				X	X	X	X	Cover
Virginia	X	Cover	X			X		X	X	Cover
Washington	X	Stress		Inclusive			X	X	X	Stress
West Virginia	X	Cover	X		X	X	X		X	Cover
Wisconsin		Stress	X							Stress
Total	**18 + DC**		**19**	**12**	**13**	**20 + DC**	**20**	**11**	**20**	

[a]If HIV education is taught in Arizona it cannot "promote" a "homosexual lifestyle" or portray homosexuality in a positive manner. Mandated HIV education in Oklahoma teaches that among other behaviors that "homosexual activity" is considered to be "responsible for contact with the AIDS virus."
[b]Localities may include topics such as contraception or STIs only with permission from the State Department of Education.
[c]Sex education shall not be medically inaccurate.
[d]State also prohibits teachers from responding to students' spontaneous questions in ways that conflict with the law's requirements.
Note: Sex education typically includes discussion of sexually transmitted infections (STIs.) HIV = human immunodeficiency virus.

SOURCE: "Content Requirements for Sex and HIV Education," in *State Polices in Brief: Sex and HIV Education*, Guttmacher Institute, September 1, 2015, http://www.guttmacher.org/statecenter/spibs/spib_SE.pdf (accessed September 22, 2015)

so-called reality television programs whose purpose was to see who "hooked up" were more likely than nonviewers of these programs to believe that "men are sex driven and that men and women are sexual adversaries."

The AAP also reveals that results of nine long-term studies found a correlation between watching sex in the media and becoming sexually active in early adolescence. These studies showed that "exposure to sexual content in TV and other media in early adolescence, particularly for white teenagers, can as much as double the risk of early sexual intercourse. Adolescents whose parents limit their TV-viewing are less likely to engage in early sex. Younger children who have viewed adult-oriented TV shows and movies are more likely to begin having sexual intercourse earlier." To diminish the negative effects of exposure to sex in the media on young teens, the AAP recommends encouraging dialogue among parents, pediatricians, and teenagers to limit such exposure; encouraging the entertainment industry to incorporate responsible and healthy sexual content and messages in its programming; urging schools to provide comprehensive sex education programs; asking the media to air advertisements for birth control products; and supporting further research into the effects of sexual content in media on adolescents and teens.

In "Overexposed and Under-prepared: The Effects of Early Exposure to Sexual Content" (*Psychology Today*, August 13, 2012), Carolyn C. Ross confirms the influence of media exposure on teens' behavior. Ross reports that the Internet, movies, and television influence teens' sexual attitudes and behaviors: the more teens were exposed to sexual content in the media, the earlier they started having sex and the more likely they were to have unprotected sex.

TRENDS IN SEXUAL RISK BEHAVIORS

Unprotected sexual intercourse and multiple sex partners place young people at risk for pregnancy as well as for HIV infection and other STIs. According to the CDC, between 1991 and 2013 there were decreases in the percentage of high school students who reported that they had: ever had sexual intercourse, had sexual intercourse before age 13, engaged in sexual intercourse with four or more people during their lifetime, and engaged in sexual intercourse during the three months prior to the survey (were currently sexually active). (See Table 5.5.) Note that when the CDC reports an increase, decrease, or no change it is making a statistical analysis

TABLE 5.5

Trends in the prevalence of sexual behaviors among high school students, selected years 1991–2013

Percentages													
1991	1993	1995	1997	1999	2001	2003	2005	2007	2009	2011	2013	Long term Change[a]	Change from 2011–2013[b]
Ever had sexual intercourse													
54.1	53.0	53.1	48.4	49.9	45.6	46.7	46.8	47.8	46.0	47.4	46.8	Decreased 1991–2013 Decreased 1991–2001 No change 2001–2013	No change
Had sexual intercourse before age 13 years (for the first time)													
10.2	9.2	8.9	7.2	8.3	6.6	7.4	6.2	7.1	5.9	6.2	5.6	Decreased 1991–2013 Decreased 1991–1997 Decreased 1997–2013	No change
Had sexual intercourse with four or more persons (during their life)													
18.7	18.7	17.8	16.0	16.2	14.2	14.4	14.3	14.9	13.8	15.3	15.0	Decreased 1991–2013 Decreased 1991–2003 No change 2003–2013	No change
Were currently sexually active (sexual intercourse with at least one person during the 3 months before the survey)													
37.5	37.5	37.9	34.8	36.3	33.4	34.3	33.9	35.0	34.2	33.7	34.0	Decreased 1991–2013	No change
Used a condom (during last sexual intercourse among students who were currently sexually active)													
46.2	52.8	54.4	56.8	58.0	57.9	63.0	62.8	61.5	61.1	60.2	59.1	Increased 1991–2013 Increased 1991–2003 Decreased 2003–2013	No change
Used birth control pills (before last sexual intercourse to prevent pregnancy among students who were currently sexually active)													
20.8	18.4	17.4	16.6	16.2	18.2	17.0	17.6	16.0	19.8	18.0	19.0	Decreased 1991–1995 Increased 1995–2013	No change
Did not use any method to prevent pregnancy (during last sexual intercourse among students who were currently sexually active)													
16.5	15.3	15.8	15.2	14.9	13.3	11.3	12.7	12.2	11.9	12.9	13.7	Decreased 1991–2013 Decreased 1991–2007 No change 2007–2013	No change
Drank alcohol or used drugs before last sexual intercourse (among students who were currently sexually active)													
21.6	21.3	24.8	24.7	24.8	25.6	25.4	23.3	22.5	21.6	22.1	22.4	Increased 1991–1999 Decreased 1999–2013	No change
Were ever taught in school about AIDS or HIV infection													
83.3	86.1	86.3	91.5	90.6	89.0	87.9	87.9	89.5	87.0	84.0	85.3	Increased 1991–1997 Decreased 1997–2013	No change
Were ever tested for HIV (not including tests done when donating blood)													
—[c]	—	—	—	—	—	—	11.9	12.9	12.7	12.9	12.9	No change 2003–2013	No change

[a]Based on linear and quadratic trend analyses using logistic regression models controlling sex, race/ethnicity, and grade, $p < 0.05$. Significant linear trends (if present) across all available years are described first followed by linear changes in each segment of significant quadratic trends (if present).
[b]Based on t-test analysis, $p < 0.05$.
[c]Not available.

SOURCE: "Trends in the Prevalence of Sexual Behaviors and HIV Testing National YRBS: 1991–2013," in *Youth Risk Behavior Surveillance System (YRBSS)*, Centers for Disease Control and Prevention, National Center for Chronic Disease Prevention and Health Promotion, Division of Adolescent and School Health, May 15, 2015, http://www.cdc.gov/healthyyouth/data/yrbs/pdf/trends/us_sexual_trend_yrbs.pdf (accessed September 22, 2015) that indicates whether the small differences (if any) from one year to the next are significant or if they are likely to be the result of random differences in the population being sampled.

Among currently sexually active high school students, the percentage who reported having used a condom the last time they had sexual intercourse increased from 46.2% in 1991 to 63% in 2003, after which it dropped slightly to 59.1% in 2013. (See Table 5.5.) The percentage of sexually active students who used alcohol or drugs before their last sexual intercourse increased between 1991 and 2001 and then decreased between 2001 and 2013.

Table 5.6 shows the responses to questions concerning the use of birth control pills and condoms. The 2013 results are broken down by race, grade, and gender. In the high school population, condom use was highest for non-Hispanic African American males in 2013, with 73% reporting condom use during their last sexual intercourse. In surveying grade-level use, condom use was highest for 11th-grade males. More high school males (65.8%) than females (53.1%) reported condom use. The use of birth control pills was not as prevalent among high school students as was condom use. The highest rate of use in 2013 was by non-Hispanic white females, at 30.7%. Use of birth control pills was highest among 12th-grade females, at 27.6%.

TABLE 5.6

Percentage of high school students who used a condom during last sexual intercourse and who used birth control pills before last sexual intercourse, by sex, race/ethnicity, and grade, 2013

	Condom use			Birth control pill use		
	Female	Male	Total	Female	Male	Total
Category	%	%	%	%	%	%
Race/ethnicity						
White*	53.2	61.8	57.1	30.7	20.1	25.9
Black*	55.3	73.0	64.7	7.3	9.0	8.2
Hispanic	50.7	66.5	58.3	7.3	10.8	9.0
Grade						
9	56.5	69.5	62.7	14.7	7.7	11.4
10	55.5	69.3	61.7	19.2	13.7	16.7
11	54.8	70.6	62.3	23.2	15.1	19.3
12	48.4	58.0	53.0	27.6	19.3	23.7
Total	**53.1**	**65.8**	**59.1**	**22.4**	**15.1**	**19.0**

*Non-Hispanic.
Notes: Among the 34.0% of students nationwide who were currently sexually active. Birth control pills and condoms were used to prevent pregnancy.

SOURCE: Laura Kann et al., "Table 67. Percentange of high School Students Who Used a Condom during Last Sexual Intercourse and Who Used Birth Control Pills before Last Sexual Intercourse, by Sex, Race/Ethnicity, and Grade—United States, Youth Risk Behavior Survey, 2013," in "Youth Risk Behavior Surveillance—United States, 2013," *MMWR*, vol. 63, no. 4, June 13, 2014, http://www.cdc.gov/mmwr/pdf/ss/ss6304.pdf (accessed September 22, 2015)

TEEN BIRTH RATES

International Comparisons

As Table 5.7 reveals, U.S. teenagers are more likely to give birth than are teenagers in most other developed countries. In 2014 the birth rate among U.S. teenagers aged 15 to 19 years was 24 per 1,000 women, a figure matched only by New Zealand and the Russian Federation. In 2014 a teenager in the United States was eight times more likely than a teenager in Switzerland to give birth; six times more likely than a teenager in Denmark, Japan, or the Netherlands; and four times more likely than a teenager in Iceland, Italy, Luxembourg, Norway, or Sweden. Overall, a teenager in the United States was at least twice as likely to give birth than a teenager in 20 of the 25 advanced countries listed in Table 5.7.

In "Why Is the Teen Birthrate in the United States So High and Why Does It Matter?" (*Journal of Economic Perspectives*, vol. 26, no. 2, Spring 2012) Melissa S. Kearney and Phillip B. Levine observe that U.S. teens are two-and-a-half times as likely to give birth as teens in Canada and about four times as likely as teens in Germany or Norway. Kearney and Levine posit that social and economic inequality in the United States and a lack of economic opportunity leads many teenage girls to have children while they are young and unmarried. The consequences—less educational attainment and less economic advancement later in life (compared with teens who do not have children)—are simply the continuation of their economic disadvantage. Kearney and Levine attribute the high rate of teen births to hopelessness—teens growing up in environments where there is little chance of social and economic advancement.

U.S. Teen Birth Rate Is at Historic Low

Although teen birth rates in the United States have been high compared with other developed countries, the birth rate for U.S. teens has been dropping in concert with the teen pregnancy rate. As Figure 5.5 shows, teen birth rates dropped dramatically between 1957, when there were 96.3 births per 1,000 females aged 15 to 19 years, and the mid-1980s. The birth rate among teens experienced a sharp rise during the late 1980s and early 1990s, but it subsequently entered another period of significant decline. Figure 5.6 reveals that, with the exception of a brief uptick around 2007, teen birth rates in the United States fell steadily between 1991 and 2014. Figure 5.7 demonstrates that this decline reached across different teenage age groups. For example, in 2013 the birth rate among females aged 15 to 17 years was 12.3 per 1,000, a decline of 68% from 1991 figures. Births among females aged 18 to 19 years decreased by 50% over this span, falling to 47.1 per 1,000 in 2013. By 2014 the birth rate among females aged 15 to 19 years had fallen to 24.2, a historic low. (See Figure 5.5.)

Table 5.8 shows declines in teen birth rates for select years between 1991 and 2013 by race and ethnicity. During

TABLE 5.7

International comparison of teen birth rates in select developed countries, selected years, 1990–2014

States	1990	2000	2006	2007	2008	2009	2010	2011	2012	2013	2014
Australia	21	18	17	17	17	16	16	16	16	15	14
Austria	21	14	12	11	11	10	10	9	9	8	7
Belgium	11	11	10	10	10	10	10	9	9	9	8
Canada	24	17	14	14	13	13	12	12	11	11	10
Denmark	9	7	6	6	6	5	5	5	4	4	4
Finland	12	10	10	9	9	8	8	8	7	7	7
France	12	10	10	10	10	10	10	10	10	9	9
Germany	16	13	10	10	9	9	9	8	8	7	7
Greece	22	11	11	12	11	10	10	9	9	8	8
Iceland	28	20	15	14	13	12	11	9	8	7	6
Ireland	16	19	17	16	15	15	14	13	12	11	11
Israel	20	17	14	14	13	13	13	12	12	11	10
Italy	9	7	7	7	7	7	7	6	6	6	6
Japan	4	5	5	5	5	5	5	5	5	4	4
Luxembourg	12	11	10	10	9	9	8	8	7	7	6
Netherlands	7	7	6	5	5	5	5	5	4	4	4
New Zealand	33	28	29	30	29	28	27	26	25	25	24
Norway	17	11	9	9	8	8	7	7	6	6	6
Portugal	24	20	17	16	15	15	14	13	12	11	10
Russian Federation	51	31	29	29	29	28	28	27	27	26	24
Spain	12	9	12	12	12	11	10	10	9	9	9
Sweden	12	7	6	6	6	6	6	6	5	6	6
Switzerland	6	5	5	5	4	4	4	4	3	3	3
United Kingdom	31	28	26	26	24	23	21	20	18	17	15
United States	57	46	40	40	38	36	34	32	30	27	24

Note: Adolescent fertility rate (births per 1,000 women ages 15–19)

SOURCE: Adapted from "Adolescent Fertility Rate (Births per 1,000 Women Ages 15–19)," in *World Development Indicators*, The World Bank, 2015, http://databank.worldbank.org/data/reports.aspx?source=2&country=&series=SP.ADO.TFRT&period=# (accessed September 23, 2015)

FIGURE 5.5

Birth rates among teens aged 15–19, 1950–2014

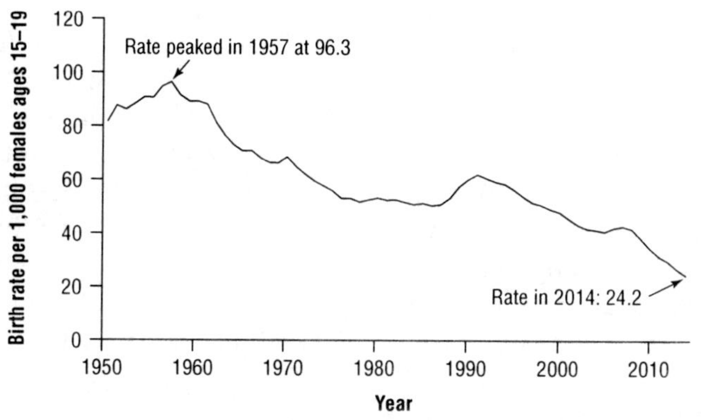

SOURCE: Carmen Solomon-Frears, "Figure 1. Teen Birth Rates (Ages 15–19), 1950–2014," in *Teenage Pregnancy Prevention: Statistics and Programs*, Congressional Research Service, June 23, 2015, https://www.fas.org/sgp/crs/misc/RS20301.pdf (accessed September 23, 2015)

this span the birth rate among females aged 15 to 19 years of Asian or Pacific Islander descent fell 68%, more than any other group. Furthermore, Asians or Pacific Islanders between the ages of 15 to 19 years consistently had the lowest birth rate of any racial or ethnic group between 1991 and 2013. For example, in 2013 the birth rate among Asians or Pacific Islanders in this age group was 8.7 per 1,000. This figure was half the rate of 18.6 per 1,000 among non-Hispanic whites, the group with the second-lowest birth rate among 15- to 19-year-olds.

Births to Unmarried Teenagers

Table 5.9 shows the number and percentage of births to unmarried women by age and race/ethnicity. The data indicate that a high percentage of teenagers who gave birth in 2014 were unmarried, which is not surprising in light of the fact that most teens are not married. That year, 88.8% of all births to women under the age of 20 years were to unmarried teens. Women aged 20 to 24 years were also more likely to be unmarried than married when they gave birth. The older age groups were all significantly more likely to be married when they gave birth than not.

State-Specific Birth Rates

In 2013 the birth rates for teens aged 15 to 19 years ranged from a low of 12.1 births per 1,000 women in Massachusetts to a high of 43.5 births per 1,000 women in Arkansas. (See Table 5.10.) Other states with relatively low teen birth rates in 2013 were New Hampshire (12.6), Connecticut (12.9), Vermont (14.5), and New Jersey (14.8). Other states with relatively high teen birth rates in 2013 were New Mexico (43.3), Oklahoma (42.9), and Mississippi (42.6).

TEEN ABORTION

Not only are U.S. teen pregnancy rates and birth rates higher than in most other industrialized countries, but the

FIGURE 5.6

Birth rates among teens aged 15–19, by race/ethnicity, 1991–2014

[Per 1,000 girls age 15–19]

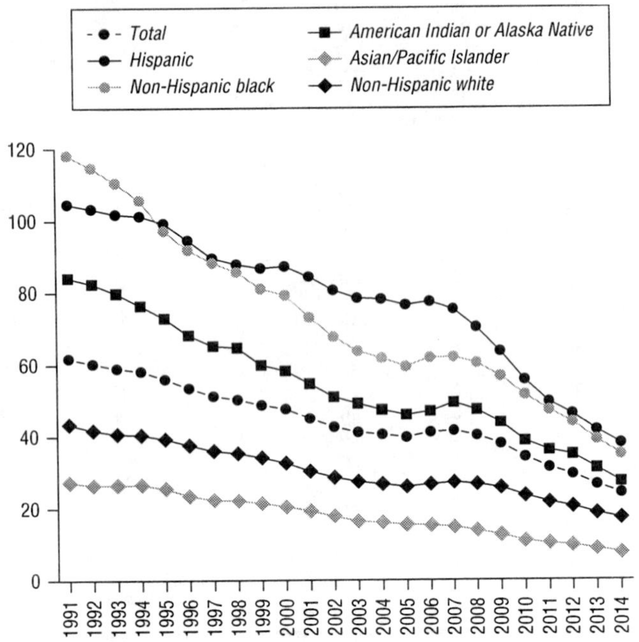

SOURCE: "Figure 1. Teen Birth Rates (per 1,000 Girls Age 15–19) 1991–2014, by Race/Ethnicity," in *Fast Facts: Teen Childbearing in the United States, 2014 Birth Data*, The National Campaign to Prevent Teen and Unplanned Pregnancy, July 2015, https://thenationalcampaign.org/sites/default/files/resource-primary-download/fast-facts-teen-childbearing-in-the-us-2014-birth-data_2.pdf (accessed September 22, 2015)

FIGURE 5.7

Birth rates for teens by age group, 1960–2013

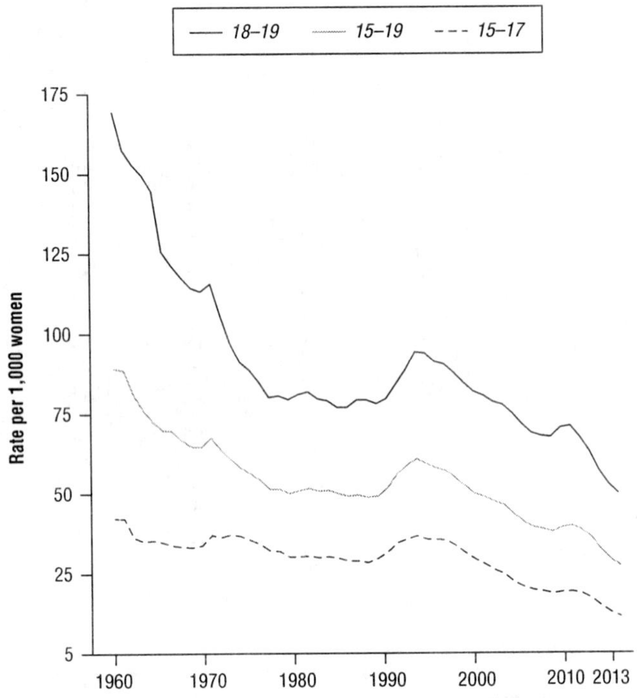

SOURCE: Joyce A. Martin et al., "Figure 3. Birth Rates for Teenagers Aged 15–19, by Age Group: United States, 1960–2013," in "Births: Final Data for 2013," *National Vital Statistics Report*, vol. 64, no. 1, January 15, 2015, http://www.cdc.gov/nchs/data/nvsr/nvsr64/nvsr64_01.pdf (accessed September 22, 2015)

United States also has higher rates of teen abortion. Having analyzed the most recent available data from more than 40 countries, Gilda Sedgh et al. of the Guttmacher Institute report in "Legal Abortion Levels and Trends by Woman's Age at Termination" (*Perspectives on Sexual and Reproductive Health*, vol. 45, no. 1, March 2013), the most recent study on this topic as of November 2015, that U.S. teens aged 15 to 19 years had an abortion rate of 19.8 in 2008 (19.8 abortions per 1,000 women in that age group). This was the fifth-highest abortion rate for adolescents out of the 41 countries included in the study. Cuba (63.9 in 2009), England/Wales (22 in 2010), New Zealand (21.6 in 2010), and Sweden (20.9) had higher rates in recent years. By comparison, over a dozen countries had teen abortion rates of 7 per 1,000 or lower in the most recent year reported in the study. Sedgh et al. conclude that higher abortion rates "probably reflect higher-than-average levels of unmet need for contraception or difficulty using methods consistently and effectively, and a stronger desire to avoid childbearing."

Although the abortion rate for teenagers in the United States was higher in 2008 than in many other countries, it was much lower than it had been during the 1990s. In "Pregnancy Rates for U.S. Women Continue to Drop" (*NCHS Data Brief*, no. 136, December 2013), Sally C. Curtin et al. indicate that in 1990 the overall abortion rate was 40.3 per 1,000 women aged 15 to 19 years. The rate had been at roughly this level since 1980. Subsequently, however, the teen abortion rate dropped every year through 2005, when it stood at 18.7. After a small uptick in 2006 the decline continued, reaching 16.3 in 2009.

Race and Ethnicity

According to Stephanie J. Ventura et al., in "Estimated Pregnancy Rates and Rates of Pregnancy Outcomes for the United States, 1990–2008" (*National Vital Statistics Report*, vol. 60, no. 7, June 20, 2012), there are significant differences in the teen abortion rate across different racial and ethnic groups. For example, non-Hispanic white teenagers had 10.4 abortions per 1,000 women in 2008. Hispanic teenagers had a rate nearly twice as high as non-Hispanic white teenagers, at 20.1 abortions per 1,000 women. The rate for non-Hispanic African American teenagers was more than four times that of non-Hispanic white teenagers, at 43.4 per 1,000 women.

TABLE 5.8

Birth rates for teens aged 10–19, by age and race and Hispanic origin, 1991, 2007, and 2011–13

[Rates per 1,000 women in specified age and race and Hispanic origin group. Population estimated as of July 1.]

Age group (years) and race and Hispanic origin of mother	Year					Percent change		
	2013	2012	2011	2007	1991	2012–2013	2007–2013	1991–2013
10–14								
All races and origins[a]	0.3	0.4	0.4	0.6	1.4	−25	−50	−79
Non-Hispanic white[b]	0.1	0.2	0.2	0.2	0.5	−50	−50	−80
Non-Hispanic black[b]	0.7	0.8	0.9	1.4	4.9	−13	−50	−86
American Indian or Alaska Native total[b, c]	0.4	0.5	0.5	0.7	1.6	−20	−43	−75
Asian or Pacific Islander total[b, c]	0.1	0.1	0.1	0.2	0.8	[e]	−50	−88
Hispanic[d]	0.5	0.6	0.7	1.2	2.4	−17	−58	−79
15–19								
All races and origins[a]	26.5	29.4	31.3	41.5	61.8	−10	−36	−57
Non-Hispanic white[b]	18.6	20.5	21.7	27.2	43.4	−9	−32	−57
Non-Hispanic black[c]	39.0	43.9	47.3	62.0	118.2	−11	−37	−67
American Indian or Alaska Native total[b, c]	31.1	34.9	36.1	49.3	84.1	−11	−37	−63
Asian or Pacific Islander total[b, c]	8.7	9.7	10.2	14.8	27.3	−10	−41	−68
Hispanic[d]	41.7	46.3	49.6	75.3	104.6	−10	−45	−60
15–17								
All races and origins[a]	12.3	14.1	15.4	21.7	38.6	−13	−43	−68
Non-Hispanic white[b]	7.4	8.4	9.0	11.9	23.6	−12	−38	−69
Non-Hispanic black[b]	18.9	21.9	24.6	34.6	86.1	−14	−45	−78
American Indian or Alaska Native total[b, c]	15.9	17.0	18.2	26.1	51.9	−6	−39	−69
Asian or Pacific Islander total[b, c]	3.7	4.1	4.6	7.4	16.3	−10	−50	−77
Hispanic[d]	22.0	25.5	28.0	44.4	69.2	−14	−50	−68
18–19								
All races and origins[a]	47.1	51.4	54.1	71.7	94.0	−8	−34	−50
Non-Hispanic white[b]	35.0	37.9	39.9	50.4	70.6	−8	−31	−50
Non-Hispanic black[b]	67.0	74.1	78.8	105.2	162.2	−10	−36	−59
American Indian or Alaska Native total[b, c]	53.3	60.5	61.6	86.3	134.2	−12	−38	−60
Asian or Pacific Islander total[b, c]	16.1	17.7	18.1	24.9	42.2	−9	−35	−62
Hispanic[d]	70.8	77.2	81.5	124.7	155.5	−8	−43	−54

[a]Includes births to race and Hispanic origin groups not shown separately, such as white Hispanic and black Hispanic women, and births with origin not stated.
[b]Race and Hispanic origin are reported separately on birth certificates. Persons of Hispanic origin may be of any race. Race categories are consistent with1977 Office of Management and Budget (OMB) standards. Forty-four states and the District of Columbia reported multiple-race data in 2013 that were bridged to single-race categories for comparability with other states. Multiple-race reporting areas vary for 2007 and 2011–2013.
[c]Includes persons of Hispanic and non-Hispanic origin, and origin not stated, according to the mother's reported race.
[d]Includes all persons of Hispanic origin of any race.
[e]Difference not statistically significant.

SOURCE: Joyce A. Martin et al., "Table A. Birth Rates for Women Aged 10–19, by Age and Race and Hispanic Origin of Mother: United States, 1991, 2007, and 2011–2013," in "Births: Final Data for 2013," *National Vital Statistics Report*, vol. 64, no. 1, January 15, 2015, http://www.cdc.gov/nchs/data/nvsr/nvsr64/nvsr64_01.pdf (accessed September 22, 2015)

The racial and ethnic differences in teen abortion rates are due in part to the fact that Hispanic and non-Hispanic African American teenagers are much more likely to become pregnant than non-Hispanic white teenagers. Ventura et al. report that, in 2008, 23.2% of all pregnancies to non-Hispanic white teenagers aged 15 to 19 years ended with an induced abortion. For Hispanic teenagers in the same age group, 17.8% of pregnancies ended with an induced abortion that year. Among non-Hispanic African American teenagers aged 15 to 19 years, 35.7% of pregnancies ended with an induced abortion in 2008. Thus, Hispanic teens were the least likely to end their pregnancies with an abortion in 2008, but they had a higher abortion rate than non-Hispanic white teens because they were more likely to become pregnant in the first place.

Susan A. Cohen reports in "Abortion and Women of Color: The Bigger Picture" (*Guttmacher Policy Review*, vol. 11, no. 3, Summer 2008) that many factors explain the high abortion rate among African American women. One primary reason is that African American women have a rate of unintended pregnancy three times that of white women. This high rate of unintended pregnancy is linked to disparities in access to and consistent use of effective contraceptives. Cohen determines that financial, geographic, educational, and personal issues contribute to using contraceptives less frequently and less consistently.

PARENTAL INVOLVEMENT IN ABORTION DECISIONS

Parental involvement in abortion decisions of minors is a contentious issue. Those in favor of parental involvement believe that if a minor becomes pregnant, she will benefit from parental support and counsel. In addition, proponents of parental involvement believe that parental involvement will increase the chance that a pregnant teen will receive the proper medical care she needs. If the

TABLE 5.9

Numbers and percentages of births to unmarried women, by age and race/ethnicity, 2013 and 2014

	Number		Percent	
Characteristic	2014	2013	2014	2013
Age of mother				
All ages[a]	1,604,495	1,595,873	40.3	40.6
Under 20	223,363	245,239	88.7	88.8
Under 15	2,755	3,072	99.4	99.2
15–19	220,608	242,167	88.6	88.7
15–17	63,887	71,394	95.7	95.4
18–19	156,721	170,773	86.0	86.1
20–24	579,653	586,874	65.7	65.4
25–29	419,618	401,876	36.7	35.9
30–34	243,041	231,598	22.5	22.3
35–39	110,026	102,412	21.6	21.2
40 and over	28,794	27,874	24.3	23.7
Race and Hispanic origin of mother				
Non-Hispanic white[b]	627,541	623,645	29.2	29.3
Non-Hispanic black[b]	417,531	417,291	70.9	71.5
American Indian or Alaska Native total[b, c]	29,540	30,543	65.7	66.4
Asian or Pacific Islander total[b, c]	46,334	45,062	16.4	17.0
Hispanic[d]	483,900	479,751	52.9	53.2

[a]Includes births to race and Hispanic origin groups not shown separately, such as white Hispanic and black Hispanic women, and births with origin not stated.
[b]Race and Hispanic origin are reported separately on birth certificates. Persons of Hispanic origin may be of any race. Race categories are consistent with the 1977 Office of Management and Budget (OMB) standards. Forty-eight states and the District of Columbia reported multiple-race data in 2014. The multiple-race data for these states were bridged to the single-race categories of the 1977 OMB standards for comparability with other states. Multiple-race reporting areas vary for 2013–2014.
[c]Includes persons of Hispanic and non-Hispanic origin, and origin not stated, according to the mother's reported race.
[d]Includes all persons of Hispanic origin of any race.
Note: Data for 2014 are based on a continuous file of records received from the states. Figures for 2014 are based on weighted data rounded to the nearest individual, so categories may not add to total.

SOURCE: Brady E. Hamilton et al., "Table 6. Births to Unmarried Women, by Age and Race and Hispanic Origin of Mother: United States, Final 2013 and Preliminary 2014," in "Births: Preliminary Data for 2014," *National Vital Statistics Report*, vol. 64, no. 6, June 17, 2015, http://www.cdc.gov/nchs/data/nvsr/nvsr64/nvsr64_06.pdf (accessed September 22, 2015)

pregnancy is a result of rape, then parents can help protect their daughter from further harm. Those against parental involvement believe that some teens would resort to having an illegal and potentially life-threatening abortion if they were forced to tell their parents or would—at the very least—delay reaching out for the help and care they need. They believe that some teens may anger their parents with the news and even face physical danger. In addition, parents may force their daughter to make a decision, either to have an abortion or to carry the pregnancy to term, rather than allowing her a choice in the matter. Thus, they emphasize the importance of providing teens with confidential reproductive services so that the teen can make an informed decision. This is especially important if the pregnancy is due to incest, in which case the pregnant teen may be in a situation in which she must have the consent of her abuser to abort the pregnancy.

Table 5.11 shows that as of September 2015, 38 states had laws in effect requiring some parental involvement before a minor had an abortion. Parental consent or notification laws generally include judicial bypass (waiver) provisions if the young woman does not want to or cannot tell her parents of her decision. In a judicial bypass, a court decides if the minor is mature enough to make the decision on her own or if the abortion would be in her best interests. Of the states that had laws requiring some parental involvement before a minor had an abortion, 37 had a judicial bypass provision. In addition, seven states had laws in which a minor could involve a grandparent or other adult relative in the decision instead of a parent.

RELINQUISHMENT FOR ADOPTION

A teenager faced with an unintended pregnancy can choose parenthood (often obtaining help from relatives), relinquishing (giving up) the infant for adoption, or abortion. Most women of any age choose to keep their infant or to have an abortion. In "Who Adopts? Characteristics of Women and Men Who Have Adopted Children" (*NCHS Data Brief*, no. 12, January 2009), the most recent report on this topic as of November 2015, Jo Jones of the CDC explains that never-married women continue to be the most likely group of women to give up an infant for adoption. Jones also reports that the percentage of infants given up for adoption by never-married women has declined from 9% of those born before 1973 to 1% of those born between 1996 and 2002, which is fewer than 7,000 infants per year.

TABLE 5.10

Birth rates for teenagers aged 15–19, by state and territory, 2013

[By place of residence. Fertility rates are births per 1,000 women aged 15 to 44; total fertility rates are sums of birth rates for 5-year age groups multiplied by 5; birth rates by age are births per 1,000 women in specified age group estimated in each area. Populations estimated as of July 1.]

	Age of mother (years)		
	15–19		
Area	Total	15–17	18–19
United States*	26.5	12.3	47.1
Alabama	34.3	15.8	61.4
Alaska	30.3	11.0	63.2
Arizona	33.1	15.3	59.7
Arkansas	43.5	18.3	82.7
California	23.6	11.1	41.9
Colorado	23.4	11.6	40.5
Connecticut	12.9	6.2	22.0
Delaware	24.7	12.3	39.9
District of Columbia	32.1	23.9	37.4
Florida	24.6	10.8	45.5
Georgia	30.5	13.9	54.9
Hawaii	25.1	10.4	48.0
Idaho	25.7	9.2	51.8
Illinois	24.6	11.7	44.0
Indiana	30.3	13.6	54.9
Iowa	22.1	9.8	38.6
Kansas	29.6	12.5	54.6
Kentucky	39.5	16.7	74.1
Louisiana	39.2	17.4	72.2
Maine	17.4	7.1	31.8
Maryland	19.4	9.1	34.1
Massachusetts	12.1	6.0	19.1
Michigan	23.6	10.6	42.5
Minnesota	16.8	7.3	30.5
Mississippi	42.6	19.5	75.4
Missouri	30.0	12.6	55.7
Montana	27.9	12.6	50.0
Nebraska	24.9	11.4	43.5
Nevada	30.3	12.4	61.5
New Hampshire	12.6	4.7	22.8
New Jersey	14.8	6.8	27.6
New Mexico	43.3	22.3	74.2
New York	17.7	8.3	30.5
North Carolina	28.4	13.1	49.8
North Dakota	24.1	9.9	40.6
Ohio	27.2	11.6	50.0
Oklahoma	42.9	20.5	76.1
Oregon	21.6	9.7	39.4
Pennsylvania	20.9	10.3	34.6
Rhode Island	17.7	9.3	26.3
South Carolina	31.6	14.5	55.0
South Dakota	29.1	13.2	51.3
Tennessee	34.7	15.1	64.0
Texas	41.0	21.1	72.0
Utah	20.6	8.6	39.0
Vermont	14.5	4.9	24.7
Virginia	20.1	8.0	36.5
Washington	20.5	8.8	38.7
West Virginia	40.1	17.1	73.4
Wisconsin	19.6	8.5	35.2
Wyoming	29.6	13.0	54.1
Puerto Rico	44.6	25.5	72.4
Virgin Islands	—	—	—
Guam	54.1	26.3	95.0
American Samoa	42.9	22.2	65.9
Northern Marianas	44.3	26.6	69.2

TABLE 5.10

Birth rates for teenagers aged 15–19, by state and territory, 2013 [CONTINUED]

—Data not available.
*Excludes data for the territories.
Note: Population data for computing birth rates were provided by the U.S. Census Bureau. Rates by state may differ from rates computed on the basis of other population estimates.

SOURCE: Adapted from Joyce A. Martin et al., "Table 12. Birth Rates, by Age of Mother: United States, Each State and Territory, 2013," in "Births: Final Data for 2013," *National Vital Statistics Report*, vol. 64, no. 1, January 15, 2015, http://www.cdc.gov/nchs/data/nvsr/nvsr64/nvsr64_01.pdf (accessed September 22, 2015)

TABLE 5.11

State policies on parental involvement in minors' abortions, September 2015

	Parental involvement			Judicial bypass				Exceptions	
State	Consent only	Notification and consent	Notification only	Available	Specific criteria	"Clear and convincing" evidence	Other adult relatives	Medical emergency	Abuse, assault, incest or neglect
Alabama	X			X				X	
Alaska			X	X				X	X
Arizona	X[c]			X	X	X		X	X
Arkansas	X[c]			X	[b]	[b]		X	X
California	▼								
Colorado			X	X		X		X	X
Delaware[e]			X[d]	X[d]			X[e]	X[e]	
Florida			X	X	X	X		X	
Georgia			X	X				X	
Idaho	X			X		X		X	X
Illinois			X	X			X	X	X
Indiana	X			X				X	
Iowa			X	X			X	X	X
Kansas	Both parents[c]			X	X	X		X	
Kentucky	X			X	X			X	
Louisiana	X[c]			X		X		X	
Maryland			X[d]						X[d]
Massachusetts	X			X				X	
Michigan	X			X				X	
Minnesota			Both parents	X				X	X
Mississippi	Both parents			X		X		X	
Missouri	X			X					
Montana	[a]		[a]						
Nebraska	X[c]			X		X		X	X
Nevada			▼						
New Hampshire			X	X				X	
New Jersey			▼						
New Mexico	▼								
North Carolina	X			X			X	X	
North Dakota	Both parents			X		X		X	
Ohio	X			X	X	X			
Oklahoma		X[c]		X		X		X	X
Pennsylvania	X			X				X	
Rhode Island	X			X				X	
South Carolina[e]	X[d]			X[e]			X[e]	X[e]	X[e]
South Dakota			X	X		X		X	
Tennessee	X			X				X	X
Texas		X[c]		X		[b]	[b]	X	
Utah		X		X[f]				X	X[g]
Virginia		X[c]		X			X	X	X
West Virginia			X[d]	X[c]				X	
Wisconsin	X[d]			X[c]			X	X	X
Wyoming		X		X		X		X	
Total	**21**	**5**	**12**	**37**	**5**	**13**	**7**	**35**	**16**

▼ Enforcement permanently enjoined by court order; policy not in effect.
[a]Enforcement temporarily enjoined by court order; policy not in effect.
[b]New laws scheduled to take effect in early 2016.
[c]Requires parental consent documentation to be notarized.
[d]Allows specified health professionals to waive parental involvement in limited circumstances.
[e]The law in Delaware applies to women younger than 16 and South Carolina's law to those younger than 17.
[f]The provision applies only to parental consent requirements.
[g]The provision applies only to the parental notice requirements.

SOURCE: "Parental Involvement in Minors' Abortions," in *State Policies in Brief: Parental Involvement in Minors' Abortions*, Guttmacher Institute, September 1, 2015, http://www.guttmacher.org/statecenter/spibs/spib_PIMA.pdf (accessed September 22, 2015)

CHAPTER 6
ABORTION CLINICS

QUALITY OF ABORTION CLINIC SERVICES

The National Abortion Federation (NAF) is a professional association of abortion providers in the United States and Canada. NAF's mission is to promote and enhance the quality of abortion services. The federation has developed clinical policy guidelines to help ensure safe, high-quality abortion care. More than 400 nonprofit and private clinics, women's health centers, Planned Parenthood Federation of America facilities, hospitals, and private physicians, as well as researchers, clinicians, and educators at universities and teaching hospitals across the United States and Canada, are members of the NAF.

In *2015 Clinical Policy Guidelines* (2015, http://prochoice.org/wp-content/uploads/2015_NAF_CPGs.pdf), the NAF addresses three types of policies: standards, recommendations, and options. Standards are applied rigidly and include directives such as, "Abortion will be provided by licensed practitioners. This category is intended to include physicians from various specialties as well as nurse midwives, nurse practitioners, physician assistants, registered nurses, and other health professionals." Recommendations allow some flexibility in clinical management but must be justified when not followed. Recommendations include items such as, "Appropriate referrals must be available for patients who cannot be cared for by a practitioner at your facility." As the name implies, options may or may not be followed, at the discretion of the provider. For example, whereas "The practitioner must ensure that appropriate personnel have a discussion with the patient in which accurate information is provided about the procedure and its alternatives, and the potential risks and benefits. The patient must have the opportunity to have any questions answered to her satisfaction prior to intervention," is a standard that must be followed, the NAF allows the option that "Information may be provided either on an individual basis or in group sessions."

Meanwhile, access to abortion services is becoming increasingly limited for a significant percentage of women in the United States. As Table 6.1 shows, in 2011 more than one-third (38%) of all American women lived in counties where there was no abortion clinic. Access to abortion was especially limited in the Midwest and South, where 53% and 49% of women, respectively, lived in counties that had no abortion clinics.

STATE LEGISLATION PROMPTS CLINIC CLOSURES

A spate of state-level legislation that began in 2010 is said by pro-choice advocates to have resulted in the closure of numerous clinics. David Crary reports in "Abortions Declining in Nearly All States" (AP.org, June 7, 2015) that between 2011 and 2015, 31 states passed a total of 267 new abortion restrictions, resulting in the closure of approximately 70 abortion clinics nationwide. In Texas alone, 27 abortion clinics were forced to close during this span.

In "Anti-abortion Laws Take Dramatic Toll on Clinics Nationwide" (HuffingtonPost.com, August 26, 2013), Laura Bassett explains that the new state laws, referred to as Targeted Regulation of Abortion Providers (TRAP) laws by their opponents, "often require abortion clinics to undergo extensive and costly renovations in order to become ambulatory surgical centers, which are essentially mini-hospitals." Clinics that cannot afford the renovations shut down instead, which pro-choice advocates argue is the true intention of the laws. The laws' supporters counter that abortion clinics are simply being forced to meet safety standards like other medical facilities. As Mary Kate Cary puts it in the editorial "Safety First for Abortion Clinics" (USNews.com, July 18, 2013), "When I read that several states have required abortion clinics to meet the same standards as ambulatory surgical centers—with doorways wide enough for ambulance gurneys, in case things go wrong—that didn't strike me as 'extremist'

TABLE 6.1

Numbers of abortion providers and abortion clinics, with percentages of women aged 15–44 living in counties not served by abortion providers, by state, 2008 and 2011

	Providers			Clinics			Counties, 2011		% of women in counties with no clinic, 2011*
Region and state	2008	2011	% change, 2008–2011	2008	2011	% change, 2008–2011	No.	% with no clinic	
U.S. total	**1,793**	**1,720**	**−4**	**851**	**839**	**−1**	**3,143**	**89**	**38**
Northeast	**500**	**453**	**−9**	**201**	**186**	**−7**	**217**	**65**	**24**
Connecticut	47	41	−13	22	21	−5	8	13	5
Maine	13	11	−15	6	5	−17	16	81	55
Massachusetts	41	40	−2	11	12	9	14	36	10
New Hampshire	11	13	18	4	5	25	10	50	23
New Jersey	75	64	−15	27	24	−11	21	48	28
New York	249	225	−10	103	94	−9	62	53	12
Pennsylvania	50	47	−6	22	20	−9	67	87	49
Rhode Island	4	4	0	2	2	0	5	80	37
Vermont	10	8	−20	4	3	−25	14	79	51
Midwest	**173**	**173**	**0**	**115**	**124**	**8**	**1,055**	**94**	**53**
Illinois	37	37	0	22	26	18	102	92	39
Indiana	12	12	0	9	10	11	92	93	61
Iowa	11	18	64	10	17	70	99	85	50
Kansas	4	3	−25	4	3	−25	105	98	74
Michigan	46	41	−11	32	30	−6	83	86	36
Minnesota	14	15	7	6	7	17	87	95	59
Missouri	6	5	−17	5	4	−20	115	97	74
Nebraska	5	5	0	2	3	50	93	97	41
North Dakota	1	1	0	1	1	0	53	98	73
Ohio	26	26	0	19	18	−5	88	91	54
South Dakota	2	2	0	1	1	0	66	98	77
Wisconsin	9	8	−11	4	4	0	72	96	67
South	**366**	**357**	**−2**	**246**	**245**	**0**	**1,423**	**93**	**49**
Alabama	8	8	0	7	6	−14	67	93	59
Arkansas	6	5	−17	4	3	−25	75	97	78
Delaware	8	8	0	4	4	0	3	33	18
DC	8	9	13	4	5	25	1	0	0
Florida	91	88	−3	72	72	0	67	73	22
Georgia	32	28	−13	17	19	12	159	96	58
Kentucky	3	3	0	2	2	0	120	98	74
Louisiana	7	7	0	7	7	0	64	92	63
Maryland	34	34	0	20	21	5	24	67	24
Mississippi	2	2	0	1	1	0	82	99	91
North Carolina	31	36	16	18	21	17	100	90	53
Oklahoma	6	5	−17	4	3	−25	77	96	55
South Carolina	6	9	50	3	3	0	46	93	72
Tennessee	13	14	8	10	9	−10	95	96	63
Texas	67	62	−7	50	46	−8	254	93	35
Virginia	40	35	−13	21	21	0	134	92	78
West Virginia	4	4	0	2	2	0	55	98	90
West	**754**	**737**	**−2**	**289**	**284**	**−2**	**448**	**79**	**16**
Alaska	8	9	13	3	4	33	29	90	37
Arizona	19	17	−11	16	15	−6	15	67	14
California	522	512	−2	169	160	−5	58	45	5
Colorado	42	42	0	24	24	0	64	78	28
Hawaii	37	33	−11	5	6	20	5	40	4
Idaho	4	4	0	3	2	−33	44	95	69
Montana	8	8	0	6	7	17	56	89	46
Nevada	13	14	8	6	8	33	17	88	10
New Mexico	12	12	0	6	7	17	33	94	60
Oregon	29	29	0	15	15	0	36	78	31
Utah	7	9	29	3	4	33	29	97	62
Washington	50	45	−10	33	32	−3	39	64	13
Wyoming	3	3	0	0	0	0	23	100	100

*Population counts are for July 1, 2011.

SOURCE: Jones RK and Jerman J, Abortion incidence and service availability in the United States, 2011, *Perspectives on Sexual and Reproductive Health, 2014*, 46(1):3–14, https://www.guttmacher.org/pubs/journals/psrh.46e0414.pdf, Table 4 (accessed September 23, 2015)

or a 'war on women.' It struck me as common sense. I've been in a situation where a gurney couldn't fit through a door to help save someone who was dying, and it was horrendous. It's also common sense to have nurses on duty, a safe blood supply, and a hospital within 30 miles. Having a doctor with hospital admitting privileges, so there won't be an hours long wait in the emergency room, seems like a good idea too."

The editorial "Wendy Davis Is a Formidable Foe of Abortion Restrictions" (WashingtonPost.com, June 28, 2013) opines that TRAP laws "offer no real safety protections to women seeking abortions, and they would cost women access to important health-care services such as contraceptive care, cancer screenings and other routine tests." The editorial recounts Texas state senator Wendy Davis's (1963–; D) 13-hour filibuster of such legislation in Texas in June 2013. Davis's filibuster drew national attention to the issue of TRAP laws and was successful in preventing passage of a TRAP bill in Texas during that legislative session. Nevertheless, Governor Rick Perry (1950–; R) subsequently called a special session of the state legislature to pass the bill and signed it into law in July 2013.

Following the passage of the new law in Texas, the *Texas Tribune* reviewed state inspection records for 36 abortion clinics in Texas and found scant evidence of violations that would compromise patient safety. In "In State Records, Little Evidence to Back Stricter Abortion Law" (TexasTribune.org, September 14, 2013), Becca Aaronson reports that "most of the state's recent inspection findings point to administrative errors as opposed to medical ones." Aaronson goes on to describe how Daniel Grossman, a principal investigator of the Texas Public Policy Evaluation Project, found "no evidence that Texas' licensed abortion facilities had unsafe conditions" during another recent study. Rather, Grossman cited self-induced abortions (women trying to end their pregnancies themselves) as the biggest safety concern and opined, "This additional burden is just going to be too much for some women. I think it's very, very likely that abortion self-induction is going to go up, and that's definitely going to be bad for women's health."

Limiting local access to abortion often forces women to travel significant distances to receive the care they need. For example, Samantha Lachman notes in "Southwestern Ohio Won't Have an Abortion Clinic If John Kasich Gets His Way" (HuffingtonPost.com, September 30, 2015) that increased regulations in Ohio forced six of the state's 15 abortion clinics to close between 2013 and 2015. These closures forced many Ohio women seeking abortions to travel to neighboring states, notably Michigan. According to Crary, the number of nonresident women receiving abortions in Michigan nearly doubled in a single year, rising from 708 in 2013 to 1,318 in 2014. Meanwhile, Lachman explains that clinics in Dayton and Cincinnati, two of the largest cities in the state, were threatened with closure as of September 2015, pending legal appeals.

ACTIONS AGAINST ABORTION CLINICS

Violence and Disruption

The NAF (June 9, 2015, http://5aa1b2xfmfh2e2mk03kk8rsx.wpengine.netdna-cdn.com/wp-content/uploads/Stats_Table_2014.pdf) has tracked instances of violence and disruption against abortion providers since 1977. NAF members report incidents regularly and their reports are supplemented with information from the media, law enforcement agencies, and abortion provider organizations.

Over the years many abortion clinics throughout the nation have experienced violence. The most serious instances have been the murder and attempted murder of abortion doctors and clinic workers. The first clinic murder occurred in 1993, when Michael Griffin (1961–) killed physician David Gunn (1946–1993) in Pensacola, Florida. Four murders occurred the following year, and two occurred in 1998. In May 2009 the Wichita, Kansas, physician George Tiller (1941–2009), one of only a few U.S. physicians who performed late-term abortions, was shot to death while in church. Besides these murders, there were 17 attempted murders of abortion providers between 1977 and 2014, including a failed attempt on Tiller in 1993, when he was shot in both arms by the activist Rachelle Shannon (1956–).

Incidents of extreme violence against abortion providers, such as murder, bombing, arson, and acid attacks, declined after the 1990s. The NAF credits the arrest and prosecution of Eric Robert Rudolph (1967–), James Charles Kopp (1954–), and Clayton Waagner (1956–), three antiabortion extremists, as key factors in the decline of severe forms of violence against abortion providers.

Bombing and arson incidents reflect the downward trend in violence directed at abortion clinics. The NAF consolidates all incidents between 1977 and 1994; there were 29 bombings during that time frame. From 1995 onward the NAF reports 13 bombings. The highest total reported for a single year is six in 1997. Between 2000 and 2014 the NAF reports two bombings, in 2001 and 2011. A total of 182 arsons at abortion clinics were reported between 1977 and 2014, of which 124 occurred before 1995. The highest number of arsons at abortion providers in a single year occurred in 1995, when there were 14 incidents. Between 2000 and 2014 there were never more than five abortion-clinic arson incidents in a single year.

Although extreme forms of violence against abortion providers declined after 1999, other forms of violence continued. The NAF reports 795 violent incidents in 2001 and 761 in 2005, the two highest totals. There were 99 identified acts of violence in 2014. This was the third-lowest number reported between 1995 and 2014, ahead of 2010 (95 incidents) and 2012 (88 incidents).

Trespassing and vandalism are the most common of the incidents that the NAF tracks and reports as violence. Between 1977 and 2014 there were 2,560 trespassing incidents reported and 1,507 acts of vandalism. In 2014 there were 78 incidents of trespassing and 12 acts of vandalism against abortion providers, the two highest totals for any form of violent incident that year.

The NAF also tracks forms of nonviolent disruption aimed at abortion clinics. Picketing was by far the most common of these activities between 1977 and 2014. Picketing increased each year between 1995 and 2006, when a high of 13,505 incidents were reported. Picketing subsequently declined substantially, dropping to 5,402 incidents in 2014. There were also 367 incidents of hate mail and harassing calls reported that year.

Many abortion clinic protests have been under the direction of Operation Rescue/Operation Save America, an organization that seeks to shut down clinics completely but denies promoting the use of violence. Operation Save America believes the United States, in permitting abortion, has lost its morality. Demonstrators claim they are not only saving the lives of the unborn but also preventing the judgment of God from being passed on the United States for murder committed through abortion.

FREEDOM OF ACCESS TO CLINIC ENTRANCES ACT

The Freedom of Access to Clinic Entrances (FACE) Act was signed into law in May 1994 in response to escalating violence against abortion clinic workers and clients. FACE prohibits physical attacks on clinic employees and patient escorts, attempted arson of clinic facilities, blockades of clinic entrances by people or vehicles, and threats of bodily harm to providers or recipients of services.

FACE's opponents challenge its constitutionality on various grounds. Some charge that FACE violates the freedom of speech and religion protections under the First Amendment, whereas others claim that Congress lacks the power to pass such a law under the commerce clause (to regulate interstate commerce) of the U.S. Constitution. However, as of November 2015 the U.S. Supreme Court had affirmed the constitutionality of FACE by refusing to hear challenges to the law. (For additional information on court cases regarding FACE and abortion clinic violence, see Chapter 2.)

The Effectiveness of FACE

In "Freedom of Access to Clinic Entrances (FACE) Act" (December 12, 2007, http://prochoice.org/wp-content/uploads/face_act.pdf), Jennifer Blasdell and Kate Goss of the NAF state that "the FACE Act is an important tool in responding to clinic violence and in deterring possible offenders." Blockades are attempts to physically prevent people from entering facilities that provide abortions. According to the NAF (June 9, 2015, http://5aa1b2xfmfh2e2mk03kk8rsx.wpengine.netdna-cdn.com/wp-content/uploads/Stats_Table_2014.pdf), there were 23 blockade incidents in 2014. By contrast, in the 18 years prior to the passage of FACE the NAF indicates there were 634 blockades, an average of more than 35 per year. FACE also spurred enhanced clinic protection by law enforcement.

FACE and the Internet

In 1999 a federal jury in Portland, Oregon, unanimously ruled that it is illegal for pro-life activists to threaten abortion providers through Wild West–style "wanted posters" and the website "Nuremberg Files." The "Nuremberg Files" listed the names of abortion doctors accused of committing "crimes against humanity." The list included the doctors' addresses and other family information. Murdered doctors were listed with lines drawn through their names.

The jury ordered the defendants (American Coalition of Life Activists, Advocates for Life Ministries, and 12 individuals) to pay the plaintiffs (Planned Parenthood Federation of America, the Portland Feminist Women's Health Center, and four abortion doctors) more than $109 million in damages. All the defendants were found guilty of violating or conspiring to violate FACE and all but two of the defendants were guilty of violating or conspiring to violate the Racketeer Influenced and Corrupt Organizations Act.

In March 2001 a three-judge panel of the U.S. Court of Appeals for the Ninth Circuit unanimously reversed the jury verdict and the injunction against continued publishing of the materials. Then in May 2002 an 11-judge panel of the U.S. Court of Appeals for the Ninth Circuit upheld the 1999 trial verdict, stating that the "Nuremberg Files" website and the wanted posters amounted to threats and intimidation that violated FACE as well as other laws. Blasdell and Goss indicate the U.S. Supreme Court has refused to hear the appeal of this or any other federal cases regarding FACE, "in essence affirming the Act's constitutionality."

State FACE Acts

FACE is a federal law and as such is enforced by federal authorities. However, some states have enacted similar laws to protect abortion providers. According to the Guttmacher Institute, 13 states and the District of Columbia had laws in place as of September 2015 that protected access to clinics in various ways. (See Table 6.2.) Some states prohibit specific activities at abortion clinic facilities, such as blocking the entrance (obstruction), threatening clinic workers or patients, damaging property, making harassing telephone calls, creating excessive noise, releasing substances with noxious odors, or having access to weapons during demonstrations. Some states require a protected bubble zone around a person entering or leaving an abortion clinic.

TABLE 6.2

States that prohibit specific actions against abortion clinics and the actions they prohibit, September 2015

State	Specific prohibited actions					Protected "bubble zone"
	Obstruction	Threat	Damage	Telephone harassment	Other	
California[a]	X	X	X		Online harassment	
Colorado						8-ft. zone within 100 ft. of door
Dist. of Columbia	X	X		X	Noise, trespassing	
Kansas	X					
Maine	X			X	Noise, odor	
Maryland	X					
Massachusetts	X	X				25 feet if ordered by police
Michigan		X				
Minnesota	X					
Montana	X					8-ft. zone within 36 ft. of door
Nevada	X					
New Hampshire						[b]
New York	X	X	X			
North Carolina	X	X			Weapon	
Oregon	X		X			
Washington	X	X		X	Noise, trespassing	
Wisconsin					Trespassing	
Total	**12 + DC**	**6 + DC**	**3**	**2 + DC**	**5 + DC**	**3**

[a]Requires the collection and analysis of data by state attorney general's office and training for law enforcement officers by experts on clinic violence.
[b]New law was scheduled to take effect in 2014; currently not enforced.

SOURCE: "Protecting Access to Clinics," in *State Policies in Brief: Protecting Access to Clinics*, Guttmacher Institute, September 1, 2015, http://www.guttmacher.org/statecenter/spibs/spib_PAC.pdf (accessed September 22, 2015)

CHAPTER 7

MEDICAL AND ETHICAL QUESTIONS CONCERNING ABORTION

ABORTION AND HEALTH

Abortion was widely practiced during the colonial period and early years of the United States but became less common between the early 1800s and 1973, during which time—under certain conditions—it was considered a criminal offense. During the period when abortion was legally banned, women of means were generally able to find doctors willing to perform supposedly therapeutic (medically necessary) abortions that were allowed by law. Many poor women, however, died or developed medical complications from self-induced abortions or abortions performed by untrained people.

Since the 1973 U.S. Supreme Court ruling on the legality of abortion in *Roe v. Wade* (410 U.S. 113), numerous studies have been conducted on the emotional, physical, and psychological impact of abortion on women. For example, the Institute of Medicine of the National Academies concludes in *Legalized Abortion and the Public Health* (1975) that "evidence suggests that legislation and practices that permit women to obtain abortions in proper medical surroundings will lead to fewer deaths and a lower rate of medical complications than [will] restrictive legislation and practices."

There is evidence of the public health benefit of safe, legal abortion. Willard Cates Jr. observes in "Abortion Policy and Science: Can Controversy and Evidence Co-exist?" (*Journal of Public Health Policy*, vol. 33, no. 3, August 2012) that the legalization of abortion not only led women to seek legal abortion but also led women to seek abortions earlier in their pregnancies, which made the procedure safer by reducing the risk of complications. Cates concludes, "Over the past four decades in the United States, we have accumulated more data about the practice of legal abortion than any other surgical procedure. This evidence has documented the public health impact of increased access to safer abortion."

Complications and Deaths

The Guttmacher Institute notes in the fact sheet "Induced Abortion in the United States" (July 2014, http://www.guttmacher.org/pubs/fb_induced_abortion.html) that legal abortion in the United States is so safe that fewer than 0.05% of patients require hospitalization for complications from the procedure. In general, the earlier in pregnancy the abortion is performed, the safer and less complicated it is. First-trimester abortion is considered minor surgery. Along with the length of pregnancy, other factors that determine the likelihood of complications include the physician's skill and training, the use of general anesthesia, the abortion method used, and the woman's overall health.

Although they occur infrequently, surgical abortions are not without health risks. Table 7.1 describes some of the health risks that may be associated with surgical abortion.

Abortions provided by professionals in the United States are generally safe, but in other parts of the world abortion carries greater risks to the mother. Gilda Sedgh et al. indicate in "Induced Abortion: Incidence and Trends Worldwide from 1995 to 2008" (*Lancet*, vol. 379, no. 9816, February 2012), the most recent study on this topic as of November 2015, that worldwide the proportion of all abortions that were unsafe increased from 44% in 1995 to 49% in 2008. They further report that 13% of maternal deaths resulted from unsafe abortions. Most of the world's abortions and nearly all deaths and serious complications attributable to abortion occurred in developing countries where abortion is often clandestine. Some of the highest rates of unsafe abortion were in Africa (97%), Latin America (95%), south-central Asia (65%), and western Asia (60%). Sedgh et al. report that the use of medical abortion (using a combination of the drugs mifespristone and misoprostol, or misoprostol alone) had increased worldwide and was thought to have helped reduce the deaths and serious health consequences associated with unsafe surgical abortion.

TABLE 7.1

Possible health risks associated with abortion

Infection—Bacteria may enter the uterus and cause infection. Although antibiotics are generally effective against infection, in some instances another procedure may be necessary. The rate of infection is less than 1% for suction curettage, 1.5% for dilation and evacuation (D&E), and 5% for induction of labor.

Heavy bleeding—Some bleeding is expected after an abortion. However, heavy bleeding is uncommon and may be treated by repeat suction, medication, or in rare instances surgery. In about 1% of women, blood clots, which cause severe cramping occur and may be removed by a repeat suction curettage.

Incomplete abortion—Should the uterus not be completely emptied, there is risk of infection and bleeding and an additional procedure may be necessary. The rate of such complications is less than 1% after a D&E.

Perforation or tears—In an estimated 1% of cases, the opening of the uterus may be torn while medical instruments pass through it to enter the uterus. In about one in 500 cases, a medical instrument may pierce the wall of the uterus. Perforation may lead to infection and/or heavy bleeding. Surgical repair of the injury may be required.

Anesthesia-related complications—Even local anesthesia, which is generally used for abortion, is not entirely risk-free. Anesthesia-related complications occur in an estimated one per 5,000 abortions.

SOURCE: Created by Barbara Wexler for Gale, © 2015

Psychological Effects

In 1987 President Ronald Reagan (1911–2004) promised right-to-life groups that he would investigate the health effects of abortion, including psychological stress. Reagan instructed the U.S. surgeon general, C. Everett Koop (1916–2013), to prepare a report. Martin Tolchin notes in "Koop's Stand on Abortion's Effect Surprises Friends and Foes Alike" (NYTimes.com, January 11, 1989) that after meetings with experts and thorough reviews of many studies for almost a year and a half, Koop reported in a January 1989 letter to Reagan that his investigation of the psychological effects of abortion was inconclusive because of methodological problems with the scientific studies he examined. Koop observed that "the data do not support the premise that abortion does nor does not cause or contribute to psychological problems."

In response to Koop's inconclusive findings, Nancy E. Adler et al. reviewed the relevant literature with "the most rigorous research designs" and reported their findings in "Psychological Responses after Abortion" (*Science*, vol. 248, no. 4951, April 6, 1990). The researchers found "consistent findings on the psychological status of women who have had legal abortions under nonrestrictive circumstances.... Although there may be sensations of regret, sadness, or guilt, the weight of the evidence from scientific studies indicates that legal abortion of an unwanted pregnancy in the first trimester does not pose a psychological hazard for most women." Adler et al. noted that "the time of greatest distress is likely to be before the abortion. Severe negative reactions after abortions are rare and can best be understood in the framework of coping with a normal life stress."

Since Adler et al.'s review, the psychological impact of abortion has been extensively and repeatedly examined. In *Report of the APA Task Force on Mental Health and Abortion* (2008, http://www.apa.org/pi/women/programs/abortion/mental-health.pdf), the Task Force on Mental Health and Abortion (TFMHA) of the American Psychological Association analyzes and summarizes literature on mental health factors that are associated with abortion and its aftermath. The task force finds that many studies were flawed methodologically (as had Koop 19 years earlier), so it emphasizes that its conclusions are formulated based on the results of the most methodologically rigorous research.

In the executive summary of its 107-page report, the task force asserts, "The best scientific evidence published indicates that among adult women who have an *unplanned pregnancy* the relative risk of mental health problems is no greater if they have a single elective first-trimester abortion than if they deliver that pregnancy. The evidence regarding the relative mental health risks associated with multiple abortions is more equivocal. Positive associations observed between multiple abortions and poorer mental health may be linked to co-occurring risks that predispose a woman to both multiple unwanted pregnancies and mental health problems."

The task force also addresses women's psychological health after having an abortion later in pregnancy due to a finding of fetal abnormality. It indicates that "terminating a wanted pregnancy late in pregnancy due to fetal abnormality appears to be associated with negative psychological reactions equivalent to those experienced by women who miscarry a wanted pregnancy or who experience a stillbirth or death of a newborn, but less than those who deliver a child with life-threatening abnormalities." When compared with the results for women having unplanned pregnancies and single elective first-trimester abortions, these results suggest that "the differing patterns of psychological experiences observed among women who terminate an unplanned pregnancy versus those who terminate a planned and wanted pregnancy highlight the importance of taking pregnancy intendedness and wantedness into account when seeking to understand psychological reactions to abortion."

The task force concludes:

> None of the literature reviewed adequately addressed the prevalence of mental health problems among women in the United States who have had an abortion. In general, however, the prevalence of mental health problems observed among women in the United States who had a single, legal, first-trimester abortion for nontherapeutic reasons was consistent with normative [normal] rates of comparable mental health problems in the general population of women in the United States.
>
> Nonetheless, it is clear that some women do experience sadness, grief, and feelings of loss following termination of a pregnancy, and some experience clinically significant disorders, including depression and anxiety. However, the TFMHA reviewed no evidence sufficient

to support the claim that an observed association between abortion history and mental health was caused by the abortion per se, as opposed to other factors.

As of November 2015, the TFMHA's report was still considered to be the most definitive work on this topic due to the scope of its literature review. In 2009, however, a study by Priscilla K. Coleman et al. found different results and ignited controversy. In "Induced Abortion and Anxiety, Mood, and Substance Abuse Disorders: Isolating the Effects of Abortion in the National Comorbidity Survey" (*Journal of Psychiatric Research*, vol. 43, no. 8, May 2009), they suggested a link between abortion and long-term mental health problems such as panic attacks, depression, substance abuse, and post-traumatic stress disorder. Alexandra Sifferlin reports in "Study Linking Abortion to Mental Health Problems Is Flawed" (Healthland.Time.com, March 8, 2012) that seven states used the 2009 study to support laws requiring women seeking abortion to receive counseling about mental health risks. She also reports, however, that by 2012 Coleman's research had been strongly criticized by the scientific community as unsound. According to Sifferlin, the *Journal of Psychiatric Research*, which published Coleman et al.'s research, later issued a commentary stating that Coleman et al.'s work "does not support assertions that abortions led to psychopathology," a charge echoed by many others. Among their complaints was that Coleman et al. failed to distinguish between women who developed mental illnesses before and after their abortions.

In "Induced First-Trimester Abortion and Risk of Mental Disorder" (*New England Journal of Medicine*, vol. 364, no. 4, January 27, 2011), Trine Munk-Olsen et al. supported the conclusion that there is no increased risk of mental disorder after a first-trimester abortion. Reviewing the records of thousands of women who had first-trimester abortions between 1995 and 2007, the researchers found similar rates of "first psychiatric contact" before and after abortion and no increased risk of mental disorders after a first-trimester abortion.

Priscilla K. Coleman generated further controversy when she published "Abortion and Mental Health: Quantitative Synthesis and Analysis of Research Published 1995–2009" (*British Journal of Psychiatry*, vol. 199, no. 3, September 2011). In this article Coleman reviewed the published literature to measure the association between abortion and indicators of poor mental health. Unlike the review conducted by Munk-Olsen et al., Coleman found increased risk of mental health problems after abortion. Coleman reported that the extent to which abortion affected mental health varied depending on the comparison group—women who had not had an abortion, women who gave birth after an intended pregnancy, or women who gave birth after an unintended pregnancy—and the type of mental health problem examined (substance abuse, anxiety, depression, or suicide attempts). Coleman stated that "the strongest effects were observed when women who had had an abortion were compared with women who had carried to term and when the outcomes measured related to substance use and suicidal behavior." Like Coleman's earlier research, this 2011 article prompted harsh criticism from many physicians and researchers, who said Coleman's research methods were not only biased and misleading but also seriously flawed. In "Abortion and Mental Health: Guidelines for Proper Scientific Conduct Ignored" (*British Journal of Psychiatry*, vol. 200, no. 1, January 2012), Louise M. Howard et al. expressed the opinions of many researchers, explaining, "Most importantly for readers of this [Coleman's] study to know, is the erroneous conclusions drawn by the author.... Abortion and mental health is a politicised issue—it is therefore essential that research in this field is methodologically robust."

ETHICAL QUESTIONS RELATED TO ABORTION

Scientific advances often raise ethical questions. Ethics is a branch of philosophy that is concerned with evaluating human action. Some distinguish ethics, what is considered right or wrong behavior based on reason, from morals, what is considered right or wrong behavior based on social custom.

Embryonic Stem Cell Research

A fetus is a developing animal (in this case human) from eight weeks after conception to birth. From conception through eight weeks, the developing organism is called a pre-embryo and then an embryo. The embryo and fetus are rich sources of cells that differentiate the variety of cell types that make up the body. These cells are called stem cells. Multipotent stem cells can give rise to only certain types of cells. Pluripotent stem cells can develop into any of the more than 200 types of cells in the body.

To develop human embryonic stem cell lines for research, cells are harvested from the inner cell mass of a week-old embryo. Cultured properly, the cells can grow and divide indefinitely. A stem cell line is a mass of cells descended from an original stem cell. It shares the original cell's genetic characteristics. Groups of cells can be separated from the cell line and distributed to researchers.

Stem cells are important for medical research because they can be used to make needed cells for medical treatment. For example, pluripotent stem cells may be used as a renewable source of replacement cells and tissues to treat diseases, conditions, and disabilities such as Parkinson's disease (a disorder that affects nerve cells in the part of the brain that controls muscle movement), spinal cord injuries, burns, multiple sclerosis (a chronic progressive disorder in which the immune system destroys the myelin sheath that protects nerve fibers), heart disease, diabetes, and arthritis.

Fetal research and the use of fetal and embryonic tissue in research is not a recent medical development. It dates back to the 1930s and was responsible, during the mid-20th century, for the development of vaccines against poliomyelitis (a highly infectious viral disease that, in its severe form, affects the central nervous system and can lead to paralysis) and rubella (German measles), as well as the preventive treatment of Rh incompatibility (a condition in which a mismatch between the blood of a pregnant woman and that of her fetus can harm the fetus).

POLITICS, ETHICS, AND THE LINK TO ABORTION. Embryonic stem cells used in research are harvested during the earliest stage of embryonic development. Most are derived from embryos that are a by-product of in vitro fertilization (IVF) treatments, in which eggs are fertilized outside of the body and then implanted in a woman's uterus. The IVF process often generates more embryos than are necessary to impregnate a woman, and some of these excess embryos have been donated for research. Thus, embryonic stem cells are not derived from embryos conceived in a woman's body, nor are they embryos destined to gestate. Nonetheless, because many people regard human embryos as human beings, or at least as potential human beings, they consider their destruction, or even using techniques to obtain stem cells that might imperil their future viability, as immoral or unethical.

Using human embryos for stem cell research is both a political and ethical issue that evokes strong emotions. The debate centers on the most basic conflict between pro-life and pro-choice positions: the fundamental disagreement about when life begins. Most people who are "pro-life" (antiabortion) believe that life begins at conception, when the sperm and egg unite. Pro-life groups oppose embryonic stem cell research because they believe it destroys human life and encourages abortion. Most people who are "pro-choice" (supportive of a woman's right to choose abortion) believe that the embryo is living tissue, but not a person. The determination of when a fetus becomes a person varies among pro-choice advocates, from when the fetus is capable of living on its own until birth. Pro-choice advocates generally support stem cell research. They argue that the embryos used in this type of research would be destroyed anyway and that the potential benefits of this research, which may include cures for debilitating diseases, justifies its pursuit.

The controversy about the use of aborted fetuses for medical research erupted after the 1973 *Roe v. Wade* decision legalized abortion. Shortly after this decision was announced, the U.S. Department of Health, Education, and Welfare (HEW; now the U.S. Department of Health and Human Services) placed a moratorium (hold) on medical research using living embryos. The following year Congress added its own moratorium on all federally funded embryonic research, including research on infertility, prenatal diagnosis (determination of diseases or conditions while the fetus is still within the uterus), and IVF. The purpose of both moratoriums was to provide time to study the issue of the creation and use of human embryos and to develop national guidelines.

HISTORICAL BACKGROUND. In 1974 Congress established the National Commission for the Protection of Human Subjects of Biomedical and Behavioral Research, and one of the topics the commission addressed was fetal and embryonic tissue. The commission developed ethical guidelines for research using fetal and embryonic tissue, and the HEW issued regulations based on the commission's recommendations. The commission then recommended the establishment of a national Ethics Advisory Board (EAB) to review research protocols for compliance with the ethical guidelines.

In 1975, with research regulations and the EAB in place, the moratorium was lifted on basic research that had no direct medical application. In 1979 the EAB recommended federal funding for research on IVF and embryo transfer up to 14 days, but the HEW rejected this recommendation. The following year funding for the EAB expired and was never reinstituted. Thereafter, no national board existed to review and recommend embryo research protocols.

In October 1987 the National Institutes of Health (NIH), which is part of the U.S. Department of Health and Human Services (HHS), received a request to fund a research study in which fetal tissue would be transplanted into the brains of patients suffering from Parkinson's disease. The HHS denied the request and in March 1988 imposed a moratorium on the use of federal funds for fetal tissue transplantation research until an expert panel could study the ethical implications of such research. In November 1989, despite the panel's finding that the use of fetal tissue in research is acceptable public policy, the HHS secretary Louis W. Sullivan (1933–) continued the moratorium. Adam Clymer reports in "Bush Vetoes Bill to Lift Ban on Money for Fetal Research" (NYTimes.com, June 24, 1992) that in 1992 President George H. W. Bush (1924–) vetoed Congress's efforts to restore public funding of fetal tissue research, fearing "its potential for promoting and legitimizing abortion."

When President Bill Clinton (1946–) took office in 1993, one of his first actions was to lift the ban on federally funded research using fetal tissue from induced abortion. That same year the NIH Revitalization Act legalized fetal tissue transplantation research. The law provided ethical guidelines that ensured informed consent, forbade payment for fetal tissue, and forbade altering the timing or method of abortion for the sake of research. In 1995, however, Congress banned the use of federal funds for research on embryos. In January 1999 the HHS ruled that stem cell research does not fall within the congressional ban on human embryo research. According to the HHS's Office of the General Counsel, because stem cells alone are not capable of developing into a human, they cannot be considered embryos.

The Clinton administration created rules for funding stem cell research, but they were never implemented. In 2000 the NIH announced that it would accept applications for stem cell projects that involved cells taken from frozen embryos developed in fertility treatments that were no longer needed. Shortly after taking office, however, President George W. Bush (1946–) put that plan on hold and began a review of the policy.

In August 2001 Bush announced his decision to allow federal funding for experiments involving stem cells already derived from embryos, but he would not allow federal funding for research that involved the destruction of more embryos. His decision did not affect private-sector embryonic stem cell research. At the same time that he announced his policy on embryonic stem cell research, Bush created the President's Council on Bioethics to monitor this research and recommend guidelines and regulations. The council included scientists, doctors, ethicists, lawyers, and theologians.

Despite scientists' arguments that additional embryonic stem cells, and entirely new lines of embryonic stem cells, were needed for research, the Bush administration instead pushed forward with alternative sources. In December 2005 Bush signed the Stem Cell Therapeutic and Research Act into law. This act provided for the collection and maintenance of human umbilical cord blood stem cells not only for the treatment of patients but also for research. The umbilical cord is made up of arteries and veins that shuttle blood to and from the developing fetus and the placenta of the mother. The placenta develops in the lining of the uterus and is where blood gases, nutrients, and wastes are exchanged. Cord blood is a source of stem cells for the treatment of a variety of conditions, diseases, and disorders and can be used for bone marrow transplantation.

The next year brought the passage of a bill that responded to fears that cells or tissues could be removed from fetuses that had been conceived solely for use in medical therapies or for research. Congress passed and Bush signed into law the Fetus Farming Prohibition Act of 2006, which prohibits the use of tissue from fetuses conceived for use in fetal tissue transplants or stem cell therapy.

In an effort to extend federal financing of embryonic stem cell research beyond previous limits set by President Bush, the U.S. Senate and the U.S. House of Representatives passed the Stem Cell Research Enhancement Act of 2007. The act would have given researchers access—with donor consent—to thousands of embryos that would otherwise be frozen or discarded by fertility clinics. However, the bill was vetoed by Bush in June 2007.

When President Barack Obama (1961–) took office in January 2009, he began undoing many Bush-era policies. He signed an executive order that lifted the limitations on embryonic stem cell research and gave the NIH 120 days to develop new guidelines for funding embryonic stem cell research. In August 2010, after the guidelines had been developed and funding proceeded, Judge Royce C. Lamberth (1943–) of the U.S. District Court for the District of Columbia placed an injunction (temporarily stopped) on federal funding of embryonic stem cell research in response to a lawsuit filed against the NIH.

The Christian Medical Association and Nightlight Christian Adoptions had sued the NIH because, they believed, the NIH guidelines violated the Dickey-Wicker Amendment. This amendment had been included in federal spending bills since 1996 and stated that federal funds could not be used for research in which a human embryo is destroyed. It carried the understanding that funds could be used for embryonic stem cell research projects that did not destroy embryos but studied the lines themselves. In September 2010 an appeals court lifted the injunction while it heard further arguments on the case. In April 2011 the appeals court ruled 2–1 that the NIH guidelines correctly interpreted the Dickey-Wicker Amendment and overturned the injunction. The case was returned to Judge Lamberth for a summary judgment (a final ruling). Bound by the reasoning of the appeals court, Judge Lamberth dismissed the case in July 2011.

In 2015 Americans generally believed that medical research using embryonic stem cells was morally acceptable. According to the Gallup Organization, in *Stem Cell Research* (2015, http://www.gallup.com/poll/21676/stem-cell-research.aspx), 64% of Americans surveyed held this opinion in 2015.

Genetic Testing

GENDER SELECTION. Advances in prenatal (pre-birth) testing have raised questions about the possible reasons for obtaining an abortion. For example, ultrasonography (using sound waves to create images of a fetus) and amniocentesis (removal of a small amount of amniotic fluid to gain information about a fetus) can be used to determine the sex of a fetus.

In some countries, such as China, India, and South Korea, many parents prefer boys and sometimes use abortion to prevent the birth of girls. Between 1979 and 2015 China implemented a one-child policy, which resulted in many Chinese couples preferring to have their one child be male rather than female. In "Distortions of Sex Ratios at Birth in the United States; Evidence for Prenatal Gender Selection" (*Prenatal Diagnosis*, vol. 31, no. 6, June 2011), James F. Egan et al. explain that the cultural preference for males in China and South Korea, and to a certain degree in India, is based in Confucianism (a Chinese ethical and philosophical system). The system mandates patrilineal inheritance, which means that family relationships are traced through the male line. Also, sons take care of the elders, whereas daughters leave the family when they marry. China's one-child policy was replaced by a two-child policy in October 2015.

A major consequence of this parental preference is that sex ratios at birth are skewed; that is, the ratio of males to females no longer approximates the worldwide average of 103 to 107 males born for every 100 females. Wei Xing Zhu, Li Lu, and Therese Hesketh note in "China's Excess Males, Sex Selective Abortion, and One Child Policy: Analysis of Data from 2005 National Intercensus Survey" (*British Medical Journal*, vol. 338, April 18, 2009) that China's sex ratio was 124 males to 100 females for births from 2000 to 2004 and then 119 males to 100 females for births in 2005. According to Prabhat Jha et al., in "Trends in Selective Abortions of Girls in India: Analysis of Nationally Representative Birth Histories from 1990 to 2005 and Census Data from 1991 to 2011" (*Lancet*, vol. 377, no. 9781, June 4, 2011), the selective abortion of girls in India has increased substantially and occurs primarily in pregnancies after a firstborn girl.

In "The Mystery of Missing Female Children in the Caucasus: An Analysis of Sex Ratios by Birth Order" (*International Perspectives on Sexual & Reproductive Health*, vol. 39, no. 2, June 2013), Marc Michael et al. note that sex ratios in some post-Soviet states—Armenia (117 boys per 100 girls), Azerbaijan (116 boys per 100 girls), and Georgia (121 boys per 100 girls)—suggest a rise in sex-selective abortions. The number of girls born in these countries in 2010 was 10% lower than the naturally expected rate.

In the United States, a technology called sperm sorting has become popular with couples that want to choose the sex of a child. The techniques used in sperm sorting were developed by the Genetics and IVF Institute, a fertility clinic in Virginia. The original purpose of the technology was to increase the chances of couples, in which the mother is a carrier of one or more of 350 X-linked recessive genetic disorders, to produce daughters. If a woman with one of these X-linked genes has a son, he will suffer from the genetic disorder. If a daughter is born to a woman with one of these genes, the daughter will carry the gene but not be affected by it. Then, with provisional approval from the U.S. Food and Drug Administration (FDA), in 2008 the Genetics and IVF Institute began to offer sperm sorting for "family balancing." That is, it used sperm sorting to try and produce pregnancies that would result in boys for families that had girls, and vice versa. However, Marcy Darnovsky of the Center for Genetics and Society indicates in "FDA Questions Sex Selection for 'Family Balancing'" (BiopoliticalTimes.org, April 11, 2011) that in 2011 the FDA notified the Genetics and IVF Institute that it could no longer enroll subjects in clinical trials for family balancing. Overall, more than 1,341 babies were born during the clinical trial of the sex selection technology.

Despite ethical concerns related to the technology, sex selection remains legal in the United States, where it has become a multimillion-dollar industry. According to Jasmeet Sidhu, in "How to Buy a Daughter" (Slate .com, September 14, 2012), approximately 4,000 to 6,000 gender selection procedures are performed every year. At costs approaching $18,000 per procedure, sex selection generates more than $100 million annually.

Another technology for gender selection is the initiation of IVF with preimplantation genetic diagnosis (PGD). With this technique, eggs are fertilized outside of the mother's body and the gender of each embryo is determined. Only those embryos with the desired sex are used, and the others are discarded.

In response to these types of sex selection, the Ethics Committee of the American Society for Reproductive Medicine (ASRM) issued three reports over several years starting in 1994 and concluded that using medical technologies to prevent children being born with genetic disorders is acceptable but that using these technologies for nonmedical reasons creates a variety of ethical questions.

In June 2015 the ASRM issued "Use of Reproductive Technology for Sex Selection for Nonmedical Reasons" (*Fertility and Sterility*, vol. 103, no. 6). Acknowledging "reasoned differences of opinion" on the issue, the committee states that:

> the ASRM Ethics Committee has not reached consensus on whether it is ethical for providers to offer ART for sex selection for nonmedical purposes. Arguments regarding patient autonomy and reproductive liberty have been offered in support of the practice. Risks and burdens of the procedure, gender bias, sex stereotyping and nonacceptance of offspring, efforts to guard against coercion, and issues of justice all raise concerns about the practice. Practitioners must take care to ensure that parents are fully informed about the risks and burdens of the procedure and that they are not being coerced to undergo it. Because the practice is so controversial, clinics are encouraged to draft and make available written policies setting forth whether and under what circumstances nonmedical sex selection will be available. When nonmedical sex selection is offered in clinical practice, clinic employees with objection to the technique must be permitted to absent themselves from its provision.

By 2009 an at-home test to determine the sex of a fetus eight weeks into a pregnancy had become available. According IntelliGender (2015, http://www.intelligender .com/gender-prediction-test-independent-studies), independent studies find the test is nearly 90% accurate.

The test works somewhat like a home pregnancy test: a pregnant woman mixes her urine with the test's chemicals, and a color change signals the sex of the fetus. IntelliGender states that the test is not a diagnostic procedure and should be used only for fun, even though the company's promotional materials tout the test's accuracy.

SCREENING FOR BIRTH DEFECTS AND HEREDITARY DISEASES. Prenatal testing through amniocentesis, ultrasound, or other methods may reveal severe defects in the fetus, such as anencephaly (absence of most of the brain), spina bifida (incomplete development of the spinal cord), and Down syndrome (a genetic disorder that usually includes mental retardation). In addition, genetic testing allows some parents to determine if the child they are carrying has the genes for certain diseases, such as Huntington's disease (an inherited disease that affects the functioning of both the body and brain), Tay-Sachs disease (a disease that is most common among people of Jewish descent and results in neurological disorders and death in childhood), cystic fibrosis (an inherited disease of the mucous glands that produces problems associated with the lungs and pancreas), or the genes BRCA1 and BRCA2, which increase a female's risk of breast and ovarian cancer. Women who discover that the fetuses they are carrying are seriously impaired or will develop debilitating diseases may face an agonizing decision about whether to have an abortion.

Some people have no problem with genetic testing if it makes possible the use of preventive therapy for a predisposed condition, or an acceptance of and preparation for a child who may be born with abnormalities that cannot be treated. However, because most genetic tests are for untreatable disorders, some fear that the screening techniques may be used for eugenic (selective breeding) purposes, preventing the birth of children affected by hereditary defects.

Many people with disabilities take issue with those who advocate abortions in cases of fetal defects and potential diseases. They argue that had late-term abortions been available to their mothers during pregnancy, they might have never had the chance for life. Some observers are also wary that the genetic information obtained from prenatal testing might eventually result in preventing the birth of children with certain traits or behavioral tendencies.

Infertility Treatments

MULTIPLE BIRTHS. Many women who are unable to conceive have turned to assisted reproductive technology (ART). There are several methods of ART, including IVF, gamete intrafallopian transfer, and zygote intrafallopian transfer. IVF is the most widely used method to help women achieve pregnancy. IVF is performed by removing the woman's eggs, fertilizing them in the laboratory, and transferring the resulting embryo or embryos back into her uterus. According to the Centers for Disease Control and Prevention, the ASRM, and the Society for Assisted Reproductive Technology, in *2013 Assisted Reproductive Technology National Summary Report* (October 2015, http://www.cdc.gov/art/pdf/2013-report/art_2013_national_summary_report.pdf), there were 93,787 ART transfer procedures that used fresh nondonor eggs or embryos in 2013. Of these, 33,425 (35.5%) resulted in a pregnancy and 27,406 (29.2%) resulted in a live-birth delivery.

The pregnancy success rate in ART decreases as the woman's age increases, as shown in Table 7.2. Therefore, to increase the chances of success in older women, doctors are likely to implant more embryos. In a number of cases, many well-publicized triplet and higher multiple births have resulted. Table 7.2 shows the outcomes of ART using each technology.

The birth of the McCaughey septuplets in 1997 in Iowa, the Chukwu octuplets in 1998 in Texas, and the Suleman octuplets in 2009 in California brought criticism from many medical professionals who thought the parents and their fertility doctors had acted irresponsibly. Some believed the mothers had taken a tremendous risk with their health and that of their children. Siblings in multiple births are at a high risk for prematurity, low birth weight, long-term mental and physical disabilities, and death.

Ethicists ask if it is justifiable to abort some fetuses when a woman is pregnant with multiples to reduce the risks to the remaining ones. This process is called selective reduction. Some people believe the parents of multiples should employ selective reduction. Those who are against selective reduction warn that the acceptance of abortion in cases of multiple births will eventually make it too easy in the future to "selectively reduce" other members of society, such as older adults or people with disabilities.

The rate of triplet and higher multiple births increased dramatically after 1980. (See Table 7.3.) In "Births: Final Data for 2013" (*National Vital Statistics Reports*, vol. 64, no. 1, January 15, 2015), Joyce A. Martin et al. of the CDC attribute this upsurge to two primary causes:

- The birth rate of women over the age of 30 years has increased significantly since the 1980s and women aged 30 years and older are more likely than women under the age of 30 years to conceive multiples spontaneously.
- The use of fertility-enhancing therapies, which increase the probability of multiple births, has increased.

However, the rate of triplet and higher multiple births declined 38.2% between 1998 and 2013. (See Table 7.3.) This decline is thought be the result of a drop in the number of embryos that were implanted during ART procedures, as

TABLE 7.2

Assisted reproductive technology national summary of cycle profiles, pregnancy success rates, and clinic services, 2013

2013 Art cycle profile

Type of ART and procedural factors[a]				Patient diagnosis[b]					
IVF	>99%	With ICSI	69%	Tubal factor	13%	Uterine factor	5%	Multiple factors:	
Unstimulated	1%	Used PGD	6%	Ovulatory dysfunction	14%	Male factor	33%	Female factors only	12%
Used gestational carrier	<1%			Diminished ovarian reserve	32%	Other factor	45%	Female & male factors	17%
				Endometriosis	9%	Unknown factor	13%		

2013 Art success rates[c] **Total number of cycles[d] : 190,773 (includes 2,655 cycle[s] using frozen eggs)**

	Age of woman					
Type of cycle	**<35**	**35–37**	**38–40**	**41–42**	**43–44**	**>44**
Fresh embryos from nondonor eggs						
Number of cycles	40,083	19,853	18,061	9,588	4,823	1,379
Percentage of cancellations (%)	5.6	8.9	12.3	15.6	18.3	23.9
Average number of embryos transferred	1.8	2.0	2.3	2.7	2.9	2.5
Percentage of embryos transferred resulting in implantation (%)	39.9	30.8	20.0	10.7	5.0	2.3
Percentage of elective single embryo transfers (eSET) (%)	21.4	12.6	5.1	1.8	0.6	0.8
Outcomes per cycle						
Percentage of cycles resulting in term, normal weight & singleton live births[e] (%)	23.8	19.6	13.7	7.8	3.9	1.2
Percentage of cycles resulting in singleton live births (%)	28.2	23.2	16.7	9.6	4.8	1.4
Percentage of cycles resulting in twin live births (%)	11.3	8.0	4.2	1.5	0.4	0.2
Percentage of cycles resulting in live births (%)	39.9	31.6	21.1	11.1	5.2	1.6
Percentage of cycles resulting in pregnancies (%)	45.9	38.0	28.6	18.8	10.2	3.8
Outcomes per transfer						
Number of transfers	33,750	15,941	13,456	6,588	3,086	750
Percentage of transfers resulting in term, normal weight & singleton live births[e] (%)	28.2	24.4	18.4	11.4	6.0	2.1
Percentage of transfers resulting in singleton live births (%)	33.5	28.9	22.5	14.0	7.6	2.5
Percentage of transfers resulting in twin live births (%)	13.4	10.0	5.6	2.2	0.6	0.4
Percentage of transfers resulting in live births (%)	47.4	39.3	28.4	16.2	8.2	2.9
Percentage of transfers resulting in pregnancies (%)	54.5	47.3	38.3	27.3	15.9	6.9
Frozen embryos from nondonor eggs						
Number of cycles	21,627	11,140	8,354	3,344	1,503	811
Number of transfers	20,423	10,374	7,713	3,005	1,329	732
Estimated average number of transfers per retrieval	1.3	1.1	0.8	0.6	0.4	0.4
Average number of embryos transferred	1.7	1.7	1.7	1.8	2.0	1.9
Percentage of embryos transferred resulting in implantation (%)	39.6	35.6	31.5	25.4	18.6	13.1
Percentage of transfers resulting in term, normal weight & singleton live births[e] (%)	28.6	27.2	24.4	21.2	15.8	8.7
Percentage of transfers resulting in singleton live births (%)	33.9	32.7	29.6	26.0	20.9	11.5
Percentage of transfers resulting in twin live births (%)	9.8	7.1	5.9	4.1	2.5	2.7
Percentage of transfers resulting in live births (%)	44.1	40.1	35.7	30.3	23.5	14.2
Percentage of transfers resulting in pregnancies (%)	54.2	50.0	46.9	42.1	34.2	23.4
Number of egg/embryo banking cycles	**7,350**	**5,437**	**6,493**	**3,918**	**2,578**	**1,788**

Donor eggs	**Fresh embryos[f]**	**Frozen embryos[f]**
Number of cycles	9,718	10,270
Number of transfers	8,597	9,499
Average number of embryos transferred	1.7	1.7
Percentage of embryos transferred resulting in implantation (%)	50.9	34.9
Percentage of transfers resulting in term, normal weight & singleton live births[e] (%)	29.8	24.2
Percentage of transfers resulting in singleton live births (%)	37.5	32.0
Percentage of transfers resulting in twin live births (%)	18.0	7.9
Percentage of transfers resulting in live births (%)	55.9	40.2
Percentage of transfers resulting in pregnancies (%)	66.0	50.1

Current services & profile **Number of reporting clinics: 467**

Percentage of clinics that allow cycles involving:				Clinic profile:	
Donor eggs	92%	Gestational carriers	86%	SART member	82%
Donor embryos	69%	Embryo cryopreservation	>99%	Verified lab accreditation	
Single women	96%			Yes	93%
				No	7%
				Pending	<1%

recommended in published guidelines written by the ASRM during the late 1990s (and later updated). The guidelines were developed in response to the rise in triplet and high multiple births and resulting poor outcomes.

TABLE 7.2

Assisted reproductive technology national summary of cycle profiles, pregnancy success rates, and clinic services, 2013 [CONTINUED]

ART = Assisted reproductive technology.
ICSI = Intracytoplasmic sperm injection.
PGD = Pre-implantation genetic diagnosis.
SART = Society for Assisted Reproductive Technology.
[a]Reflects features of fresh nondonor cycles. If IVF is <100%, the remaining cycles are GIFT, ZIFT, or a combination of these procedures with IVF.
[b]Total patient diagnosis percentages may be greater than 100% because more than one diagnosis can be reported for each ART cycle.
[c]Multiple-infant births (e.g., twins) with at least one live infant are counted as one live birth.
[d]Total cycle number includes those using frozen eggs. It excludes 67 cycle(s) evaluating new procedures. Both cycle types are excluded from ART success rates.
[e]In this report, births are defined as term if at least 37 full weeks gestation and normal birth weight if at least 2,500 grams (approximately 5 pounds, 8 ounces).
[f]All ages are reported together because previous data show that patient age does not materially affect success with donor eggs.

SOURCE: "2013 National Summary," in *2013 Assisted Reproductive Technology Fertility Clinics Success Rates Report*, Centers for Disease Control and Prevention, American Society for Reproductive Medicine, Society for Assisted Reproductive Technology, August 2015, http://www.cdc.gov/art/pdf/2013-report/art-2013-fertility-clinic-report.pdf (accessed September 22, 2015)

FROZEN EMBRYO TRANSFERS. Couples who undergo IVF treatments will sometimes produce additional fertilized embryos, which can subsequently be frozen and stored. This process is known as cryopreservation or frozen embryo transfer. These frozen embryos can be used in cases where an earlier implantation fails or if a couple decides to have additional children in the future. However, in instances where couples separate or divorce, the question of what to do with their frozen embryos can become a contentious legal issue, particularly if one member of the couple decides that he or she wants the embryos destroyed.

One high-profile case occurred in April 2015, when stories emerged that the actress Sofia Vergara (1972–) was being sued by her former fiancé, the businessman Nicholas M. Loeb (1975–), over the fate of embryos the couple had frozen in 2013. Jaqueline Hurtado and Michael Martinez report in "Sofia Vergara Reportedly Sued by Ex-fiance over Their Frozen Embryos" (CNN.com, April 21, 2015) that Loeb filed suit to prevent the embryos from being destroyed, in part because of his personal conviction that human life begins at conception. Indeed, the case raised a number of ethical issues concerning the origins of human life. "When does life begin? Are these embryos alive?" California-based attorney Vance Owen told Hurtado and Martinez. "To Catholics, for example, conception marks the beginning of life. To abortion advocates, the child has to be in a more advanced state, perhaps the third trimester, so it's a very interesting time to be discussing these life issues." In "After a Divorce, What Happens to a Couple's Frozen Embryos?" (NPR.org, August 22, 2015), Jennifer Ludden notes that these legal cases have forced courts to consider unprecedented legal situations, as judges must determine whether or not frozen embryos represent property or children.

"Morning-After" Pills

After a man and woman have sexual intercourse it typically takes several days for a man's sperm to reach an egg and for that egg to implant in the woman's uterus, thereby establishing a pregnancy. Medications have been developed that, if taken during this period, may prevent the pregnancy from occurring. These medications have come to be known as morning-after pills, Plan B contraception, or emergency contraception. Because they prevent pregnancy from occurring, as opposed to ending a pregnancy that has already happened, their use does not bring about an abortion. Some pro-life advocates nevertheless object to their use, however, because they object to interfering with the process that leads to pregnancy or because they disagree with the medical definition of when pregnancy begins.

Michael D. Shear and Pam Belluck indicate in "U.S. Drops Bid to Limit Sales of Morning-After Pill" (NYTimes.com, June 10, 2013) that the drug Plan B One-Step first became available in the United States in 1999 and quickly became one of the most popular forms of the morning-after pill. Over the years, as it demonstrated its safety and effectiveness, pressure mounted for the drug to be made available over the counter (OTC; without a prescription). In 2006 the FDA approved it for OTC sale to women aged 18 years and older. Lawsuits and other pressure continued, and in 2009 the age limit was dropped to 17 years. In December 2011 the FDA appeared ready to lift the age limit entirely but was blocked by Kathleen Sebelius (1948–), head of the FDA's parent agency, HHS. President Obama supported the decision because, as Shear and Belluck put it, "as the father of two young girls, the idea of making the drug available to them without a prescription made him uncomfortable."

Sebelius's decision was challenged in court, and Judge Edward R. Korman (1942–) of the U.S. District Court of the Eastern District of New York ordered that the age limits on OTC sales be lifted. Faced with continued criticism from the Planned Parenthood Federation of America and like-minded groups over the age limits, and with uncertain prospects on appeal, Shear and Belluck report that the Obama administration announced on June

TABLE 7.3

Twin, triplet, and higher-order multiple births, by race and Hispanic origin, 1980–2013

Year and race and Hispanic origin of mother	Total births	Twin births	Triplet and higher-order births	Multiple birth rate[a]	Twin birth rate[b]	Triplet and higher-order birth rate[c]
All races[d]						
2013	3,932,181	132,324	4,700	34.8	33.7	119.5
2012	3,952,841	131,024	4,919	34.4	33.1	124.4
2011	3,953,590	131,269	5,417	34.6	33.2	137.0
2010	3,999,386	132,562	5,503	34.5	33.1	137.6
2009	4,130,665	137,217	6,340	34.8	33.2	153.5
2008	4,247,694	138,660	6,268	34.1	32.6	147.6
2007	4,316,233	138,961	6,427	33.7	32.2	148.9
2006	4,265,555	137,085	6,540	33.7	32.1	153.3
2005	4,138,349	133,122	6,694	33.8	32.2	161.8
2004	4,112,052	132,219	7,275	33.9	32.2	176.9
2003	4,089,950	128,665	7,663	33.3	31.5	187.4
2002	4,021,726	125,134	7,401	33.0	31.1	184.0
2001	4,025,933	121,246	7,471	32.0	30.1	185.6
2000	4,058,814	118,916	7,325	31.1	29.3	180.5
1999	3,959,417	114,307	7,321	30.7	28.9	184.9
1998	3,941,553	110,670	7,625	30.0	28.1	193.5
1997	3,880,894	104,137	6,737	28.6	26.8	173.6
1996	3,891,494	100,750	5,939	27.4	25.9	152.6
1995	3,899,589	96,736	4,973	26.1	24.8	127.5
1994	3,952,767	97,064	4,594	25.7	24.6	116.2
1993	4,000,240	96,445	4,168	25.2	24.1	104.2
1992	4,065,014	95,372	3,883	24.4	23.5	95.5
1991	4,110,907	94,779	3,346	23.9	23.1	81.4
1990	4,158,212	93,865	3,028	23.3	22.6	72.8
1989	4,040,958	90,118	2,798	23.0	22.3	69.2
1988	3,909,510	85,315	2,385	22.4	21.8	61.0
1987	3,809,394	81,778	2,139	22.0	21.5	56.2
1986	3,756,547	79,485	1,814	21.6	21.2	48.3
1985	3,760,561	77,102	1,925	21.0	20.5	51.2
1984	3,669,141	72,949	1,653	20.3	19.9	45.1
1983	3,638,933	72,287	1,575	20.3	19.9	43.3
1982	3,680,537	71,631	1,484	19.9	19.5	40.3
1981	3,629,238	70,049	1,385	19.7	19.3	38.2
1980	3,612,258	68,339	1,337	19.3	18.9	37.0
Non-Hispanic white[e]						
2013	2,129,196	78,072	3,134	38.1	36.7	147.2
2012	2,134,044	78,449	3,264	38.3	36.8	152.9
2011	2,146,566	78,638	3,670	38.3	36.6	171.0
2010	2,162,406	79,728	3,842	38.6	36.9	177.7
2009	2,212,552	81,954	4,457	39.1	37.0	201.4
2008	2,267,817	82,903	4,493	38.5	36.6	198.1
2007	2,310,333	83,632	4,559	38.2	36.2	197.3
2006	2,308,640	83,108	4,805	38.1	36.0	208.1
2005	2,279,768	82,223	4,966	38.2	36.1	217.8
2004	2,296,683	83,346	5,590	38.7	36.3	243.4
2003	2,321,904	81,691	5,922	37.7	35.2	255.0
2002	2,298,156	79,949	5,754	37.3	34.8	250.4
2001	2,326,578	77,882	5,894	36.0	33.5	253.3
2000	2,362,968	76,018	5,821	34.6	32.2	246.3
1999	2,346,450	73,964	5,909	34.0	31.5	251.8
1998	2,362,462	71,270	6,206	32.8	30.2	262.8
1997	2,333,363	67,191	5,386	31.1	28.8	230.8
1996	2,358,989	65,523	4,885	29.8	27.8	207.1
1995	2,382,638	62,370	4,050	27.9	26.2	170.0
1994	2,438,855	62,476	3,721	27.1	25.6	152.6
1993	2,472,031	61,525	3,360	26.2	24.9	135.9
1992[f]	2,527,207	60,640	3,115	25.2	24.0	123.3
1991[f]	2,589,878	60,904	2,612	24.5	23.5	100.9
1990[g]	2,626,500	60,210	2,358	23.8	22.9	89.8

10, 2013, that it would comply with the judge's order. The FDA gave Plan B One-Step approval for OTC use for all women of reproductive age on June 20, 2013. Other forms of morning-after pills, involving treatment regimens that the FDA considered less appropriate for young women, remained under age restrictions.

Some states have laws regarding access to emergency contraception. Table 7.4 shows that, as of September 2015, 17 states and the District of Columbia required that emergency departments provide information on emergency contraceptives to any sexual assault victims that they treat, and 13 states and the District of Columbia

TABLE 7.3

Twin, triplet, and higher-order multiple births, by race and Hispanic origin, 1980–2013 [CONTINUED]

Year and race and Hispanic origin of mother	Total births	Twin births	Triplet and higher-order births	Multiple birth rate[a]	Twin birth rate[b]	Triplet and higher-order birth rate[c]
Non-Hispanic black[e]						
2013	583,834	22,346	623	39.3	38.3	106.7
2012	583,489	21,545	629	38.0	36.9	107.8
2011	582,345	21,681	634	38.3	37.2	108.9
2010	589,808	21,804	574	37.9	37.0	97.3
2009	609,584	23,159	644	39.0	38.0	105.6
2008	623,029	22,924	569	37.7	36.8	91.3
2007	627,191	23,101	612	37.8	36.8	97.6
2006	617,247	22,702	580	37.7	36.8	94.0
2005	583,759	21,254	616	37.5	36.4	105.5
2004	578,772	20,605	577	36.6	35.6	99.7
2003	576,033	20,010	631	35.8	34.7	109.5
2002	578,335	20,064	591	35.7	34.7	102.2
2001	589,917	19,974	531	34.8	33.9	90.0
2000	604,346	20,173	506	34.2	33.4	83.7
1999	588,981	18,920	561	33.1	32.1	95.2
1998	593,127	18,589	518	32.2	31.3	87.3
1997	581,431	17,472	523	30.9	30.0	90.0
1996	578,099	16,873	425	29.9	29.2	73.5
1995	587,781	16,622	340	28.9	28.3	57.8
1994	619,198	17,934	357	29.5	29.0	57.7
1993	641,273	18,115	314	28.7	28.2	49.0
1992[f]	657,450	18,294	346	28.4	27.8	52.6
1991[f]	666,758	18,243	367	27.9	27.4	55.0
1990[g]	661,701	17,646	306	27.1	26.7	46.2
Hispanic[h]						
2013	901,033	21,511	643	24.6	23.9	71.4
2012	907,677	20,505	636	23.3	22.6	70.1
2011	918,129	21,236	723	23.9	23.1	78.7
2010	945,180	21,359	721	23.4	22.6	76.3
2009	999,548	22,481	835	23.3	22.5	83.5
2008	1,041,239	23,266	834	23.1	22.3	80.1
2007	1,062,779	23,405	857	22.8	22.0	80.6
2006	1,039,077	22,698	787	22.6	21.8	75.7
2005	985,505	21,723	761	22.8	22.0	77.2
2004	946,349	20,351	723	22.3	21.5	76.4
2003	912,329	19,472	784	22.2	21.3	85.9
2002	876,642	18,128	737	21.5	20.7	84.1
2001	851,851	17,257	710	21.1	20.3	83.3
2000	815,868	16,470	659	21.0	20.2	80.8
1999	764,339	15,388	583	20.9	20.1	76.3
1998	734,661	15,015	553	21.2	20.4	75.3
1997	709,767	13,821	516	20.2	19.5	72.7
1996	701,339	13,014	409	19.1	18.6	58.3
1995	679,768	12,685	355	19.2	18.7	52.2
1994	665,026	12,206	348	18.9	18.4	52.3
1993	654,418	12,294	321	19.3	18.8	49.1
1992[f]	643,271	11,932	239	18.9	18.5	37.2
1991[f]	623,085	11,356	235	18.6	18.2	37.7
1990[g]	595,073	10,713	235	18.4	18.0	39.5

[a]Number of live births in all multiple deliveries per 1,000 live births.
[b]Number of live births in twin deliveries per 1,000 live births.
[c]Number of live births in triplet and other higher-order deliveries per 100,000 live births.
[d]Includes races other than white and black and origin not stated.
[e]Race and Hispanic origin are reported separately on birth certificates. Persons of Hispanic origin may be of any race. Race categories are consistent with 1977 Office of Management and Budget standards. Forty-four states and the District of Columbia reported multiple-race data for 2013 that were bridged to single-race categories for comparability with other states. Multiple-race reporting areas vary for 2003–2013.
[f]Excludes data for New Hampshire, which did not report Hispanic origin.
[g]Excludes data for New Hampshire and Oklahoma, which did not report Hispanic origin.
[h]Includes all persons of Hispanic origin of any race.

SOURCE: Joyce A. Martin et al., "Table 27. Twin, Triplet, and Higher-Order Multiple Births, by Race and Hispanic Origin of Mother: United States, 1980–2013," in "Births: Final Data for 2013," *National Vital Statistics Report*, vol. 64, no. 1, January 15, 2015, http://www.cdc.gov/nchs/data/nvsr/nvsr64/nvsr64_01.pdf (accessed September 22, 2015)

required that such drugs be provided to sexual assault victims on request. Some states also allowed pharmacists to provide prescription-only emergency contraceptives without a doctor's prescription under various circumstances. Conversely, three states had excluded, or were seeking to exclude, emergency contraceptives from coverage under Medicaid or other health programs in the state.

TABLE 7.4

State policies on emergency contraception (EC), September 2015

State	Expanding access: Emergency rooms required to: Provide information about EC	Expanding access: Emergency rooms required to: Dispense EC upon request	Expanding access: Pharmacist may dispense EC without prescription under: Collaborative practice agreement	Expanding access: Pharmacist may dispense EC without prescription under: State-approved protocol	Expanding access: Must fill valid prescriptions: Pharmacy	Expanding access: Must fill valid prescriptions: Pharmacist	Restricting access: State law excludes EC from: Medicaid family planning expansion	Restricting access: State law excludes EC from: Contraceptive coverage mandate	Restricting access: State law allows refusal to dispense EC by: Pharmacist	Restricting access: State law allows refusal to dispense EC by: Pharmacy	Restricting access: Requires prescription: 16 and Younger
Alaska			X[b]								
Arizona									X	X	
Arkansas	X							X	X	c	
California	X	X	X	X		X					
Colorado	X								c	c	
Connecticut	X[d]	X[d]									
District of Columbia	X	X									
Florida									c		
Georgia									X		
Hawaii	X	X	X								
Idaho									X		
Illinois	X				X				c	X	
Maine				X					c	c	
Massachusetts	X	X	X								
Minnesota	X	X									
Mississippi									X	X	
New Hampshire			X								
New Jersey	X	X			X						
New Mexico	X	X		X							
New York	X	X									
North Carolina								X			
Ohio	f	f									
Oklahoma											a
Oregon	X	X									
Pennsylvania	X	g									
South Carolina		X									
South Dakota									X		
Tennessee									c	c	
Texas	X						X[e]				
Utah	X	X									
Vermont			X								
Washington	X	X	X		X						
Wisconsin	X	X			X						
Total	**17 + DC**	**13 + DC**	**7**	**3**	**4**	**1**	**1**	**2**	**6**	**3**	

[a]Permanently enjoined; law not in effect.
[b]Pharmacists may dispense any prescription drug, including emergency contraception.
[c]A broadly worded refusal policy may apply to pharmacists or pharmacies, but does not specifically include them.
[d]A hospital may contract with an independent medical professional in order to provide the emergency contraception services.
[e]The law explicitly excludes emergency contraception in Texas.
[f]Policy does not include an enforcement mechanism.
[g]A hospital may refuse based on religious or moral beliefs to provide emergency contraception when requested by a woman who has been sexually assaulted. However, a refusing hospital is then required to immediately transport the woman to the closest medical facility that will provide her with the medication.
EC = Emergency contraception.

SOURCE: "Emergency Contraception Policies," in *State Polices in Brief: Emergency Contraception*, Guttmacher Institute, September 1, 2015, http://www.guttmacher.org/statecenter/spibs/spib_EC.pdf (accessed September 22, 2015)

Refusal to Provide Abortion, Contraception, or Other Services

Some health care providers do not want to provide abortions, contraception, or other forms of health care that they find objectionable for moral, religious, or other reasons. The Guttmacher Institute notes in "Refusing to Provide Health Services" (November 1, 2015, http://www.guttmacher.org/statecenter/spibs/spib_RPHS.pdf) that most states have policies that allow health care practitioners and institutions to refuse to provide abortion, contraception, or sterilization services. In states without such provisions, health care providers are often protected by law from being compelled to offer services in conflict with their religious beliefs. A few states have laws that allow pharmacists to refuse to fill prescriptions to which they object on moral or religious grounds, the drugs used for medical abortions being one example.

Table 7.5 lists state policies that give health care providers the ability to refuse to provide abortion services. Forty-five states allow any individual health care provider to refuse to provide abortion services, and 43 states allow some or all institutions to refuse as well.

Table 7.4 shows that as of September 2015, six states permitted individual pharmacists to refuse to provide

TABLE 7.5

State policies allowing health care providers to refuse providing abortion, contraception, or sterilization services, September 2015

	Refusal						
	Abortion		Contraception			Sterilization	
State	**Individual provider**	**Institution**	**Individual provider**	**Pharmacist**	**Institution**	**Individual provider**	**Institution**
Federal policy	X	X				X	X
Alaska	X	Private					
Arizona	X	X	X	X	X		
Arkansas	X	X	X	X	Private	X	X
California	X	Religious					
Colorado			X	[a]	Private		
Connecticut	X						
Delaware	X	X					
Florida	X	X	X	[a]			
Georgia	X	X		X		X	X
Hawaii	X	X					
Idaho	X	X	X	X		X	X
Illinois	X	X	X	[a]	X	X	X
Indiana	X	Private					
Iowa	X	Private					
Kansas	X	X	[a, b]	[a, b]		X	X
Kentucky	X	X				X	
Louisiana	X	X					
Maine	X	X	X	[a]	Private	X	X
Maryland	X	X				X	X
Massachusetts	X	Private			Private	X	Private
Michigan	X	X					
Minnesota	X	Private					
Mississippi	X	X	X	X	X	X	X
Missouri	X	X					
Montana	X	Private				X	Private
Nebraska	X	X					
Nevada	X	Private					
New Jersey	X	Private				X	Private
New Mexico	X	X					X
New York	X	X					
North Carolina	X	X					
North Dakota	X	X					
Ohio	X	X					
Oklahoma	X	X					
Oregon	X	Private					
Pennsylvania	X	Private				X	Private
Rhode Island	X					X	
South Carolina	X	Private					
South Dakota	X	X		X			
Tennessee	X	X	X	[a]	Private		
Texas	X	Private					
Utah	X	X					
Virginia	X	X					
Washington	X	X	X	X		X	X
West Virginia						X	X
Wisconsin	X	X				X	X
Wyoming	X	Private					
State total	**45**	**43**	**10**	**7**	**8**	**17**	**16**

[a]A broadly worded refusal clause may apply. In Illinois a state court held that a regulation requiring pharmacies to provide emergency contraception cannot be enforced against pharmacies that refuse to dispense the medication.
[b]The law permits refusal if the provider "reasonably believes" the drug or device "may result" in an abortion.
Note: Unless indicated, the right to refuse applies to all institutions—private, religious and public.

SOURCE: "Policies Allowing Providers to Refuse," in *State Policies in Brief: Refusing to Provide Health Services*, Guttmacher Institute, September 1, 2015, http://www.guttmacher.org/statecenter/spibs/spib_RPHS.pdf (accessed September 22, 2015)

morning-after pills. Another three states permitted pharmacies, as institutions, to refuse to provide such drugs. In contrast, there were four states that specifically required pharmacies to fill any valid prescription, even for emergency contraceptives, and one state that placed this requirement on individual pharmacists.

Many professional associations have weighed in on the issue of health care providers' and pharmacists' refusal to provide abortion and contraception services and medications, balancing the provider's right to refuse with the responsibility to provide appropriate health care. Most professional association statements concur that providers have the right not to perform services or provide medicines that may go against their moral or religious beliefs, but that they have a responsibility to refer the patient to a provider who can provide that service or medication.

FETAL RIGHTS

Fetal rights is the view that the unborn deserve the same legal protections as children. Since its 1973 decision in *Roe v. Wade*, the U.S. Supreme Court has consistently ruled that the woman's right to health and life outweighs the state's interest in the fetus, even after viability. In recent years, however, there have been a number of attempts to elevate the status of the fetus to that of a child.

In 2007 the Supreme Court ruled 5–4 in *Gonzales v. Carhart* (550 U.S. 124) that the federal Partial-Birth Abortion Ban Act of 2003 was constitutional. (See Chapter 2.) The act imposes civil and criminal penalties on physicians who knowingly perform the intact dilation and extraction abortion procedure, which can be used for abortions at 21 or more weeks of gestation. Justice Ruth Bader Ginsburg (1933–) noted in her dissenting opinion, "Today's decision is alarming.... It tolerates, indeed applauds, federal intervention to ban nationwide a procedure found necessary and proper in certain cases by the American College of Obstetricians and Gynecologists (ACOG).... For the first time since *Roe*, the Court blesses a prohibition with no exception safeguarding a woman's health." Thus, this ruling does not directly decree that the fetus is a child, but it does put the interests of the life of a fetus before the life of the women bearing the fetus.

The Fetus as a Victim of a Crime

UNBORN VICTIMS OF VIOLENCE ACT OF 2004. The Unborn Victims of Violence Act of 2004 is the first federal law to recognize the fetus as a victim of a crime. The law makes it "a separate offense" to injure or cause the death of "a child, who is in utero [in the womb] at the time the conduct takes place." The act applies only to federal offenses, such as crimes that are committed on federal properties, against certain federal officials and employees, and by members of the military. It does not apply to crimes that are prosecuted by the individual states. Although the law does not seek the prosecution of "conduct relating to an abortion," abortion advocates claim that it sets the stage for dismantling the legal right to abortion.

THE STATES AND UNBORN VICTIMS. The National Right to Life Committee indicates in "State Homicide Laws That Recognize Unborn Victims" (May 24, 2014, https://www.nrlc.org/federal/unbornvictims/statehomicidelaws092302) that in 2014, 29 states had homicide laws that recognize unborn children as victims throughout the entire prenatal period. Another eight states had homicide laws that recognize unborn children as victims during part of the prenatal development.

Fetal Rights versus Parents' Rights

If a pregnant woman's behaviors during pregnancy are detrimental to the fetus, should this be considered child abuse? As shown in Table 7.6, 18 states answered "yes" to this question in September 2015 and had laws stating that substance abuse during pregnancy is considered child abuse. These laws were civil laws not criminal laws, except in South Carolina, where the state supreme court has held that a viable fetus is a person.

Opponents of fetal rights believe that if a fetus is granted the same legal rights that are traditionally granted to people, the law will be forced to embark on the "slippery slope" of how much control the state should have over women (and men). If substance use can be prohibited, then everything a woman does that might potentially harm a fetus could be regulated. Her eating and drinking, her work, or her health habits could all be scrutinized. Could a woman who inadvertently harmed a fetus before she knew she was pregnant be held liable? Could a woman be criminally prosecuted for failing to seek prenatal care?

Results of medical research reveal increasing evidence that a woman's behavior is not the only influence on the fetus. Men who smoke, abuse drugs (including marijuana) and alcohol, or work with toxic chemicals may be damaging their sperm, thereby causing genetically defective fetuses. Men, however, have not yet been charged with abuse of the unborn.

TABLE 7.6

State policies on substance abuse during pregnancy, September 2015

State	Substance abuse during pregnancy considered: Criminal act	Substance abuse during pregnancy considered: Child abuse	Substance abuse during pregnancy considered: Grounds for civil commitment	When abuse suspected, state requires: Reporting	When abuse suspected, state requires: Testing	Drug treatment for pregnant women: Targeted program created	Drug treatment for pregnant women: Pregnant women given priority access in general programs	Drug treatment for pregnant women: Pregnant women protected from discrimination in publicly funded programs
Alabama		X[a]						
Alaska				X				
Arizona				X			X	
Arkansas		X				X		
California						X		
Colorado		X				X		
Connecticut						X		
Florida		X				X		
Georgia							X	
Illinois		X		X		X		
Indiana		X						
Iowa		X		X	X			X
Kansas							X	X
Kentucky					X	X	X	
Louisiana		X		X		X		
Maine				X				
Maryland				X		X	X	
Massachusetts				X				
Michigan				X				
Minnesota		X	X	X	X	X		
Missouri							X[d]	X
Montana				X				
Nebraska						X[b]		
Nevada		X		X				
New York						X		
North Carolina						X		
North Dakota				X	X			
Ohio						X		
Oklahoma		X		X			X	X
Oregon						X[c]		
Pennsylvania				X		X		
Rhode Island		X		X		X	X	
South Carolina		X[a]						
South Dakota		X	X					
Tennessee	X	X					X	
Texas		X					X	
Utah				X			X	
Virginia		X		X		X		
Washington						X		
Wisconsin		X	X				X	
Total	**1**	**18**	**3**	**18**	**4**	**19**	**12**	**4**

[a]The Alabama Supreme Court held that drug use while pregnant is considered chemical endangerment of a child. The South Carolina Supreme Court held that a viable fetus is a "person" under the state's criminal child-endangerment statute and that "maternal acts endangering or likely to endanger the life, comfort, or health of a viable fetus" constitute criminal child abuse.
[b]Applies only to women and newborns eligible for Medicaid.
[c]Establishes requirements for health care providers to encourage and facilitate drug counseling.
[d]Priority applies to pregnant women referred for treatment.

SOURCE: "State Policies on Substance Abuse during Pregnancy," in *State Policies in Brief: Substance Abuse during Pregnancy*, Guttmacher Institute, September 1, 2015, http://www.guttmacher.org/statecenter/spibs/spib_SADP.pdf (accessed September 22, 2015)

CHAPTER 8
ABORTION AROUND THE WORLD

Women are fertile for almost half of their lives, and because many women have unwanted pregnancies at one time or another, women in all countries and cultures have relied on abortion as a method of terminating unwanted pregnancies. Additionally, abortion is often used as a method of birth control. Abortion rates (the number of abortions per 1,000 women aged 15 to 44 years) around the world generally reflect the prevailing religious and political attitudes in the country, the cultural values, and the availability of contraception.

The major organizations that compile international abortion statistics are the Guttmacher Institute, which supports a woman's right to choose abortion, and the World Health Organization (WHO) of the United Nations (UN). It is difficult for these organizations to obtain current and accurate worldwide abortion statistics for a variety of reasons. In countries where abortion is illegal or severely restricted, abortions are not a part of the medical record. In addition, it is impossible to know how many women get private abortions and how many of those who turn up at the hospital with a spontaneous abortion (miscarriage) actually induced the abortion through a home method. Many countries in which abortion is legal do not keep complete medical records; as a result, estimates are made. Moreover, there are sometimes legal and confidentiality issues surrounding abortion data.

The Guttmacher Institute reports in "Facts on Induced Abortion Worldwide" (January 2012, https://www.guttmacher.org/pubs/fb_IAW.pdf), the most recent report as of November 2015, that after nearly a decade of decline, the worldwide abortion rate leveled off between 2003 and 2008, when it was 28 abortions per 1,000 women of childbearing age (aged 15 to 44 years). In 2008 the abortion rate in the developed world was 24 per 1,000 women of childbearing age. In developing countries the rate stood at 29 per 1,000. There were a total of 43.8 million abortions in 2008, of which 6 million took place in the developed world and 37.8 million in the developing world.

ABORTION LAWS WORLDWIDE

The Center for Reproductive Rights, which supports a woman's right to choose, indicates in the fact sheet "The World's Abortion Laws 2014" (July 2014, http://www.reproductiverights.org/sites/crr.civicactions.net/files/documents/AbortionMap2014.PDF) that in 2014 more than 60% of people lived in countries where abortion is permitted for a wide range of reasons or without restriction as to reason. Conversely, more than 25% of the world's population lived in countries that generally forbid abortion. Countries are categorized based on the restrictiveness of their abortion laws, as follows:

- Prohibited altogether or permitted only to save the woman's life: In 2014 there were 66 countries in this category. (See Table 3.6 in Chapter 3.) Roughly 25.6% of the world's population lived in these countries. As Figure 8.1 shows, in July 2014 most countries with highly restrictive laws were in Central and South America, Africa, the Middle East, and Southeast Asia.
- To preserve the woman's physical health (and to save her life): In 2014, 59 countries allowed an abortion if the pregnancy threatened a woman's physical health. These types of laws sometimes required that the potential injury be either serious or permanent. Many African and South American nations were in this category in 2014.
- Socioeconomic grounds (as well as to protect a woman's physical or mental well-being): 13 countries considered a woman's economic resources, her age, whether she is married, and the number of children she already has in determining if an abortion was permissible in 2014. These laws were usually interpreted liberally.

FIGURE 8.1

Abortion restrictions worldwide, July 2014

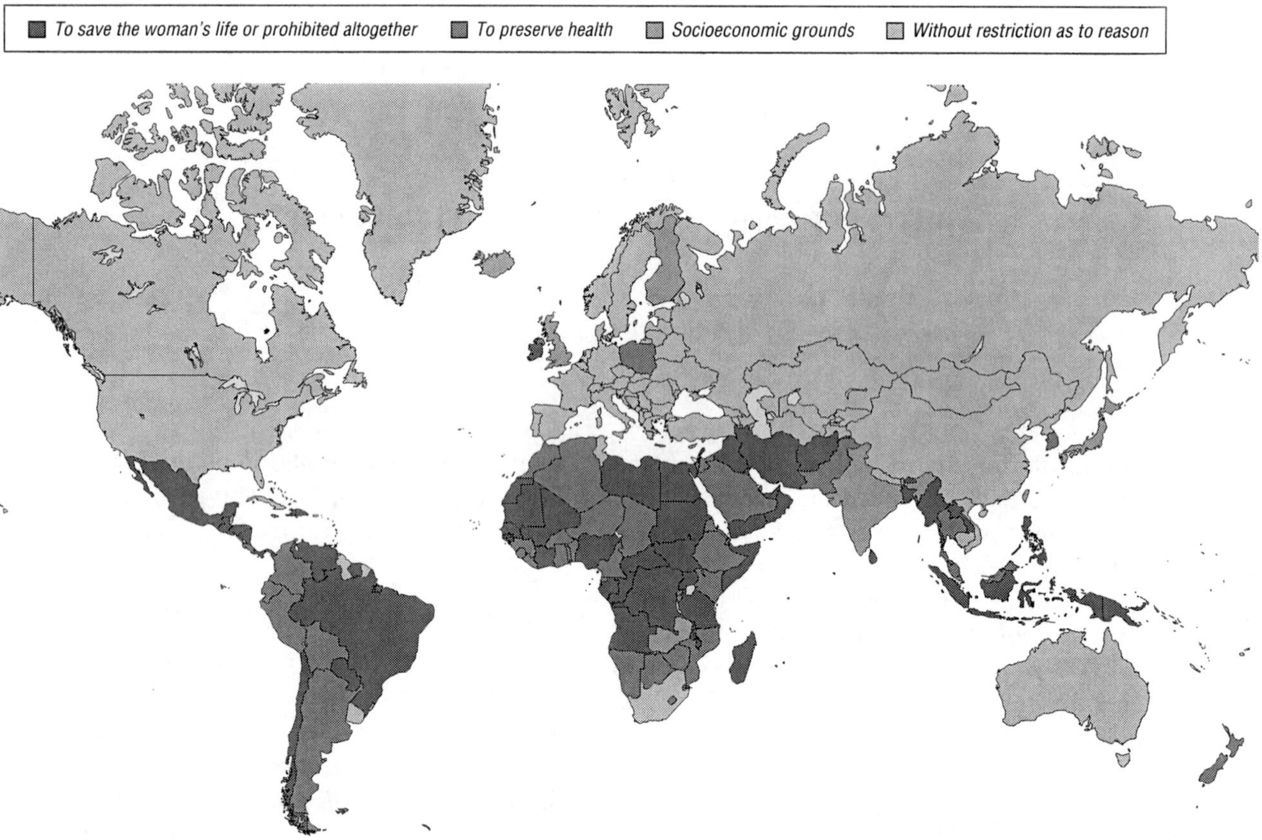

SOURCE: Adapted from *The World's Abortion Laws 2014*, Center for Reproductive Rights, July 2014, http://www.reproductiverights.org/sites/crr.civicactions.net/files/documents/AbortionMap2014.PDF (accessed September 22, 2015)

- Without restriction as to reason: In 2014, 61 countries allowed abortion without limiting the reasons for pregnancy termination. China, Russia, the United States, and much of Europe were in this category in 2014.

In addition, in some countries a woman may obtain a legal abortion based on "juridical grounds" (e.g., rape or incest) or "fetal impairment grounds" (probable genetic defects). Countries that recognize these grounds for legal abortion may be classified under any of the categories of restrictiveness.

Abortion Limitations Even When Laws Are Liberal

In the countries where abortion is not restricted as to reason and in the countries that allow abortion based on socioeconomic grounds, the laws usually mandate certain conditions for allowing the abortion. These countries may impose gestational limits; consent, counseling, and waiting-period requirements; fetal-age restrictions; limitations on advertising abortion services; and limitations on the place of abortion and the person performing the procedure. For example, a woman in Turkey must present her marriage certificate in most hospitals to get an abortion, and if she is married she must have her husband's permission. Most countries that permit abortions without restriction as to reason have gestational limits. Most commonly these restrict abortions after the fetus has reached 12 to 14 weeks gestation.

Safe and Unsafe Abortion and the Law

According to Susheela Singh et al. of the Guttmacher Institute, in *Abortion Worldwide: A Decade of Uneven Progress* (2009, http://www.guttmacher.org/pubs/Abortion-Worldwide.pdf), the WHO defines unsafe abortions as those "performed by individuals without the necessary skills, in an environment that does not conform to the minimum medical standards, or both." The researchers note that whether abortions are performed legally or illegally, safety can vary. In some countries where abortion is legal, safe medical services may not be available to all women, and these women may resort to using unqualified or unskilled people in unsafe conditions. The situation is worse in countries with restrictive abortion laws. Singh et al. explain that "abortions that occur outside the legal framework are frequently performed by unqualified and unskilled providers, or are self-induced; such abortions often take place in unhygienic conditions and involve dangerous methods or incorrect administration of medications." Women in such situations will probably not get proper follow-up care or have access to backup help if an emergency occurs during the procedure. "Thus," note Singh et al., "the risk of unsafe abortion varies not only according to the provider's skills and the method used, but is also linked to the de facto [actual] application of the law."

In *Health Worker Roles in Providing Safe Abortion Care and Post-Abortion Contraception* (2015, http://apps.who.int/iris/bitstream/10665/181041/1/9789241549264_eng.pdf?ua=1&ua=1), the WHO outlines recommended tasks for health workers when offering safe abortions and post-abortion care. As the WHO notes, providing access to safe abortions relies heavily on the availability of skilled health workers. The ratios of skilled health workers to the general population are lowest in Africa, South Asia, and other parts of the developing world.

Abortion Laws and Rates

Table 8.1 shows the numbers of legal abortions by age for various countries for the most recent year available. The table shows that in most, but not all, countries, the highest number of abortions were performed on women that were aged 20 to 24 years.

Worldwide, women have abortions whether laws are restrictive or not, and WHO estimates suggest the rate of abortion is generally lower in countries where abortion is permitted. In "Safe and Unsafe Induced Abortion" (2012, http://apps.who.int/iris/bitstream/10665/75174/1/WHO_RHR_12.02_eng.pdf), the most recent report as of November 2015, the WHO estimates the number of abortions, both safe and unsafe, that occurred worldwide and by region during 2008 and prior years. For the year 2008 WHO considered every region outside of Europe and North America to have restrictive abortion laws, except for eastern Asia, Australia, and New Zealand. Among the 11 regions with restrictive abortion laws, only two, southern Africa (15) and northern Africa (18), had abortion rates below 20. By comparison, among the six regions with liberal abortion laws, only two, Eastern Europe (43) and eastern Asia (28), had rates above 20. In other words, countries with restrictive abortion laws were estimated to have higher abortion rates, on average, than those with liberal laws.

ILLEGAL AND UNSAFE WORLDWIDE ABORTION STATISTICS

Regional Estimates of Unsafe Abortions

According to the Center for Reproductive Rights, in *Abortion Worldwide: 20 Years of Reform* (2014, http://

TABLE 8.1

Number of legal abortions, by age, selected countries, selected years 2004–12

Continent, country or area, year and age	Number of previous live births Total
America, North	
Canada[a]	
2006	
Total	**91,310**
0–14	267
15–19	15,217
20–24	28,358
25–29	20,315
30–34	13,615
35–39	9,444
40+	3,938
Unknown	156
Mexico[b]	
2012	
Total	**294**
0–14	4
15–19	46
20–24	53
25–29	59
30–34	58
35–39	45
40–44	9
45–49	—
50+	—
Unknown	20
Asia China, Hong Kong SAR (Special Administrative Region) RAS	
2011	
Total	**11,863**
0–14	32
15–19	1,011
20–24	2,504
25–29	2,548
30–34	2,320
35–39	2,208
40–44	1,126
45+	114
Israel[c]	
2011	
Total	**18,974**
0–14	51
15–19	2,174
20–24	3,898
25–29	3,845
30–34	3,733
35–39	3,448
40–44	1,682
45–49	140
50+	3
Japan	
2012	
Total	**196,639**
0–14	400
15–19	20,259
20–24	43,269
25–29	40,900
30–34	38,362
35–39	36,112
40–44	16,133
45–49	1,163
50+	14
Unknown	27

TABLE 8.1

Number of legal abortions, by age, selected countries, selected years 2004–12 [CONTINUED]

Continent, country or area, year and age	Number of previous live births Total
Europe,	
Belgium	
2011	
Total	**19,578**
0–14	87
15–19	2,575
20–24	5,027
25–29	4,688
30–34	3,745
35–39	2,454
40–44	923
45–49	78
50+	1
Croatia	
2012	
Total	**3,571**
0–14	6
15–19	291
20–24	616
25–29	777
30–34	841
35–39	696
40–44	307
45–49	26
50+	1
Unknown	10
Czech Republic	
2012	
Total	**23,032**
0–14	31
15–19	1,703
20–24	4,213
25–29	4,608
30–34	5,359
35–39	5,071
40–44	1,857
45–49	187
50+	3
Denmark[d]	
2006	
Total	**15,053**
15–19	2,518
20–24	3,138
25–29	2,861
30–34	2,973
35–39	2,373
40–44	1,107
45–49	83
50+	—
Germany	
2012	
Total	**106,815**
0–14	373
15–19	10,116
20–24	25,625
25–29	24,888
30–34	22,199
35–39	15,469
40–44	7,440
45–49	688
50+	17

TABLE 8.1

Number of legal abortions, by age, selected countries, selected years 2004–12 [CONTINUED]

Continent, country or area, year and age	Number of previous live births Total
Hungary	
2012	
Total	**36,118**
0–14	172
15–19	4,353
20–24	7,219
25–29	7,237
30–34	7,522
35–39	6,952
40–44	2,500
45–49	158
50+	5
Unknown	—
Italy[e]	
2009	
Total	**114,793**
0–14	236
15–19	9,603
20–24	20,950
25–29	23,302
30–34	25,699
35–39	22,916
40–44	10,228
45–49	955
50+	25
Unknown	879
Norway[f]	
2006	
Total	**14,132**
0–14	37
15–19	2,307
20–24	3,740
25–29	2,904
30–34	2,495
35–39	1,877
40–44	694
45–49	55
50+	—
Unknown	23
Poland[g]	
2012	
Total	**752**
0–19	23
20–24	82
25–29	189
30–34	217
35+	241
Romania	
2012	
Total	**87,975**
0–14	476
15–19	7,547
20–24	18,990
25–29	20,210
30–34	19,635
35–39	14,751
40–44	5,880
45–49	464
50+	22
Unknown	—

www.reproductiverights.org/sites/crr.civicactions.net/files/documents/20Years_Reform_Report.pdf), of the approximately 22 million unsafe abortions performed annually worldwide, 98% occur in developing countries, where restrictive abortion laws predominate. Although the Center for Reproductive Rights notes that many countries, notably

TABLE 8.1

Number of legal abortions, by age, selected countries, selected years 2004–12 [CONTINUED]

Continent, country or area, year and age	Number of previous live births: Total
Russian Federation	
2011	
Total	**1,124,880**
0–14	585
15–19	66,275
20–24	264,346
25–29	309,875
30–34	248,494
35–39	168,461
40–44	60,768
45–49	5,904
50+	172
Unknown	—
Spain	
2004	
Total	**84,985**
0–14	369
15–19	11,677
20–24	22,461
25–29	20,309
30–34	15,212
35–39	10,572
40–44	4,072
45–49	313
50+	—
Unknown	—
2012	
Total	**112,390**
0–14	460
15–19	13,198
20–24	24,339
25–29	25,584
30–34	24,298
35–39	17,389
40–44	6,600
45+	522
Sweden[h]	
2010	
Total	**37,693**
0–14	191
15–19	6,199
20–24	10,068
25–29	7,495
30–34	6,124
35–39	5,073
40–44	2,248
45–49	238
50+	56
Unknown	1
United Kingdom of Great Britain and Northern Ireland[i]	
2012	
Total	**197,569**
0–14	910
15–19	32,967
20–24	58,367
25–29	44,612
30–34	32,139
35–39	19,651
40–44	8,199
45–49	697
50+	237
Unknown	—
Oceania	
New Zealand	
2011	
Total	**15,863**
0–14	68
15–19	2,822
20–24	5,160
25–29	3,340
30–34	2,220
35–39	1,593
40–44	605
45–49	55
50+	—

*Provisional.
^Indicates an open-ended group, for example 4+.
[a]Data refer to resident population only. Significant undercoverage of medically induced abortions in clinics in 2006 due to non response in some provinces.
[b]Data refer to abortions prescribed by a physician. Data refer to 'Therapeutic Abortions'. According to the Mexican law, only the induced abortions, prescribed by medical reasons and induced because of pregnancy coming from sexual agression, are considered as legal. Refers to residence of the mother. To calculate the total number of abortions, foetal deaths of less than 20 weeks of gestation were considered.
[c]Includes data for East Jerusalem and Israeli residents in certain other territories under occupation by Israeli military forces since June 1967. Data refer to applications to commissions for termination of pregnancy and not to authorizations.
[d]Excluding Faeroe Islands and Greenland shown separately, if available. Unrevised data.
[e]Data are incomplete for Abruzzo, Campania, Basilicata, Sicilia and Sardegna regions.
[f]Unrevised data.
[g]Based on hospital and polyclinic records.
[h]Data refer to abortions by previous deliveries of mother rather than previous live births of mother.
[i]Excluding Channel Islands (Guernsey and Jersey) and Isle of Man, shown separately, if available. Excluding Northern Ireland.

SOURCE: Adapted from "14. Legally Induced Abortions by Age and Number of Previous Live Births of Women: Latest Available Year, 2004–2013," in *United Nations Demographic Yearbook 2013*, United Nations Department of Economic and Social Affairs, Statistics Division, 2014, http://unstats.un.org/unsd/demographic/products/dyb/dyb2013/Table14.pdf (accessed September 22, 2015). © 2014 United Nations. Reprinted with Permission of the United Nations

in Africa and Asia, liberalized their abortion laws between 1994 and 2014, there were some notable exceptions. For example, in 2013 Macedonia passed legislation imposing new restrictions on women seeking to obtain abortions, including mandatory biased counseling, ultrasounds, and three-day waiting periods.

Deaths and Complications Due to Unsafe Abortions

Abortion is among the safest medical procedures when performed under proper conditions. As with all medical procedures, however, it is unsafe when performed by untrained providers in unsanitary conditions. For many women worldwide with unwanted pregnancies, a safe abortion may be too expensive, unavailable, or illegal. Because of these obstacles, women may delay abortions until later in pregnancy, when the risk of complications increases.

In *Abortion Worldwide: 20 Years of Reform*, the Center for Reproductive Rights estimates that each year about 5 million women sustain injuries and 47,000 women die worldwide due to unsafe abortions. The most common complications of unsafe abortion include incomplete abortion, tears in the cervix, perforation of the uterus, fever, infection, septic shock (severe system-wide infection), and severe hemorrhaging. Other serious long-term health consequences may also occur, including chronic pelvic pain, problems getting and staying pregnant, infertility, blockage of a fallopian tube, and ectopic pregnancy (a pregnancy outside of the uterus, usually in a fallopian tube).

ABORTION IN SELECTED COUNTRIES AND REGIONS

Poland

The collapse of communism in Poland in 1989 led to the prohibition of abortion, which had been legal since 1956. As soon as the Solidarity Party gained control of Parliament, it amended the existing abortion law. Strongly supported by the Roman Catholic Church, the new statute severely restricted access to abortion by requiring a woman requesting a state-funded abortion to present written approval from three physicians and a psychologist from a state-approved list of doctors.

The new abortion provision granted physicians and hospital staffs in public hospitals the right to refuse to perform abortions. In addition, the state stopped funding contraceptives for the poor, and funding was reduced for the Polish affiliate of the International Planned Parenthood Association, resulting in the closing of half of its offices in Poland.

In March 1993 a new antiabortion law granting protection to a fetus from the moment of conception went into effect. The law allowed abortion only if the pregnancy seriously threatened a woman's life or health, in cases of rape or incest, or if the fetus had irreparable abnormalities. Private clinics were forbidden to perform abortions, and physicians performing illegal abortions could be imprisoned for up to two years. Should a woman die of complications from an illegal abortion, a physician could face up to 10 years' imprisonment. The new law also required that the Catholic Church be involved in reproductive services. As a result, little information about contraception was delivered by health professionals other than information on natural family planning methods (e.g., abstaining from sexual intercourse during the time of the month when a woman is most likely to conceive), which are accepted by the Catholic Church.

In November 1996 the Polish government again legalized abortion, but in May 1997 Poland's highest court, the Constitutional Tribunal, struck down the 1996 abortion law. In December 1997 the newly elected Parliament, which was dominated by pro–Catholic Church legislators, reinstated the strict 1993 antiabortion law.

In late 2004 the UN Human Rights Committee concluded a review of Poland's compliance with the International Covenant on Civil and Political Rights, demanding that the nation liberalize its abortion laws. During the 2005 elections, however, the conservative Law and Justice Party was voted into power. The party proposed a range of constitutional amendments, from those banning abortion to those making it harder to weaken existing antiabortion legislation. In April 2007 the Parliament rejected these amendments. Nonetheless, Poland still had some of the strictest abortion laws in Europe.

Table 8.2 shows that in 2004 there were 199 legal abortions performed in Poland. That number rose to 225 in 2005 and continued to climb to 752 in 2012. In "Curbs on Abortion Spread across East Europe" (IPSnews.net, July 12, 2013), Pavol Stracansky reports that an estimated 200,000 illegal abortions are performed in Poland each year because many women cannot afford to travel to countries where the procedure is legal. Stracansky observes that an unintended consequence of Poland's stringent antiabortion law is that the birth rate has steadily declined between 1993 and 2012. Wanda Nowicka, a Polish women's rights campaigner and member of a UN task force on population and development, is quoted as saying, "What happens is that when a woman is unsure about her reproductive choices she decides not to have children." Stracansky states that a number of other eastern European countries were considering new restrictions on abortion in the summer of 2013. Besides the situation in Macedonia discussed earlier, Belarus also passed legislation in 2013 that imposed new limits on women seeking abortion after the 12th week of pregnancy, allowing abortions after that time only in cases of rape, or when a woman's parental rights have been terminated by law.

Romania

During the rule of the communist dictator Nicolae Ceauşescu (1918–1989), abortion was banned (beginning in 1967), except for women who were older than 45 years and had at least five children. Access to modern contraception was also severely restricted. Ceauşescu had hoped to build his country into a powerful nation based on population growth. Birth rates increased initially and then declined.

Patricia Stephenson et al. note in "Commentary: The Public Health Consequences of Restricted Induced Abortion—Lessons from Romania" (*American Journal of Public Health*, vol. 82, no. 10, October 1992) that it was only after Ceauşescu's regime was overthrown that the situation in Romania was revealed to the world. Many parents could not support their children because of poverty, so the children were placed in state care. Without contraception, women often resorted to illegal abortion to prevent unwanted births. During Ceauşescu's rule an

TABLE 8.2

Legal abortions worldwide, by country, 2004–13

Continent and country or area	2004	2005	2006	2007	2008	2009	2010	2011	2012	2013
					Number					
Africa										
Réunion	4,155	4,421	4,523	—	—	—	—	—	—	—
Seychelles	435	413	443	446	453	471	556	—	553	515
America, North										
Anguilla	26	21	—	—	—	—	—	—	—	—
Bermuda	215	237	222	90	283	303	284	278	278	275
Canada[a]	100,039	96,815	91,310[b]	—	—	—	—	—	—	—
Costa Rica[c]	8,801	8,411	8,367	8,504	8,733	7,848[d]	7,697[d]	—	—	—
Cuba	67,277	62,530	67,903	66,008	74,905	84,724	71,398	83,943	83,682	—
Dominican Republic	26,438	29,167	—	—	—	—	—	—	—	—
Greenland	905	899	904	887	899	799	858*	—	—	—
Martinique	2,426	2,304	2,392	—	—	—	—	—	—	—
Mexico[e]	748	729	793	833	764	867	986	1,041	294	—
Puerto Rico[f]	9,215	6,904	5,538[g]	—	—	—	—	—	—	—
Turks and Caicos Islands[h]	43	32	—	—	—	—	—	—	—	—
United States of America[i]	839,226	820,151	852,385	827,609	825,564	—	—	—	—	—
America, South										
Chile	1,510	1,841	—	—	—	—	—	—	—	—
French Guiana	1,639	1,612	1,661	—	—	—	—	—	—	—
Asia										
Armenia	10,487	10,925	11,132	11,501	12,469	13,797	—	—	—	—
Azerbaijan	19,798	19,577	20,864	22,323	25,247	24,554	26,799	27,787	31,037	—
Bahrain[j]	1,505	2,078	2,297	2,014	2,575	2,394	2,525	2,452	2,463	—
China, Hong Kong SAR	15,882	14,192	13,510	13,515	13,199	12,028	11,231	11,863	—	—
Georgia	17,210	19,681	21,204	20,644	22,062	24,311	25,585	30,590	—	—
Israel[k]	19,712	19,090	19,452	19,470	19,638	19,849	19,575	18,974	—	—
Japan	301,673	289,127	276,352	256,672	242,326	226,878	212,694[l]	202,106	196,639	—
Kyrgyzstan[m]	19,984	20,035	19,762	21,884	20,800	22,088	21,675	—	—	—
Mongolia	8,919	9,064	12,594	15,817	10,688	12,602	12,492	—	—	—
Qatar	172	169	—	—	—	—	—	—	—	—
Singapore	12,070	11,482	12,032	11,933	12,222	12,318	12,082	11,940	10,624	9,282
Tajikistan	20,495	19,418	17,489	18,986	18,481	19,470	19,510	17,503	16,618	—
Europe										
Åland Islands	59	68	53	73	67	68	70	73	60	—
Albania	10,517	9,403	9,552	9,030	8,335	—	—	—	—	—
Belarus	71,700	64,655	58,516	46,285	42,197	35,967	33,262	32,031	28,628	—
Belgium	16,024	16,696	17,640	18,033	18,595	18,870	19,095	19,578	—	—
Bulgaria	47,223	41,795	37,272	37,594	36,593	33,733	31,548	31,716	29,992	—
Croatia	5,232	4,563	4,733	4,573	4,497	4,450	4,043	4,347	3,571	—
Czech Republic	27,574	26,453	25,352	25,414	25,760	24,636	23,998	24,055	23,032	—
Denmark[n]	15,231	15,183	15,197	16,071	16,776	16,657	16,362	—	—	—
Estonia[a]	10,074	9,610	9,378	8,883	8,409	7,542	7,068	6,668	6,056	—
Faeroe Islands	44	29	41	46	—	—	—	—	—	—
Finland	11,162	10,969	10,645	10,533	10,423	10,359[o]	10,172[o]	10,418[o]	10,001[o]	—
France[p]	209,907	205,392	214,360	212,285	208,242	208,939	210,813	206,722	—	—
Germany	129,650	124,023	119,710	116,871	114,484	110,694	110,431	108,867	106,815	—
Greece	16,135	16,495	—	—	—	—	—	—	—	—
Hungary	52,539	48,689	46,324	43,870	44,089	43,181	40,449	38,443	36,118	—
Iceland	889	868	904	905	959	981	977	970[q]	980	—
Italy	137,140[r]	129,272[s]	125,782[t]	125,116[u]	118,891[v]	114,793[w]	112,463[x]	—	—	—
Latvia	13,723	12,785	11,825	11,814	10,425	8,881	7,443	7,089	6,197	—
Lithuania	10,644	9,972	9,536	9596	9,031	8,024	6,989	6,205	6,033	—
Montenegro	—	1,952	—	—	—	—	—	—	—	—
Norway	14,071	13,989	14,417	15,165	16,054	15,774	15,735	15,343	—	—
Poland[y]	199	225	339	328	506	538	644	669	752	—
Portugal	710	798	1,215	4,325	13,541	17,932	17,261	17,351	—	—
Republic of Moldova	17,965	16,642	15,742	15,843	15,900	14,634	14,785	15,710	14,838	—
Romania	191,038	163,359	150,246	137,226	127,907	116,060	101,915	103,386	87,975	—
Russian Federation	1,797,567	1,675,693	1,582,398	1,479,010	1,385,600	1,292,389	1,186,108	1,124,880	1,063,982	—
Serbia[z]	29,650	26,645	25,665	24,273	22,867	—	—	—	—	—
Slovakia	15,307	14,427	14,243	13,424	13,394	13,240	12,582	11,789	11,214	—
Slovenia	6,403	5,851	5,632	5,176	4,946	4,653	4,328	4,263	4,106	—
Spain	84,985	91,664	1,01,592	112,138	115,812	111,482	113,031	118,359	112,390	—
Sweden	34,454	34,978	36,045	37,205	38,049	37,524	37,693	37,696	—	—
Switzerland	10,959	10,818	10,594	10,035[bb]	10,310[aa]	10,187[aa]	10,650[aa]	10,715[aa]	10,477[aa]	—
Ukraine	289,065	263,590	229,618[bb]	225,336[bb]	217,413	194,845	176,774	169,131	153,147	—
United Kingdom of Great Britain and Northern Ireland[cc]	206,960	207,018	214,340	219,376	216,062	208,854	209,048	208,636	203,419[dd]	—

TABLE 8.2

Legal abortions worldwide, by country, 2004–13 [CONTINUED]

Continent and country or area	2004	2005	2006	2007	2008	2009	2010	2011	2012	2013
Oceania					Number					
Guam	—	—	—	—	327	266	269	295	275	213
New Zealand	18,211	17,531	17,934	18,382	17,940	17,550	16,630	15,863	—	—

*Provisional.
[a]Data refer to resident population only.
[b]Significant undercoverage of medically induced abortions in clinics in 2006 due to non response in some provinces.
[c]Number of abortions the woman had before the birth of the registered child.
[d]Excluding abortions performed in private hospitals.
[e]Data refer to "Therapeutic Abortions." According to the Mexican law, only the induced abortions, prescribed by medical reasons and induced because of pregnancy coming from sexual agression, are considered as legal. Data refer to abortions prescribed by a physician. Refers to residence of the mother. To calculate the total number of abortions, foetal deaths of less than 20 weeks of gestation were considered.
[f]Data refer to the fiscal year from 1 July to 30 June.
[g]Excluding abortions performed in a clinic which closed operations without reporting the data.
[h]Data refer to abortions performed in hospitals at Grand Turk and Providenciales.
[i]Includes areas that reported abortion counts every year during the period of analysis. Excludes states that did not report abortion numbers: Alaska (1998–2002), California (1997–2008), Louisiana (2005), Maryland (2006–2008), New Hampshire (1998–2008), Oklahoma (1998–1999), and West Virginia (2003–2004).
[j]Data refer to spontaneous abortions and miscarriages.
[k]Includes data for East Jerusalem and Israeli residents in certain other territories under occupation by Israeli military forces since June 1967. Data refer to applications to commissions for termination of pregnancy and not to authorizations.
[l]Excluding data of cities and towns in the jurisdiction of Sousou Public Health and Welfare Office of Fukushima Prefecture due to the impact of the Great East Japan Earthquake.
[m]Based on administrative reporting of the Ministry of Health.
[n]Excluding Faeroe Islands and Greenland shown separately, if available.
[o]Excluding Åland Islands.
[p]Data refer to women between 15 and 49 years of age.
[q]Definition of localities was revised in 2011 causing a break with the previous series.
[r]Data are incomplete for Sicilia region.
[s]Data are incomplete for Friuli-Venezia Giulia, Campania, Molise and Sicilia regions.
[t]Data are incomplete for Friuli-Venezia Giulia, Campania and Sicilia regions.
[u]Data are incomplete for Campania and Sicilia regions.
[v]Data are incomplete for Campania, Calabria, Sicilia and Sardegna regions.
[w]Data are incomplete for Abruzzo, Campania, Basilicata, Sicilia and Sardegna regions.
[x]Data are incomplete for Umbria, Campania and Sicilia regions.
[y]Based on hospital and polyclinic records.
[z]Excludes data for Kosovo and Metohia. Data refer to institutions included in the Health Institutions Network Plan in the Republic of Serbia.
[aa]Data refer to termination of pregnancy for women who are Switzerland residents.
[bb]Data refer to the recorded events in Ministry of Health institutions only.
[cc]Excluding Northern Ireland. Excluding Channel Islands (Guernsey and Jersey) and Isle of Man, shown separately, if available.
[dd]Including provisional data for Scotland.

SOURCE: "13. Legally Induced Abortions, 2004–2013," in *United Nations Demographic Yearbook 2013*, United Nations Department of Economic and Social Affairs, Statistics Division, 2014, http://unstats.un.org/unsd/demographic/products/dyb/dyb2013/Table13.pdf (accessed September 22, 2015).

estimated 10,000 women died from illegal abortions, either self-induced or induced by untrained people. Between 1979 and 1989, when Ceauşescu fell from power, Romania had the highest maternal mortality rate in Europe, 10 times higher than any other European country.

After the revolution Romania's interim government made abortion available on request through the 12th week of pregnancy. Abortions up to the 24th week of pregnancy were permitted in cases of rape, incest, and endangerment of the woman's life if she were to carry her pregnancy to term. Cynthia Dailard of the Guttmacher Institute explains in "Issues in Brief: Abortion in Context—United States and Worldwide" (May 1999) that when abortion became legal in Romania in 1990, abortion-related mortality fell to one-third of its highest level, which had occurred the previous year.

With the shift in policy allowing abortion on demand, Romanians resorted to abortion as a principal method of birth control. According to the article "Romania: Abortions Continue to Exceed Live Births" (LifeSiteNews.com, February 10, 2004), in 2003 Romania had the second-highest abortion rate in Europe (after Russia). However, the article "Newborns Exceed Abortions in Romania First Time since 1989" (Agence France Presse, March 29, 2006) reports that by 2005, for the first time since the fall of the communist regime, the number of newborns in Romania exceeded the number of abortions. Table 8.2 shows that the number of abortions fell from 163,359 in 2005 to 87,975 in 2012.

Russia

Abortion was first legalized in Russia in 1920 and remained legal under the communist regime that formed the Soviet Union in 1922. Many women had abortions because contraception was not widely available and abortion was the primary method of family planning. By the mid-1930s there were three abortions for every birth, so Soviet leader Joseph Stalin (1879–1953) banned abortions to encourage more births. In 1955, two years after Stalin's death, abortion law was liberalized in the country to once again make the procedure safe and reduce maternal mortality. Abortions were allowed on demand through the 12th week of pregnancy and for medical and social reasons through the 22nd week. Because modern methods of contraception were still not available in Russia, most women again relied on abortion to control childbirth.

During the late 1960s contraceptive methods such as the intrauterine device became available in Russia, but the quality of contraceptives was poor and the side effects from high-dosage hormonal methods were many. Although the abortion rate fell, many women still relied on abortion as a method of birth control. This remained true even after the fall of Soviet communism in 1991. According to Robert Greenall, in "Russia Turns Spotlight on Abortion" (BBC.co.uk, September 16, 2003), by 2003 Russia's abortion ratio had dropped to 130 abortions for every 100 live births, but its abortion rate was still the highest in Europe. Greenall notes that in August 2003—for the first time since abortion laws were liberalized in 1955—the Russian government tightened abortion laws by reducing the circumstances under which a woman could legally have the procedure, hoping to thereby reduce the abortion rate.

Svetlana Osadchuk reports in "Simply an Issue of Control" (MoscowTimes.com, April 16, 2008) that by 2008 Russian women were using various forms of contraception, although sales of the birth control pill were low; the high-dose hormone pills of Russia's past had biased women against this method of contraception. During this time the number of abortions fell 39%, from 1.8 million in 2004 to just under 1.1 million in 2012, but many women still used early abortion as their primary method of birth control. (See Table 8.2.)

In 2011 an antiabortion movement slowly took shape in Russia after Prime Minister Vladimir Putin (1952–) announced measures to boost the country's birth rate. In "Putin Drops Strongest Hint Yet of Bid for Presidency" (Independent.co.uk, April 21, 2011), Shaun Walker reports that in an April 2011 speech, Putin announced his plan to solve the country's "demographic crisis." The "crisis" that Putin referred to was the population decline experienced by Russia in the years after the fall of the Soviet Union. Putin revealed his plan to boost the birth rate by 25% to 30% from 2006 levels via the use of cash grants, longer paid maternity leaves, and day care subsidies. Although Putin did not mention placing more restrictions on abortion, an antiabortion movement backed by the Russian Orthodox Church began to gain momentum. The Center for Reproductive Rights notes in *Abortion Worldwide: 20 Years of Reform* that in 2011 Russia passed a law imposing new waiting periods on women seeking abortions during the first trimester of pregnancy. Two years later, the Russian Ministry of Health and Social Affairs implemented new regulations prohibiting all forms of abortion advertising.

Ireland

Ireland is the only western European country that still bans abortion except in cases where the mother's life is threatened. (See Figure 8.1.) Both the Republic of Ireland and Northern Ireland, which is part of the United Kingdom and separate governmentally from the rest of Ireland (the Republic of Ireland), ban abortion.

The article "Q&A: Abortion in NI" (BBC.co.uk, June 13, 2001) explains that the ban on abortion in Northern Ireland began in 1861, much earlier than in the Republic of Ireland. That same year the Offenses against the Person Act made abortion illegal in all of the United Kingdom. This law was amended in Northern Ireland in 1945 to allow abortion in cases in which the mother's life, physical health, or mental health was in danger. In 1967 abortions became legal under a broader set of conditions in England and Wales, but not in Northern Ireland. In 2008 an amendment was added to the Human Fertilization and Embryology Bill that would legalize abortion in Northern Ireland, but it was withdrawn in response to pressure from antiabortion groups.

In 1983 the constitution of the Republic of Ireland was amended to ban abortion. In 1992, however, the Irish Supreme Court ruled that an Irish woman could legally obtain an abortion in another country if there was a threat to her life, including the threat of suicide. Shortly after this ruling, Irish voters approved a law giving women the right to obtain information regarding abortion services abroad and allowing women to travel abroad to get abortions. In May 1995 the Irish Supreme Court ruled constitutional a measure allowing doctors and clinics to provide women with information about foreign abortion clinics.

In 2010 there were some signs that the Republic of Ireland's abortion laws may become less strict. By early 2010 a public opinion poll found that "78 percent supported access to abortion in Ireland if the pregnancy endangered health or was the result of abuse, rape or incest." Then in December 2010 the European Court of Human Rights ruled that the Republic of Ireland was in violation of the European Convention on Human Rights because the country prohibited abortion.

In July 2013 Ireland's president Michael Higgins signed the Protection of Life during Pregnancy law, which permits abortion when a woman's life is at risk due to medical complications or the threat of suicide. The new law does not, however, permit abortion in instances of rape or incest. In "Abortion in Ireland Becomes Legal in Certain Circumstances" (Guardian.com, July 30, 2013), Henry McDonald reports that the legislation was unlikely to stop the flow of women who travel to Britain to obtain abortions, estimated at 4,000 women annually, including more than 100 young women under the age of 18 years.

China

In China abortion is allowed without restriction as to reason. (See Figure 8.1.) During the 1970s China initiated a stringent family planning program that has resulted in one of the fastest fertility declines in the world. For decades, the program promoted one-child families in urban areas and two-child families in rural areas and for ethnic minorities. In October 2015 the Chinese government changed the policy to allow for two-child families throughout the country. Chapter 7 discusses the effects of China's family planning program along with a cultural parental preference for boys. A consequence of this parental preference is that sex ratios at birth are skewed; that is, the ratio of males to females no longer approximates the worldwide average of 103 to 107 males born for every 100 females. Critics of China's family planning laws feel that a cultural preference for boys in China, coupled with the limitation on the number of births per family, endangers females. Every year, many girls are abandoned, killed, aborted, or hidden from family planning authorities.

In *World Factbook: China* (October 28, 2015, https://www.cia.gov/library/publications/the-world-factbook/geos/ch.html), the Central Intelligence Agency (CIA) estimates that the sex ratio at birth in China was 115 boys per 100 girls in 2015. Population data show that in China males outnumbered females by about 39.4 million in 2015.

India

The Indian government started providing family planning services in 1952 and was one of the first developing countries to promote population control. However, the policy was not aggressive, and the population continued to grow. In 1971 India legalized abortion with the enactment of the Medical Termination of Pregnancy Act. Abortion is permitted in India to save a woman's life, physical health, and mental health, as well as in cases of rape or fetal impairment. (See Figure 8.1.)

Education about India's population problem became part of the school curriculum, and during the 1980s an increased number of family planning programs were implemented, including financial assistance for families in need of such help. Government programs promote two children as an "ideal" total number, but many Indian couples, especially those in rural areas where they work the land, continue having children until two sons are born.

Much like China, a high rate of sex-selective abortion occurs in India, although the Indian government condemns this practice via the Pre-natal Diagnostic Techniques (Regulation and Prevention of Misuse) Act. Sex-selection abortion occurs anyway due to a strong cultural and socioeconomic preference for sons in India. This is evidenced by a skewed sex ratio at birth. The CIA estimates in *World Factbook: India* (October 28, 2015, https://www.cia.gov/library/publications/the-world-factbook/geos/in.html) that the Indian sex ratio at birth was 112 boys per 100 girls in 2015. Population data show that in India males outnumbered females by 47.3 million in 2015.

Sushanta Banerjee et al. observe in "Evaluation of a behavior change communication (BCC) intervention on abortion knowledge, attitudes and practices . . . in Bihar and Jharkhand, India" (November 5, 2013, https://apha.confex.com/apha/141am/webprogram/Paper282320.html) that "four million unsafe abortions occur annually in India, and 13% of maternal mortality in south and central Asia is due to unsafe abortion." Banerjee et al. report that an education intervention using signs, street plays, counseling, and communication materials improved women's knowledge about and access to safe abortion.

Latin America

Latin America consists of the Spanish-, Portuguese-, and French-speaking countries of the Western Hemisphere that lie south of the United States. In many Latin American countries abortion is illegal under all circumstances. In some Latin American countries, however, exceptions exist, such as endangerment of the woman's life, rape, incest, and fetal abnormality. Regardless, women rarely seek legal abortions using these exceptions because they do not know they are eligible, nor do they know the legal requirements for obtaining an abortion. In addition, they may not be able to afford a legal abortion. Hence, abortions have become secret and generally unsafe in Latin America.

In 2007 the Mexico City legislature passed a law legalizing abortion during the first 12 weeks of pregnancy, a law that was upheld by the Mexican Supreme Court in 2008. As Allyn Gaestel and Allison Shelley write in "Mexican Women Pay High Price for Country's Rigid Abortion Laws" (Guardian.com, October 1, 2014), by 2014 more than 100,000 legal abortions had been performed since the law's passage. Abortion, however, was still restricted in other Mexican states and, in a backlash to the law, 16 Mexican states had passed legislation outlawing abortion. According to Gaestel and Shelley, between 2009 and 2011 roughly 679 Mexican women were "reported or sentenced" for having an abortion.

South Africa

When South Africa was under apartheid (a policy of racial segregation that involved political, legal, and social discrimination against nonwhites) between 1948 and 1991, abortion was illegal except in cases where the pregnancy threatened the woman's mental health. Because black people vastly outnumbered white people, the government used tax credits to encourage white women to have children. Nonetheless, many upper- and middle-income women with unwanted pregnancies sought abortions in private physicians' offices or abroad. Many poor women with unwanted pregnancies, however, either terminated their own pregnancies or used the services of unqualified abortionists.

Reacting to pressures from the medical profession and women's groups, the legislature enacted the Abortion and Sterilization Act of 1975, which legalized abortion. Many women continued seeking illegal abortions, however, because of the stringent provisions of the law, such as requiring the approval of two physicians and a psychiatrist.

In November 1996 South Africa's first democratically elected Parliament passed a new abortion law, the most liberal abortion law in Africa, the Choice of Termination of Pregnancy (CTOP) Act. Under the law, women can receive state funding for abortions up to the 12th week of pregnancy. From the 13th to the 20th week of pregnancy, abortion is legal in cases of danger to the mother's physical or mental health, rape, incest, and fetal defect. The law also allows abortion if continuing the pregnancy would affect the woman's social or economic circumstances. Abortion after 20 weeks of pregnancy is allowed if a physician or trained midwife finds that continuation of the pregnancy would threaten the woman's health or result in fetal abnormality. Adolescents are counseled to consult their parents, but the law allows them to have abortions without parental knowledge.

In 2004 CTOP was amended. This legislation designated facilities to provide abortion services to women, decentralized and improved the efficiency of the abortion process, and allowed registered nurses and midwives who have undergone appropriate training to perform abortions. However, the South African Constitutional Court struck down the amendment, ruling that Parliament had not sufficiently involved the public when it passed the abortion law amendment bill. The court gave Parliament 18 months to conduct public hearings. In "Call for Better Abortion Services for HIV-Positive Women" (AllAfrica.com, August 10, 2007), Tamar Kahn reports that researchers determined that since the implementation of the amendment there had been a 91% decline in deaths from abortion-related causes. Parliament held the hearings and the bill was finally passed in January 2008.

Despite these liberalizations, access to abortion, especially in rural areas, is not always available. In "Abortion in a Progressive Legal Environment: The Need for Vigilance in Protecting and Promoting Access to Safe Abortion Services in South Africa" (*American Journal of Public Health*, vol. 103, no. 3, March 1, 2013), Karen A. Trueman and Makgoale Magwentshu report that access to abortion differs depending on a woman's ability to pay for services. Women who can afford to pay the fees can access safe abortion services in private health care facilities, but poor women who cannot afford the fees have to rely on the state or on illegal and often unsafe providers. Trueman and Magwentshu state that "there is evidence that gains made in the first 10 years of our democracy are gradually being eroded, and that the country's poor women are no better off than they were before the CTOP Act."

A WORLDWIDE PLAN FOR REPRODUCTIVE HEALTH

At the landmark International Conference on Population and Development (ICPD) sponsored by the UN in Cairo, Egypt, in September 1994, 179 nations reached consensus on a 20-year plan to achieve reproductive health and rights for all. The plan was wide ranging and included ideas about increased contraceptive services, fewer maternal deaths, better education for girls, and greater equality for women. The Cairo conference was the first in which the pervasiveness of abortions throughout the world was openly discussed.

According to the UN Department of Public Information, in "Summary of the Programme of Action" (March 1995), the international community agreed on a position regarding abortion: "In no case should abortion be promoted as a method of family planning. All Governments and relevant intergovernmental and non-governmental organizations are urged to strengthen their commitment to women's health, to deal with the health impact of unsafe abortion . . . as a major public health concern and to reduce the recourse to abortion through expanded and improved family planning services. Prevention of unwanted pregnancies must always be given the highest priority and all attempts should be made to eliminate the need for abortion. Women who have unwanted pregnancies should have ready access to reliable information and compassionate counselling."

In July 1999, 179 countries met to assess the progress of the Programme of Action. The five-year review process, known as ICPD+5, found that nations implementing the program recommendations had improved conditions within their countries. For example, the UN Population Fund (UNFPA; July 31, 2003, http://www.un.org/popin/unpopcom/32ndsess/gastatements.htm) reports that more than 40 countries had introduced reproductive health services, and nearly half the countries had addressed the issue of adolescent reproductive health needs. Nonetheless, the delegates agreed that much work still needed to be done.

In 2014 the ICPD marked its 20th anniversary. That year, the UN released *Framework of Actions for the Follow-Up to the Programme of Action of the International Conference on Population and Development beyond 2014: Report of the Secretary-General* (February 12, 2014, http://icpdbeyond2014.org/uploads/browser/files/93632_unfpa_eng_web.pdf), in which it reiterated the need to continue expanding reproductive health services throughout the developing world. According to the report, 70,000 adolescent girls in developing countries die each year giving birth, and maternity-related complications are the leading cause of death among women of childbearing age in Africa and South Asia. The report states: "In the area of sexual and reproductive health and reproductive rights, less than two-thirds of countries (63 per cent) have promulgated and enforced a law protecting the right to the highest attainable standard of physical and mental health, including sexual and reproductive health (Asia: 66 per cent; Oceania: 62 per cent; the Americas: 58 per cent; Africa: 55 per cent); the percentage increases to 80 per cent in Europe."

CHAPTER 9

PUBLIC ATTITUDES TOWARD ABORTION

The results of public opinion polls should be viewed cautiously. Public opinion polls are not absolutely accurate; their findings are snapshots of the attitudes of the survey respondents at a given time. As such, survey and poll results vary, even those conducted within days of one another. Typically, well-conducted surveys are accurate to about plus or minus three percentage points.

Historically, abortion has been a highly charged, emotional, and divisive political issue. However, in "Roe v. Wade at 40: Most Oppose Overturning Abortion Decision" (January 16, 2013, http://www.pewforum.org/2013/01/16/roe-v-wade-at-40), the Pew Research Center indicates that in 2013 abortion was a less important issue to some than it had been in the past. A Pew Research Center survey conducted in 2006 found that more than one-quarter (28%) of Americans said abortion was a critical issue, and 38% said it was one among many important issues. By 2013 only 18% described abortion as critical, and 27% named it an important issue among many. That year more than half (53%) of survey respondents said abortion "is not that important compared with other issues," up from 32% in 2006.

AMERICANS SUPPORT LANDMARK ABORTION DECISION

A Gallup Organization poll found that 40 years after the *Roe v. Wade* (410 [1973] U.S. 113) decision the majority of Americans (53%) wanted the decision to stand rather than be overturned (29%). In *Majority of Americans Still Support Roe v. Wade Decision* (January 22, 2013, http://www.gallup.com/poll/160058/majority-americans-support-roe-wade-decision.aspx), Lydia Saad reports that between 1989 and 2013, Americans' attitudes toward *Roe v. Wade* saw only modest changes. The majority consistently opposed overturning the decision, and although the level of support found in 2013 was down from a high of 66% in 2006, the percentage of Americans who wanted the law overturned was also lower than it had been in 2008. The most noticeable change in 2013 was the highest-ever percentage of respondents (18%) who expressed no opinion. Saad also explains that young adults between the ages of 18 and 29 years were most likely to say they have no opinion. She posits that this age group may not have strong opinions about the decision because they did not witness some of the fiery debates about abortion that took place in the late 1980s and early 1990s.

The Pew Research Center survey reported in "Roe v. Wade at 40," conducted just weeks after the Gallup survey, found even greater support for *Roe v. Wade*. More than 63% of survey respondents were opposed to overturning the landmark decision. Like the Gallup poll, the Pew Research Center survey found that 29% of the public wanted the U.S. Supreme Court to completely overturn *Roe v. Wade*.

AMERICANS' VIEWS ABOUT THE LEGALITY OF ABORTION

Despite this strong support for upholding *Roe v. Wade*, Americans remained deeply divided on the issue of abortion's legality. As Table 9.1 shows, in 2015 less than one-third (29%) of all Americans thought that abortion should be legal "under any circumstances," whereas more than one-third (36%) believed that abortion should be legal "only in a few circumstances." Nearly one in five (19%) of Americans held that abortion should be illegal in all circumstances in 2015.

Views about the legality of abortion vary by race and political affiliation. As Table 9.2 shows, white respondents (54%) were more likely than U.S.-born Hispanic (51%) or African American (47%) respondents to believe that abortion should be legal in all or almost all circumstances in 2014. Slightly more than one-third (35%) of foreign-born Hispanics held the same view. By contrast, 60% of foreign-born Hispanics responded that abortion should be illegal in almost all cases, compared with 46% of African

Americans, 43% of U.S.-born Hispanics, and 41% of whites. As Figure 9.1 shows, 66% of Asian Americans supported the idea that abortion should be legal in most or all circumstances, whereas 79% of biracial Asian whites supported legal abortions in all or most cases.

Table 9.3 provides an overview of attitudes toward existing abortion laws based on party identification. Between 2012 and 2015, nearly half (47%) of Democrats surveyed said they were satisfied with the nation's abortion laws. By contrast, only one-quarter (26%) of Republicans expressed satisfaction with existing abortion laws during that period. Whereas 43% of Republicans wanted abortion laws to become more restrictive during these years, only 13% of Democrats held the same view; 15% of Democrats wanted abortion laws to become less restrictive. Among independents, 40% were satisfied with abortion laws between 2012 and 2015, whereas one-quarter (25%) were dissatisfied because they thought abortion laws were not restrictive enough.

PRO-CHOICE/PRO-LIFE IDENTIFICATION

Between 1995 and 2015 the Gallup Organization examined trends on pro-choice/pro-life identification using the consistent stand-alone question: "With respect to the abortion issue, would you consider yourself to be pro-choice or pro-life?" According to Lydia Saad, in *Americans Choose "Pro-Choice" for First Time in Seven Years* (May 29, 2015, http://www.gallup.com/poll/183434/americans-choose-pro-choice-first-time-seven-years.aspx?g_source=ABORTION&g_medium=topic&g_campaign=tiles), those identifying themselves as pro-choice ranged from a high of 56% in 1995 to a low of 41% in 2012. (See Figure 9.2.) Those responding that they were pro-life ranged from a low of 33% in 1995 to a high of 51% in 2009. Between 1995 and 2008 the percentage of Americans who identified as pro-choice was generally higher than the percentage who identified as pro-life. Between 2009 and 2013 responses fluctuated, but the percentage of pro-life supporters was most often higher than that of pro-choice supporters. By 2015 the proportion of pro-choice Americans rose to 50%, whereas the proportion of those expressing pro-life views dipped to 44%.

In general, women are more likely than men to identify as pro-choice. (See Figure 9.3.) Younger Americans are also more likely to have pro-choice views than older Americans. As Figure 9.4 shows, 53% of Americans aged 18 to 34 years were pro-choice in 2015, compared with 52% of Americans aged 35 to 55 years and 47% of Americans aged 55 years and older. In contrast, the proportion of pro-choice Americans between the ages of 18 and 34 years actually fell by two percentage points between 2001 and 2015, whereas the proportion of pro-choice Americans between the ages of 35 and 55 years increased by five percentage points and the proportion of pro-choice Americans 55 years of age and older

TABLE 9.1

Public opinion on the degree to which abortion should be legal, May 2015

[Results among U.S. adults, and by self-identified abortion position]

	U.S. adults	"Pro-choice"	"Pro-life"
	%	%	%
Legal under any circumstances	29	50	4
Legal in most circumstances	13	21	5
Legal in only a few circumstances	36	23	51
Illegal in all circumstances	19	4	37
No opinion	2	2	3

SOURCE: Lydia Saad, "Americans' Preference for the Extent to Which Abortion Should Be Legal," in *Americans Choose "Pro-Choice" for First Time in Seven Years*, The Gallup Organization, May 29, 2015, http://www.gallup.com/poll/183434/americans-choose-pro-choice-first-time-seven-years.aspx?g_source=ABORTION&g_medium=topic&g_campaign=tiles (accessed September 23, 2015).

TABLE 9.2

Opinions of registered voters and of general population on degree to which abortion should be legal, by race and Hispanic origin, 2014

[% saying abortion should be...]

	Registered voters				Total U.S. adults					
	All	Hispanic	White	Black	All	Hispanic	White	Black	U.S.-born Hispanic	Foreign-born Hispanic
Legal in all/most cases	52	48	53	49	51	44	54	47	51	35
Some restrictions	31	28	33	26	31	26	34	24	31	21
Never restricted	20	21	19	23	19	17	19	23	20	14
Illegal in all/most cases	42	44	41	44	43	51	41	46	43	60
Some allowances	28	29	29	27	28	30	28	28	27	35
Never allowed	12	14	11	17	14	20	12	17	15	26
Sample size	2,665	169	2,027	270	3,341	301	2,407	348	182	117

Note: Hispanics are of any race. Whites and blacks include only non-Hispanics. "Don't know/refused" responses not shown.

SOURCE: Mark Hugo Lopez et al., "Table 8. Views of Abortion," in *Latino Voters and the 2014 Midterm Elections*, Pew Research Center, October 16, 2014, http://www.pewhispanic.org/2014/10/16/latino-voters-and-the-2014-midterm-elections/ (accessed September 23, 2015)

FIGURE 9.1

Opinions of Asians and whites on whether or not abortion should be legal, by biracial and single race status, 2015

[% saying abortion should be … in all/most cases]

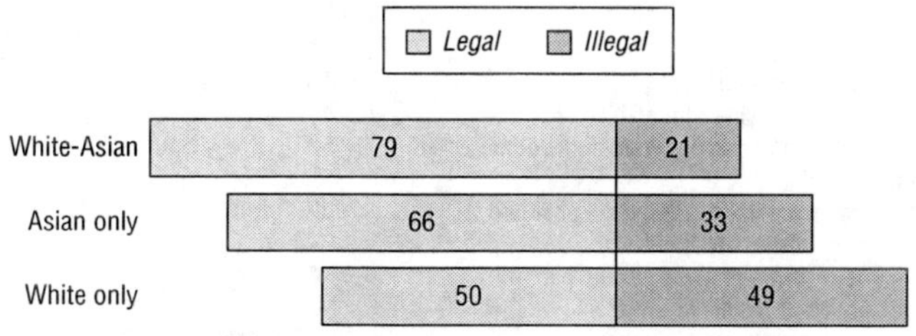

Note: All races and Hispanic origin based on backgrounds of self, parents or grandparents. Biracial white and Asian adults are two races and non-Hispanic (sample = 88). Single-raced groups are one race and non-Hispanic. Those who gave no answer are not shown. February 6–April 6, 2015, sample = 1,555 multiracial adults; sample = 1,495 adults in the general public.

SOURCE: Kim Parker et al., "Biracial Whites and Asians More Likely Than Component Single-Race Groups to Say Abortion Should Be Legal," in *Multiracial in America*, Pew Research Center, June 11, 2015, http://www.pewsocialtrends.org/files/2015/06/2015-06-11_multiracial-in-america_final-updated.pdf (accessed September 23, 2015)

FIGURE 9.2

Positions of Americans on abortion issue, 1995–2015

QUESTION WORDING: WITH RESPECT TO THE ABORTION ISSUE, WOULD YOU CONSIDER YOURSELF TO BE PRO-CHOICE OR PRO-LIFE?

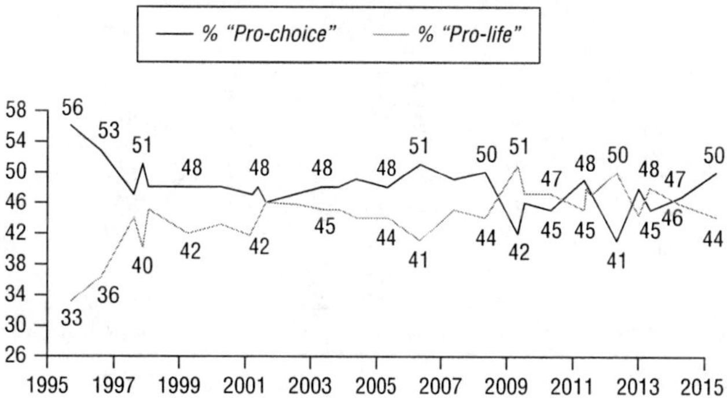

SOURCE: Lydia Saad, "U.S. Adults' Self-Identified Position on the Abortion Issue," in *Americans Choose "Pro-Choice" for First Time in Seven Years*, The Gallup Organization, May 29, 2015, http://www.gallup.com/poll/183434/americans-choose-pro-choice-first-time-seven-years.aspx?g_source=ABORTION&g_medium=topic&g_campaign=tiles (accessed September 23, 2015). Copyright © 2015 Gallup, Inc. All rights reserved. The content is used with permission; however, Gallup retains all rights of republication.

TABLE 9.3

Positions of Americans on abortion laws, by party affiliation, 2002–08 and 2012–15

(ASKED OF THOSE WHO ARE DISSATISFIED) WOULD YOU LIKE TO SEE ABORTION LAWS IN THIS COUNTRY MADE MORE STRICT, LESS STRICT, OR REMAIN AS THEY ARE?

	Average under Bush (2002–2008)	Average under Obama (2012–2015)
Republicans		
% Satisfied	42	26
% Dissatisfied, want stricter laws	38	43
% Dissatisfied, want less strict laws	5	7
% Dissatisfied, want laws to remain the same	7	12
Democrats		
% Satisfied	46	47
% Dissatisfied, want stricter laws	16	13
% Dissatisfied, want less strict laws	15	15
% Dissatisfied, want laws to remain the same	12	10
Independents		
% Satisfied	42	40
% Dissatisfied, want stricter laws	23	25
% Dissatisfied, want less strict laws	11	9
% Dissatisfied, want laws to remain the same	10	9

Note: 2001 was excluded from averages because President Bill Clinton was in office at the time polling was conducted, in January of that year.

SOURCE: Rebecca Rifkin, "Republicans Have Become More Likely to Want Stricter Laws since 2008," in *Fewest Americans Satisfied with Abortion Policies since 2001*, The Gallup Organization, February 9, 2015, http://www.gallup.com/poll/181502/fewest-americans-satisfied-abortion-policies-2001.aspx?g_source=ABORTION&g_medium=topic&g_campaign=tiles (accessed September 23, 2015). Copyright © 2015 Gallup, Inc. All rights reserved. The content is used with permission; however, Gallup retains all rights of republication.

FIGURE 9.3

Americans identifying as "pro-choice" on abortion, by gender, 2001–15

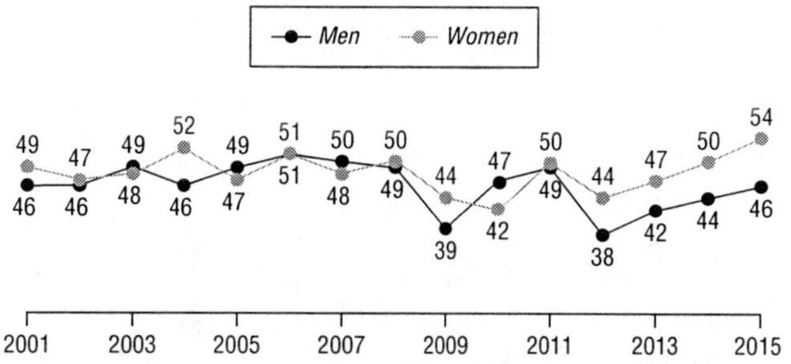

SOURCE: Lydia Saad, "Trend in Percentage Identifying as 'Pro-Choice' on Abortion, by Gender," in *Americans Choose "Pro-Choice" for First Time in Seven Years*, The Gallup Organization, May 29, 2015, http://www.gallup.com/poll/183434/americans-choose-pro-choice-first-time-seven-years.aspx?g_source=ABORTION&g_medium=topic&g_campaign=tiles (accessed September 23, 2015). Copyright © 2015 Gallup, Inc. All rights reserved. The content is used with permission; however, Gallup retains all rights of republication.

increased by seven percentage points over the same period. (See Figure 9.4.) Democrats (68%) were considerably more likely than Republicans (31%) to identify as pro-choice in 2015. (See Figure 9.5.)

MORAL ACCEPTABILITY OF ABORTION

In *Americans Continue to Shift Left on Key Moral Issues* (May 26, 2015, http://www.gallup.com/poll/183413/

FIGURE 9.4

Americans identifying as "pro-choice" on abortion, by age, 2001–15

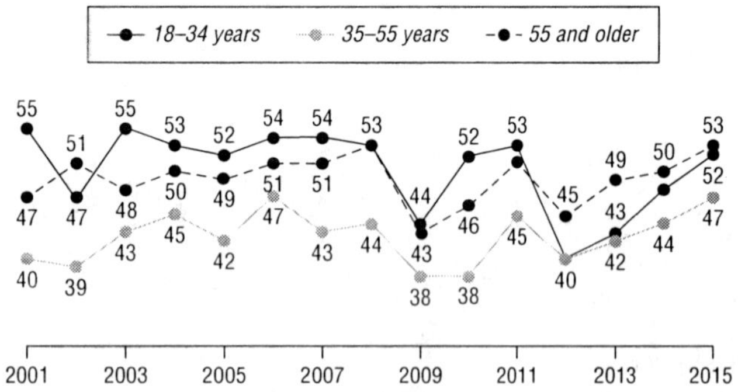

SOURCE: Lydia Saad, "Trend in Percentage Identifying as 'Pro-Choice' on Abortion, by Age," in *Americans Choose "Pro-Choice" for First Time in Seven Years*, The Gallup Organization, May 29, 2015, http://www.gallup.com/poll/183434/americans-choose-pro-choice-first-time-seven-years.aspx?g_source=ABORTION&g_medium=topic&g_campaign=tiles (accessed September 23, 2015). Copyright © 2015 Gallup, Inc. All rights reserved. The content is used with permission; however, Gallup retains all rights of republication.

FIGURE 9.5

Americans identifying as "pro-choice" on abortion, by party affiliation, 2001–15

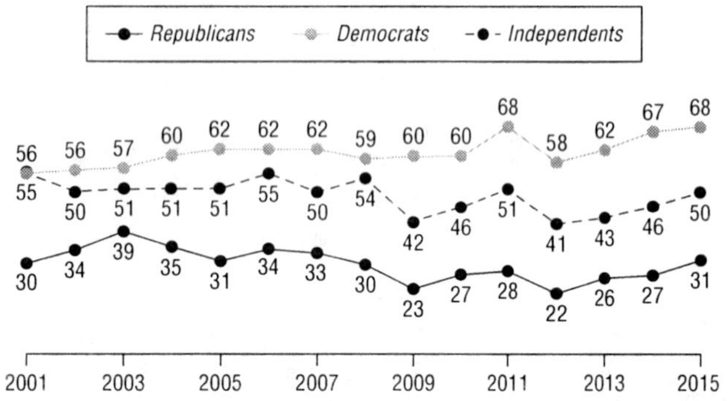

SOURCE: Lydia Saad, "Trend in Percentage Identifying as 'Pro-Choice' on Abortion, by Party ID," in *Americans Choose "Pro-Choice" for First Time in Seven Years*, The Gallup Organization, May 29, 2015, http://www.gallup.com/poll/183434/americans-choose-pro-choice-first-time-seven-years.aspx?g_source=ABORTION&g_medium=topic&g_campaign=tiles (accessed September 23, 2015). Copyright © 2015 Gallup, Inc. All rights reserved. The content is used with permission; however, Gallup retains all rights of republication.

americans-continue-shift-left-key-moral-issues.aspx?g_source=medical%20%20research&g_medium=search&g_campaign=tiles), Frank Newport of the Gallup Organization observes that Americans' views of many moral issues changed between 2001 and 2015. During that span, the proportion of Americans who believed abortion was morally acceptable rose slightly, from 42% to 45%. (See Table 9.4.)

TABLE 9.4

Public opinion on the morality of 16 moral issues including abortion, 2001 and 2015

[% morally acceptable]

	2001 %	2015 %	Change (pct. pts.)
Gay or lesbian relations	40	63	23
Having a baby outside of marriage[a]	45	61	16
Sex between an unmarried man and woman	53	68	15
Divorce	59	71	12
Medical research using stem cells obtained from human embryos[a]	52	64	12
Polygamy (when a married person has more than one spouse at the same time)[b]	7	16	9
Cloning humans	7	15	8
Doctor-assisted suicide	49	56	7
Suicide	13	19	6
Gambling[b]	63	67	4
Abortion	42	45	3
Cloning animals	31	34	3
Buying and wearing clothing made of animal fur	60	61	1
Married men and women having an affair	7	8	1
The death penalty	63	60	−3
Medical testing on animals	65	56	−9

[a]First measured in 2002.
[b]First measured in 2003.
Note: Sorted by change in the percentage saying each is "morally acceptable"; unless otherwise marked, issues first measured in 2001.

SOURCE: Frank Newport, "Moral Acceptability: Changes over Time," in *Americans Continue to Shift Left on Key Moral Issues*, The Gallup Organization, May 26, 2015, http://www.gallup.com/poll/183413/americans-continue-shift-left-key-moral-issues.aspx?g_source=medical%20%20research&g_medium=search&g_campaign=tiles (accessed September 23, 2015). Copyright © 2015 Gallup, Inc. All rights reserved. The content is used with permission; however, Gallup retains all rights of republication.

Table 9.4 also shows that the issues Americans found less morally acceptable than abortion in 2015 included married men and women having affairs, cloning humans or animals, polygamy, and suicide.

As the Pew Research Center reports in *Global Views on Morality* (April 15, 2014, http://www.pewglobal.org/2014/04/15/global-morality/table/abortion), Americans were more likely than citizens of other advanced countries to find abortion morally unacceptable. As shown in Table 9.5, 49% of Americans said that abortion was morally unacceptable in 2013, compared with 17% who said it was morally acceptable, and 23% who did not consider abortion a moral issue at all. By comparison, roughly one-quarter (26%) of Canadians said that abortion was morally unacceptable, whereas one-quarter (26%) said it was morally acceptable, and 37% believed it was not a moral issue.

The Pew Research Center survey also found that opinions about the morality of abortion varied by religion. For a majority of Catholics, for example, abortion represents a sin. Indeed, as Table 9.6 shows, 57% of Catholics believe that abortion is a sin, compared with 44% who believe that homosexual behavior is a sin, or 41% who consider it sinful to acquire luxury goods

TABLE 9.5

Views on moral acceptability of abortion, by country, 2013

DO YOU PERSONALLY BELIEVE THAT HAVING AN ABORTION IS MORALLY ACCEPTABLE, MORALLY UNACCEPTABLE, OR IS NOT A MORAL ISSUE?

Country	Unacceptable	Acceptable	Not a moral issue
Philippines	93%	2%	4%
Ghana	92%	2%	2%
Indonesia	89%	1%	1%
Uganda	88%	2%	6%
El Salvador	85%	2%	3%
Pakistan	85%	1%	4%
Bolivia	83%	6%	4%
Kenya	82%	3%	8%
Nigeria	80%	2%	10%
Malaysia	79%	4%	8%
Brazil	79%	7%	9%
Venezuela	77%	8%	6%
Tunisia	77%	4%	6%
Chile	64%	15%	9%
Mexico	63%	16%	12%
Egypt	62%	5%	22%
South Africa	61%	10%	8%
India	58%	17%	10%
South Korea	58%	19%	12%
Lebanon	56%	8%	18%
Argentina	56%	16%	11%
Greece	54%	16%	11%
Palestinian ter.	54%	7%	13%
Jordan	53%	4%	36%
Turkey	52%	18%	14%
Senegal	52%	14%	22%
United States	49%	17%	23%
Poland	47%	13%	13%
Russia	44%	25%	10%
Italy	41%	25%	11%
China	37%	29%	20%
Israel	35%	25%	23%
Japan	28%	44%	19%
Spain	26%	35%	28%
Australia	26%	29%	32%
Canada	26%	26%	37%
Britain	25%	27%	28%
Germany	19%	43%	25%
Czech Republic	18%	49%	18%
France	14%	38%	47%

SOURCE: Adapted from "Abortion," in *Global Views on Morality*, Pew Research Center, April 15, 2014, http://www.pewglobal.org/2014/04/15/global-morality/table/abortion/ (accessed September 23, 2015)

without donating to the poor. Among Catholics who regularly attend mass, women (59%) are more likely than men (55%) to consider abortion a sin. (See Table 9.7.) Among various Christian denominations, white evangelicals (72%) are most likely to consider abortion a sin, followed by African American Protestants (59%). (See Table 9.8.)

Availability of Abortion

In "Attitudes about Abortion" (January 18, 2013, http://publicreligion.org/2013/01/graphic-of-the-week-attitudes-about-abortion), Cristina Stanojevich of the Public Religion Research Institute (PRRI) asserts that public opinion about abortion cannot be adequately assessed simply by determining views about the legality and morality of abortion. The organization observes that attitudes are a

TABLE 9.6

Views of Catholics and general population on which behaviors are sinful, 2015

WHICH BEHAVIORS ARE SINFUL?

	Among Catholics		Among U.S. general public	
	Yes	No	Yes	No
Do you think it is sinful to ...	%	%	%	%
Have an abortion	57	23	48	22
Engage in homosexual behavior	44	39	45	29
Buy luxuries without giving to poor	41	42	35	38
Remarry after divorce without annulment	35	49	n/a	n/a
Live with romantic partner outside marriage	33	54	36	40
Use energy w/out considering environment	23	61	19	56
Get a divorce	21	61	19	51
Use contraceptives	17	66	10	63
Drink alcohol	12	71	15	58
Live in house larger than needed	12	73	11	64

Notes: Figures do not add to 100%; those who say they don't believe in the concept of sin and those saying they don't know whether each behavior is sinful are not shown.

SOURCE: "Which Behaviors Are Sinful?" in *U.S. Catholics Open to Non-Traditional Families*, Pew Research Center, September 2, 2015, http://www.pewforum.org/files/2015/09/Catholics-and-Family-Life-09-01-2015.pdf (accessed September 23, 2015)

TABLE 9.7

Attitudes among Catholics toward sinfulness of abortion and contraception, by sex, age, Hispanic origin, marital status, political affiliation, and frequency of attending Mass, 2015

[Based on all Catholics]

	Sinful to have an abortion?		Sinful to use contraceptives?	
	Yes	No	Yes	No
	%	%	%	%
All Catholics	57	23	17	66
Men	55	25	18	64
Women	59	21	17	67
Ages				
18–29	60	26	19	65
30–49	61	20	16	69
50–64	54	25	18	67
65+	53	22	20	60
White	52	26	15	69
Hispanic	68	15	22	60
Married	58	22	18	67
Not married	57	23	17	64
Republican	66	21	21	68
Democrat	48	29	14	69
Independent	58	21	16	67
Mass attendance				
Weekly or more	73	14	31	57
Less often	47	28	9	71
Monthly/yearly	50	27	9	73
Seldom/never	40	30	9	66

Notes: Figures do not add to 100%; those who say they do not believe in the concept of sin and those saying they don't know whether each behavior is sinful are not shown. Whites include non-Hispanics; Hispanics can be of any race.

SOURCE: Adapted from "Even among Regular Mass-Attending Catholics, Most Say Contraception Is Not a Sin," in *U.S. Catholics Open to Non-Traditional Families*, Pew Research Center, September 2, 2015, http://www.pewforum.org/files/2015/09/Catholics-and-Family-Life-09-01-2015.pdf (accessed September 23, 2015)

TABLE 9.8

Attitudes toward sinfulness of abortion and contraception, by Christian denomination, age, race/ethnicity, and political affiliation, 2015

[Based on all respondents]

	Sinful to have an abortion?		Sinful to use contraceptives?	
	Yes	No	Yes	No
	%	%	%	%
Catholics	57	23	17	66
Cultural Catholics	39	33	11	67
Ex-Catholics	43	19	7	56
U.S. general public	48	22	10	63
Protestants	60	20	10	74
White evangelical	72	13	9	78
White mainline	39	35	5	78
Black Protestant	59	20	15	65
Unaffiliated	22	21	7	39
Ages				
18–29	43	22	12	49
30–49	54	19	10	67
50–64	48	25	9	71
65+	42	21	11	60
White	44	23	7	65
Black	53	22	15	61
Hispanic	65	14	20	59
Republican	61	19	11	72
Democrat	38	26	10	59
Independent	47	21	10	63

Notes: Figures do not add to 100%; those who say they don't believe in the concept of sin and those saying they don't know whether each behavior is sinful are not shown. Whites and blacks include non-Hispanics; Hispanics can be of any race.

SOURCE: Adapted from "Religious and Demographic Differences on Sinfulness of Abortion, Homosexual Behavior and Contraception," in *U.S. Catholics Open to Non-Traditional Families*, Pew Research Center, September 2, 2015, http://www.pewforum.org/files/2015/09/Catholics-and-Family-Life-09-01-2015.pdf (accessed September 23, 2015)

FIGURE 9.6

Americans' views on importance of abortion as a political issue, 1997–2015

THINKING ABOUT HOW THE ABORTION ISSUE MIGHT AFFECT YOUR VOTE FOR MAJOR OFFICES, WOULD YOU—ONLY VOTE FOR A CANDIDATE WHO SHARES YOUR VIEWS ON ABORTION (OR) CONSIDER A CANDIDATE'S POSITION ON ABORTION AS JUST ONE OF MANY IMPORTANT FACTORS (OR) NOT SEE ABORTION AS A MAJOR ISSUE?

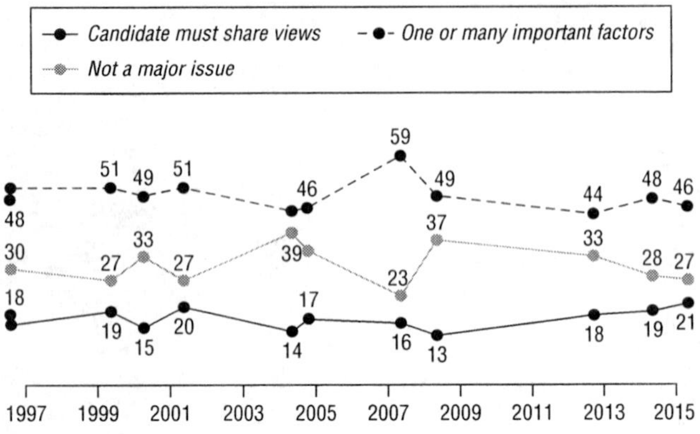

SOURCE: Rebecca Riffkin, "Most Americans Do Not Consider Abortion Top Issue When Voting," in *Abortion Edges up as Important Voting Issue for Americans*, The Gallup Organization, May 29, 2015, http://www.gallup.com/poll/183449/abortion-edges-important-voting-issue-americans.aspx?g_source=ABORTION&g_medium=topic&g_campaign=tiles (accessed September 23, 2015). Copyright © 2015 Gallup, Inc. All rights reserved. The content is used with permission; however, Gallup retains all rights of republication.

complex interplay of views about the morality, legality, and availability of abortion. PRRI's survey findings reveal that in 2011 majorities of Americans believed that abortion should be legal in all or some cases (56%). Similarly, nearly six in 10 (58%) survey respondents believed that at least some health care professionals in their communities should provide abortions. However, only 40% believed that abortion was morally acceptable.

Stanojevich points out that millennials (people born between 1980 and 2000) were unusual in that they supported access to abortion at a notably higher level (68%) than they did the legality of abortion (60%). Stanojevich observes that "limiting the abortion debate strictly to questions about legality provides for an incomplete picture of public opinion, and masks important differences among Americans on this important topic."

OPINIONS ON GOVERNMENT ABORTION POLICY

In general, a candidate's position on abortion is not the sole factor in determining how most Americans vote. As Figure 9.6 shows, in 2015 roughly one out of five Americans (21%) thought that a candidate must share their views on abortion, compared to roughly half (46%) who considered abortion only one of several important issues. Pro-life Americans (23%) were slightly more likely than pro-choice Americans (19%) to vote for a candidate only if they shared their position on abortion. (See Figure 9.7.)

One of the first items on the presidential agenda of Barack Obama (1961–) when he took office in January 2009 was to rescind the Mexico City Policy, which had been put into place by President Ronald Reagan (1911–2004). This policy had been enforced by executive order for almost a decade before being rescinded by President Bill Clinton (1946–). It was later reinstated by President George W. Bush (1946–). The Mexico City Policy stated that the United States would not provide financial support for private family planning groups overseas that performed or promoted abortion. By reversing this policy, Obama made his pro-choice stance on abortion clear. (See Chapter 3.)

In May 2009, after President Obama had been in office for 100 days, CNN and the Opinion Research Corporation conducted a poll on the new president's performance and reported the findings in "CNN Poll: Abortion Not Hurting

FIGURE 9.7

Percentage of Americans who vote based on candidate's position on abortion, 2001–15

THINKING ABOUT HOW THE ABORTION ISSUE MIGHT AFFECT YOUR VOTE FOR MAJOR OFFICES, WOULD YOU—ONLY VOTE FOR A CANDIDATE WHO SHARES YOUR VIEWS ON ABORTION (OR) CONSIDER A CANDIDATE'S POSITION ON ABORTION AS JUST ONE OF MANY IMPORTANT FACTORS (OR) NOT SEE ABORTION AS A MAJOR ISSUE?

[% only vote for candidate who shares views]

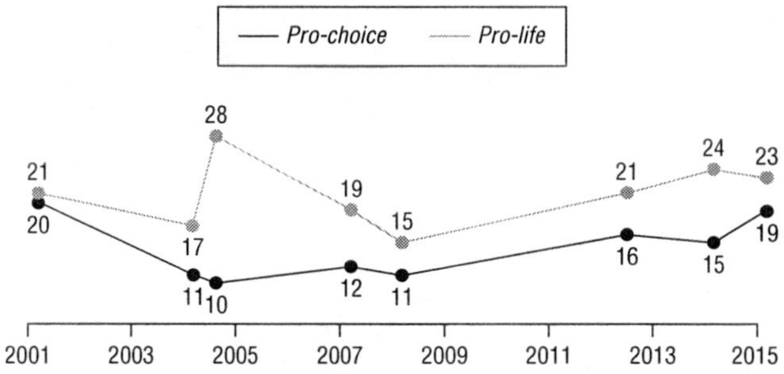

SOURCE: Rebecca Riffkin, "Importance of Abortion to Votes of Pro-Life and Pro-Choice Americans," in *Abortion Edges up as Important Voting Issue for Americans*, The Gallup Organization, May 29, 2015, http://www.gallup.com/poll/183449/abortion-edges-important-voting-issue-americans.aspx?g_source=ABORTION&g_medium=topic&g_campaign=tiles (accessed September 23, 2015). Copyright © 2015 Gallup, Inc. All rights reserved. The content is used with permission; however, Gallup retains all rights of republication.

FIGURE 9.8

Percentage of Americans expressing satisfaction with government policies on abortion, by political affiliation, 2001–15

NEXT, WE'D LIKE TO KNOW HOW YOU FEEL ABOUT THE STATE OF THE NATION IN EACH OF THE FOLLOWING AREAS. FOR EACH ONE, PLEASE SAY WHATEVER YOU ARE—VERY SATISFIED, SOMEWHAT SATISFIED, SOMEWHAT DISSATISFIED, OR VERY DISSATISFIED. HOW ABOUT THE NATION'S POLICIES REGARDING THE ABORTION ISSUE?

[% very/somewhat satisfied]

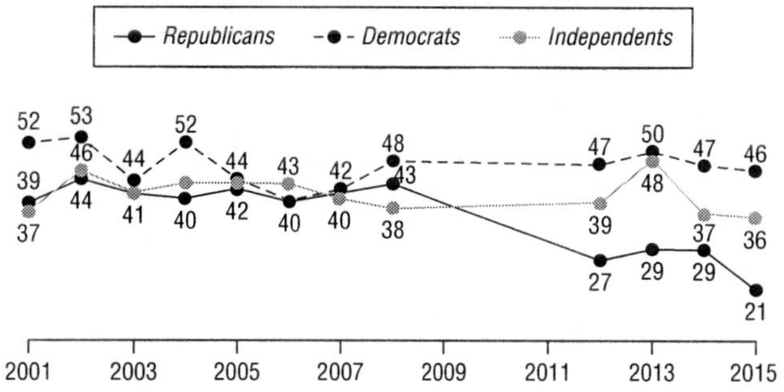

SOURCE: Rebecca Rifkin, "Satisfaction with U.S. Abortion Policies, by Political Affiliation," in *Fewest Americans Satisfied with Abortion Policies since 2001*, The Gallup Organization, February 9, 2015, http://www.gallup.com/poll/181502/fewest-americans-satisfied-abortion-policies-2001.aspx?g_source=ABORTION&g_medium=topic&g_campaign=tiles (accessed September 23, 2015). Copyright © 2015 Gallup, Inc. All rights reserved. The content is used with permission; however, Gallup retains all rights of republication.

Obama" (May 18, 2009, http://politicalticker.blogs.cnn.com/2009/05/18/cnn-poll-abortion-not-hurting-obama). Pollsters asked 1,010 adult Americans whether President Obama's views on abortion changed their view of him and the job he was doing as president. A majority (57%) of respondents answered that the president's pro-choice stance had no effect on their opinion of him. By comparison, 27% said his views on abortion made them think less favorably of him, and 14% said his views made them think more favorably of him.

In April 2013 President Obama stated his views about abortion at the time of the trial of Kermit Gosnell. Gosnell, a physician who ran an abortion clinic in Philadelphia, was ultimately sentenced to life in prison without parole for the murders of several babies born alive after botched abortions, as well as for involuntary manslaughter relating to the death of a patient. In "Obama: Abortion Violators Should Be Prosecuted" (WashingtonTimes.com, April 17, 2013), Dave Boyer reports that when asked about his own views, the president said, "I think President Clinton said it pretty well when he said abortion should be safe, legal and rare." Boyer also quotes Obama as saying that "if an individual carrying out an abortion, operating a clinic or doing anything else is violating medical ethics, violating the law, then they should be prosecuted."

As Figure 9.8 shows, however, overall satisfaction with government abortion policies has declined steadily

FIGURE 9.9

Percentage of Americans expressing satisfaction with government policies on abortion, 2001–15

NEXT, WE'D LIKE TO KNOW HOW YOU FEEL ABOUT THE STATE OF THE NATION IN EACH OF THE FOLLOWING AREAS. FOR EACH ONE, PLEASE SAY WHATEVER YOU ARE—VERY SATISFIED, SOMEWHAT SATISFIED, SOMEWHAT DISSATISFIED, OR VERY DISSATISFIED. HOW ABOUT THE NATION'S POLICIES REGARDING THE ABORTION ISSUE?

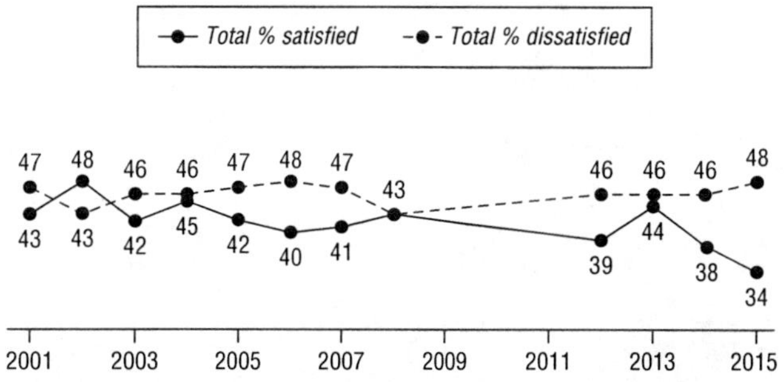

SOURCE: Rebecca Rifkin, "Satisfaction with U.S. Abortion Policies," in *Fewest Americans Satisfied with Abortion Policies since 2001*, The Gallup Organization, February 9, 2015, http://www.gallup.com/poll/181502/fewest-americans-satisfied-abortion-policies-2001.aspx?g_source=ABORTION&g_medium=topic&g_campaign=tiles (accessed September 23, 2015). Copyright © 2015 Gallup, Inc. All rights reserved. The content is used with permission; however, Gallup retains all rights of republication.

since Obama took office. In 2008 roughly an equal proportion of Americans expressed satisfaction or dissatisfaction with government abortion policies, at 43% for each view. By 2015 the percentage of Americans who were satisfied with the government's policies on abortion had fallen to 34%, whereas the proportion of those who were dissatisfied rose to 48%. Whereas support for Obama's abortion policies has remained relatively steady among Democrats, approval of abortion policies has declined dramatically among Republicans over the course of Obama's presidency, falling from 43% in 2008 to 21% in 2015. (See Figure 9.9.)

CHAPTER 10

ABORTION: THE ONGOING DEBATE

On January 22, 1973, the U.S. Supreme Court handed down a landmark decision in the now famous *Roe v. Wade* (410 U.S. 113) legal battle. The ruling made it legal for a woman and her doctor to choose abortion without restrictions during the earlier months of pregnancy and with restrictions during the later months.

The 42nd anniversary of *Roe v. Wade* in 2015 prompted supporters and opponents of the decision to reflect on the landmark decision. The excerpts and statements presented in this chapter reflect the positions of both pro-life and pro-choice politicians and activists on whether or not *Roe v. Wade* should be reconsidered. The chapter also includes statements expressing both opposition and support for new laws that would ban late-term abortions.

THE *ROE V. WADE* DECISION SHOULD BE RECONSIDERED

Speech of Arizona Representative Trent Franks (1957–; R) on the 42nd Anniversary of the *Roe v. Wade* Decision, January 22, 2015

Mr. Speaker, another legislative day has come to an end, and sunset approaches fast in Washington, D.C. And as I have so many years, I stand before you in this House with what I call a Sunset Memorial, because, you see, Mr. Speaker, before the sun sets today in America, almost 4,000 more defenseless unborn children will be killed by abortion on demand in the land of the free and the home of the brave. That is more than the number of innocent lives lost on September 11 in this country by a multitude of thousands. And it happens every day.

It has now been 42 years since the tragedy called *Roe v. Wade* was first handed down. Since then, the very foundation of this Nation has been stained by the blood of almost 56 million of its own unborn children. Some of them, Mr. Speaker, cried and screamed as they died, but because it was amniotic fluid going over the vocal cords instead of air, we couldn't hear them.

All of them had at least four things in common, Mr. Speaker. First, they were just little babies who had never done anything wrong to anyone. Each one of them died a nameless and lonely death. And each one of their mothers, whether she realizes it or not, will never quite be the same. All the gifts that these children might have brought for humanity and to humanity are now lost forever.

Yet, Mr. Speaker, even in the glare of such tragedy, this generation still clings to this blind, invincible ignorance while history repeats itself over and over again, and our silent genocide mercilessly annihilates the most helpless of all victims—those yet unborn.

We should remember the quotes of President Abraham Lincoln when he said:

> Those who deny freedom to others deserve it not themselves, and under a just God, cannot long retain it.

Mr. Lincoln called upon all of us to remember America's Founding Fathers when he said:

> Their enlightened belief was that nothing stamped with the divine image and likeness was sent into the world to be trodden on or degraded and imbruted by its fellows.

He reminded those he called posterity—and that is us, Mr. Speaker:

> When in the distant future some man, some factions, some interests should set up a doctrine that some were not entitled to life, liberty, and the pursuit of happiness that their posterity—again, Mr. Speaker, that is us—might look up again to the Declaration of Independence and take courage to renew the battle which their fathers began.

Mr. Speaker, when authorities entered the clinic of Dr. Kermit Gosnell, they found a torture chamber for little babies that defies description within the constraints of the English language.

According to the grand jury report:

Dr. Kermit Gosnell had a simple solution for unwanted babies: he killed them. Now, he didn't call it that. He called it "ensuring fetal demise." And the way he ensured fetal demise was by sticking scissors in the back of the baby's neck and cutting the spinal cord. He called it snipping. Over the years there were hundreds of snippings.

Mr. Speaker, Ashley Baldwin, one of Dr. Gosnell's employees, said she saw babies breathing, and she described one as two feet long that no longer had eyes or a mouth, but, in her words, was making like this screeching noise. She said: "It sounded like a little alien."

For God's sake, Mr. Speaker, is this who we really are?

Kermit Gosnell now rightfully sits in prison for killing a mother and murdering innocent, pain-capable children like the one I just described. Yet if he had killed them only five minutes earlier and before they had passed through the birth canal, it would have all been perfectly legal in many of the United States of America, including here in the District of Columbia.

If there is one thing we must not miss about this unspeakably evil episode it is that Kermit Gosnell is not an anomaly. He is just the visible face of this lucrative enterprise of murdering pain-capable unborn children in America. Mr. Speaker, more than 18,000 very late-term abortions are occurring in America every year, placing the mothers at exponentially greater risk and subjecting their pain-capable unborn babies to torture and death without anesthesia. It is the worst atrocity in America today, and this in the land of the free and the home of the brave.

Throughout history there has often been great intensity surrounding the debates of protecting the innocent lives of those who, through no fault of their own, find themselves obscured in the shadows of humanity. It encourages me greatly that in nearly all of those cases the collective conscience was finally moved in favor of the victims.

The same thing is beginning to happen in this debate related to innocent, unborn children, Mr. Speaker, especially those that are pain capable. We are beginning to ask ourselves the real question: Does abortion take the life of a child? We are especially asking the question recently: Does very late-term abortion torture and take the life of a pain-capable baby? And we are finally beginning to realize as human beings that it does.

Ultrasound technology now demonstrates to all reasonable observers both the humanity of the victim and the inhumanity of what is being done to them. And we are beginning to realize as Americans that taking brutally the lives of the innocent unborn does not liberate anyone and that 56 million children, Mr. Speaker, is enough.

Ironically I have heard Barack Obama speak such poignant words that, whether he knows it or not, apply so profoundly to the tragedy of abortion on demand in America. Let me quote excerpted portions of his comments. He said:

This is our first task—caring for our children. It is our first job. If we don't get that right, we don't get anything right. That is how, as a society, we will be judged.

He went on to say:

And by that measure, can we truly say, as a nation, that we are meeting our obligations? Can we honestly say that we are doing enough to keep our children—all of them—safe from harm? Can we say that we are truly doing enough to give all the children of this country the chance they deserve to live out their lives with happiness and purpose?

The President went on to say:

I have been reflecting on this the last few days, and if we are honest with ourselves, the answer is no. We are not doing enough. And we will have to change.

Oh, how true the President's words are, Mr. Speaker.

The President also said:

We can't tolerate this anymore. These tragedies must end. And to end them, we must change.

And then the President asked:

Are we really prepared to say that we are powerless in the face of such carnage, that the politics are too hard? Are we prepared to say that such violence visited on our children year after year after year is somehow the price of freedom?

Mr. Speaker, is this not the most relevant of questions we should all be asking in the midst of this genocidal murder of thousands of unborn babies in America every day?

The President has said: "Our journey is not complete until all our children" ... are "cared for and cherished and always safe from harm."

Finally, he said: "That is our generation's task—to make these words, these rights, these values of life and liberty and the pursuit of happiness real for every American."

Mr. Speaker, never have I so deeply agreed with any words ever spoken by President Barack Obama as those I have just quoted, and yet this President in the most merciless distortion of logic and reason and humanity itself refuses to apply these majestic words to helpless unborn babies.

Oh, how I wish somehow that Mr. Obama and all of us could open our hearts and our ears to his words and ask ourselves in the core of our own soul why his words that should apply to all children cannot apply to the most helpless of all children.

Mr. Speaker, we honor Abraham Lincoln most because he found the courage as President of the United States in the days of slavery, and he found the humanity within himself to recognize the image of God stamped on the soul of slaves that the Supreme Court said were not human and that the tide of public opinion didn't recognize as protectable under the law.

Could it still be that President Barack Obama might consider that perspective as well as his own legacy, and even eternity itself, and recognize that those little unborn children look so desperately to him now for help?

Could it be that the President might finally remember that on the pages of the Bible on which he laid his hands were the words written in red: "Inasmuch as you have done it unto one of the least of these My brethren, you have done it unto Me"?

Whether he does or not, it is time for those of us in this Chamber to remind ourselves of why we are really all here. Thomas Jefferson said:

The care of human life and its happiness and not its destruction is the chief and only object of good government.

The phrase in the 14th Amendment capsulizes our entire Constitution. It says:

No State shall deprive any person of life, liberty or property, without the due process of law.

The 14th Amendment tells us that we should have equal protection of the laws for all. Mr. Speaker, protecting the lives of all Americans and their constitutional rights is why we are all here.

The bedrock foundation of this Republic is that clarion declaration of the self-evident truth that all human beings are created equal and endowed by their Creator with unalienable rights, the rights of life and liberty and the pursuit of happiness. Every conflict and battle our Nation has ever faced can be traced to our commitment to this core self-evident truth. It has made us the beacon of hope for the entire world. Mr. Speaker, it is truly who we are.

Yet today another day has passed. As so many sunset memorials that I have given, another day has passed, and we in this body have failed again to honor that foundational commitment. We have failed our sworn oath and our God-given responsibility as we broke faith with nearly 4,000 more innocent, unborn babies who died today without the protection we should have given them.

So, Mr. Speaker, let me conclude this sunset memorial in the hope that perhaps someone new who heard it will finally embrace the truth that abortion really does kill little babies, that it hurts mothers in ways that we can never express, and that it is time we stood up together again and looked up to the Declaration of Independence, and that we remember that we are the same America that rejected human slavery and marched into Europe to arrest the Nazi Holocaust, and we are still the courageous and compassionate Nation that can find a better way for mothers and their unborn children than abortion on demand.

It is still not too late for us to make a better world and for America to be the one that leads the rest of the planet, just as we did in the days of slavery, from this tragic genocide of murdering nearly 4,000 of our own children every day.

So now, Mr. Speaker, as we consider the thousands, the hundreds of thousands out on The Mall marching to protect these little babies, as we consider the plight of the unborn for 42 years under *Roe v. Wade*, maybe we can each remind ourselves that our own days in this sunshine of life are all numbered and that we, too, each one, shall walk from these Chambers one day for the very last time.

If it should be that Congress is allowed to convene on yet another day, may that be the day when we finally hear the cries, when we finally hear the cries of innocent, unborn children. May that be the day when we find the humanity and the constitutional duty to protect these, the least of our tiny little American brothers and sisters, from this murderous scourge upon our Nation called abortion on demand.

Mr. Speaker, it is now 42 years to the day since *Roe v. Wade* first stained the foundation of this Nation with the blood of its own children—this, in the land of the free and the home of the brave. (https://www.congress.gov/crec/2015/01/22/CREC-2015-01-22.pdf)

Speech of Utah Senator Orrin Hatch (1934–; R) on the 42nd Anniversary of the *Roe v. Wade* Decision, January 22, 2015

Mr. President, today is the anniversary of a tragedy. Forty-two years ago today, the Supreme Court announced its creation of a right to abortions for virtually any reason at all virtually at any time. The result of that decision is a tragedy for our society, for our culture, and for our precious life lost.

Since even before America's founding, the law was on a steady march toward protecting human beings before birth. In the 19th century, medical professionals and civil rights activists led a movement that succeeded in prohibiting abortion in every State except to save the mother's life. America had reached a consensus on the importance of protecting the most vulnerable. Unfortunately, the Supreme Court swept all of that aside, imposing upon the country a permissive abortion regime that the American people to this day have never chosen or accepted.

The debate over the morality and legality or policy of abortion begins with one inescapable fact—every abortion kills a living human being. Many have tried mightily to avoid, obscure, distract from, or ignore that fact, but it will not go away. Every abortion kills a living human being. That fact informed President Ronald Reagan when he wrote a moving essay titled "Abortion and the Conscience of the Nation" in 1983.

He wrote, "We cannot diminish the value of one category of human life—the unborn—without diminishing the value of all human life." The real question, President Reagan said, is not about when human life begins, but about the value of human life. I believe that remains the real question today.

Today the United States is one of only seven nations in the world to allow abortion into the sixth month of pregnancy and beyond. That list of nations includes such champions of human rights as China and North Korea. Yet, in 1948, the United States voted in favor of the Universal Declaration of Human Rights, which recognizes in its preamble the inherent dignity and inalienable rights of "all members of the human family."

Article 3 of the declaration states that "everyone has a right to life." Words such as "universal" and "inherent" and "all" are unambiguous and clear.

Our embrace of the inherent dignity and worth of all human beings in 1948 stands in jarring contrast to the Supreme Court's decision in *Roe* just 25 years later, that the life of any human being may be ended before birth.

The Supreme Court might have thought in 1973 that it was settling the abortion issue. By 1992, however, the Court conceded that the rules it created in *Roe* simply did not work and issued revised regulations in a case titled *Planned Parenthood v. Casey*. The Court said then that the contending sides in the abortion controversy should "end their national division by accepting a common mandate rooted in the Constitution."

National division on any issue, let alone one so profound as the taking and the value of human life, will not end simply because the Court says so. The division over abortion not only continues, but has remained largely unchanged even after dozens of Supreme Court decisions and four decades of insisting that abortion is a constitutional right.

The Supreme Court can render opinions on constitutionality, but it is limited in its ability to forge lasting consensus. That is the provenance of our great deliberative bodies where the people are truly represented.

More than 70 percent of Americans believe abortion should be illegal in most or all circumstances. That figure has not changed in 40 years. What has changed is that more Americans today identify themselves as pro-life than pro-choice. Large majorities favor a range of limitations on abortion and last November elected scores of new pro-life Senators at both the State and Federal level.

We must not avoid the fundamental question of the value of human life, for no question is more important. Do we still, as we once did, believe that every human being has inherent dignity and worth?

Two nights ago, in his State of the Union Address, President Obama spoke about the values that are at stake in the public policy choices we must make. Is there any value more important than life itself? He spoke about expanding opportunities for individuals, but the first opportunity that must be secured is the opportunity for life itself.

For many, the right to abortion is a symbol of progress. However, the idea that an act resulting in killing a living human being should be held up as a step forward, as a light to guide our way, strikes me as deeply misguided. We should instead be deepening the conviction that all human beings have inherent dignity and worth. That has been and should remain the foundation of our culture, society, and even our politics.

In his 1983 essay, President Reagan wrote that "we cannot survive as a free nation when some men decide that others are not fit to live and should be abandoned to abortion."

Today's tragic anniversary is a reminder of how our Nation's survival depends on respecting the essential dignity and worth of every human individual. Resting in the balance is how we ultimately define who we are as a people and what we strive to be as a nation.

This is an important issue. It is not one that should be slighted over. It is an issue that should strike at the heart of every person in this body. It is an issue that we all should stand up to strengthen and fight against in the case of this issue of abortion.

I am so grateful that so many people feel the same way, and that more and more people in this country are starting to realize every human life is important and that this society has sometimes gotten off track and not respected the rights of human beings. I think *Roe v. Wade* led us there, and we should be let out of *Roe v. Wade* by those who know there is a better way to have the sensitivity that society deserves to have, should have, and I believe will have in the future. (https://www.congress.gov/crec/2015/01/22/CREC-2015-01-22.pdf)

THE *ROE V. WADE* DECISION SHOULD NOT BE RECONSIDERED

Statement of Washington Senator Patty Murray (1950–; D) on the 42nd Anniversary of the *Roe v. Wade* Decision, January 22, 2015

Forty-two years ago today the Supreme Court issued a constitutional guarantee in *Roe v. Wade* to women across the country, affirming their fundamental right to make their own choices about their own bodies. *Roe v. Wade* was a critical step forward for equality and opportunity for women across America.

It is deeply disappointing that decades later, Republicans in Congress and in state governments continue to push for policies that threaten the basic rights of every woman. Last night, in fact, House Republican leaders were forced to pull a bill from the floor that was so extreme and harmful some women in their own caucus withdrew their support, despite voting for the same measure last year. Unfortunately, rather than stepping back from their attacks, House Republicans doubled down and replaced that bill with yet another damaging legislative threat to women's health access, safety, and choice.

In November, Majority Leader [Mitch] McConnell [1942–; R-KY] told the American people he was committed to working across the aisle to create jobs and grow the economy. I truly hope this means he will refuse to take up partisan, harmful legislation that would turn back the clock on women's rights and choice. I hope we can all focus on moving forward, not backward, for women and work together to prevent unwanted pregnancies, improve access to preventive health services, and protect the basic premise that a woman's health care decisions are hers alone to make.

But let me be very clear: if Majority Leader McConnell chooses to go down the partisan path we've seen from Republicans before on women's health, Democrats and women and men across the country will be ready to stand up and fight back. We're not going anywhere, and that's why bills that threaten women's fundamental rights aren't either. (http://www.murray.senate.gov/public/index.cfm/2015/1/murray-statement-on-roe-v-wade-anniversary-continued-gop-attacks-on-women-s-health-care-decisions)

Statement of President Barack Obama (1961–; D) on the 42nd Anniversary of the *Roe v. Wade* Decision, January 22, 2015

Forty-two years ago today, the U.S. Supreme Court issued its ruling in *Roe v. Wade*, a decision that protects a woman's freedom to make her own choices about her body and her health, and reaffirms a fundamental American value: that government should not intrude in our most private and personal family matters.

I am deeply committed to protecting this core constitutional right, and I believe that efforts like H.R. 7, the bill the House considered today, would intrude on women's reproductive freedom and access to health care and unnecessarily restrict the private insurance choices that consumers have today. The federal government should not be injecting itself into decisions best made between women, their families, and their doctors. I am also deeply committed to continuing our work to reduce unintended pregnancies, support maternal and child health, promote adoptions, and minimize the need for abortion.

Today, as we reflect on this critical moment in our history, may we all rededicate ourselves to ensuring that our daughters have the same rights, freedoms, and opportunities as our sons. (https://www.whitehouse.gov/the-press-office/2015/01/22/statement-president-42nd-anniversary-roe-v-wade)

Speech of California Senator Barbara Boxer (1940–; D) on the 42nd Anniversary of the *Roe v. Wade* Decision, January 22, 2015

Before *Roe v. Wade* was decided in the 1970s, women died because they could not end a pregnancy even if they were raped. There are bodies buried in America, and we don't know the cause of death because if a woman tried to end an unwanted pregnancy—sometimes as a result of rape or even incest—she would be considered a criminal. And that is what you hear from my colleagues on the other side. They say, let's go back to the last century— let's undo *Roe v. Wade*.

It is hard for me to believe that here I stand in this century arguing that women should be respected, that families should be respected, and that everyone's religion should be respected. I support a woman's right to choose, and that means if your religion says you will never end an unwanted pregnancy, I support you.

I believe this decision should be between a woman, her doctor, her family, and her God. I don't think any Senator should get in the middle of a woman's private life. It is dangerous to do so, it is wrong to do so, and to do so in the name of doing something that is going to help the family—it doesn't make sense to me.

The Republican Party used to be the party of individual freedom and individual rights. When I was on the board of Planned Parenthood so many years ago, before *Roe v. Wade*, do you know who was very active and on their board? George Herbert Walker Bush [1924–]. This was an issue that was embraced by Republicans and Democrats—individual respect and rights for women and caring about a woman's health. It was not a partisan issue.

I don't see how interfering with a woman's health, or her right to choose, in any way is helpful to her in a time of need. It should be her decision within the law. We don't want to go back to the last century.

I was glad to see that the Republicans in the House pulled a bill off the floor because it was so nasty to women. It didn't even allow women the right to terminate a pregnancy at a certain date if the woman was a victim of rape. They pulled it, but then they replaced it with another terrible bill that also limits a woman's right to choose.

My Republican friends would make doctors criminals and put them in jail for years and years. They would make women criminals. They have even had a bill that said that a grandmother should be put in jail if she helps her granddaughter. As a grandmother, that was too much for me. How dare some Senator come down here and tell a grandma what to do for her granddaughter? This is the party of individual freedom that always decries too much government? Come on. This is putting the government right in the middle of our most personal decisions. It never used to be that way, but that is the way it is now.

Everyone deserves respect for their views. They should not be taunted for their views, and that is why the right to choose makes so much sense. You don't tell someone that the government says you must do A, B, or C. You tell the person within the law—within *Roe*, which was a modest decision at the time—you make a decision, we respect that decision, and we don't need to know about it.

Putting Senators in the middle of our private lives is not why I came to the Senate. We have a lot of work to do. We have to work on good jobs. We have to pass a highway bill. We have to make sure this planet is habitable for people. Talk about kindness. Think about future generations who have to live on a planet that is increasingly inhospitable. Scientists tell us if we don't do anything about climate, at the end of the day it may be an uninhabitable planet.

We have a lot of work to do. We all do. It seems to me we should start off by doing what government should do, not putting ourselves in the middle of private lives.

Again, I greatly respect my colleagues whose views are different than mine. All I ask them to think about is this: If we embrace the right to choose, then we are saying to women all over America that this is a tough decision and we understand that. Make it with your God. Make it with your loved ones. But we are not going to be right there in the middle of people's living rooms telling them what we think is right, because that is not why we were elected.

I am glad I happened to be on the floor to follow the remarks of Senator Hatch. I feel very strongly about this. As many of my colleagues know, the Democratic women of the Senate and several of our Republican women colleagues will continue to fight against saying to a woman that she has no right to make a most private, most personal decision without satisfying U.S. Senators, most of whom are men, by the way. It is just not right.

Speaking of polls, because I think Senator Hatch mentioned one, people want us to have a moderate approach on this. They don't want abortion on demand and neither does any prochoice Senator. *Roe v. Wade* spelled it out. In the early stages we know a woman has that right; later, only if her health or her life is threatened. It is pretty modest. It makes sense. Leave it alone. That decision was made in 1973. Don't turn the clock back in this century. (https://www.congress.gov/crec/2015/01/22/CREC-2015-01-22.pdf)

Speech of Tennessee Representative Steve Cohen (1949–; D) on the 42nd Anniversary of the *Roe v. Wade* Decision, January 22, 2015

Madam Speaker, I, too, am against this bill for I am for a woman's right to choice. This bill is the second bill that has been brought in the last few days to show the Republican side's intent to repeal *Roe v. Wade*. That is what they would like to do: repeal *Roe v. Wade*.

What is most important is to understand the theater that this bill has shown that the majority party has made this historic hallowed hall of Congress today.

Today is the March for Life, lots of pro-lifers here. They wanted to give them something, so they scheduled a bill—we could be legislating on jobs, on minimum wage, on infrastructure. They wanted to give them something, so they came with a bill called "fetal pain" to get around the viability requirements of the Supreme Court.

Their caucus found that bill too extreme to get the votes—even their caucus. Now, the leadership wouldn't listen to the Democrats of the Rules Committee, and it wouldn't listen to the Democrats on the floor, and they didn't have the good sense to realize it would make them look as they are: antiwoman and out-of-step with reality.

It took some women and maybe a few men—but mostly women—in their caucus to finally go "no," so they brought up a retread of a bill. That was a retread too, but they brought up another one, a substitute bill, because they had to have something to give as a gift for the March for Life pro-life caucus.

This is theater. This is drama. That is what this has become. A woman's right should not be theater; it shouldn't be drama. A woman's right should be preserved. If any case, if there is any question about them, it should go through regular process, go through committees.

Let the Members know about the bill with notice, not have, within 72 hours, a bill brought to this floor. Regular order has been destroyed because of theater and messaging, and that is what you are going to see for the next two years.

The American people will be very disappointed in this Congress because it has become the theater of the absurd. (https://www.congress.gov/crec/2015/01/22/CREC-2015-01-22.pdf)

Speech of Florida Representative Lois Frankel (1948–; D) on the 42nd Anniversary of the *Roe v. Wade* Decision, January 22, 2015

Madam Speaker, I thank the gentlewoman from New York for yielding. I, too, rise in opposition to the rule and the underlying bill.

Today, on the 42nd anniversary of *Roe v. Wade*, we should be celebrating it, not dismantling it. I heard my colleagues on the other side of the aisle talk about pain.

Well, do you want to know about pain? Think back in horror to the perils for our mothers, our daughters, and our sisters in the days before the Supreme Court ruled that women have a constitutional right to make our own personal health care decisions.

Back then, our country faced a public health crisis as women were maimed, made sterile, and lost their lives as a result of self-inflicted or illegal abortions. I remember finding a friend who was near death as a result of a back alley procedure.

Since *Roe v. Wade*, State after State, including Florida, my home State, has passed onerous laws criminalizing doctors, requiring unnecessary tests, and other insidious obstructions to prevent access to abortion.

Today, Congress again piles on to the damage hurting the poorest of our citizens. (https://www.congress.gov/crec/2015/01/22/CREC-2015-01-22.pdf)

LATE-TERM ABORTIONS SHOULD BE ILLEGAL

In 2007 the U.S. Supreme Court issued its decision in *Gonzales v. Carhart* (550 U.S. 124). At issue was the constitutionality of the Partial-Birth Abortion Ban Act of 2003. This law had outlawed late-term abortions of a type referred to as "partial-birth abortions" by their detractors. Lower courts had ruled the law unconstitutional and prevented it from being enforced, in part because the ban did not include any exceptions, even to protect the health of the mother. The Supreme Court, however, ruled 5–4 that the act is constitutional. Excerpts of the majority and dissenting opinions of the case are presented in Chapter 2.

Since the 2007 *Gonzales v. Carhart* ruling, several state legislatures have moved to ban late-term abortions. In 2010, for example, Nebraska banned abortions conducted at 20 or more weeks, based on the scientifically disputed "fetal pain" theory. In June 2013 pro-life members of the U.S. House of Representatives introduced H.R. 1797, the Pain-Capable Unborn Child Protection Act. The bill would prohibit abortion after 20 weeks of pregnancy—making it the most restrictive abortion bill to come to a vote in Congress since the Partial-Birth Abortion Ban Act in 2003. The bill passed the House but was not voted on by the (pro-choice majority) Senate during 2013. The bill was reintroduced by Representative Trent Franks of Arizona in January 2015 as H.R. 36. Although the bill again passed the House in May 2015, it was defeated in the Senate by a pro-choice filibuster in September of that year.

The following passages express support for the bill and explain the position of many who believe late-term abortions should be banned.

Letter of Seán Cardinal O'Malley (1944–) to the U.S. Congress in Support of the Pain-Capable Unborn Child Protection Act, January 20, 2015

As chairman of the U.S. bishops' Committee for Pro-Life Activities, I am writing today to urge your support for H.R. 36, the Pain-Capable Unborn Child Protection Act introduced by Reps. Trent Franks (R-AZ) and Marsha Blackburn (R-TN) on January 6.

The Catholic Church's teaching concerning abortion is well known. We hold that every child, at every moment of existence, deserves love and the protection of the law. We do not believe any person or government has the right to take the life of an innocent human being—and we hold that the real problems that lead women to consider abortion should be addressed with solutions that support both mother and child. We understand that not everyone agrees with the Church's teaching and that there are other views regarding these matters.

It is widely recognized that our citizens were deeply shaken by the revelations of Dr. Kermit Gosnell's actions, which led in 2013 to his being convicted of murder and other crimes committed in the course of providing abortions. This tragic circumstance led many Americans to realize that our permissive laws and attitudes have allowed the abortion industry to undertake these procedures. All decent and humane people are repulsed by the callous and barbarous treatment of women and children in Gosnell's clinic, and in other clinics that abort children after 20 weeks. Among the lessons learned are these:

1. The Supreme Court's past insistence that unborn children must be "viable" to deserve even nominal protection is not meaningful or workable. "Viability" is a prediction about whether a given child would have survived indefinitely outside the womb if given medical support. Some children killed by Dr. Gosnell were surely "viable" in this sense— though that can be difficult to prove if they are killed at birth. The reality, as attested by eyewitnesses at the clinic, is that the children were born alive and crying or screaming in pain, until their lives were intentionally and deliberately ended.

2. These procedures after the middle point of pregnancy also pose serious dangers to women—as evidenced by Dr. Gosnell's own manslaughter conviction for one woman's death, and news about the death or serious complications of other women undergoing such procedures.

3. Some have tried to argue that such difficult and risky procedures should instead be done in more "mainstream" abortion clinics. This misses the point. Many women were sent to Gosnell by those very clinics, because they wanted

nothing to do with abortions performed at such a late stage in the child's development. What does it say about us as a nation, if we will not act against abortions that even full-time abortionists find abhorrent?

For all these reasons, the proposed ban on abortions at 20 weeks after fertilization is a place to begin uniting Americans who see themselves as "pro-life" and as "pro-choice." On behalf of our country and the children whose lives are at stake, I urge you to support the common-sense reform offered by H.R. 36 and to oppose all weakening amendments. (http://nchla.org/datasource/idocuments/LtrHR36.15.pdf)

Speech of Arkansas Senator Tom Cotton (1977–; R) before the U.S. Senate in Support of the Pain-Capable Unborn Child Protection Act, September 21, 2015

Over the last year, I've learned a lot about the magic of human life—from conception to growth in the mother's womb to childbirth to newborn development. This wasn't part of my legislative work or public duties. And my newfound knowledge didn't come from a course of study, reading scientific journals, or consulting with medical experts. Instead, like many parents, I learned through experience, the blessing of my first child.

My wife Anna gave birth to our very own little angel, Gabriel, almost five months ago. Since then, Gabriel has joined me on this very floor, at this very desk. Many of you have met our little man, and happily agreed that he appears to take after his mother.

Gabriel has been a part of our family from the beginning—long before he was born. I remember when Anna and I first discovered that she was pregnant. We were so excited, yet—like so many new parents—also apprehensive for his health and safety. Then, a year ago this week, we had our first appointment with the OB/GYN in Russellville. We couldn't believe when we heard his little heartbeat on the ultrasound at barely nine weeks. Anna recalls that she "almost started crying," though I don't recall an "almost" for either one of us.

Just four weeks later, as the first trimester concluded, we got one of those perfect ultrasound shots. We saw Gabriel in profile, lying on his back, hands near his face, feet and legs kicked up in the air. We now know how much of his personality and habits had already developed by that point, because that position is how we usually find him when he wakes up from a nap. Soon after, he began to flip around, kick, and hiccup, which he also likes to do to this day.

All these things happened before the halfway point in Anna's pregnancy—before Gabriel reached 20 weeks. And while he's precious and one of a kind for us, it's quite normal for a typical baby, as expecting parents can tell you and as modern medical science can now document.

While Anna carried Gabriel to term and he was born happy and healthy, many babies aren't as lucky. But thanks to the miracle of medical science, babies aged just 20 weeks after fertilization can increasingly survive if born at that extremely premature age. A remarkable study published earlier this year in the *New England Journal of Medicine* concluded that babies aged 20–22 weeks could survive, with skilled and proper—though not extraordinary—medical intervention and treatment.

Likewise, advances in perinatology have made fetal surgery more common and successful, sometimes as early as 16 weeks. These breakthroughs can help correct or ameliorate certain fetal conditions. So not only can 20-week-old babies survive outside the womb, but they also can undergo successful surgery inside the womb. And it's common practice in these surgeries to administer anesthesia not just to the mother, but specifically to the baby in utero, to prevent both from feeling pain.

In other words, medical science increasingly confirms the common experience of parents and the religious and ethical belief of the ages: an unborn baby is just as much a person as you, as I, as each of us—only more innocent, more helpless, and therefore even more deserving of protection. Especially by the halfway point of a pregnancy, they feel pain and they seek life.

So it's particularly heartbreaking that such babies are killed in our country. By some estimates, 10,000 babies 20 weeks or older are aborted each year. By this point, most Americans have seen the gruesome videos of Planned Parenthood officials callously discussing the dismemberment of babies to harvest and sell their organs. They cavalierly talk about using "less crunchy" procedures to preserve the organs, subjecting the baby to excruciating pain and death for profit.

This is a sad reality in America today. Just two miles from where I stand—just five blocks from the White House—is an abortionist who advertises on his website for abortions without restrictions up to 26 weeks—right up to the third trimester—far past the medically accepted point of viability. Who knows how many other abortionists do the same, just more discreetly?

It's past time to end this barbaric practice and protect these innocent babies. I therefore strongly support the Pain-Capable Unborn Child Protection Act and urge my fellow senators to do the same. This legislation would stop the abortion of babies 20 weeks or older, with certain reasonable and widely supported exceptions.

I understand that abortion provokes strong feelings on both sides of the question. I acknowledge that reasonable people of good will disagree about the wisdom and morality of early-first-term abortions. But I'm mystified as to why we cannot come together and agree to protect babies who feel pain and who can survive outside the womb.

And it's not just I and large majorities of the American people who feel this way; the civilized world overwhelmingly rejects this kind of late-term abortion. Only seven countries allow elective abortion after 20 weeks, including communist dictatorships like China and North Korea, which also inflict forced abortion and sterilization on their people.

By contrast, countries to our left, like France, and Germany heavily restrict or ban abortion after the first trimester. So does Belgium, home of the European Union. Even Russia bans elective abortion after the first trimester. Our abortion policy is one case where we should be ashamed of our international isolation and follow Europe's lead in protecting innocent life.

In our country, founded as it is on the equal rights of mankind and the unalienable right of life, it's deeply disappointing that the laws don't protect those most innocent lives among us, particularly when medical science now has the ability to do so. These scientific advances, like life itself, are miracles. These days, it may sometimes seem like a miracle when a law passes around here. If that is the case, as a father, an American and a lawmaker, I think a miracle is called for now if it ever was. (http://www.cotton.senate.gov/?p=speech&id=208)

Speech of Kentucky Senator Mitch McConnell before the U.S. Senate in Support of the Pain-Capable Unborn Child Protection Act, September 21, 2015

Mr. President, ask a family to show you the first picture of their child these days, and you are likely to get a black-and-white image with delicate fingers and tiny toes. Maybe it is their precious Christine. Maybe it is their little guy Brett. But one thing's for sure—that baby is their child.

Scientific advances like the sonogram are helping pull back the curtain on the mystery of life, they are helping foster a new spirit of compassionate protection for the most defenseless, and they are providing new opportunities to bridge old political divides.

We in this Chamber are never going to agree completely on the abortion question, but we should at least be able to agree that if an unborn child has reached the point where he or she can feel pain, that child's life deserves protection. Science is telling us that a child can reach this stage around 20 weeks—in other words, five months. This is when unborn children can react—even recoil—to stimuli an adult would recognize as painful. This is when doctors even administer fetal anesthesia during surgery.

As the *New England Journal of Medicine* study recently demonstrated, babies delivered at this age can survive outside the womb. So even if we differ on the larger abortion issue, can't we at least agree that children at this late stage of development deserve our protection? The American people seem to think so. Polls show that American women and American men oppose abortions after five months. The fact is that we are now one of just seven nations—among them countries such as North Korea and China—that allow elective abortions at such a late stage. Can't we do better than this as a country? The Pain-Capable Unborn Child Protection Act would allow America to finally join the ranks of the most civilized nations on this issue.

Just this past weekend in Louisville, hundreds of Kentuckians gathered to spread a message of dignity and hope. They marched for those who may not meet them. They marched for those who may not hear them. But I hope Americans across the country, including participants in the 37th annual Walk for Life, will be encouraged to know that their voices of humanity and of respect are finally being heard again in a Senate under new leadership.

The executive director of Kentucky Right to Life said the issue before us is "critical." She said, "We have worked tirelessly to give these defenseless babies some protection." Several States have already taken action to protect these children. So has the House of Representatives. Now it is up to each of us to show where we stand. We are seeing how science is changing this debate.

So what I am asking every colleague is this: Look in your hearts and help us stand up for the most innocent life, help us protect that beating heart in that sonogram. (https://www.congress.gov/crec/2015/09/22/CREC-2015-09-22.pdf)

NO NEW LIMITATIONS SHOULD BE PLACED ON LATE-TERM ABORTION PROCEDURES

The following testimony by Wendy Davis (1963–; D) is excerpted from her filibuster of House Bill 2. The statements by the Obama administration and the American Civil Liberties Union were issued in opposition to the Pain-Capable Unborn Child Protection Act.

Speech of Texas State Senator Wendy Davis before the Texas Senate Regarding a Bill Proposing New Regulations of Abortion Providers, June 25, 2013

This is the omnibus piece of legislation that contains these elements of bills that were filed in the 83rd session: the 20-week ban, the abortion-inducing drugs provision, the ambulatory surgical center standards, and the hospital admitting privileges. The alleged reason for the bill is to enhance patient safety. But what they really do is create provisions that treat women as though they are not capable of making their own medical decisions. They weaken standards of care because as we all know, every member on this floor knows that the provisions of the ambulatory surgical center standards will immediately place 37 of the 42 abortion clinics in Texas out of compliance. And though the arguments on the senate floor were made that the reason for those standards was for patient safety, not a single instance, not a single instance, could be demonstrated to illustrate why those ambulatory surgical standards were important in assuring women's safety. Not a single example was provided where women had been provided a less safe atmosphere in the existing clinical setting today than they would receive in that setting. What this bill really does, is to threaten the doctor-patient relationship, and we know that we received a great deal of information from doctors' groups which I'll read into the record in a little while about the intrusion on that relationship and we know that in no other instance has this legislature chosen to place itself between a woman and her doctor, or any patient and their doctor. We know that these additional standards are unnecessary. They're unsupported by scientific evidence, including unnecessary requirements that may be extremely difficult and in some cases impossible to meet without a basis in public health or safety. . . .

The 20-week ban on abortion, we've heard a great deal of testimony about that particular provision and I want to hit a few highlights of what has been shared with us. Number one, and most importantly, from our medical community we've heard the concern that this interferes with the practice of medicine. As important, we know that concerns have been raised that this ban interferes with a woman's healthcare decision before she and her doctor may have important health information about her own health and the health of the pregnancy. The ban will have devastating consequences when a woman is experiencing medical complications, and unfortunately it bans abortion before a woman may receive important information about her own health and the health of her pregnancy. Fewer than 2% of abortions occur after 20 weeks and while they are uncommon, it is important that a woman and her doctor have every medical option available. . . .

Let's talk about the parts of the bill that are medically unnecessary. First of all, I think each of us would agree that as patients we trust our doctors, not the government, to determine what medical equipment and what sized room is necessary to provide us with good care. It is medically unnecessary to require health centers to build a hospital-grade operating room for an abortion procedure when one is not required for this type of procedure. And in fact, we know there are many outpatient clinical procedures that are more invasive, have higher incidences of problems, that today are allowed to take place in clinical settings such as doctor's office without the standards that are being required in this bill. Texas, of course, as I said a moment ago, already requires that abortions performed after 16 weeks be performed at ambulatory surgical centers. This provision, the provision in these bills, goes further by requiring that all health centers that provide abortions comply with regulations that are equivalent to the governing places where surgery takes place. The vast majority of abortions, however, are outpatient procedures that can be performed in a health center, making those requirements inappropriate, unnecessary, and not at all about the health of women.

We also have written testimony provided to the health and human services committee by Robin Wallace, M.D.M.A.S., who is a leadership training academy fellow with physicians for reproductive health. She testified before the Texas Senate committee on health and human services on Senate Bill 537 during a regular session on March 19th, 2013, and she provided this written testimony, which I think is compelling.

"I am pleased to submit this testimony and opposition to SB 537 on behalf of physicians for reproductive health. SB 537 is harmful to women. As a physician who takes care of women every single day, I cannot stress enough how dangerous these laws are to the health and well-being of my patients. Women need timely access to safe abortion care. SB 537 imposes medically unnecessary standards on abortion facilities. SB 537 would require abortion facilities to become ambulatory surgical centers (ACSs), which are the setting for complicated and invasive surgical procedures. Abortion, especially early abortion, in the first 12 weeks, is a safe medical procedure with inherently low-risk in outpatient settings without hospital-like facilities. Serious complications arising from surgical abortions at any gestational age are uncommon. By comparison, pregnancy and childbirth are significantly more dangerous to women than abortion. For example, CDC [Centers for Disease Control and Prevention] data indicates that the pregnancy related mortality ratio in the United States is 15.2 deaths per 100,000 live births compared to 0.64 deaths per 100,000 legal abortions," and she provides a footnote for that from the CDC, in a report that was compiled in 2011. "The requirements imposed by this bill are simply medically unnecessary, unsupported by scientific evidence, and contrary to the standards of care."

. . . And then this statement, by the American Congress of Obstetricians and Gynecologists: "Texas ACOG Statement Opposing Texas Fetal Pain Legislation"—and this comes from District 11 of that particular organization. "The Texas District of the American Congress of Obstetricians and Gynecologists, Texas ACOG, opposes HB 16 by Representative [Jodie] Laubenberg [1957–; R]. Texas ACOG opposes HB 16 and other legislative proposals that are not based on sound science or that attempt to prescribe how physicians should care for their individual patients. As a district of the nation's leading authority on women's health, our role is to ensure that policy proposals accurately reflect the best available medical knowledge." (http://counterpathpress.org/let-her-speak-transcript-of-texas-state-sentaor-wendy-daviss-june-25-2013-filibuster-of-the-texas-state-senate)

Statement of Policy by the Obama Administration Regarding the Pain-Capable Unborn Child Protection Act, January 20, 2015

The Administration strongly opposes H.R. 36, which would unacceptably restrict women's health and reproductive rights and is an assault on a woman's right to choose. Women should be able to make their own choices about their bodies and their health care, and Government should not inject itself into decisions best made between a woman and her doctor.

Over the past 40 years, since *Roe v. Wade*, the Supreme Court has affirmed a woman's constitutional right to privacy, including the right to choose. H.R. 36 is a direct challenge to the Supreme Court's holdings on abortion. Not only is the basis for H.R. 36 scientifically disputed, the bill disregards women's health and rights, the role doctors play in their patients' health care decisions, and the Constitution. Furthermore, the provision that requires rape and incest survivors to report the crime to a law enforcement agency or child welfare authority in order to have access to an abortion after the 20-week mark demonstrates a complete disregard for the women who experience sexual assault and the barriers they may face in reporting. Research indicates that the majority of survivors have not reported their sexual assaults to law enforcement.

The Administration is continuing its efforts to reduce unintended pregnancies, expand access to contraception, support maternal and child health, and minimize the need for abortion. At the same time, the Administration is committed to the protection of women's health and reproductive freedom and to supporting women and families in the choices they make.

If the President were presented with this legislation, his senior advisors would recommend that he veto this bill. (https://www.whitehouse.gov/sites/default/files/omb/legislative/sap/114/saphr36r_20150120.pdf)

Speech of Massachusetts Senator Elizabeth Warren (1949–; D) before the U.S. Senate in Opposition to the Pain-Capable Unborn Child Protection Act, September 21, 2015

Mr. President, I will be honest. I am deep-down furious at the Republican scheme to defund Planned Parenthood. I didn't think the Republican leadership could sink any lower than trying to defund women's cancer screenings and access to birth control, but then I saw the bill we are voting on tomorrow and I felt sick to my stomach. Here we are just days away from another reckless Republican government shutdown, and the Republicans think the best use of our time is to vote on a bill to give the government the power to intrude on the most wrenching, intimate, private medical decisions a woman will ever make.

The Republicans want a debate over a 20-week abortion ban, so let's talk about exactly what that means. Nearly 99 percent of all abortions take place within the first 21 weeks of a woman's pregnancy. Let me repeat. Nearly 99 percent are in the first 21 weeks. So based on statistics alone, this bill won't make a big difference in the number of abortions, but for the women who get hit, the consequences can be truly horrific.

Let's start with the research. Who are these women? Who are the 1 percent who get an abortion after 20 weeks? Who? Women or girls who are the victims of rape, incest, or domestic violence and were to frightened to ask for help any sooner. Who? Women whose doctors have told them that if they don't end their pregnancy—pregnancies they really wanted—their kidneys could fail or their hearts could give out or they couldn't get the chemotherapy they may need to save their lives. Who? Women who go for an ultrasound and get the worst possible news—that their fetus has a giant hole in its stomach or organs outside its body or a deformed head and the fetus either has no chance of survival or has a severe abnormality that would mean a short life filled with pain. Research also shows that women who have had later abortions are more likely to be young—very young girls, really—and didn't understand they were pregnant. They are more likely to live in places where getting an abortion means driving three hours or more to find a doctor who will perform one. They are more likely to be poor and need to save up money to pay for the procedure. That is who gets hit by this.

I have taken a close look at the Republican bill to see just how hard they get hit. I want to put it right out here in the open for everyone to see.

There are no—I repeat—no exceptions in this bill for the condition of the fetus. Even if a woman knows at 20 weeks that her child will die immediately after birth, she would still be required to carry that pregnancy for months.

An 18-year-old survivor of rape or incest must wait until she can provide written proof that she received counseling from a doctor, and then that counseling is loaded with hurdles: The counseling must come only from a doctor who refuses to perform abortions and who doesn't work in an office with another doctor who does. Think about it. Prolong the pain and anxiety, and for anyone who lives in a rural area or anyone who is making it barely paycheck to paycheck and cannot miss multiple days of work, make it twice as hard to get any help.

If the victim of rape or incest is a minor, it gets even worse. A girl—a girl who is 10, 12, 14 years old—this girl must face the same challenges and must provide written proof that she reported the crime to the police, even if turning in a family member or announcing to the world that she has been raped could destroy her life in a million different ways. I cannot imagine that the Senate would pass a law to require a frightened 12-year-old girl to submit written proof that she had called the police to report a rape by her mother's boyfriend before she could terminate that pregnancy. That kind of cruelty is barbaric, and it has no place in our laws.

But this is not just about the tiny number of people who must seek abortions after 20 weeks; this horrifying bill that we will vote on tomorrow is just one more piece of a deliberate, methodical, orchestrated rightwing plan to attack women's health and reproductive rights. A funding cut here, a new restriction here, month after month, year after year, and *Roe v. Wade* will be chipped away to nothing. That is what this is all about. That is what this has always been all about.

We have lived in an America where women died in back-alley abortions. We have lived in an America where high school girls tried poisons and coat hangers to try to end pregnancies. We have lived in an America where young woman who faced unwanted pregnancies took their own lives. We have lived in that America, and we are not going back—not now, not ever.

We stand here on the brink of another reckless Republican government shutdown. We all remember what happened the last time the Republicans shut the government down: $24 billion was flushed down the drain for a political stunt—$24 billion that could have gone to help mothers and their babies with prenatal care, better infant nutrition, Head Start classes, medical research on birth abnormalities. Instead, the money was flushed away by Republicans who want to play political games more than they want to help children and families all across this country.

I urge my colleagues to vote no on this terrible bill. Stand up to this rightwing assault on women and families. Instead of trying to do the job of physicians and telling women what is best for their own medical care, Republicans in the Senate should start doing the job of legislators and get to work on this Nation's budget. (https://www.congress.gov/crec/2015/09/21/CREC-2015-09-21.pdf)

IMPORTANT NAMES AND ADDRESSES

American Association of University Women
1111 16th St. NW
Washington, DC 20036
(202) 785-7700
1-800-326-2289
FAX: (202) 872-1425
E-mail: connect@aauw.org
URL: http://www.aauw.org/

American Civil Liberties Union
125 Broad St., 18th Floor
New York, NY 10004
(212) 549-2500
URL: http://www.aclu.org/

American Congress of Obstetricians and Gynecologists
409 12th St. SW
Washington, DC 20024-2188
(202) 638-5577
1-800-673-8444
URL: http://www.acog.org/

American Life League
PO Box 1350
Stafford, VA 22555
(540) 659-4171
FAX: (540) 659-2586
URL: http://www.all.org/

American Medical Association
AMA Plaza
330 N. Wabash Ave.
Chicago, IL 60611-5885
1-800-621-8335
URL: http://www.ama-assn.org/ama/

Catholics for Choice
1436 U St. NW, Ste. 301
Washington, DC 20009-3997
(202) 986-6093
FAX: (202) 332-7995
URL: http://www.catholicsforchoice.org/

Center for Reproductive Rights
199 Water St.
New York, NY 10038
(917) 637-3600
FAX: (917) 637-3666
E-mail: info@reprorights.org
URL: http://www.reproductiverights.org/

Centers for Disease Control and Prevention Division of Reproductive Health
1600 Clifton Rd.
Atlanta, GA 30329-4027
1-800-232-4636
URL: http://www.cdc.gov/reproductivehealth/index.htm

Centers for Disease Control and Prevention National Center for Health Statistics
1600 Clifton Rd.
Atlanta, GA 30329-4027
1-800-232-4636
URL: http://www.cdc.gov/nchs

Christian Coalition of America
PO Box 37030
Washington, DC 20013
(202) 479-6900
URL: http://www.cc.org/

Family Research Council
801 G St. NW
Washington, DC 20001
1-800-225-4008
URL: http://www.frc.org/

Feminist Majority Foundation
1600 Wilson Blvd., Ste. 801
Arlington, VA 22209
(703) 522-2214
FAX: (703) 522-2219
URL: http://www.feminist.org/

Guttmacher Institute
125 Maiden Ln., Seventh Floor
New York, NY 10038
(212) 248-1111
1-800-355-0244
FAX: (212) 248-1951
URL: http://www.guttmacher.org/

Human Life International
4 Family Life Ln.
Front Royal, VA 22630
1-800-549-5433
URL: http://www.hli.org/

Institute of Medicine
500 Fifth St. NW
Washington, DC 20001
(202) 334-2352
FAX: (202) 334-1412
E-mail: iomwww@nas.edu
URL: http://iom.nationalacademies.org/

International Planned Parenthood Federation
4 Newhams Row
London, SE1 3UZ
United Kingdom
(011-44) 20-7939-8200
FAX: (011-44) 20-7939-8300
E-mail: info@ippf.org
URL: http://www.ippf.org/

Kaiser Family Foundation
2400 Sand Hill Rd.
Menlo Park, CA 94025
(650) 854 9400
FAX: (650) 854 4800
URL: http://www.kff.org/

Medical Students for Choice
PO Box 40188
Philadelphia, PA 19106
(215) 625-0800
FAX: (215) 625-4848
E-mail: students@msfc.org
URL: http://www.msfc.org/

NARAL Pro-Choice America
1156 15th St. NW, Ste. 700
Washington, DC 20005
(202) 973-3000
FAX: (202) 973-3096
URL: http://www.prochoiceamerica.org/

National Abortion Federation
1660 L St. NW, Ste. 450
Washington, DC 20036
(202) 667-5881
Hotline: 1-800-772-9100
FAX: (202) 667-5890
E-mail: naf@prochoice.org
URL: http://www.prochoice.org/

National Campaign to Prevent Teen and Unplanned Pregnancy
1776 Massachusetts Ave. NW, Ste. 200
Washington, DC 20036
(202) 478-8500
FAX: (202) 478-8588
URL: http://thenationalcampaign.org/

National Institutes of Health
9000 Rockville Pike
Bethesda, MD 20892
(301) 496-4000
E-mail: NIHinfo@od.nih.gov
URL: http://www.nih.gov/

National Organization for Women
1100 H St. NW, Ste. 300
Washington, DC 20005
(202) 628-8669
URL: http://www.now.org/

National Right to Life Committee
512 10th St. NW
Washington, DC 20004
(202) 626-8800
URL: http://www.nrlc.org/

National Women's Health Network
1413 K St. NW, Fourth Floor
Washington, DC 20005
(202) 682-2640
FAX: (202) 682-2648
E-mail: nwhn@nwhn.org
URL: http://www.nwhn.org/

National Women's Political Caucus
PO Box 50476
Washington, DC 20091
(202) 785-1100
FAX: (202) 370-6306
E-mail: info@nwpc.org
URL: http://www.nwpc.org/

Pan American Health Organization
525 23rd St. NW
Washington, DC 20037
(202) 974-3000
FAX: (202) 974-3663
URL: http://www.paho.org/hq/

Planned Parenthood Federation of America
1110 Vermont Ave. NW
Washington, DC 20005
(202) 973-4800
FAX: (202) 296-3242
URL: http://www.plannedparenthood.org/

Population Action International
1300 19th St. NW, Ste. 200
Washington, DC 20036-1624
(202) 557-3400
FAX: (202) 728-4177
E-mail: info@pai.org
URL: http://pai.org/

Population Council
One Dag Hammarskjold Plaza
New York, NY 10017
(212) 339-0500
1-877-339-0500
FAX: (212) 755-6052
E-mail: pubinfo@popcouncil.org
URL: http://www.popcouncil.org/

Population Reference Bureau
1875 Connecticut Ave. NW, Ste. 520
Washington, DC 20009
1-800-877-9881
FAX: (202) 328-3937
E-mail: popref@prb.org
URL: http://www.prb.org/

Religious Coalition for Reproductive Choice
1413 K St. NW, 14th Floor
Washington, DC 20005
(202) 628-7700
FAX: (202) 628-7716
E-mail: info@rcrc.org
URL: http://www.rcrc.org/

United Nations Population Fund
605 Third Ave.
New York, NY 10158
(212) 297-5000
FAX: (212) 370-0201
E-mail: hq@unfpa.org
URL: http://www.unfpa.org/

U.S. Conference of Catholic Bishops Committee for Pro-Life Activities
3211 Fourth St. NE
Washington, DC 20017
(202) 541-3000
URL: http://www.usccb.org/about/pro-life-activities/

RESOURCES

The three primary sources of abortion statistics used in this book are the Centers for Disease Control and Prevention (CDC), the Guttmacher Institute, and NARAL Pro-Choice America. The CDC publishes its "Abortion Surveillance" reports annually. The most current information on abortion data from the CDC used in the preparation of this book was "Abortion Surveillance—United States, 2011" (Karen Pazol et al., November 2014). Other CDC publications used in preparing this volume include "Births: Final Data for 2013" (Joyce A. Martin et al., January 2015), "Births: Preliminary Data for 2014" (Brady E. Hamilton et al., June 2015), "Pregnancy Rates for U.S. Women Continue to Drop" (Sally C. Curtin et al., December 2013), *NCHS Data on Teen Pregnancy* (April 2014), *Youth Risk Behavior Surveillance System (YRBSS)* (May 2015), *2013 Assisted Reproductive Technology Fertility Clinics Success Rates Report* (August 2015), *U.S. Teen Pregnancy Outcomes by Age, Race and Hispanic Ethnicity* (2013), and "Youth Risk Behavior Surveillance—United States, 2013" (Laura Kann et al., June 2014).

The Guttmacher Institute is the major nongovernmental source of abortion statistics in the world. It strongly supports a woman's right to choose abortion. The institute publishes *Perspectives on Sexual and Reproductive Health*, a quarterly journal that provides research and analysis on sexual and reproductive health and rights in the United States and other developed countries. Other Guttmacher publications cited in this book include "Publicly Funded Contraceptive Services in the United States" (July 2015), "Facts on Induced Abortion in the United States" (July 2014), *State Policies in Brief: Bans on "Partial-Birth" Abortion* (September 2015), *State Policies in Brief: Emergency Contraception* (September 2015), *State Policies in Brief: Minors' Access to Contraceptive Services* (September 2015), *State Policies in Brief: An Overview of Abortion Laws* (September 2015), *State Policies in Brief: Parental Involvement in Minors' Abortions* (September 2015), *State Policies in Brief: Protecting Access to Clinics* (September 2015), *State Policies in Brief: Sex and HIV Education* (September 2015), *State Policies in Brief: State Funding of Abortion under Medicaid* (September 2015), and *State Policies in Brief: State Policies on Later Abortions* (September 2015).

NARAL Pro-Choice America publishes information on the status of abortion in the individual states in *Who Decides? The Status of Women's Reproductive Rights in the United States* (January 2015). This document was an excellent source of statistics and information for this book.

The National Campaign to Prevent Teen and Unplanned Pregnancy provides a wealth of information about teen pregnancy, including *What Works 2011–2012: Curriculum-Based Programs That Prevent Teen Pregnancy* (Katy Suellentrop, October 2011), as well as the results of public opinion surveys about informing teens about delaying sex and contraception.

International birth rates were drawn from the Central Intelligence Agency's *World Factbook* (October 2015), and international abortion statistics were provided by the World Health Organization and the Center for Reproductive Rights.

The National Abortion Federation (NAF), a national association of abortion providers and a strong abortion advocate, tabulates statistics on incidents of violence against abortion providers. The NAF publishes a wide range of consumer education materials on abortion and operates a nationwide toll-free consumer hotline to answer questions and make referrals to qualified abortion providers throughout the United States and Canada.

The Gallup Organization, the Pew Research Center, and the Public Religion Research Institute publish surveys on American attitudes toward abortion, as do various news media.

INDEX

Page references in italics refer to photographs. References with the letter t *following them indicate the presence of a table. The letter* f *indicates a figure. If more than one table or figure appears on a particular page, the exact item number for the table or figure being referenced is provided.*

B

D

E

F

G

K

L

M

N

Q

R

S

T

U

CPSIA information can be obtained
at www.ICGtesting.com
Printed in the USA
FFOW01n0927300616
25522FF

9 781573 026642